22-95

CW01650586

Mastering Amí Professional®

Other Titles of Interest from Wiley

Advanced Excel for the IBM PC, PS/2 and Compatibles, Ashley and Fernandez
Advanced WordPerfect: A Power User's Guide, Farrell
WordStar Professional Release 5: An Advanced Book, Ashley and Fernandez
R:BASE for DOS: A Business User's Guide, Condliffe
Paradox 3.0: A Business User's Guide, Condliffe
Using dBASE IV: Basics for Business, Brownstein
The PC Upgrader's Manual: How to Build and Extend Your System, Held
IBM PS/2 User's Reference Manual, Held
OS/2: Features, Functions, and Applications, Krantz, Mizell, and Williams
OS/2: A Business Perspective, Conklin
OS/2 Presentation Manager Programming, Cheatham, Reich, and Robinson
Ventura Publisher for the IBM PC: Mastering Desktop Publishing, Jantz
Desktop Publishing with WordPerfect 5.0, Tevis
Desktop Publishing with PageMaker 3.0: IBM PC AT, PS/2, and Compatibles, Bove and Rhodes
Desktop Publishing with PageMaker 3.02: Macintosh, Bove and Rhodes
The Power of Quattro: A Business User's Guide, Salkind
Using Lotus Agenda, Goodman and Wolf
Macros, Menus, and Miracles for Lotus 1-2-3, Lunsford
Lotus 1-2-3 Release 2.2, Williams
Lotus 1-2-3 Release 3, Williams
Mastering Enable OA: Office Automation Software, Spezzano
Hard Disk Smarts: Everything You Need to Know to Choose and Use Your Hard Disk, Bosshardt
Inside Allways: The Spreadsheet Publisher, Sandler and Badgett
Advanced Lotus 1-2-3 Release 3, Yu and Harrison
The New DOS 4.0, Christopher, Feigenbaum, and Saliga
DOS 4.0 Reference, Christopher, Feigenbaum, and Saliga
Excel: A Business User's Guide—IBM and Macintosh, Salkind
Designing Intelligent Front Ends for Business Software, Shafer

MASTERING AMÍ PROFESSIONAL®

Pamela S. Beason
Stephen Guild

John Wiley & Sons, Inc.

New York Chichester Brisbane Toronto Singapore

Publisher: Therese A. Zak
Editor: Katherine Schowalter
Managing Editor: Ruth Greif
Editing, Design, and Production: Impressions Publishing Services, Inc.

Library of Congress Cataloging-in-Publication Data

Beason, Pamela S.
Mastering AMÍ Professional / Pamela S. Beason, Stephen Guild.
p. cm.
ISBN 0-471-51992-8
1. Desktop publishing. 2. AMÍ Professional (Computer program)
I. Guild, Stephen. II. Title.
[Z286.D47B43 1990]
686.2'2544536—dc20 89-77145
CIP

Printed in the United States of America

90 91 10 9 8 7 6 5 4 3 2

To Larry, Jo, April, and Brian.—P.B.

To my good friend and business partner, Millard Mott.—S.G.

Contents

Foreword

Samna Amí Professional charts a new course in the world of word processing. Combining a rich core of basic features with advanced capabilities, Amí Professional will set new standards in producing professional-looking documents.

We have developed Amí Professional specifically for the individual needing such powerful features as merge, tables, indexing, and integrated charting and drawing. As the "big brother" product in the Amí word processing line, Amí Professional provides speed, flexibility, and tools to the full range of documents.

Above all, we have made Amí Professional easy to use. Even though it is full of advanced features, all of this power is very accessible. This book, *Mastering Amí Professional*, provides new or experienced users with valuable information, hints, tips, and tricks that will make using Amí Professional just that much easier. With its clear writing style, step-by-step procedures, and graphic examples, *Mastering Amí Professional* will be an indispensable reference to the Amí Professional user.

I invite you to use Amí Professional and this book to produce professional-looking documents.

Said Mohammadioun
Chief Executive Officer
Samna Corporation
Atlanta, Georgia

Acknowledgments

Often acknowledgments pay polite attention to individuals who have been involved in the production of a book such as this. In this case, these are heartfelt expressions of appreciation for the time and effort spent to help us make this a better book.

Teri Zak at John Wiley & Sons worked with us from beginning to end, offering advice, prodding when necessary, and always supporting our work. We were very lucky to have the book edited by Lynn Brown. She was as diligent about catching our mistakes as she was about keeping us to our promised schedule!

In writing about a product in process, there are many questions and issues that need answers. At Samna Corporation, we found a cooperative staff who helped us at every step along the way to clarify procedures, solve problems, and explain the particular features of Amí Professional. We are expecially grateful to Said Mohammadioun, the CEO at Samna, for his support of this project. Bill Jones, product manager, was particularly helpful throughout the writing of the book. He answered our many questions, offering comments and suggestions, and reviewed the entire manuscript. We also would like to thank each of the individuals in Samna Technical Support who helped us work through often detailed and somewhat complicated problems.

As always, there are those closer to home who contributed to the book: our families—Mike, Pat, Darren, and Sue Anne. We are thankful for their encouragement and support as well as their patience.

TRADEMARK ACKNOWLEDGMENTS

Amí is a trademark and Amí Professional is a registered trademark of Samna Corporation.

dBASE is a registered trademark of Ashton-Tate.

DisplayWrite is a trademark and IBM, Personal System/2, and PC/AT are registered trademarks of International Business Machines Corporation.

Enable is a trademark of The Software Group.

Lotus and 1-2-3 are registered trademarks of Lotus Development Corporation.

MultiMate is a registered trademark of Multimate International Corporation, an Ashton-Tate company.

Hewlett-Packard and LaserJet are registered trademarks of Hewlett-Packard Company.

Advantage is a trademark of AST Research.

Helvetica is a registered trademark of Linotype AG and its subsidiaries.

Microsoft Windows is a trademark and Microsoft, MS-DOS, Multiplan, and the Microsoft logo are registered trademarks of Microsoft Corporation.

WordPerfect is a trademark of WordPerfect Corporation.

WordStar is a registered trademark of MicroPro International Corporation.

PC Paintbrush is a registered trademark of ZSoft Corporation.

PostScript is a registered trademark of Adobe Systems, Inc.

SuperCalc is a registered trademark of Computer Associates, Inc.

All other brand and product names are trademarks of their respective companies.

Introduction

In this book you'll find all the basic procedures you'll need to use Amí Professional to create a variety of documents, as well as tips and tricks to speed up your work and optimize the program's performance. We know that most Amí Professional users are experienced computer users. Therefore, to keep this book down to a readable number of pages, we made several assumptions about our readers.

OUR ASSUMPTIONS ABOUT YOU

First, we assume that you're using the full version of Microsoft Windows® rather than the SAE (Single Application Environment) version shipped with Amí Professional. If you *are* using SAE Windows, you'll still find a wealth of helpful information in this book, but you won't be able to take advantage of a few procedures that describe using multiple Windows applications at once (such as transferring data from a Windows spreadsheet to Amí Professional). This book doesn't fully describe how to use the Microsoft Windows program, but we provide a summary of Windows operations in Appendix A.

Next, we assume that you're at least somewhat familiar with your computer's operating system, disk drives, and keyboard. If you have a mouse (optional), we're assuming you know how to move it and how to recognize a mouse pointer on the screen. We provide basic instructions for keyboard and mouse use in Chapter 2, but if you're a novice, you may need to refer to your computer's hardware manual, your operating system manual, and your mouse manual for additional information.

Finally, we assume that you've installed all the software you need (Windows, Amí Professional, and any other programs you use) and hooked up all your hardware (mouse, keyboard, monitor, and printer). You can find all the information you need for these tasks in the Windows, Amí Professional, and other software setup instructions, and in your computer and printer manuals.

CONVENTIONS WE USED

To help you find your way around in this book, we use specific style conventions to set off various types of information. Speed tips and helpful hints are clearly labeled, so you can find them at a glance. When we show what the computer displays on the screen, it's in a special font, like this:

```
C>
```

When we want you to type something, we put that text in bold, like this:

Type **win amipro** after the prompt.

In the few instances where we can't tell you exactly what to type, we put variable names in bold italics. For example,

Type **win amipro *filename*** after the prompt.

means that you need to supply the filename (for example, **win amipro letter.sam**).

HOW THIS BOOK IS ORGANIZED

This book is organized as follows:

Chapters	**Description**
Chapters 1–3	Introduce Amí Professional's features and explain the basics of using the program's commands and file structures.
Chapters 4–8	Describe the basic word processing and editing procedures you'll need to create your documents.

Chapters 9–16	Describe styles, tables, and other formatting features that control the way your pages look on the screen and when printed, as well as detailing Amí Professional's drawing and charting abilities.
Chapters 17–19	Detail advanced features such as merge techniques, numbering schemes, and creation of tables of contents and indexes.
Chapters 20–21	Show you how to use macros and other options to customize Amí Professional for your own use.
Appendix A	Summarizes commands and keystrokes used with Microsoft Windows.
Appendix B	Summarizes helpful hints used throughout the book.
Appendix C	Summarizes use of keys with Amí Professional.
Appendix D	Summarizes use of the mouse with Amí Professional.
Appendix E	Lists file extensions created and used by Amí Professional.

You'll find this book easy to read and packed with all the instructions and tips you'll need to become an Amí Professional expert. We wish you all the best as you explore the power and versatility that this exciting program has to offer.

1

Welcome to Amí Professional

Amí Professional is a word processing program that runs under Microsoft Windows. But this program has a lot more to offer serious word processor users than just standard features such as cut and paste, search and replace, spell checking, and text formatting (although of course Amí Professional includes those functions, too!). This chapter provides an overview of Amí Professional and helps you get started using one of Amí's most powerful features: windows.

UNIQUE FEATURES OF AMÍ PROFESSIONAL

Before you begin your mastery of this rich word processing system, take a look at the following description of its most powerful and flexible features.

Five Ways to Look at Documents

One of the qualities you'll notice first about Amí Professional is that it offers multiple ways to look at a document—five, to be exact. You can select standard view (for compatibility with other Windows applications), enlarged view (for precise positioning and drawing), full-page view (to see complete pages), facing-pages view (to see two facing pages at once), and working view, the view you'll use most often.

Two Modes to Display Documents

In addition to all the different ways you can view your document, you can use two modes to speed up your work. If you're just working with words, you'll find that draft mode is the faster way to enter and revise text. If you want to make those words look perfect on the page, you'll want to use layout mode. You will learn all about views and modes in Chapter 3.

Put Your Thoughts in Electronic Notes

Did you ever wonder how we got along before those yellow sticky notes were invented? With Amí Professional, you don't have to attach physical notes all over your papers or your monitor screen—you can put notes right in your documents, hide them when you don't want to see them, and display them when you do. Figure 1–1 shows just what we mean.

If you want to get technical about notes, you can easily add professional-looking footnotes to your Amí Professional documents. You don't have to worry about keeping dozens of footnotes in order—Amí Professional does it for you.

Figure 1–1
Amí Professional's handy "sticky" notes.

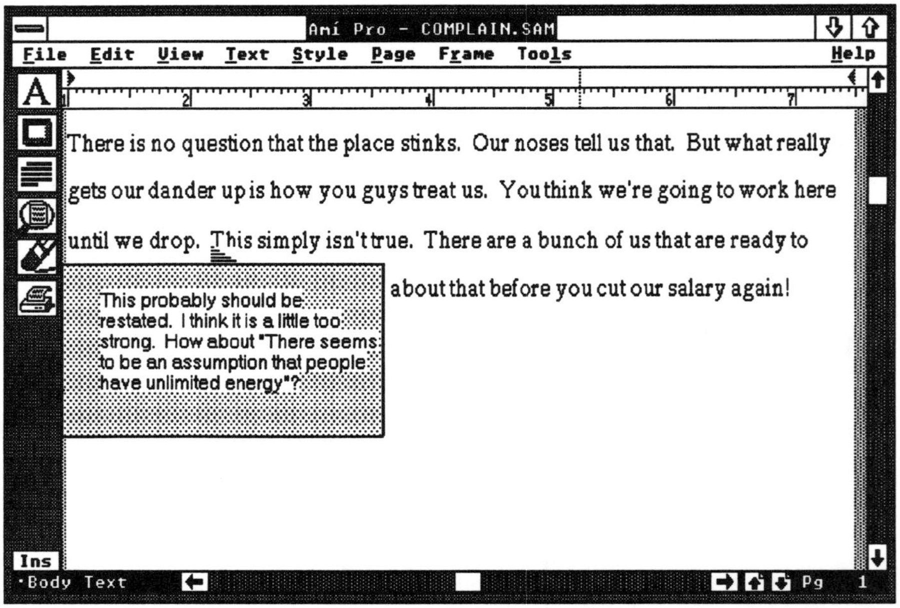

A Picture Is Worth a Thousand Words

If Windows is a graphic user interface, Amí Professional is *the* graphic word processor to run with Windows! Whenever you make changes in dialog boxes, you get to see exactly what your change will look like before you make it. This graphic use of sample pages and sample text is the answer to prayers of users frustrated by the try-and-try-again methods most other programs use. Figure 1–2 shows an example of the dialog boxes that display your selection as it will print.

Amí Professional uses graphics in dialog boxes and makes it easy for you to use graphics in your document. Not only can you use Amí Professional to import, crop, scale, and rotate pictures that you've created with other applications, but you can add to imported pictures or create your own graphics with Amí Professional's powerful drawing features. No more closing down your word processing program to go to the drawing program; you can do it all right here. Figure 1–3 shows a graphic created in Amí Professional.

And if you're looking for charts, Amí Professional has them covered, too. Imagine what sophisticated charts can do for your sales forecasts and your progress reports. As Figure 1–4 shows, you can create a wide variety of charts right in Amí Professional, change their colors, and add text and shading until everything looks perfect.

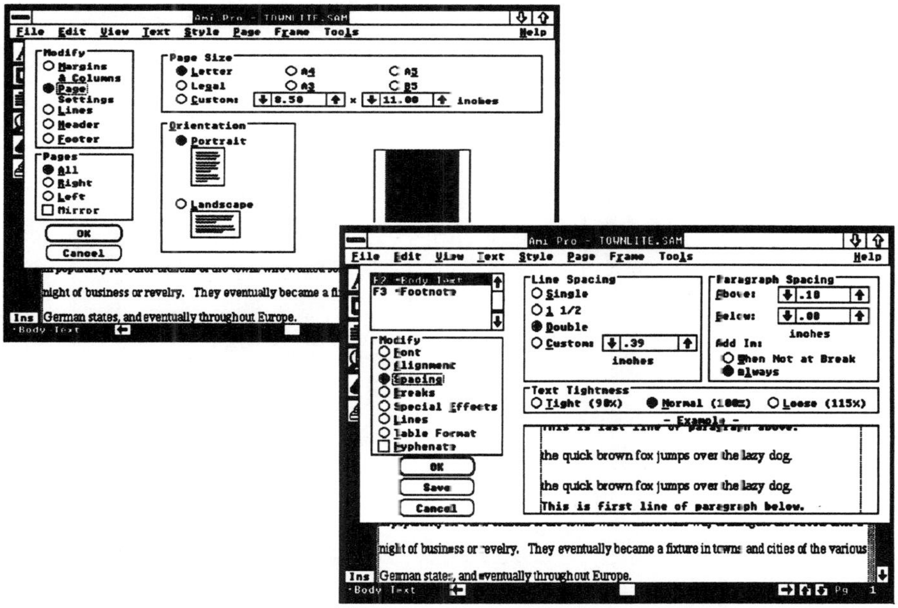

Figure 1–2
Amí Professional uses sample pages and sample text in dialog boxes to show how your changes will look *before* you make them.

Figure 1–3
A drawing created with Amí Professional.

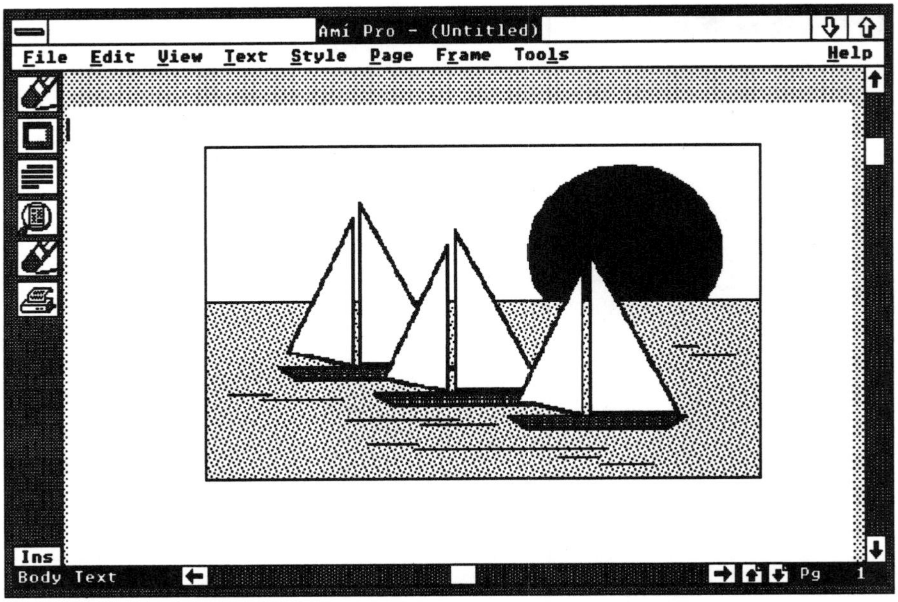

Figure 1–4
A chart created with Amí Professional.

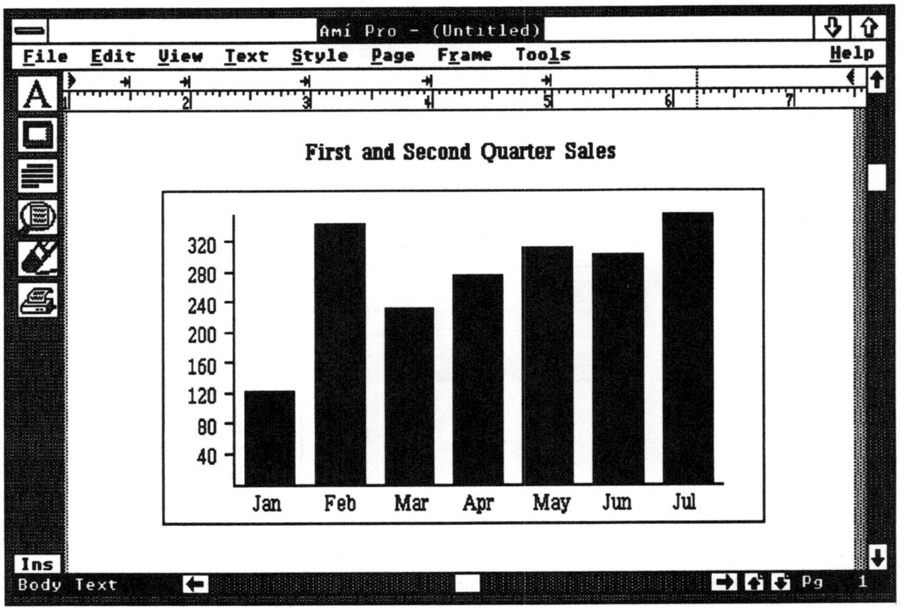

Do It with Styles

Styles are the basics of Amí Professional formatting. Many other word processing programs use styles, but Amí goes one better because you save text along with styles in your style sheets. This way you can create templates of commonly used text blocks to use over and over again.

Put It in a Table

No more fussing around using tabs when you try to line up text in rows and columns. Now there are tables! You can use Amí Professional's tables to create spreadsheet-type tables, to place paragraphs side by side, and to create interesting page layouts. Add or subtract text, and the table automatically adjusts. And you can add a wide variety of lines, frames, and shading to accentuate the data you want people to notice. Figure 1–5 shows just a sample of the table designs we're talking about.

Frame It and Hang It Wherever You Want

Whenever you want to control the position of an object or of paragraphs of text, put them in a frame. You can change the size of frames, move

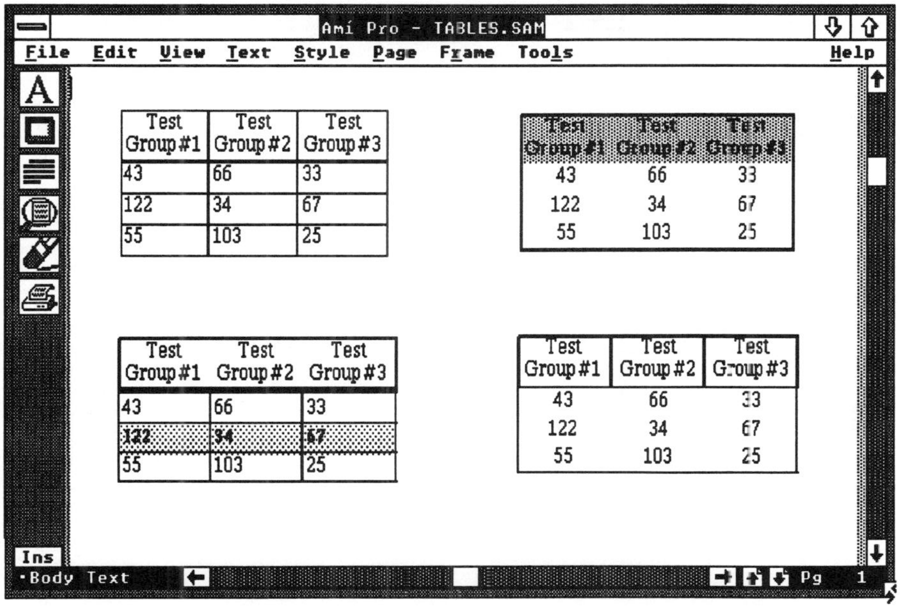

Figure 1–5 Sample of the tables you can create in Amí Professional.

them around the page, and control how text wraps around them. Figure 1–6 gives a sample. At last, now you can put whatever you want wherever you want it.

Much, Much More! . . .

Amí Professional is too full-featured to mention all of its highlights here. After all, that's why we wrote this book! In future chapters you'll find out about many more exciting capabilities, such as merging and linking, glossaries, and index and table-of-contents generation, just to name a few.

AMÍ PROFESSIONAL IS A WINDOWS PROGRAM

Amí Professional is designed to run under Microsoft® Windows, so the program uses multiple *windows* to display your documents and its tools. You can use the Windows interface to change the position and size of Amí Professional's windows, turn windows into icons and back into windows, and close windows. If you're not familiar with Windows, you'll want to

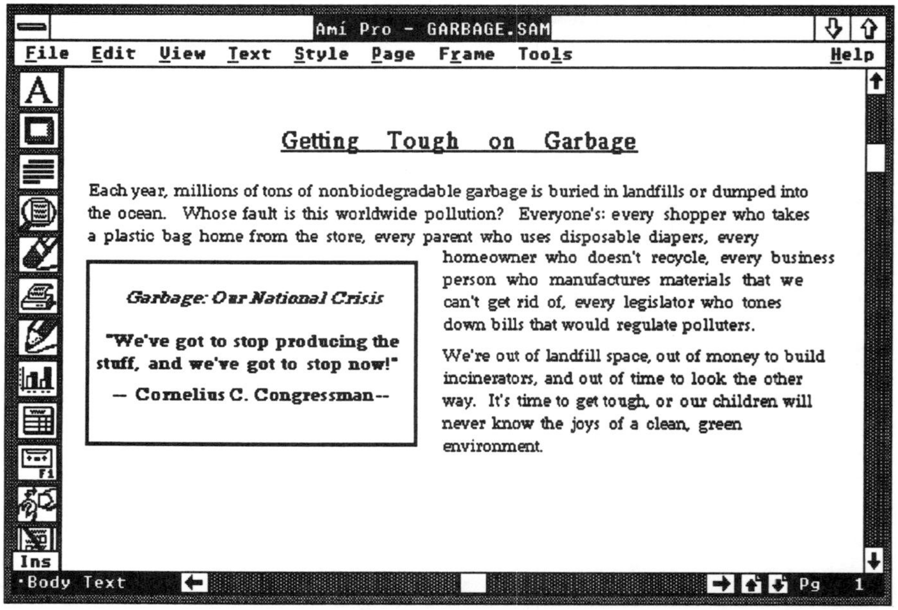

Figure 1–6 Framed objects can be positioned anywhere on a page. You control how text wraps around the frame.

read Appendix A, "Windows Basics," which explains Microsoft Windows terminology and lists the program's key combination and mouse procedures. Chapter 2 covers some Windows basics that you'll use when working with Amí Professional. Chapter 2 also explains a few procedures that are unique to Amí Professional.

2

Using Commands, Dialog Boxes, and Help

Although there are many common elements and procedures to most word processors, each has a slightly different approach to streamlining text processing. To fully use Amí Professional's power, you need to know some basics before you can begin to explore the program. This chapter describes the basics of operating Amí Professional, including

- how to start and quit Amí Professional
- how to choose commands and use dialog boxes
- how to use Amí Professional's help system

If you're new to Windows and to Amí Professional, read this chapter thoroughly before going on.

AMÍ PROFESSIONAL, WINDOWS, AND THE OPERATING SYSTEM

When you use Amí Professional for Windows, you're really dealing with three layers of software, all running at the same time, as illustrated in Figure 2–1.

Amí Professional runs under Microsoft Windows, so you can use the Windows Control Panel to control the colors and other aspects of the Amí Professional window, and to install fonts and printers. As in any other Windows application, you can change the size of the Amí Professional window, making it larger or smaller or shrinking it to an icon.

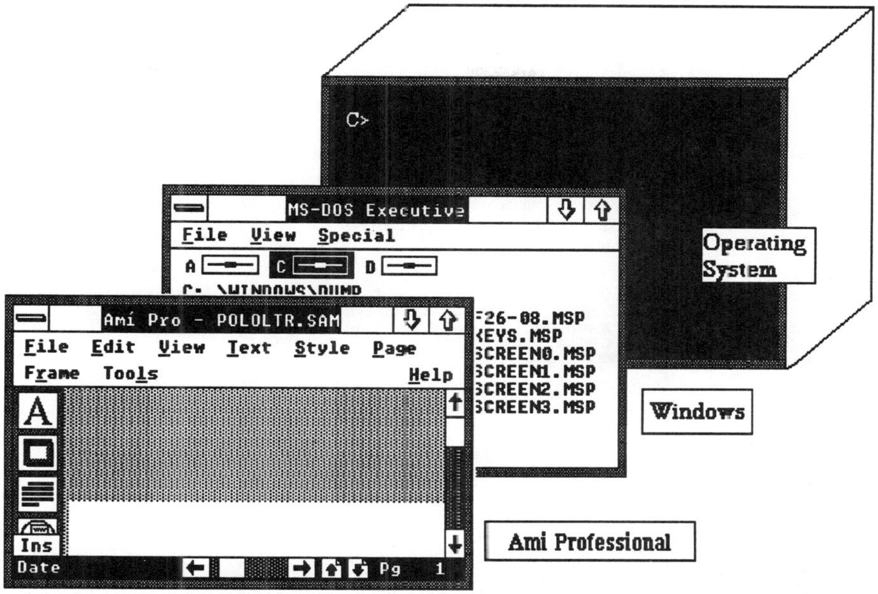

Figure 2-1
You use three levels of software when you run Amí Professional for Windows.

The Windows software runs under your operating system (MS-DOS or PC-DOS), which controls the hardware (reading from and writing to disk, sending information to the printer, and so forth). Because Amí Professional and Windows interact with the operating system, you must follow the operating system's naming conventions when you name files created with Amí Professional. You should understand the operating system's tree structure and know how to use its path name conventions when you refer to files in different directories or on different drives. For more information about your operating system, see the manuals that came with your computer.

STARTING AMÍ PROFESSIONAL

After you've started Windows, you can start Amí Professional in any of three ways:

- Use the arrow keys to highlight the AMIPRO.EXE name in the MS-DOS Executive window, then press **Enter**; or use the mouse to double-click AMIPRO.EXE.

- Use the arrow keys to highlight the name of any file created with Amí Professional (see Figure 2-2), then press **Enter**; or use the

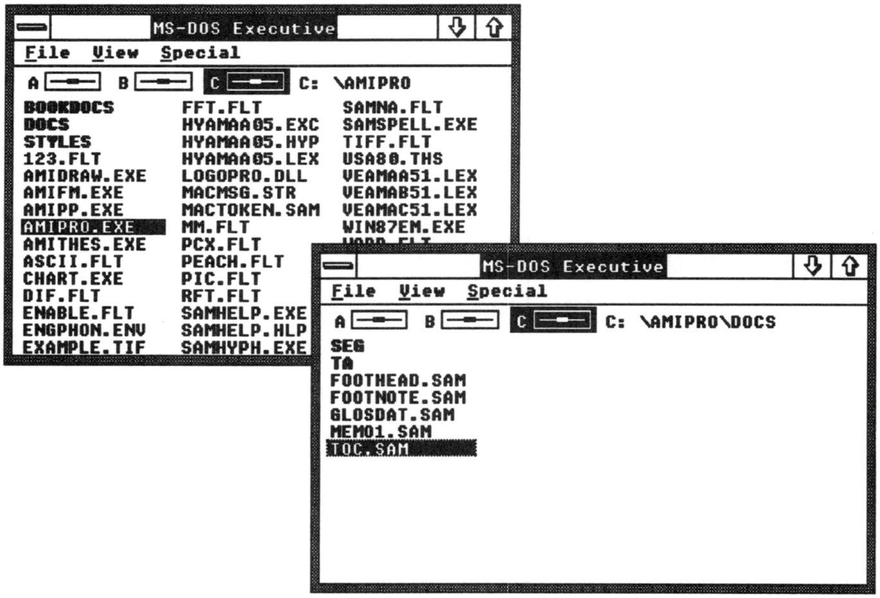

Figure 2-2
You can start Amí Professional several ways from the MS-DOS Executive Window.

mouse to double-click the name of an Amí Professional file. This starts Amí Professional and opens the document at the same time.

- Choose the File Run command in the MS-DOS Executive window, type **amipro** in the dialog box, then press **Enter**.

Outside of Windows, you can start Amí Professional by typing **win amipro** at the operating system prompt (usually C>). You type **win386 amipro** instead if you have Windows 386 or type just **amipro** if you're using SAE Windows. To start the program this way, Windows and Amí Professional directories must be on your path (see your operating system manual for more information about paths).

Speed Tips

You can speed up the starting process by typing **/L** at the startup command. For example, **win amipro/L** tells the program not to display the logo. You can also open a document at the same time by typing the file name at the end of the startup command. For example, **win amipro/L letter.sam** both starts Amí Professional without the logo display and loads the file LETTER.SAM.

A TOUR OF THE AMÍ PROFESSIONAL WINDOW

Amí Professional first opens in working view, the view you'll use most often. Take a look at Figure 2–3, which points out different parts of the Amí Professional window in working view. You'll see these terms throughout this book.

If you didn't open a specific document when you started Amí Professional, you'll notice that (Untitled) appears in the title bar. This is Amí Professional's default name for a new document. You can enter text to create a new document, then save it with the name you want. Alternatively, you can close this empty document and open another document you've already created. In the upper right corner of the Amí Professional window, you'll see the styles box—a small window with ~DEFAULT.STY in the title bar. You'll learn more about styles, style sheets, and the styles box in Chapter 9.

USING THE MOUSE

As with most Windows applications, you can use the mouse or keyboard, or a combination of both to choose commands and perform common tasks with Amí Professional. You may already be familiar with using the mouse,

Figure 2–3
The Amí Professional window in working view.

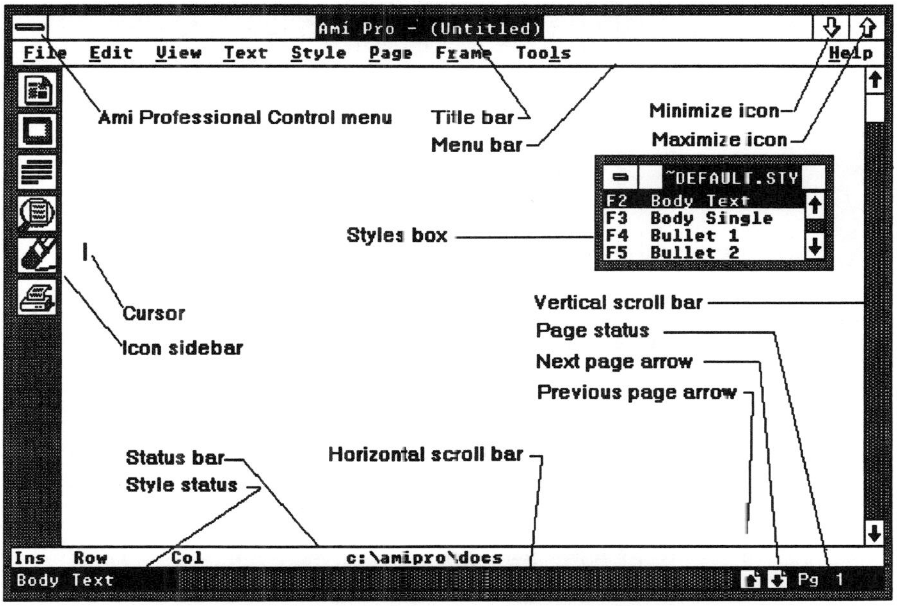

but just in case you need a reminder, here are the mouse terms used in this book.

Term	Meaning
Point	Slide the mouse on your desk to move the mouse pointer to a specific location in the Amí Professional window.
Click	Quickly press and release the mouse button while the pointer is in a specific location. For example, "Click the OK button" means move the mouse pointer to the OK button, then press and release the mouse button. You always click the left mouse button; the right mouse button has no effect on text or graphics.
Double-click	Quickly press and release the mouse button twice while the pointer is in a specific location.
Drag	Hold down the mouse button while you move the mouse. You frequently use this action to move an object on the screen. For example, "Drag the tab icon" means point to the tab icon, then hold down the mouse button while you move the mouse to drag the tab stop icon to a new location.

The mouse pointer takes on a different shape depending on the kind of action that is being performed. For instance, it's an outlined arrow when you're selecting commands from the menu, an hourglass when Amí Professional is saving a file, and a question mark when you press Shift+F1 to use it as a help pointer.

USING KEYS IN AMÍ PROFESSIONAL

Because Amí Professional is a word processing program, you'll obviously be using the keyboard to enter text. As previously mentioned, you can use the mouse or the keyboard to choose Amí Professional commands and perform other tasks. Most of the time, it's easiest to use a combination of both keyboard and mouse techniques, choosing whichever is faster for the task at hand. However, if you're more comfortable using the keyboard or you don't have a mouse, you can use the keyboard to do all tasks in Amí Professional.

To make sure you won't be confused by the keyboard instructions in this book, you should know the location of and the name this book uses for these important keys:

Key Name	**Description**
Shift	Marked with the word *Shift* and/or with an Up arrow. Generally makes letters uppercase.
Tab	Marked with the word *Tab* and/or arrows pointing left and right. Generally inserts a tab character, shifting text to the right.
Backspace	Marked with the word *Backspace* and with an arrow pointing left. Generally erases the character to the left.
Delete	Marked with the letters *Del* or the word *Delete*. Does not perform the same action as the Backspace key. Generally, Delete deletes selected characters.
Insert	Marked with the letters *Ins* or the word *Insert*. Controls the insertion of information.
Control	Marked with the letters *Ctrl* or the word *Control*. Generally used in combination with other keys.
Alt	Marked with the letters *Alt*. Generally used in combination with other keys.
Function keys	Marked with the letter *F* followed by a number, such as F6 and F10. Most newer keyboards have 12 function keys. Generally used as "shortcut keys," sometimes in combination with other keys.
Escape	Marked with the letters *Esc*, the word *Escape*, or the word *Cancel*. Generally used to cancel an operation.
Enter	Marked with the word *Enter*, the word *Return*, and/or with a bent arrow to indicate that this key creates a new line. Generally used to create a new paragraph or to carry out a command.

Arrow keys	Marked with arrows pointing left, right, up, and down. Your keyboard may have one or two sets of arrow keys. Generally used to move the cursor on the screen. In this book these cursor movement keys are referred to as the Up, Down, Right, and Left arrow keys.
Numeric keypad	The 10-key pad found at the right side of most keyboards. Generally used to insert numbers (when NumLock is on) or to move the cursor (when NumLock is off).

When this book tells you to press several keys at once, the key combination is shown with a plus sign (+) between the key names. For example,

Ctrl+C

means hold down the Control key while you press the C letter key. We use uppercase letters throughout this book to more clearly show alphabetic keys in key combinations, but you don't need to press Shift to make the letter uppercase—the lowercase letter works just as well.

When you need to press and release keys in sequence (press and release one key, then press and release the next, and so on), you'll see the key combinations written with commas between the key names. For example,

Alt, F, N

means press and release the Alt key, press and release the F key, and then press and release the N key.

CHOOSING COMMANDS

If you've used a Windows-based program before, you're probably already familiar with choosing commands from menus. This section contains both mouse and keyboard instructions.

In this book, we combine menu names and command names when we refer to commands. For example, when we say "Choose the File Open command," we mean "Pull down the File menu, then choose the Open command."

If a command is dimmed ("grayed") on a menu, that command is not available for use at this time. You cannot choose dimmed commands. Take a look at Figure 2–4 to see the visual difference between active and dimmed (inactive) commands.

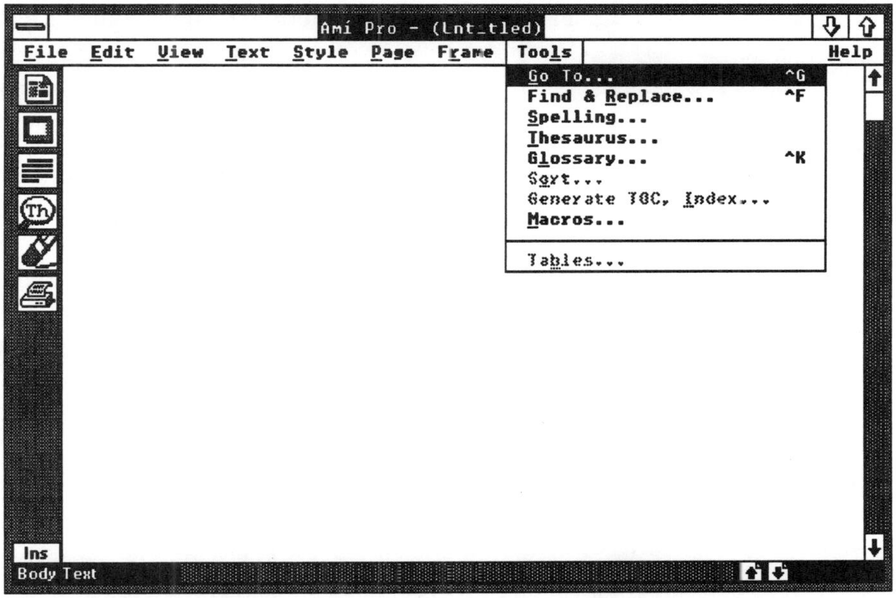

Figure 2-4
Bold commands are active; dimmed commands are not available.

Choosing Commands with the Mouse

To choose a command with the mouse:

1. Point to the menu name and hold down the mouse button to pull down the menu.
2. Drag the mouse pointer down the menu until the command you want is highlighted.
3. Release the mouse button.

If you pull down a menu, then decide not to choose a command, just drag the mouse pointer off the menu, then release the button.

Choosing Commands with the Keyboard

To choose a command with the keyboard:

1. Press **Alt, *Letter*** to pull down the menu. Each menu name has one underlined letter to indicate which letter to use with the Alt key. For example, the letter *F* in the File menu is underlined, so you'd press **Alt, F** to pull down the File menu; the letter *R* in the Frame menu is underlined, so you'd press **Alt, R** to pull down the Frame menu.

2. Press the underlined letter in the command name. For example, the letter *N* in the New command on the File menu is underlined, so you'd pull down the menu, then press **N** to choose the New command.

Amí Professional has one exception to the underlined-letter procedure: The Amí Professional Control menu in the Amí Professional window's upper left corner is represented by an icon (picture) rather than by a menu name. The Amí Professional Control menu icon is meant to look like the Spacebar on the keyboard—this is supposed to remind you that you use Alt, Spacebar to pull down that menu.

If you pull down a menu and then decide not to choose a command, press the **Escape** key to retract the menu.

Using Shortcut Keys to Choose Specific Commands

Many commands also have a key combination displayed beside the command name on the menu, as shown in Figure 2–5. The caret (^) stands for the Ctrl key—for example, ^M means press Ctrl+M. When you see a key combination beside a command, you can use the key combination to choose the command without first pulling down the menu.

For example, to choose the Draft Mode command from the View menu, you could use the mouse to pull down the menu and highlight the command

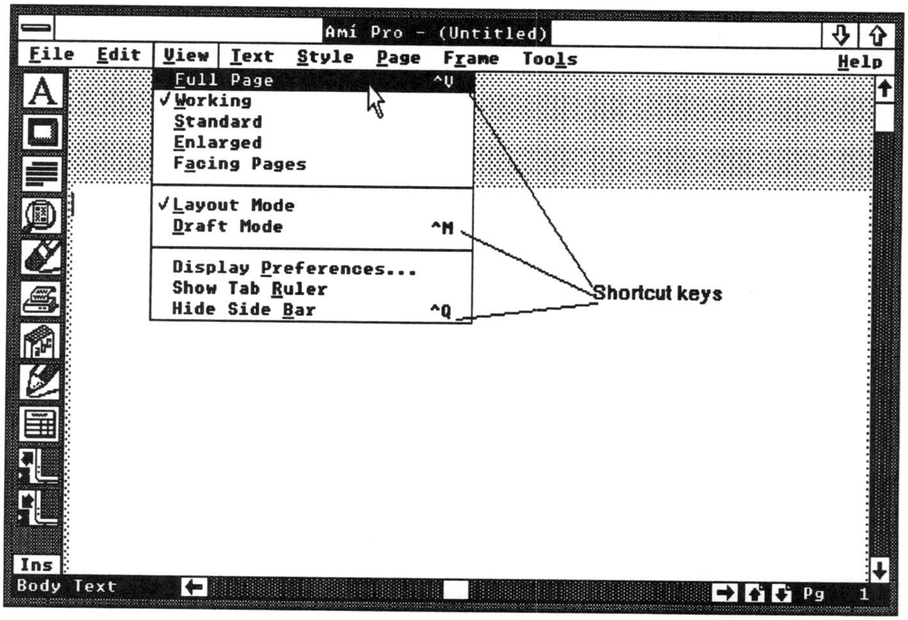

Figure 2–5
Choosing a command with the mouse.

as described earlier, or you could press **Alt, V, D** or press **Ctrl+M**, the shortcut key combination. You'll find that memorizing the shortcut keys for frequently used commands speeds up your work with Amí Professional.

CHOOSING OPTIONS IN DIALOG BOXES

Some Amí Professional commands take effect as soon as you choose them. Other Amí Professional commands display dialog boxes to ask you for more information about what you want to do. Commands that display dialog boxes are followed by three dots on the menu to represent an ellipsis. Figure 2–6 shows how the Text Font command displays a dialog box.

When a dialog box is displayed on the screen, you have to choose an option in the dialog box or close the dialog box before you can choose another command or type text in a document. If you try to do something outside of the dialog box, Amí Professional beeps to remind you to close the dialog box first.

Dialog boxes are filled with options you can choose to affect your document. Amí Professional has different types of dialog box options, as shown in Figures 2–7 and 2–8.

When you open a dialog box for the first time, you'll see that some options are selected, and sometimes you'll see a file name or a measurement

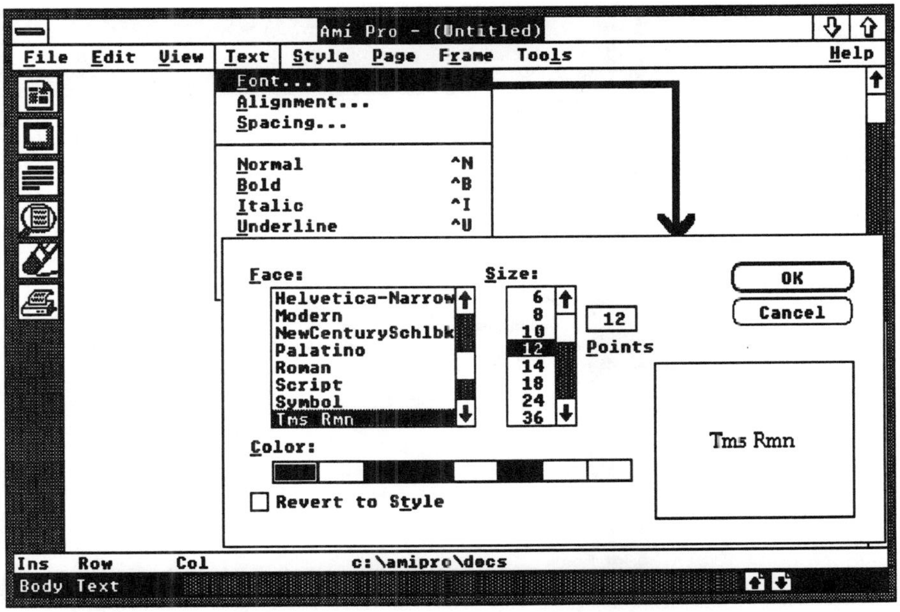

Figure 2–6
The Text Font command is followed by an ellipsis to show that it displays a dialog box.

Figure 2-7
Options in the File Open dialog box.

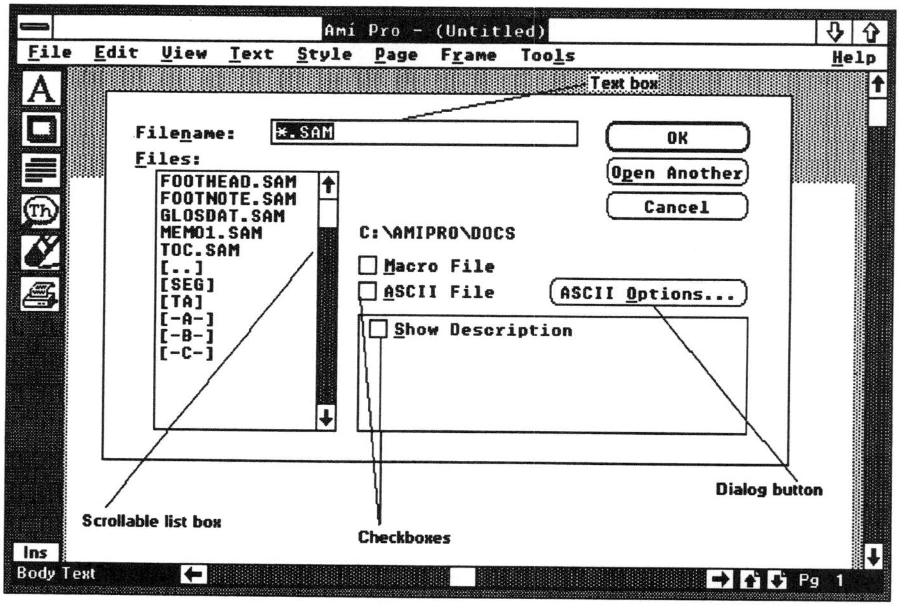

Figure 2-8
Options in the Tools Go To dialog box.

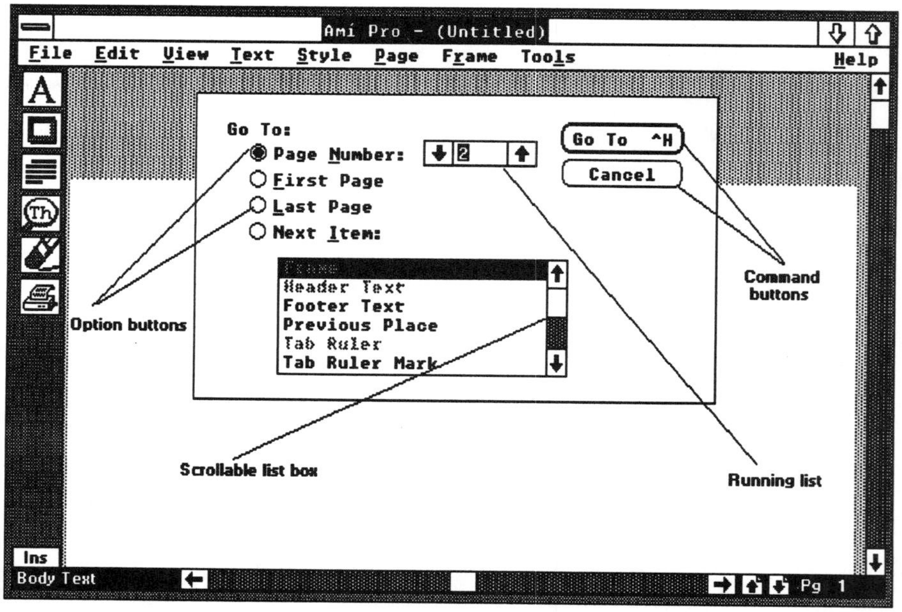

in a box. These choices come from Amí Professional's default settings—the settings Amí Professional assumes you'll want to use most of the time. Amí Professional's default settings are part of the ~DEFAULT.STY file.

You can either accept the default settings in a dialog box by leaving them alone or you can choose new options to affect that particular document. Generally speaking, choosing new options in a dialog box doesn't change the default settings—they'll appear again the next time you choose a command in a new document. (You can, however, control many default settings with the Edit Defaults and View Display Preferences commands.)

This section gives you the general procedure for choosing dialog box options with the mouse or with the keyboard. (If you open a dialog box to practice, click the Cancel button or press **Escape** to close it when you're finished.)

To choose an option in a dialog box:

1. Click the option with the mouse.
   or
   Press **Alt**+the underlined ***letter*** in the option name. If the option is an option button, this selects the option, as shown in Figure 2–9.
   If the option is a check box (an option that can be turned on or off), this "turns on" the option and places an *X* in the box, or "turns off" the option and removes the *X*. Figure 2–10 shows check boxes in both states.

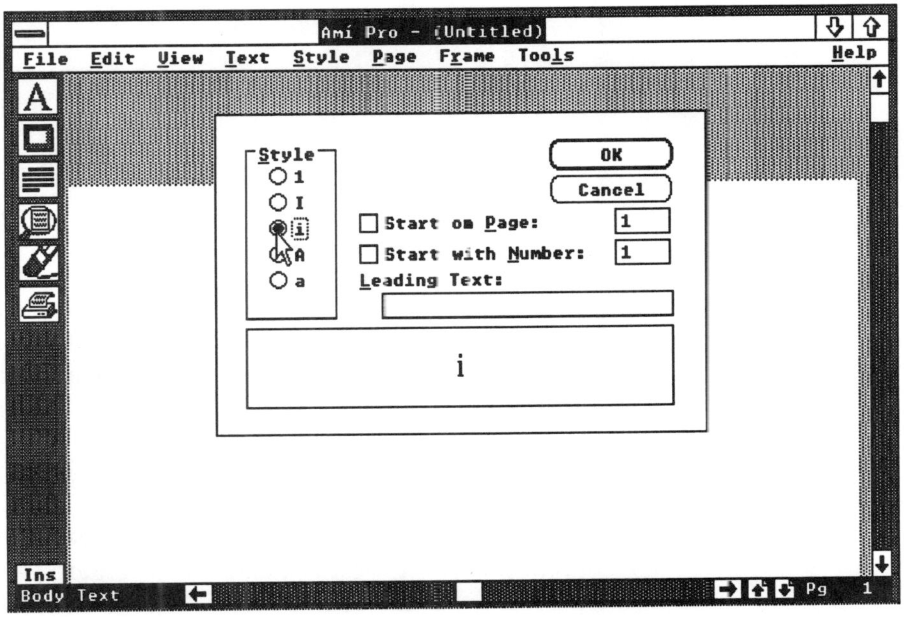

Figure 2–9
You can select only one option button from the same group.

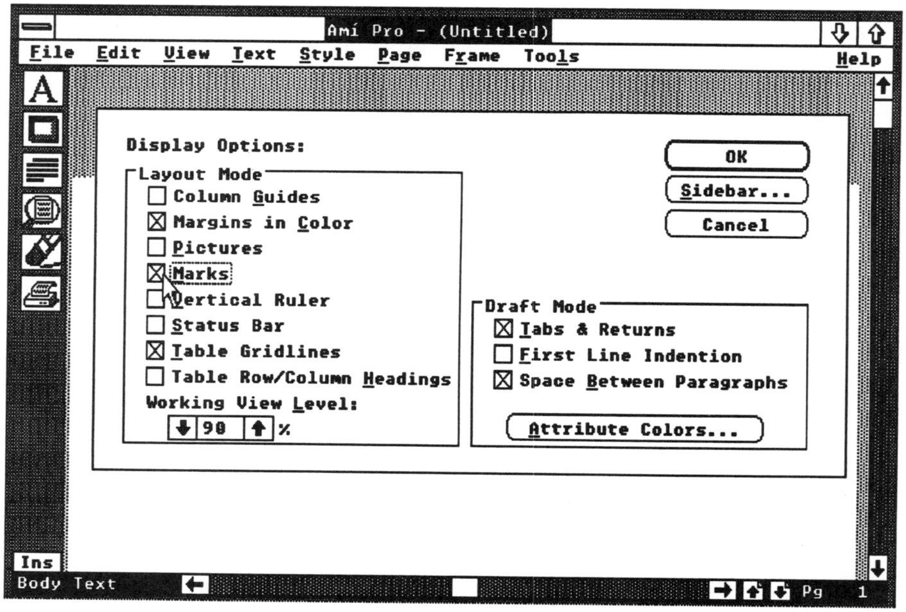

Figure 2-10
An X in a check box means the option is turned on; a blank check box means the option is turned off.

If the option is a dialog button (sometimes called a *tunnel button*), Amí Professional displays another dialog box, shown in Figure 2-11.

If the option is a command button, Amí Professional carries out the command and closes the dialog box.

2. Choose one of the following actions if necessary:

- If the option is a scrollable list box, use the scroll bar if needed to scroll the list, then click an item in the list to highlight it. To scroll one line at a time, click the Up or Down arrow in the scroll bar or press the **Up** or **Down arrow** key. To scroll one windowful at a time, click in the gray area above or below the scroll box or press the **PgUp** or **PgDn** key.

- If the option is a running list box, point to the Down or Up arrow on either side and click the mouse button, or press the **Down** or **Up arrow** key to display the next option or the previous option in the list. To scroll quickly through the list, hold down the mouse button or arrow key until the option you want appears in the middle box. You can also type a new option in the middle box.

- If the option is a text box, type new text or edit the existing text, as shown in the Filename box in Figure 2-12. If you type more characters than Amí Professional can fit in the box, the text scrolls

Figure 2-11
Clicking a dialog button in a dialog box displays another dialog box. In this example, choosing the Options button in the Edit Defaults dialog box displays the Document Defaults dialog box.

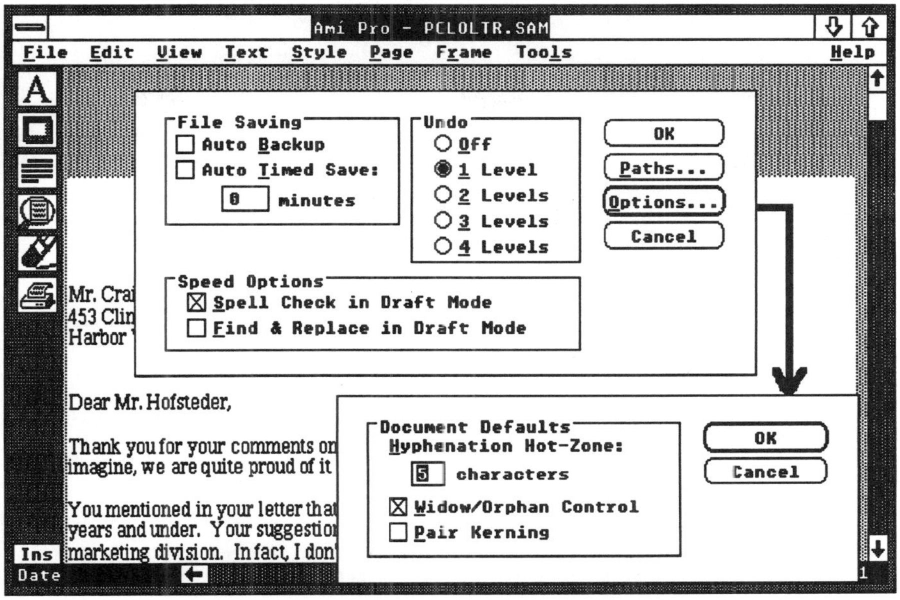

Figure 2-12
You can type new text or edit the existing text in text boxes.

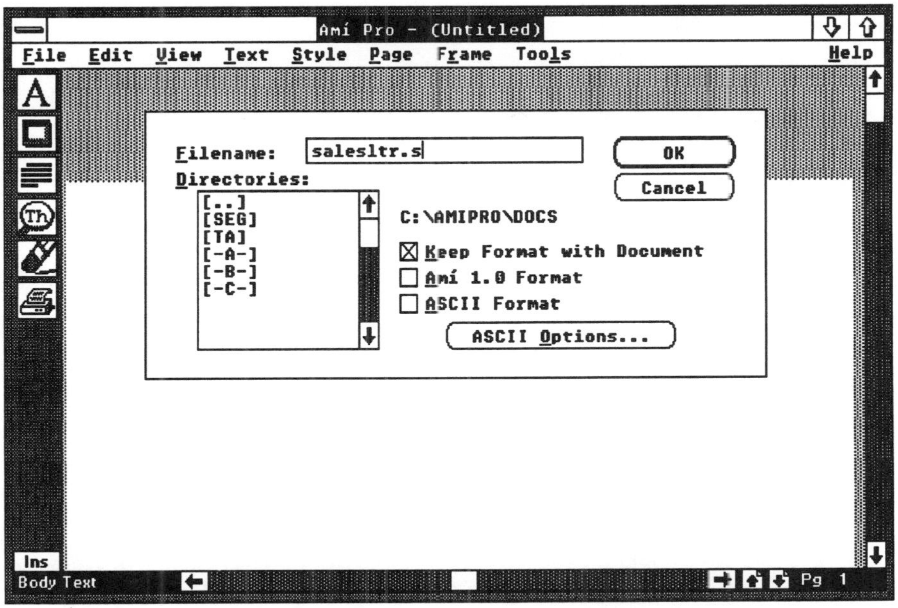

so you can see what you're typing. You can use the arrow keys to scroll back. You'll learn more about editing text in Chapter 4, "Editing Your Amí Professional Files."

3. If you've chosen all the options you want in the dialog box and you're ready for your changes to take effect, click OK or press **Enter**.

   or

   If you made a mistake and you don't want your changes to take effect, click the Cancel button or press **Escape**.

Keyboard Speed Tip

In scrollable list boxes that contain long lists, you can quickly find the item you're looking for by typing the first letter of its name. This makes the highlight "jump" to the appropriate section of the list. For example, if you were looking for a list item named "Time," you could go to the scrollable list box and type **T** to move the highlight to the first item beginning with the letter *T*. Then you could quickly find the item named Time.

Mouse Speed Tip

In scrollable list boxes, you can use the mouse to double-click a list item, which selects the list item, chooses the default command button, and closes the dialog box, all at the same time.

Moving Dialog Boxes

If a dialog box is hiding part of your document that you need to refer to, you can use this procedure to move the dialog box to a new location in the Amí Professional window:

1. Press **Alt+F7**.
2. Use the arrow keys to move the dialog box to the new location.
3. Press **Enter** to set the new position of the dialog box or press **Escape** if you change your mind and want to return to the original position.

GETTING HELP

Amí Professional has an extensive help system you can use whenever you need more information about commands, a task, or a dialog box option. Here's how it works:

To	Do This
Browse through the help system	Choose the Indexed Help command from the Help menu to display a list of help topics, as shown in Figure 2–13. To get instructions about using the help system, choose the How to Use Help topic in the Help window.
Get information about a specific command or dialog box option	Choose the command to display the dialog box, then press F1 to see specific help about that command and dialog box option, as shown in Figure 2–14.
Use a mouse pointer to click a command or screen area and display help information	Press **Shift+F1**, then use the mouse help pointer (the question mark with the arrowhead shown in Figure 2–15) to click a command or screen area you want to see help about.

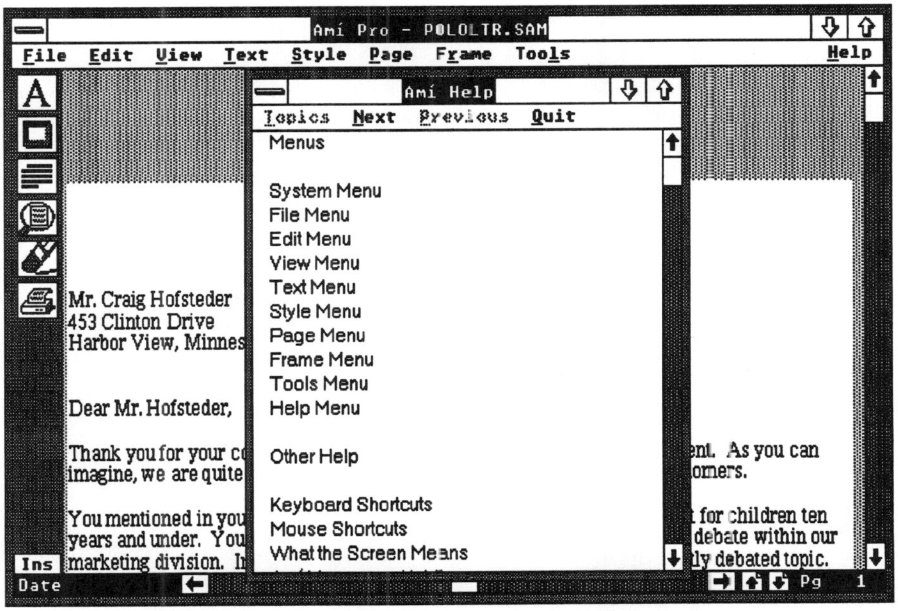

Figure 2–13
Choosing from an index of help topics displayed with the Indexed Help command.

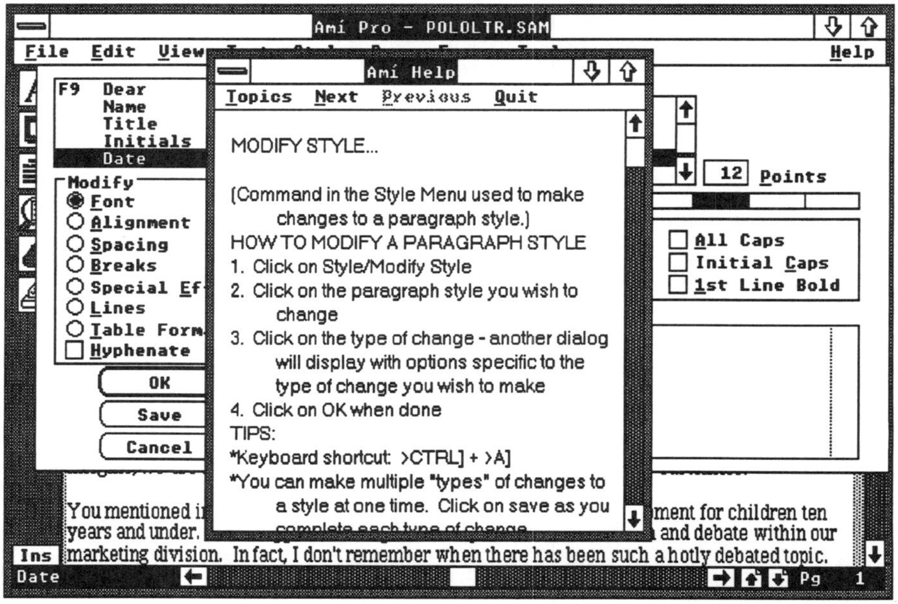

Figure 2-14 Specific help about a dialog box displayed with the F1 key.

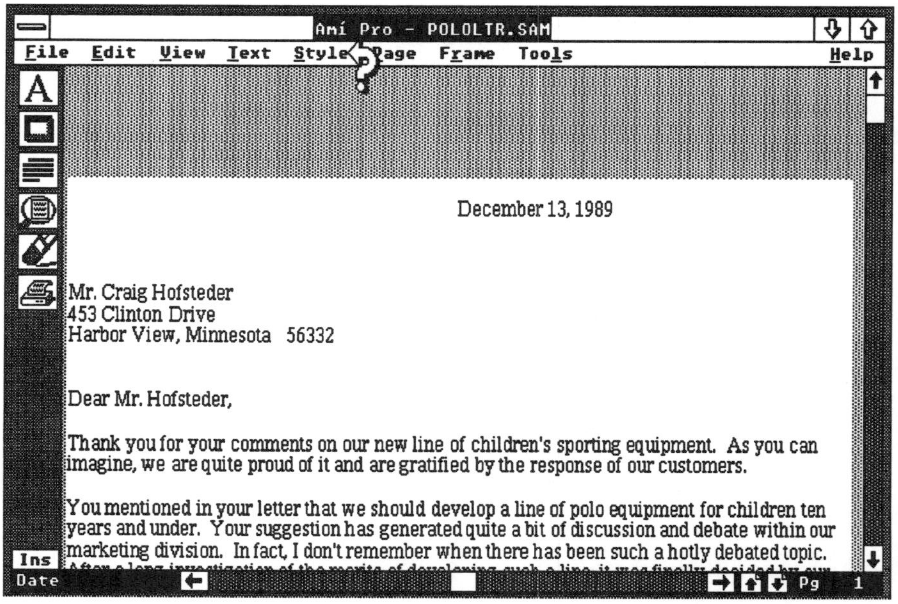

Figure 2-15 Using the mouse help pointer (displayed by pressing Shift+F1) to get help.

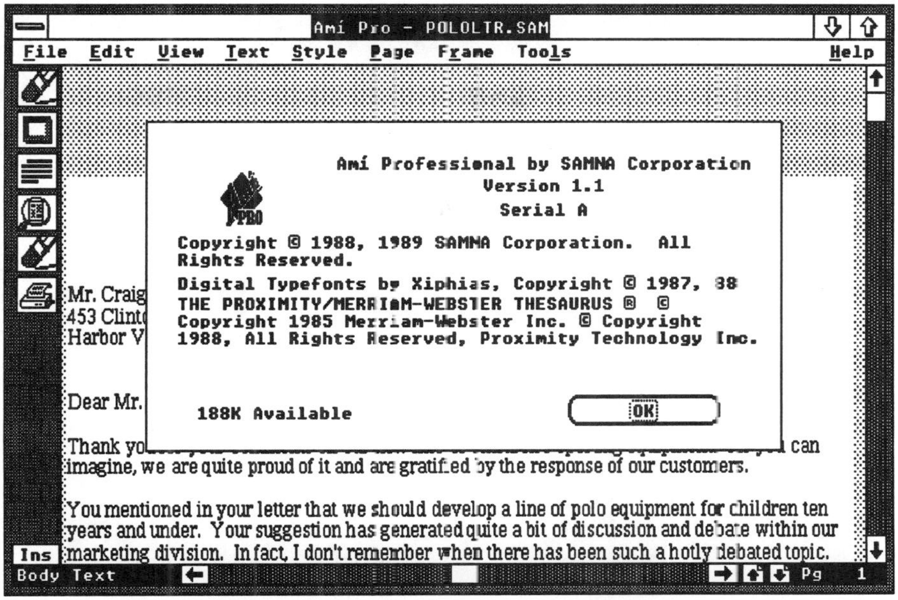

Figure 2–16 The information displayed by the Help About Amí command.

Display the Amí Professional version number and information about disk space and memory available on your computer	Choose the About Amí command from the Help menu. Click OK or press **Enter** when you're through reading. Figure 2–16 shows the opening About Amí information.

Using the Help Window

The Help window is a separate window—you can move it, change its size, turn it into an icon, and use the scroll bars to scroll through the information in the window, just like you can manipulate the Amí Professional window (or any other Windows window). If you're not familiar with these techniques, see Appendix A.

In the Help window, you'll notice that some text is bold or displayed in a different color. These bold or colored labels are jump terms, which display the help topic they name when you click on them or highlight them with the arrow keys and press **Enter**.

You can scroll through all the help files at your leisure, or you can use the four commands on the menu bar in the Help window to move efficiently through the help system.

Use This Command	To
Topics	Display the index of help topics.
Next	Display the next help topic in the list.
Previous	Display the previous topic you chose.
Quit	Close the Help window. (You can also double-click the Control menu icon in the upper left corner of the Help window.)

QUITTING AMÍ PROFESSIONAL

You can quit Amí Professional using any of the following methods:

- Choose the File Exit command (**Alt, F, X**).

or

- Choose the Close command from the Amí Professional Control menu (**Alt, Spacebar, C** or **Alt+F4**).

or

- Double-click the Amí Professional Control menu icon.

If you've made any changes that haven't been saved, Amí Professional asks you whether to save changes before quitting.

3

Using Different Modes and Views

Amí Professional provides two modes and five views for composing your documents. This chapter explains the purpose and uses for

- draft mode
- layout mode
- working view
- standard view
- enlarged view
- full-page view
- facing-pages view

DRAFT MODE VERSUS LAYOUT MODE

Amí Professional offers two modes of displaying text on the screen:

- draft mode, which displays one long file of text without margins or formatting. Amí Professional operates faster in draft mode.
- layout mode, which displays separate pages with margins, text, graphics, and formatting just as they will appear when printed.

When you want to enter a lot of text, you can switch to draft mode to speed things up. If you want to format your text (add bold, italic, underlines, and so forth), you'll want to switch to layout mode so that you can see how the finished pages will look. Figures 3–1 and 3–2 show the same document; in Figure 3–1 it appears in draft mode; in Figure 3–2, in layout mode.

Switching Between Display Modes

To switch between draft and layout modes:

- Click the mode icon (it looks like a formatted page in draft mode, like a capital letter *A* in layout mode).

or

- Choose the Draft Mode command or the Layout Mode command from the View menu, as shown in Figure 3–3.

Keyboard Shortcut

To quickly switch between draft and layout modes:

- Press **Ctrl**+**M**.

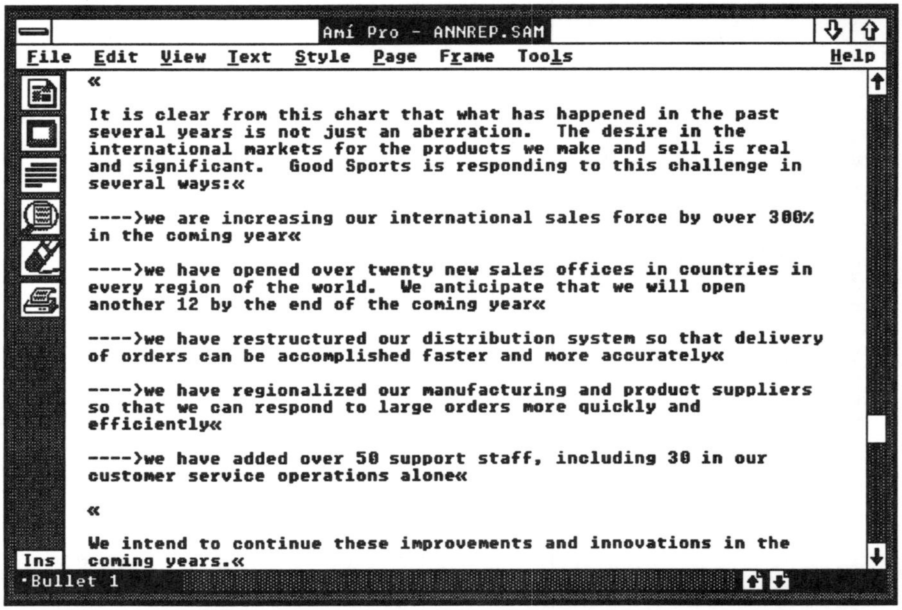

Figure 3–1 A sample document in draft mode. The double angle brackets (<<) are paragraph marks; the dashes and arrows are tab characters.

Figure 3–2
A sample document in layout mode.

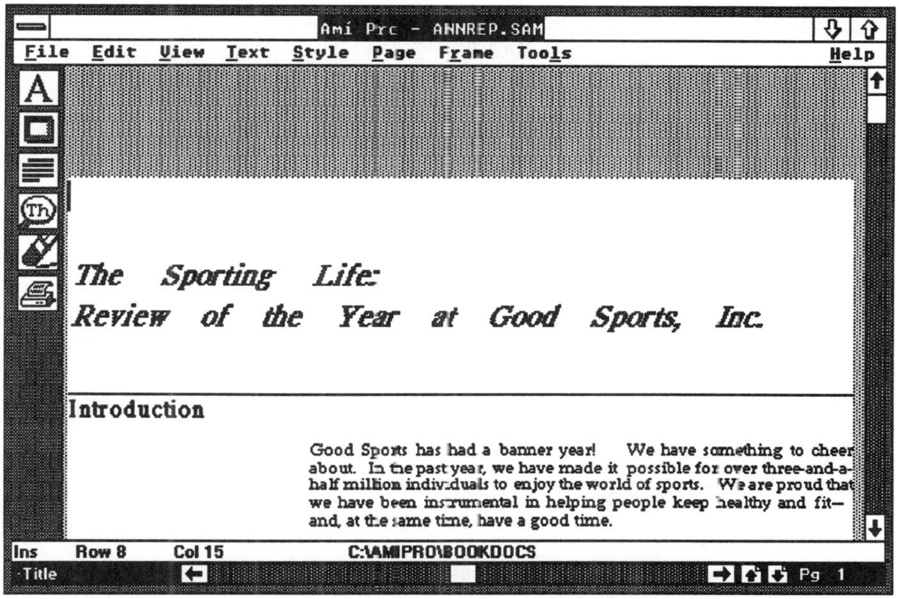

Figure 3–3
Switching to layout mode with the View Layout Mode command.

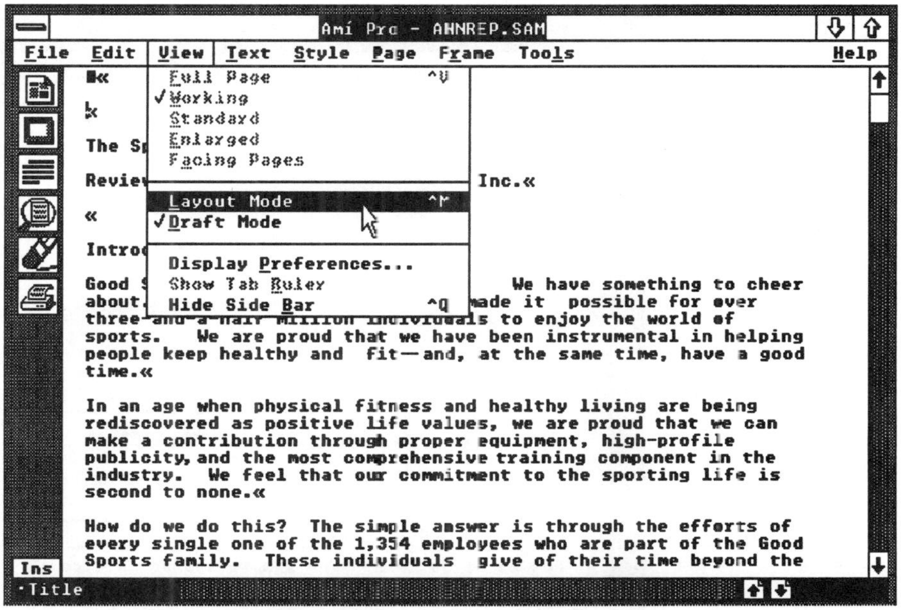

Using Draft Mode

As mentioned previously, you'll use draft mode primarily for speed typing. When you use draft mode, many commands and icons are not available for use. However, you can set options to help you easily distinguish parts of your document on the screen. None of these options affect the printed pages. You can choose to

- show tab characters and paragraph marks (shown in Figure 3–1).
- indent the first lines of paragraphs.
- display a blank line between paragraphs.
- display different types of formats (such as bold, italic, underline, and so forth) in different colors. (Obviously, this is useful only if you have a color monitor.)

To choose options for draft mode:

1. Choose the View Display Preferences command.
2. Turn on the options you want in the Draft Mode box.
3. To set colors for formatted text, choose the Attribute Colors button to display the dialog box shown in Figure 3–4, select the type of

Figure 3–4
Using the View Display Preferences command to change the color in which italic text will be displayed in draft mode.

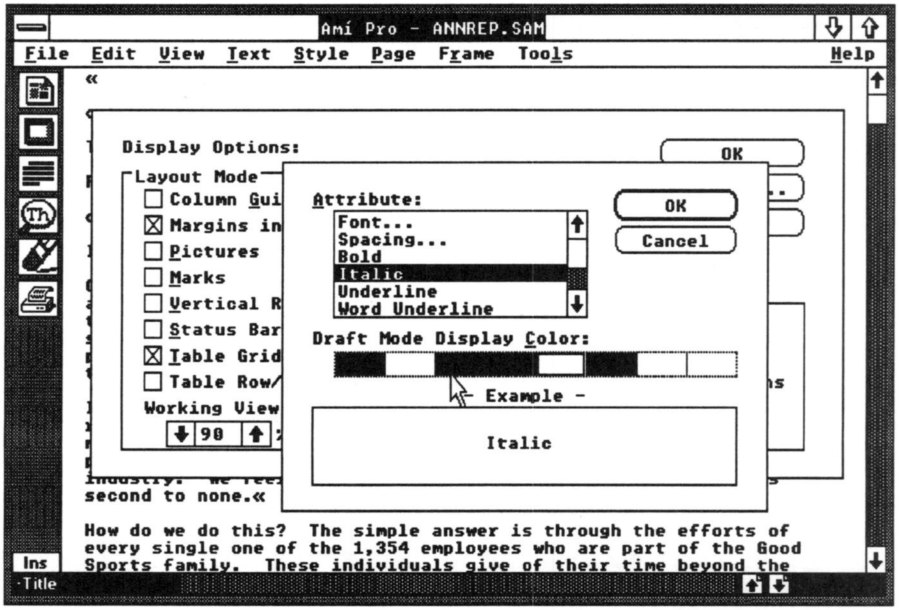

formatting from the Attribute list, then click the color you want in the color bar. The sample text at the bottom of the dialog box changes to show your choice. When you've set all the colors you want, click OK or press **Enter** to close the Attribute Colors dialog box.

4. Click OK or press **Enter**.

Using Layout Mode

Layout mode shows you individual pages of your document, including margins and formatting. When you use layout mode, you can also choose from five different views, as explained in the next section.

You can choose several options that affect layout mode. You can choose

- whether to display column guides (the dotted vertical lines shown in Figure 3–5) when you are working with multiple columns.
- whether to display colored margins (the default) or white margins (colored margin is shown as a dotted strip along the right edge in Figure 3–5).
- whether to display pictures or mark their positions with empty boxes.

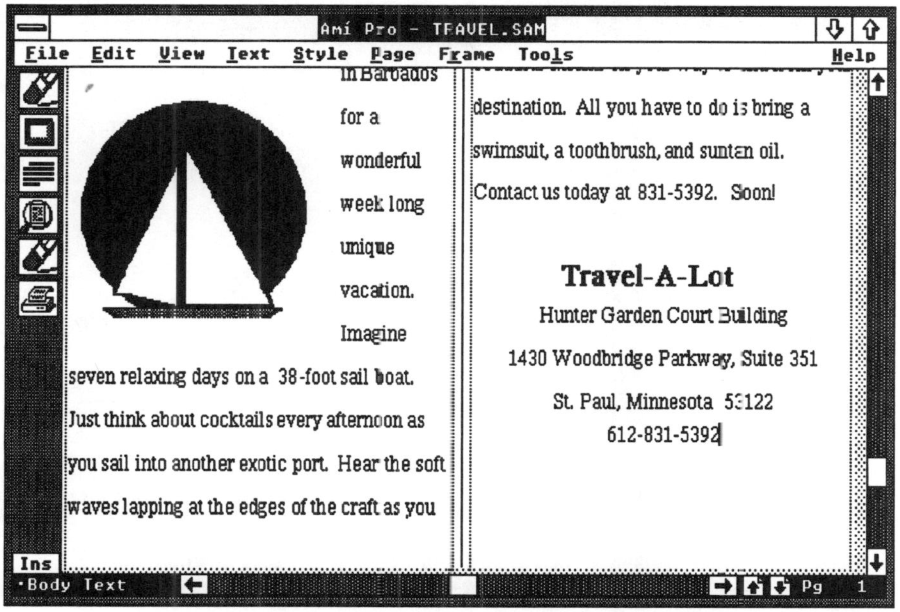

Figure 3–5 Column guides and graphics displayed in layout mode.

(Amí Professional works faster when graphics are not displayed.) Figure 3–5 shows a graphic displayed in layout mode.

- whether to display marks for notes, tab rulers, floating headers, or floating footers.
- whether to display a vertical ruler at the left of the document (shown along the left in Figure 3–6).
- whether to display a status bar at the bottom of the document window. The status bar (shown in Figure 3–6) lists the column and line number of the cursor's position.
- whether to display table gridlines to outline table cells, and row and column headings for tables. (See Chapter 14 for more information about tables.)
- whether to set a new display percentage. This controls the size of the page in working view as expressed as a percentage of standard view. Working view is set by default at 91 percent, which enables you to see complete lines of text on the screen when the Amí Professional window is maximized. By changing the percentage, you can display pages in any size you want, customizing the view to the size that works best for you. This has no effect on the printed document.

To choose options that affect layout mode:

Figure 3–6 The vertical ruler and status bar displayed in layout mode.

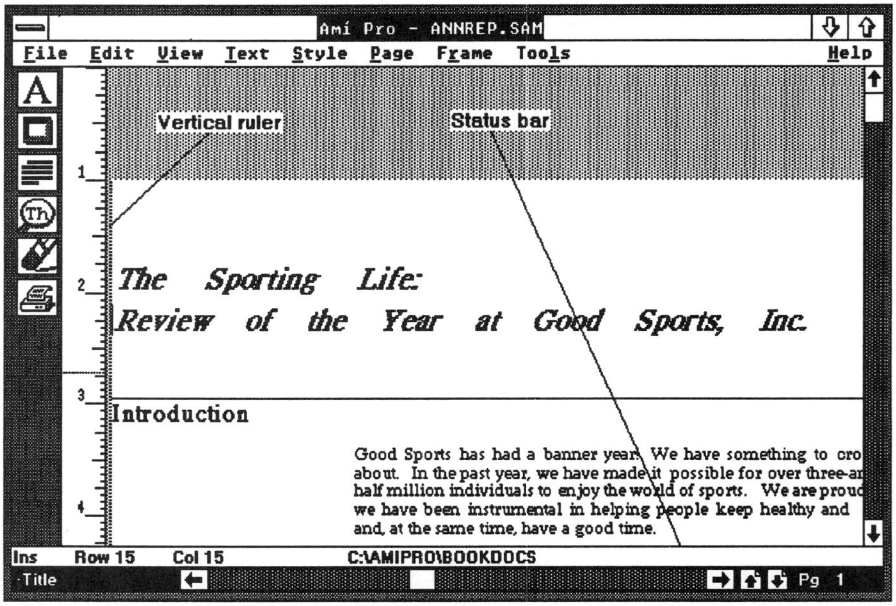

1. Choose the View Display Preferences command.
2. Turn on the options you want in the Layout Mode box. An *X* in the check box next to the dialog box indicates that the option is in effect.
3. To set a new layout percentage for working view, type or select a new number in the Working View Level running list box. This option sets the size of the page displayed in working view, expressing the size as a percentage of the printed page (which is shown in standard view). If you use a low number for this option, you may not be able to read text on the screen. If you use a high number for this option, you'll have to scroll horizontally to see all of your text on a page.
4. Click OK or press **Enter**.

USING AMÍ PROFESSIONAL'S FIVE VIEWS

When you are using layout mode, Amí Professional has five views you can use to display text:

- Working view—shows text as a percentage of the printed document. By default, this view is set to 91 percent, which means you can see both ends of the text on the screen when the Amí Professional window is maximized. You can change the percentage as described in the previous section. Working view is the view you'll probably use most often. Figure 3–7 shows a document in working view.
- Standard view—shows pages in the default size used by other Windows applications. Unless your document has large margins, you'll probably have to scroll to see the ends of lines at the right side of pages. Figure 3–8 shows a document in standard view.
- Enlarged view—shows a portion of a page enlarged on the screen so that you can see small fonts, precisely position frames, and edit in fine detail. Figure 3–9 shows a document in enlarged view.
- Full-page view—shows entire pages in miniature, one page at a time, so you can see how each page will look before printing. Figure 3–10 shows a document in full-page view.
- Facing-pages view—shows miniature pages in pairs, with even-numbered pages on the left side and odd-numbered pages on the right, so that you can see the visual balance of facing pages. Figure 3–11 shows a document in facing-pages view.

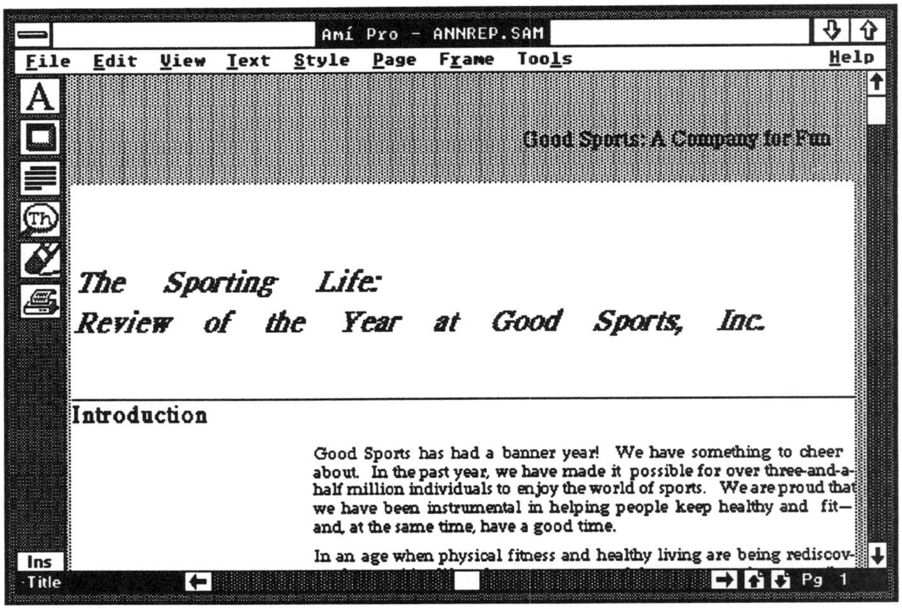

Figure 3–7 Working view.

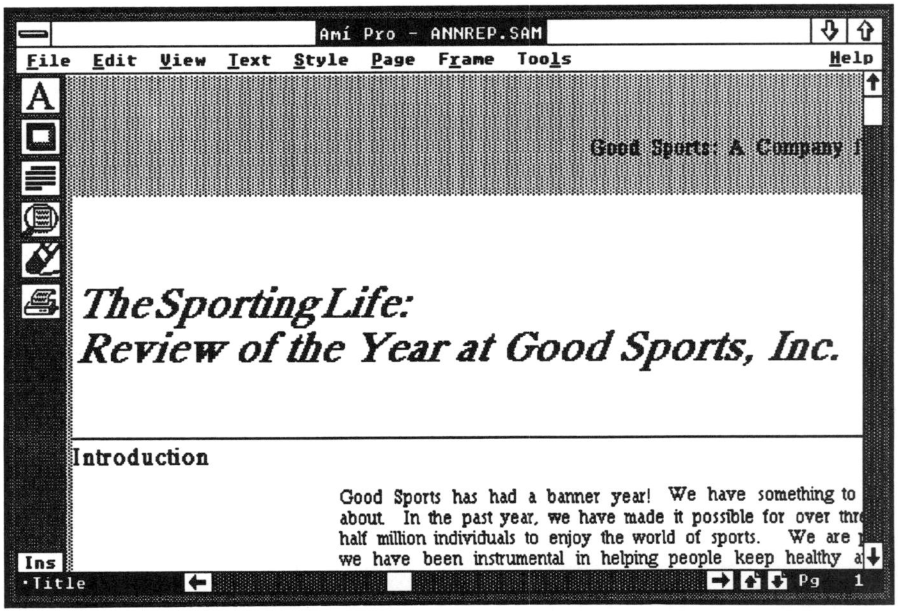

Figure 3–8 Standard view.

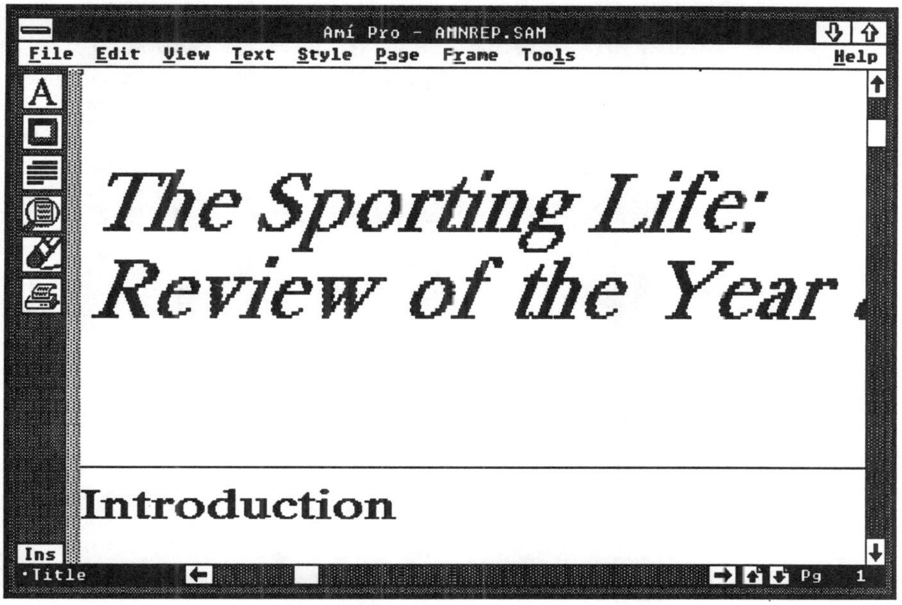

Figure 3–9
Enlarged view.

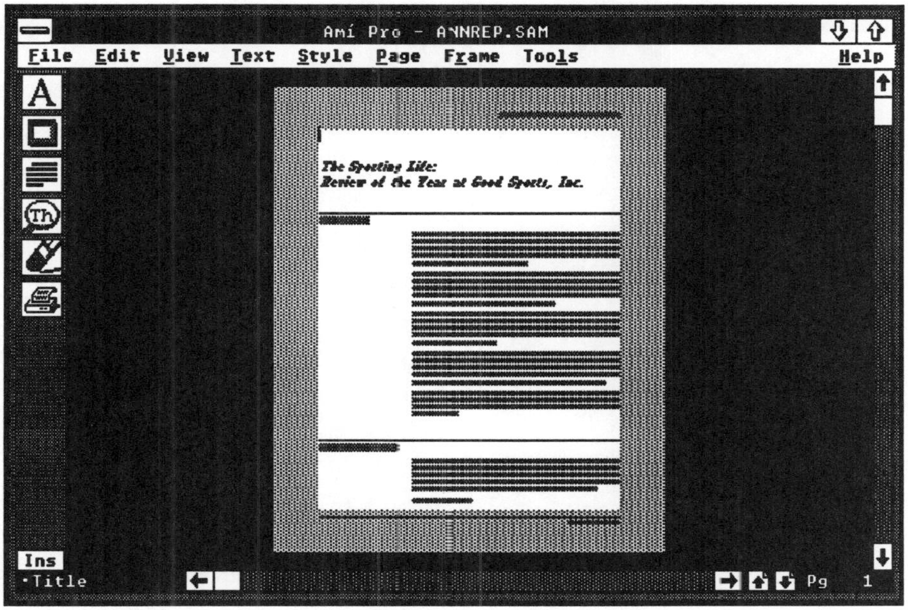

Figure 3–10
Full-page view.

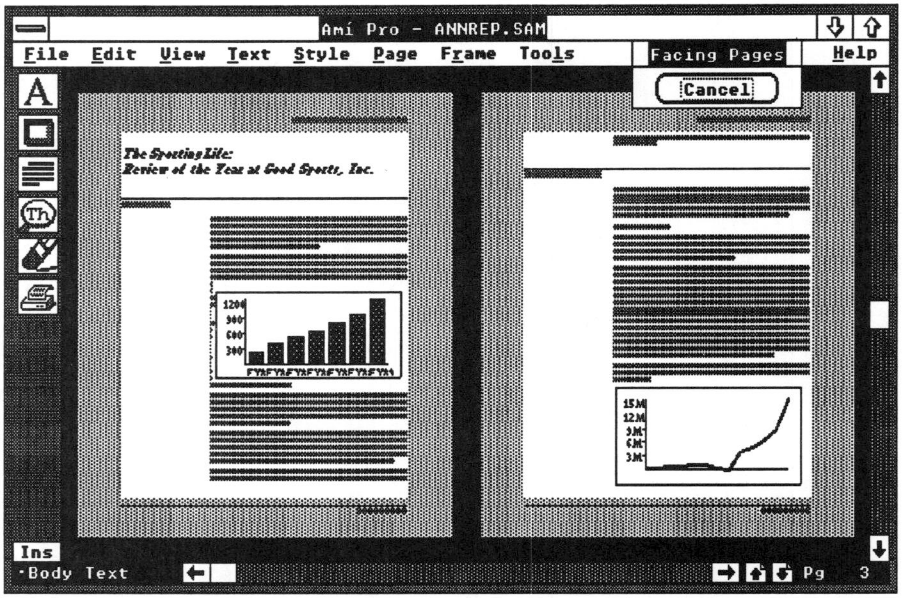

Figure 3–11
Facing-pages view.

Except for facing-pages view, no matter which view you have displayed on the screen, you use the same Amí Professional menu commands and icons to edit and format text, change the page layout, or print your document.

Switching Views

Except for facing-pages view, you can switch between the different views by choosing a command from the View menu.

Shortcuts

To toggle quickly back and forth between your current view and full-page view, you can also:

- Click the view icon (the magnifying glass) in the sidebar to the left of the document.

or

- Press **Ctrl**+**V**.

4

Managing Your Files

Because all Amí Professional documents are stored in files, understanding how to create, load, save, and manage Amí Professional files is essential. This chapter describes

- the rules for naming Amí Professional files
- the relationship between documents and style sheets in Amí Professional
- creating new files
- opening and saving different files and file formats
- using the File Manager to manipulate files
- using the document description box to provide information about files

ABOUT AMÍ PROFESSIONAL FILE NAME RULES

When you name an Amí Professional file, you must obey the operating system's rules for file names. If you try to type an invalid file name in Amí Professional or any other program running with DOS (MS-DOS or PC-DOS), you'll see a message something like:

```
Filename too long
```

or

```
Filename contains invalid characters
```

The names of all files you use with DOS must conform to the following rules:

- The file names must contain no more than eight characters in the basic file name before a period, and no more than three characters in the file name extension after the period. No spaces are allowed in file names.
- You can't use any of the following characters in a file name:

*	Asterisk
\	Backslash
:	Colon
,	Comma
.	Period
?	Question mark
;	Semicolon
/	Slash

All Amí Professional document files must have the extension .SAM, and all Amí Professional style sheet files must have the extension .STY. If you don't specify an extension or a period after the basic file name, Amí Professional adds a .SAM extension to a file name. For example, if you tell Amí Professional you want a file named PLAY, it assumes you want the file named PLAY.SAM.

When you want Amí Professional to find or put a file in a directory or a disk drive that's different than the one you're working in, type a path name in front of the file name as explained later in this chapter. For more information about file names, path names, disk drives, and operating system rules, see the operating system manual that came with your computer and the "Guide to Windows" that came with your Amí Professional program.

DOCUMENTS AND STYLE SHEETS

When you use Amí Professional, you'll work with two basic types of files: *documents* and *style sheets.* A document is a simple word-processing file:

it might be a letter, a chapter from a novel, an outline for a newspaper article, or any other sort of file that contains words.

Every Amí Professional document is based on a style sheet. A style sheet is a file that contains *styles*—named sets of formatting instructions that you can use over and over. Using a style is simple. Say you've formatted a paragraph to look like this:

CHAPTER 2

The text is bold, the font is New Century Schoolbook, the size is 14 points, the paragraph is indented from the left and right margins, and the text is centered and has lines above and below it. To use this format for all chapter headings, you could define this format as a style named *chapter*, then apply the *chapter* style to all your chapter heading paragraphs to make them look alike.

Using style sheets can save you a lot of time, because one style can contain a great deal of formatting. Styles can include bullets, lines above or below, indents, line spacing, fonts, bold formatting, italic formatting, and many other formats.

All paragraphs in an Amí Professional file have a style attached to them. If you haven't chosen a new style sheet or attached styles of your own, all paragraphs have Amí Professional's default style, the Body Text style.

Amí Professional comes with dozens of style sheets, including a standard style sheet called ~DEFAULT.STY that contains all the default settings. When you start Amí Professional, the styles in ~DEFAULT.STY are listed in the styles box in the upper right corner of the Amí window. Amí automatically bases new documents on the last style sheet used, so you don't really need to concern yourself with creating style sheets if you don't want to. If you don't like the ~DEFAULT.STY settings, you can use another provided style sheet, create your own style sheets, or you can change the ~DEFAULT.STY settings.

As well as containing styles, style sheets can also include text and graphics. So if you use a standard format for certain types of documents, such as memos, letters, or invoices, you'll probably want to create many of your own style sheets. When you've created and saved your style sheets, you can base new documents of the same type on a specific style sheet to create documents with the same basic look. You'll find out more about manipulating the styles box and about creating your own styles and style sheet files in Chapter 9.

CREATING NEW AMÍ PROFESSIONAL FILES

Amí Professional is flexible. You specify exactly what options you want when you create new documents, or you can change your mind and specify different options when you save a document. So don't worry if you don't know exactly what layout you want when you start a new file; you can always change the format later.

If you don't open an existing document when you start Amí Professional, the program opens a new, empty document for you so you can start typing right away. Amí Professional labels the document `(Untitled)` on the screen. When you save the `(Untitled)` file later, you give it the name you want and Amí Professional replaces `(Untitled)` with the name you choose.

If you have already started Amí Professional and opened an existing document, you can use the File New command to open a new, empty document.

To create a new document:

1. Choose the File New command.
2. If you want to use a style sheet other than the one selected, select a new style sheet from the list in the dialog box. (You can find out more about using style sheets in Chapter 9.)
3. Click OK or press **Enter**.
4. Type and format the text.
5. Save the file.

ENTERING TEXT

Entering text is easy—just type! You don't need to press **Enter** when you come to the end of a line. Amí Professional automatically begins a new line when the text reaches the right margin. This feature is commonly called *wordwrap*.

To begin a new paragraph, press **Enter**. To back up and erase errors, press the **Backspace** key.

OPENING EXISTING AMÍ PROFESSIONAL FILES

To open a file:

1. Choose the File Open command. Amí Professional displays the dialog box shown in Figure 4-1.

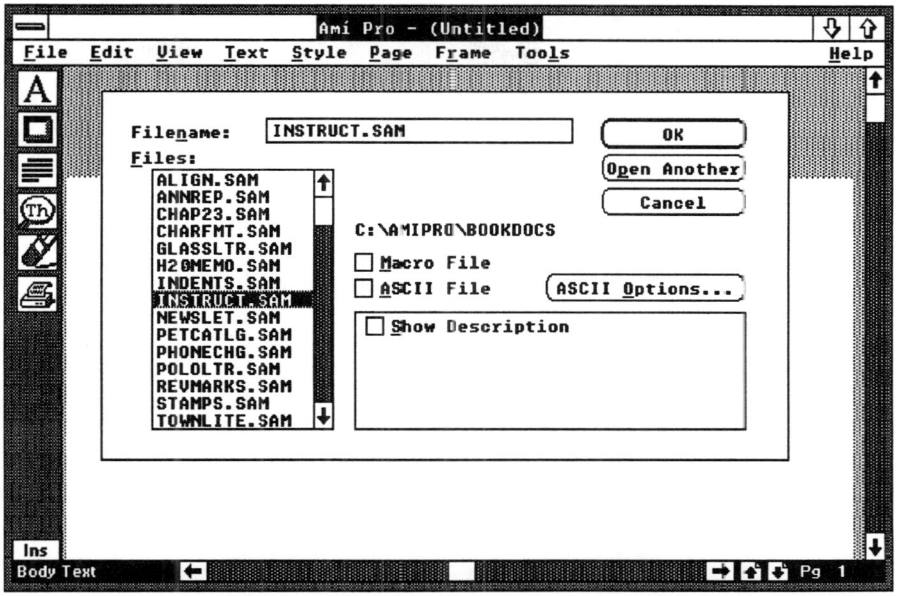

Figure 4-1
Using the File Open dialog box.

2. Select the name of the file you want to open from the list. The list displays the names of files in the active disk drive and directory. To see names of other files, you may need to type a drive name or directory names in the text box. For example, to see a list of Amí Professional files in the LETTERS directory on drive A, you would type **a:\letters** in the text box.

3. Click OK or press **Enter** to open the file and close the dialog box.

Mouse Speed Tip

To quickly open a file, you can double-click the name of the file in the File Open dialog box to select it and close the dialog box at the same time.

If you're using the full version of Windows, you can also start Amí Professional and open an Amí Professional document at the same time by selecting the document's name in the MS-DOS Executive window as long as it is in the same directory as or in a subdirectory below the AMIPRO.EXE file.

If you've saved a description of the file, you can turn on the Show Description option in the File Open dialog box to see a description of the selected file before you open it. Later, this chapter describes how you use the Document Description command and the File Manager window to save descriptions and manage files.

IMPORTING DATA CREATED BY OTHER PROGRAMS

Amí Professional can import data from files that have any of the following formats:

- AdvanceWrite
- ASCII
- dBASE®
- DCA/FFT (includes DisplayWrite™ and Display Writer)
- DCA/RFT (Revisable Form Text)
- Enable™ (text)
- Enable (spreadsheet)
- EPS (Encapsulated PostScript®)
- Excel
- Lotus® 1-2-3® and PIC
- Microsoft® Word for DOS
- MultiMate® and Advantage II
- Navy DIF
- PCX
- Peachtext
- SAMNA Word and Plus
- SuperCalc®
- TIFF
- Microsoft® Windows Write
- WordPerfect® 4.2 and 5.0
- WordStar® Releases 3.0, 4.1, and 5.0
- WordStar® 2000 1.0 and 3.0

You can use the File Save command to save the imported data in a normal Amí Professional file or use the File Import/Export command again to save it (export it) in another format.

When you save information from files that were created in other applications, Amí Professional automatically converts the text to the Amí Professional file format but does its best to retain the look of the original file. The imported information appears at the cursor position, so you may want to use the File New command to open an empty file first to avoid merging files.

To import data from an existing file created by another program:

1. Choose the File Import/Export command. Amí Professional displays the dialog box shown in Figure 4–2.

2. Select the file's current format from the File Type list box.

3. Select the name of the file from the Filename list. The list displays the names of files in the active disk drive and directory. To see names of other files, you may need to type a drive name, directory names, or file name indicators in the Import File text box, then press **Enter** to display a new list. For example, to see a list of files with .DOC extensions in the WORD directory on drive A, you would type **a:\word*.doc** in the text box, then press **Enter**.

4. Click OK or press **Enter**.

Figure 4–2 illustrates using the dialog box to import a Microsoft Word file from the WORD\RP directory.

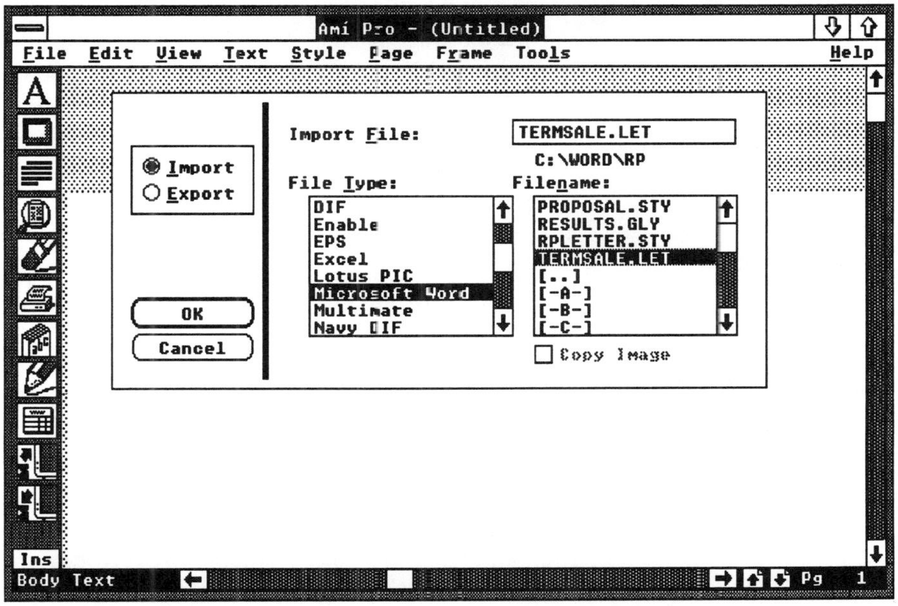

Figure 4–2 Using the File Import/Export command to import a file created in Microsoft Word into Amí Professional.

Amí Professional automatically looks for any additional files used by the original application, such as style sheet files, printer files (for fonts), footnote files, and glossary files. If the program can't locate these files, it displays a dialog box asking you to supply the correct path to the file. If this happens, correct the path name or choose the Cancel or Ignore button to proceed without using that file.

Similarly, if the imported file contains styles, Amí Professional displays a dialog box asking what you want to do with the styles. The choices are Keep Style Names, which tells the program to convert the original styles to Amí Professional styles having the same names; Use Styles, which attaches all the formatting contained in the styles to the document; and Ignore Styles, which does just that. After you respond to all dialog boxes that appear, Amí Professional displays the information contained in the file.

The Copy Image option is used for importing graphics files into frames. See Chapter 12 for more information about working with graphics.

ABOUT ASCII AND ANSI FILES

You can use Amí Professional to open files saved in ASCII and ANSI formats. To do this, you can do either of the following:

- Use the File Open command and turn on the ASCII File option in the dialog box, type or select the file name, or choose the ASCII Options button to display the dialog box shown in Figure 4–3, then choose options to specify whether to put carriage return/line feed characters (CR/LF) at the end of each line or at the end of each paragraph and to choose the current format of the file (7-bit, 8-bit, ANSI).
- Use the File Import/Export command and choose ASCII from the list.

SAVING AMÍ PROFESSIONAL FILES

Amí Professional doesn't save any of the work you've done until you choose a Save command. To minimize the risk of losing your work, it's a good idea to save frequently. A good rule of thumb is to save every 15 minutes.

You can use Amí Professional's autosave feature, described later in this chapter, to save your work automatically at time intervals you specify.

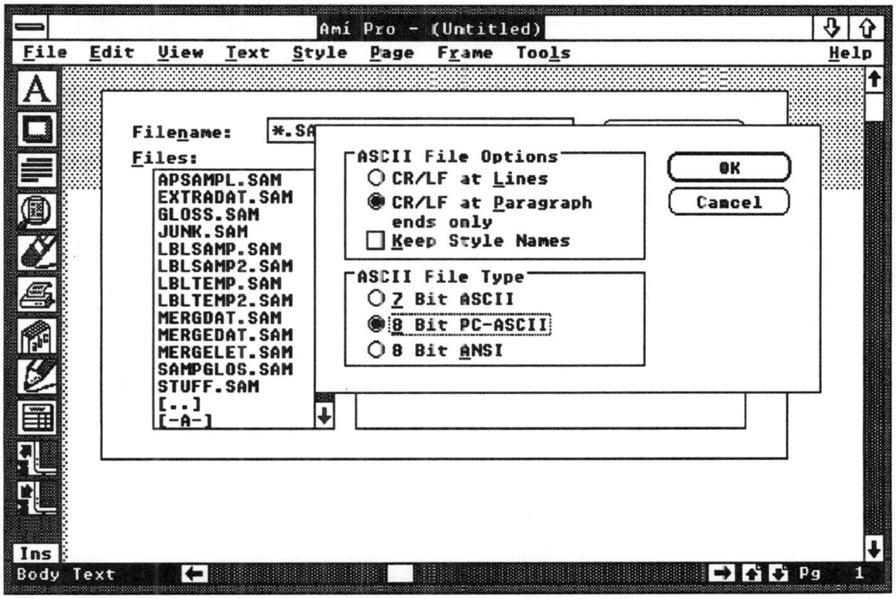

Figure 4–3
Specifying the format for opening an ASCII file with the File Open command.

Amí Professional has two File menu commands you use to save documents.

Use	**To**
Save	Name a document the first time you save it and subsequently save the document using the same name.
Save As	Name a document the first time you save it or save a document with a different name.

Both commands use the same dialog box shown in Figure 4–4, if you are saving the file for the first time.

After you've saved your document once, the File Save command saves your file without displaying the dialog box. If at any time you decide to save your file with a different name, use the File Save As command.

Saving an Amí Professional File for the First Time

To save your Amí Professional file for the first time:

1. Choose the File Save command or the File Save As command. Both commands use the same dialog box the first time you save.

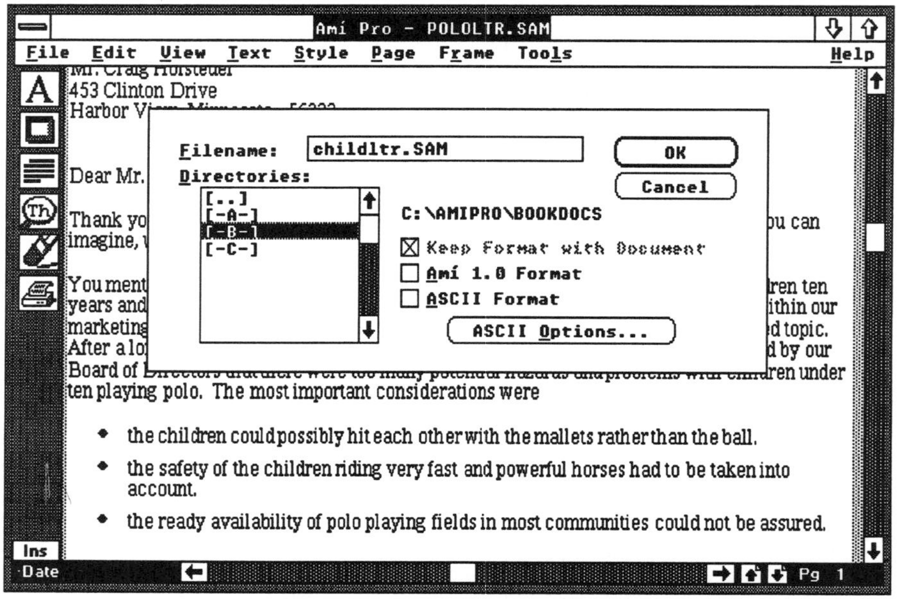

Figure 4-4 The Save and Save As dialog box.

2. To save in a different location, type a drive name or directory name(s). For example, to save a file in the PERSONAL directory on drive A, you would type **a:\personal** before the file name in the text box.

3. Type a name for your document in the Filename box. For example, to name your document TEST.SAM, type **test** in the box. Amí Professional automatically adds the extension .SAM to a document's file name, and the extension .STY to a style sheet's file name. If you type a name that another file already is using, Amí Professional asks whether you want to overwrite that document with the document you're saving.

4. If you want to save the style sheet formatting with the document instead of in a separate file, turn on the Keep Format with Document option.

5. Click OK or press **Enter** to close the dialog box and save your file.

Saving an Edited File

To save a document in the same file with the same name without opening a dialog box, choose the File Save command.

Keyboard Shortcut

To quickly save the active file (using the same file name) without choosing a command from a menu:

- Press **Ctrl+S**

You won't see a dialog box when you save a file this way.

Saving in a Different File

Sometimes you'll want to save a version of a document or style sheet with a different name in a different file, leaving the original file intact. For example, to update a monthly report that shows cumulative sales for the year, you might open a file called APRSALES.SAM, update it for May, and save the updated file as MAYSALES.SAM. Then you'd have both files for your records: APRSALES.SAM and MAYSALES.SAM.

To save a document in a different file:

1. Choose the File Save As command.
2. Type a new name for the file in the Filename box. To save in a different location, type a drive name or directory name(s) in front of the file name. For example, to save a file as CHAPTER1.SAM in the NOVEL directory on drive A, you would type **a:\novel\chapter1** in the text box.
3. Click OK or press **Enter**.

Amí Professional saves the file with the new name, leaving the original file intact.

Saving a File in a Different Format

Amí Professional can save your documents in different file formats so you can use them with other programs. If you want to save in ASCII format or in Amí 1.0 format, use the File Save As command. To save a document in another format, use the File Import/Export command.

To save files in ASCII format or in Amí 1.0 format:

1. Choose the File Save As command.
2. Type the file name in the Filename box. To store the file in a different location, type a drive name or directory name(s) in front of the file

name. For example, to save a file as SUMMARY.TXT in the THESIS directory on drive B, you would type **b:\thesis\summary.txt** in the text box.

3. Do one of the following:

   - To save in ASCII format, turn on the ASCII Format option. Then choose the ASCII Options button and choose options in the dialog box to specify the type of ASCII format you want.

   or

   - To save in Amí 1.0 format, turn on the Amí 1.0 Format option.

4. Click OK or press **Enter**.

To save in a format for another program, use the File Import/Export command. You can export in these formats:

- AdvanceWrite
- ASCII (using default ASCII options)
- DCA/FFT: includes DisplayWrite and Display Writer
- DCA/RFT
- Enable (text)
- Microsoft Word for DOS
- MultiMate and Advantage II
- Navy DIF
- Peachtext
- SAMNA Word and Plus
- Microsoft Windows Write
- WordPerfect 4.2 and 5.0
- WordStar Releases 3.0, 4.1, and 5.0
- WordStar 2000 1.0 and 3.0

To save a document with File Import/Export:

1. Choose the File Import/Export command. Amí Professional displays the dialog box shown in Figure 4–5.
2. If you want to use a different file name, type a new name in the text

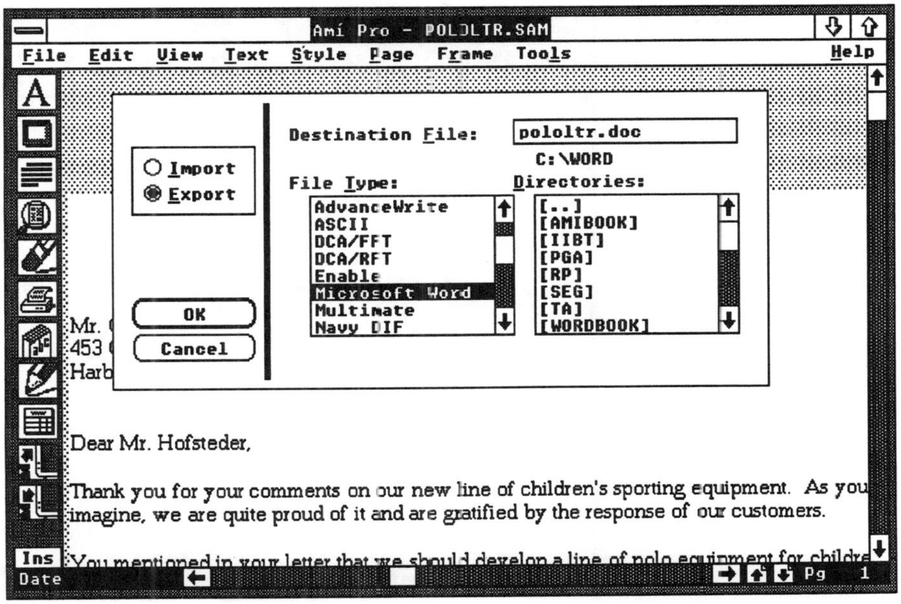

Figure 4–5 Filling out the File Import/Export dialog box to save a file in a different format.

box. To save in a different location, type a drive name or directory name(s) in front of the file name. For example, to save a file as REPORT.DOC in the WORK directory on drive B, you would type **b:\work\report.doc** in the text box.

3. Choose Export. Amí Professional changes the File Type list.
4. Select the type of file format you want from the list box.
5. Click OK or press **Enter**.

Figure 4–5 illustrates filling out the dialog box to save a file named POLOLTR.DOC as a Microsoft Word file in the \WORD directory.

Setting Up Amí Professional to Save Automatically

Instead of trying to remember to save frequently, you can set up Amí Professional to automatically save at regular time intervals. Here's how:

1. Choose the Edit Defaults command. Amí Professional displays the dialog box shown in Figure 4–6.
2. In the File Saving box, choose the Auto Timed Save option.
3. Type a time in minutes for how often you want your work saved

Figure 4–6
The Edit Defaults dialog box controls the autosave frequency.

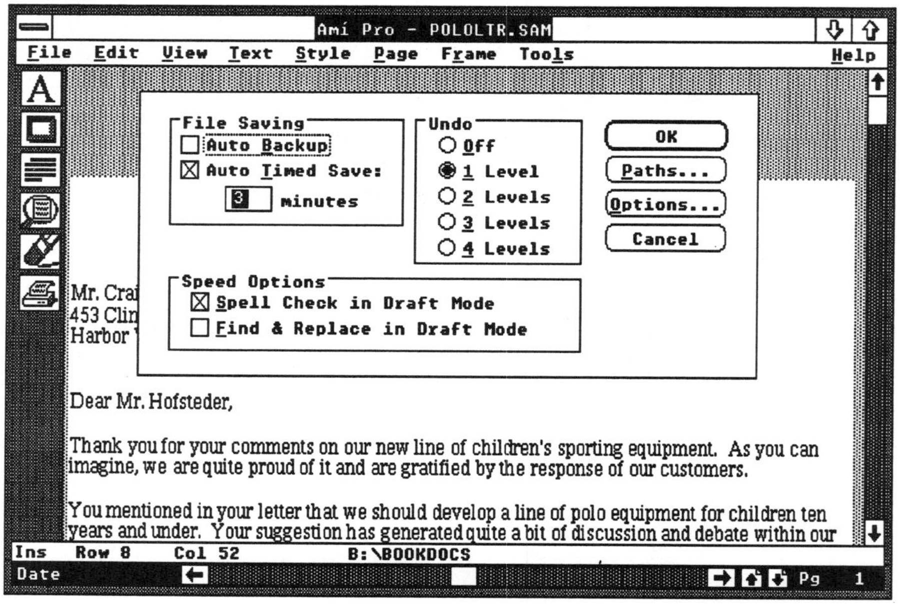

automatically. (Every 10 to 15 minutes is a good rule of thumb.) **Note:** The number you type can't include a decimal.

4. Click OK or press **Enter**.

If you decide later that you want to turn off the autosave feature, choose the Edit Defaults command again and turn off the Auto Timed Save option.

Changing the Directory for Storing Documents

By default, Amí Professional saves document files in a directory called DOCS beneath the AMIPRO directory. You can always save a file in a different directory by typing a path name in front of the file name when you save it. You can also tell the program to automatically save files in a different directory this way:

1. Choose the Edit Defaults command.
2. Choose the Paths button.
3. In the Document box, type the path name for the directory where you want Amí Professional to save your documents. Figure 4–7 illustrates changing the path name for the document directory.

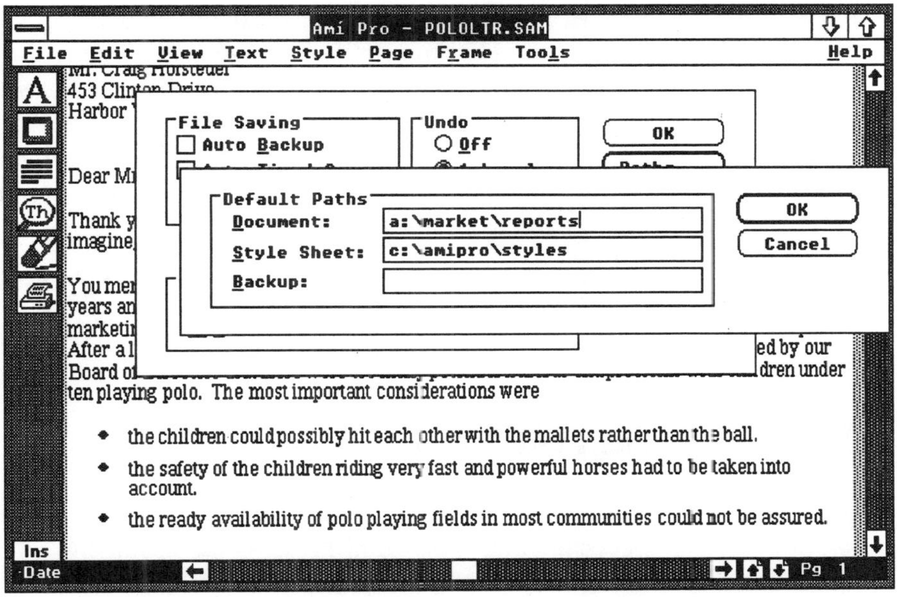

Figure 4-7
Changing the path name for the document directory with the Edit Defaults command.

4. Click OK or press **Enter** to close the Paths dialog box.

5. Click OK or press **Enter** to close the Edit Defaults dialog box. Amí Professional always saves document files and looks for document files in the directory you specify with Edit Defaults unless you type a different path in front of the file name as you save.

Creating Backup Copies

You can set Amí Professional to automatically make a separate backup copy of your file every time you save. Creating a backup copy is a safety measure—if a disaster happens to the original file, you can load the backup file (the previously saved version) and recover most of your work. Creating backup files has one obvious drawback, however: your documents will take up more disk space, because Amí Professional keeps two versions of the file every time you save.

To set up Amí Professional to automatically create backup files:

1. Choose the Edit Defaults command.

2. Turn on the Auto Backup option.

3. Choose the Paths button.

4. In the Backup box, type the directory you want Amí Professional to store backup copies in, as shown in Figure 4–8. The backup directory *must* be a *different* directory than the directory shown in the Document box, because Amí Professional creates backup files using the same name as the original files. Thus, if you don't specify a different directory, the program overwrites your newer versions of files with the older backup files.
5. Click OK or press **Enter** to close the Paths dialog box.
6. Click OK or press **Enter** to close the Edit Defaults dialog box.

INSERTING ONE FILE IN ANOTHER

When you want to use an Amí 1.0, ASCII, or another Amí Professional document in your Amí Professional document, you can easily add all the text with the File Append command. (If the file is in a different format, you can use the File Import/Export command to do this, as described earlier in this chapter.)

You can add all the text in one document to another document this way:

1. Place the cursor where you want to insert the text from the other document.

Figure 4–8 Setting up Amí Professional to make backup copies with the Edit Defaults command.

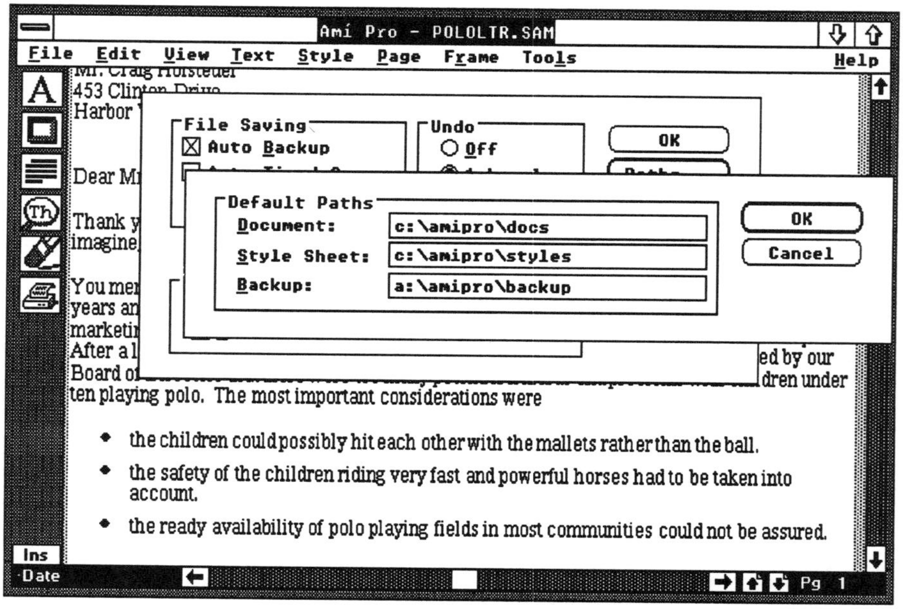

2. Choose the File Append command.
3. Select the file that you want to insert from the list. The list displays the names of files in the active disk drive and directory. To see names of other files, you may need to type a drive name or directory names in the text box. For example, to see a list of Amí Professional files in the LETTERS directory on drive A, you would type **a:\letters** in the text box.
4. Click OK or press **Enter** to insert the text.

USING THE FILE MANAGER

Amí Professional comes with a File Manager application that you can use to display and manipulate lists of files without closing the Amí Professional window.

To display the File Manager window:

- ◻ Choose the File Management command from the File menu.

Figure 4–9 shows the File Manager window. Like Help and the styles box, the File Manager is a separate window—you can move it, change its size, and close the window using standard Windows methods. See Appendix A for more information about manipulating windows.

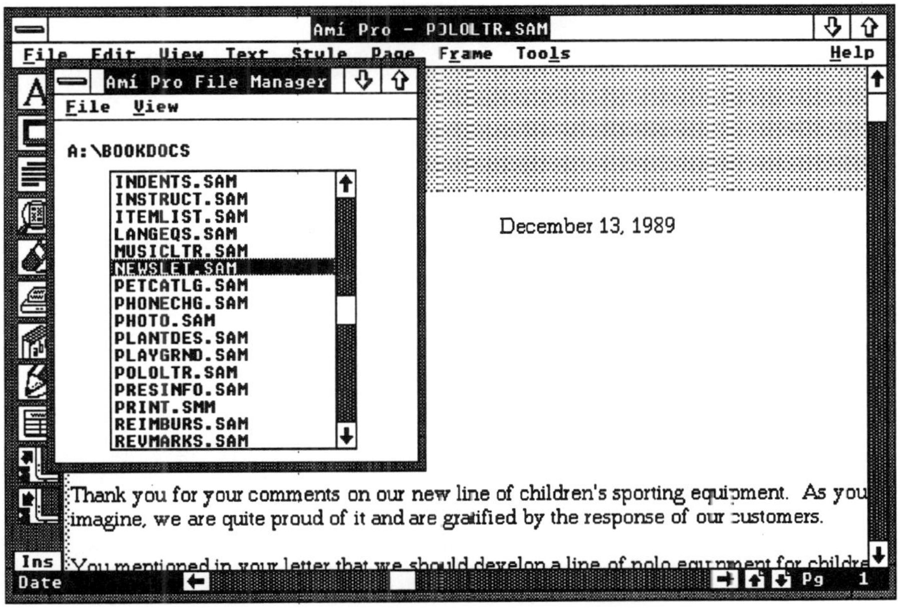

Figure 4–9 The File Manager window lets you manipulate lists of files.

The File Manager has its own menus and commands. When you type in the File Manager's dialog boxes, you use your operating system's rules for path names and file names. If you need more information about file names, path names, drive names, or the directory structure, see the manual that came with your operating system.

Displaying Different Files

In the File Manager window, you can use the commands on the View menu and the File Change Directory command to control which files are displayed in the list.

To display a different list of files in the File Manager window:

1. If you want to list files that are stored in a different location, choose the File Change Directory command and type a new path name in the text box. For example, to see files in the \LETTERS directory on drive B, you'd type **b:\letters** in the dialog box.
2. To control which files in the directory are displayed, do one of the following:

   - To display all Amí Professional files ending with .SAM or .SMM, choose the View *.S?M Files command.

   or

   - To display a list of all files in the directory, choose the View All command.

   or

   - To display only certain files in the directory, choose the View Partial command, then type wildcards and other characters to tell the File Manager which files to display. (You can use the * wildcard, which stands for any number of characters, or the ? wildcard, which stands for one character. For example, to display all files ending with .STY extensions, you'd type ***.sty** in the dialog box. To display a list of files that begin with CHAPTER followed by one number and the extension .SAM, you'd type **chapter?.sam** in the box.)

Selecting Files

To select one file in the File Manager window:

- Click the file name.

or

- Use the arrow keys to highlight the file name.

To select multiple files:

1. Select the first file name.
2. Hold down the Shift key.
3. Click with the mouse or use the arrow keys to highlight more file names.

Copying or Moving Files

You can use either of two methods to move or copy files with the File Manager. Figure 4–10 illustrates the first method, in which you select the files you want to copy or move:

1. Use the procedures described in the preceding sections to display and select the names of the files you want to copy or move.
2. Choose the File Copy or File Move command.
3. Type the drive letter and the directory name(s) as necessary in the To: box to specify where you want to copy or move the files.

Figure 4–10
Copying selected files to another disk drive with the File Manager.

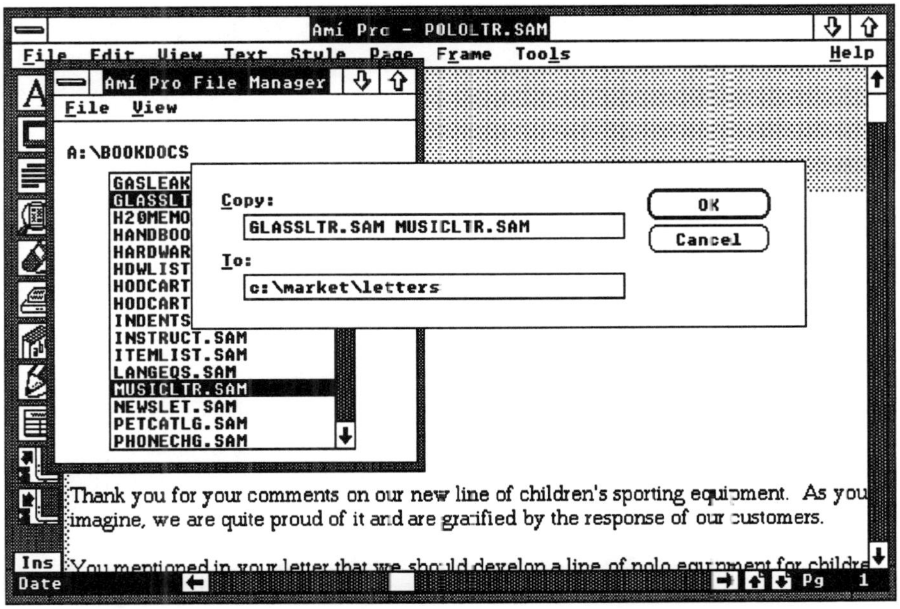

4. Click OK or press **Enter**.

Figure 4–11 illustrates the second method, in which you type the name(s) of the files:

1. Choose the Copy or Move command.
2. Type the name(s) of the file(s) you want to copy or move, including any necessary drive letters and directory names, in the Copy or Move box.
3. Type the drive letter and the directory name(s) as necessary in the To: box to specify where you want to copy or move the files.
4. Click OK or press **Enter**.

If you're using the Move command, another dialog box appears with the following options for you to choose from:

Option	**Description**
Take Associated Graphics Files	Turn option on if a file you're moving includes imported graphics files and you want to move the graphics files, too.

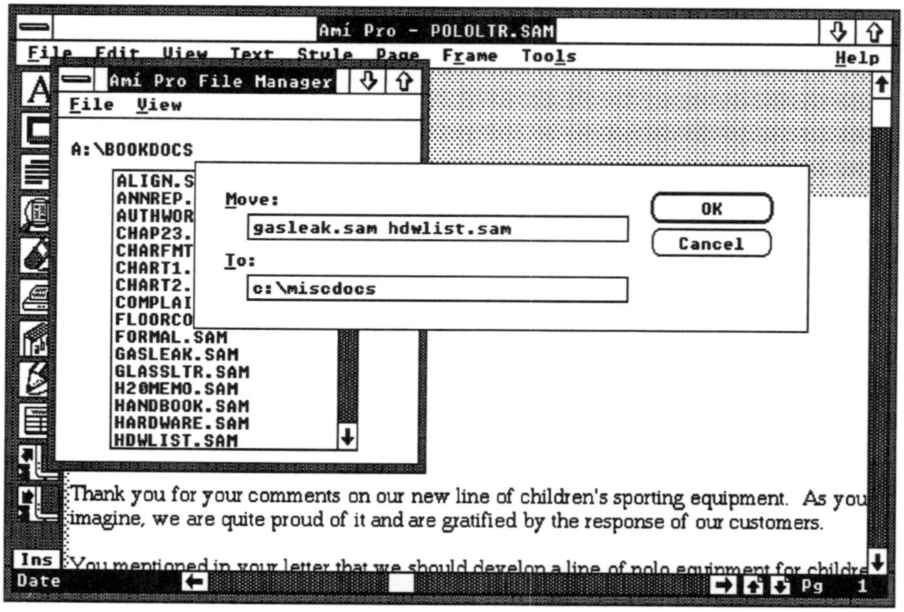

Figure 4–11
Using the File Manager to move files to a new directory.

Take Associated Style Sheet	Turn option on if a file you're moving uses a separate style sheet file and you want to move the style sheet file, too.
Maintain Format But Do Not Take Associated Style Sheet	Turn option on if you want to attach the style formatting to the file you're moving, but leave the style sheet file in its original location.

Deleting Files

The File Manager makes it easy for you to delete files. Deleting permanently erases the files, so be careful not to inadvertently delete information you want to keep. Just as when you copy or move files, you can use two methods to delete files with the File Manager:

1. Use the procedures described to display and select the names of the files you want to delete. Make sure that you've selected *only* the files you want to delete.
2. Choose the File Delete command.
3. Click OK or press **Enter**.

or

1. Choose the File Delete command.
2. Type the name(s) of the file(s) you want to delete, including any necessary drive letters and directory names, in the dialog box.
3. Click OK or press **Enter**.

Figure 4–12 illustrates deleting files selected in the File Manager window.

Renaming Files

To rename a file with the File Manager, use one of the following procedures:

1. Use the procedures described earlier to display and select the name of the file you want to rename.
2. Choose the File Rename command.

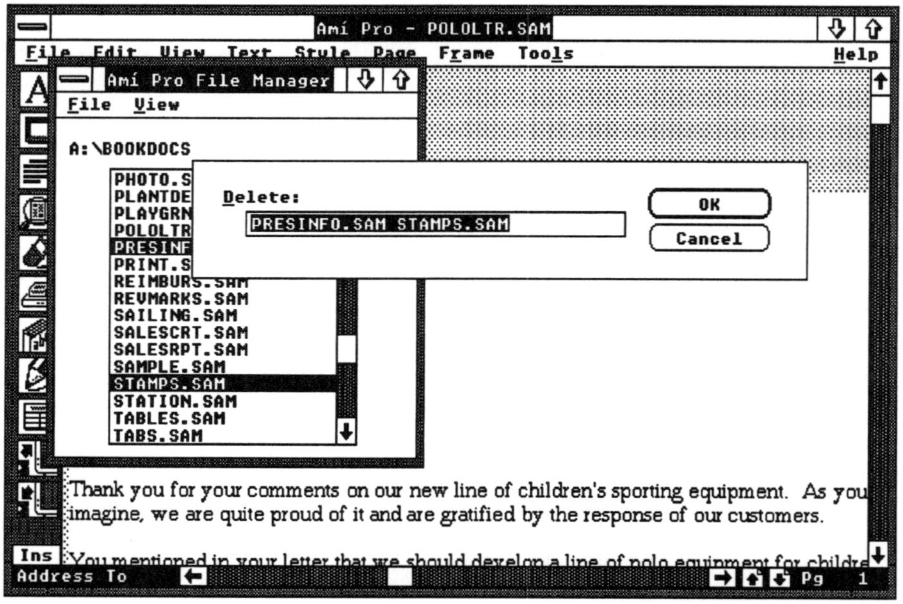

Figure 4–12 Deleting selected files with the File Manager.

3. Type the new name for the file in the To: box.
4. Click OK or press **Enter**.

or

1. Choose the File Rename command.
2. Type the name of the file you want to rename in the dialog box, including any necessary drive letter and directory names.
3. Type the new name for the file in the To: box. Figure 4–13 illustrates renaming a file.
4. Click OK or press **Enter**.

Assigning Read-Only or Read-Write Attributes

You can use the File Manager window to assign access attributes to your files. By default, Amí Professional creates files that have a read-write attribute, which means that an Amí Professional user can both read (display) and write (change or delete) the files. You can change the attribute for a file to read-only, which means that users can display but not change the file.

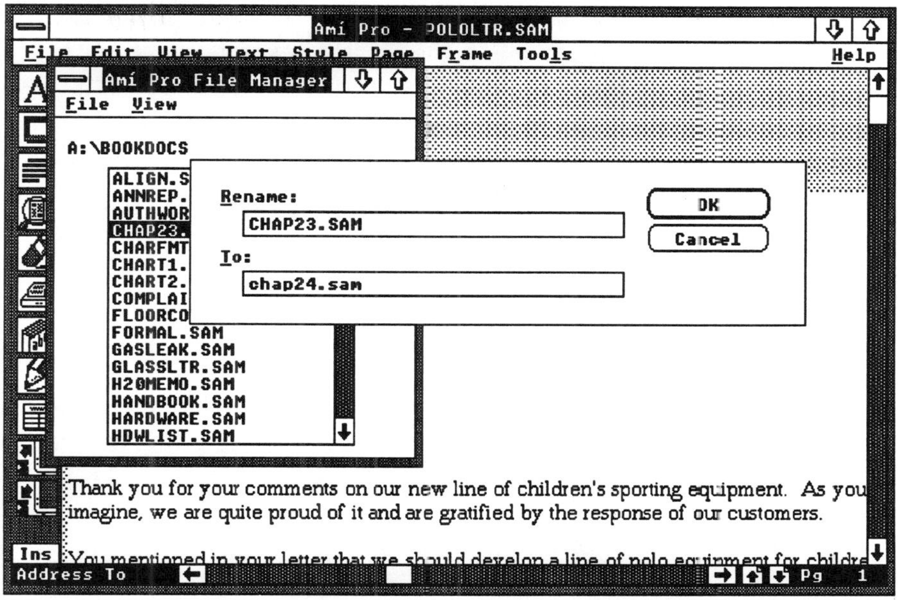

Figure 4–13
Renaming a file with the File Manager.

To change file attributes in the File Manager window:

1. Select the name of the file whose attribute you want to change. If you want to change several files at once, you must select files that share the same attribute (for example, all must be read-write files).
2. Choose the File Attributes command.
3. Choose the Read-Only option or the Read-Write option.
4. Click OK or press **Enter**.

Closing the File Manager Window

To close the File Manager window:

- Choose the File Exit command, double-click the Control menu icon in the upper left corner of the File Manager window, or press **Alt+F4**.

USING DOCUMENT DESCRIPTIONS

Whenever you save a file for the first time in Amí Professional, the program records information about the file in a document description box.

As shown in Figure 4–14, the document description always lists information about the file, including its name, path, style sheet, imported files used, the date it was created, the date of the last revision, and the total number of revisions for the file. You can also add information of your own in the Document Description box and in the four fields.

You can display or print the document description to keep a record of the file's history.

Displaying the Document Description Box

You can display a document description box for the active file in the Amí Professional window or for a file you have selected in the File Manager window.

To display a document description box for the active file in the Amí Professional window:

1. Choose the File Document Description command.
2. When you're finished reading the information in the box, click OK or press **Enter**.

To display a document description box for a file in the File Manager window:

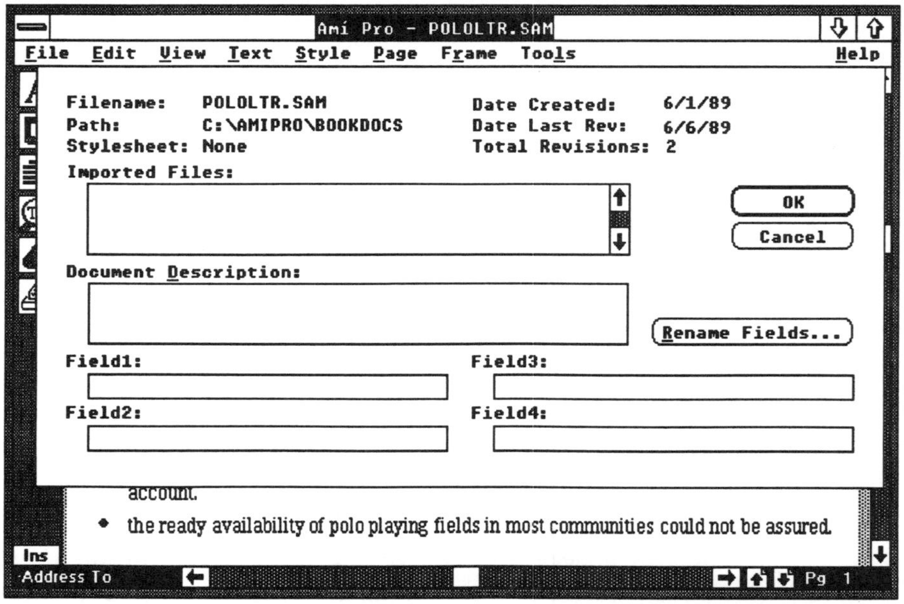

Figure 4–14 The Document Description box.

1. Use the procedures described earlier for the File Manager to display and select the name of the file you want to see a description for.
2. Choose the View Description command.
3. When you're finished reading the information in the box, click OK or press **Enter**.

Adding Information to the Document Description Box

You can add information to the Document Description box by typing in the box and in the four fields. You can display the information you add to the box when you turn on the Show Description option in the File Open dialog box, as shown in Figure 4–15. This can help you find the file you want.

You can rename the fields and fill them in to add useful information to the description. For example, you might want to keep a record of the person who created each file, that person's phone number and work group name, and the name of the project. To do this, you could rename the fields to Writer, Phone, Group, and Project. These fields would then be displayed in every document description box. You can also use the Edit Insert Variable command, described in a later chapter, to insert these fields in documents if you like.

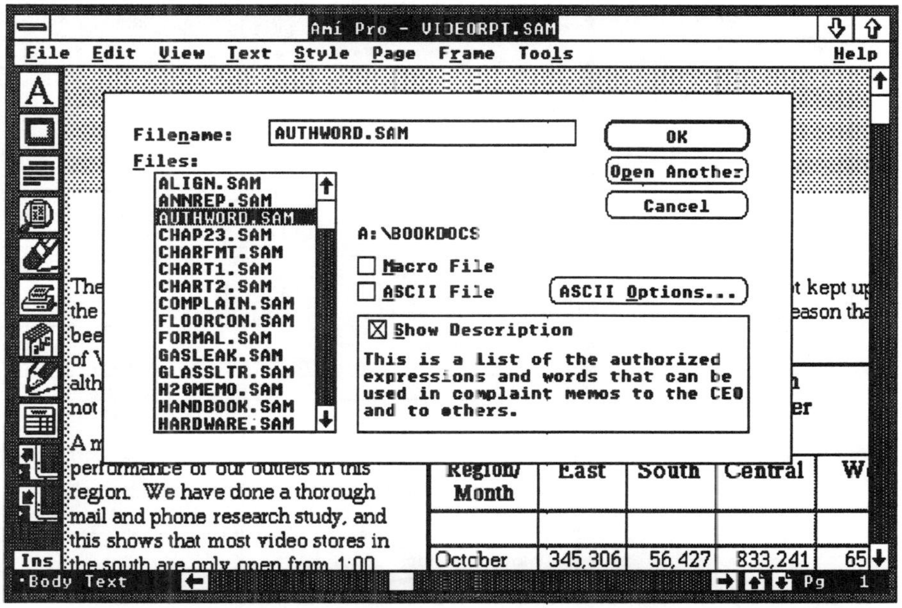

Figure 4–15 With the Show Description option, you can display information from the Document Description box in the File Open dialog box.

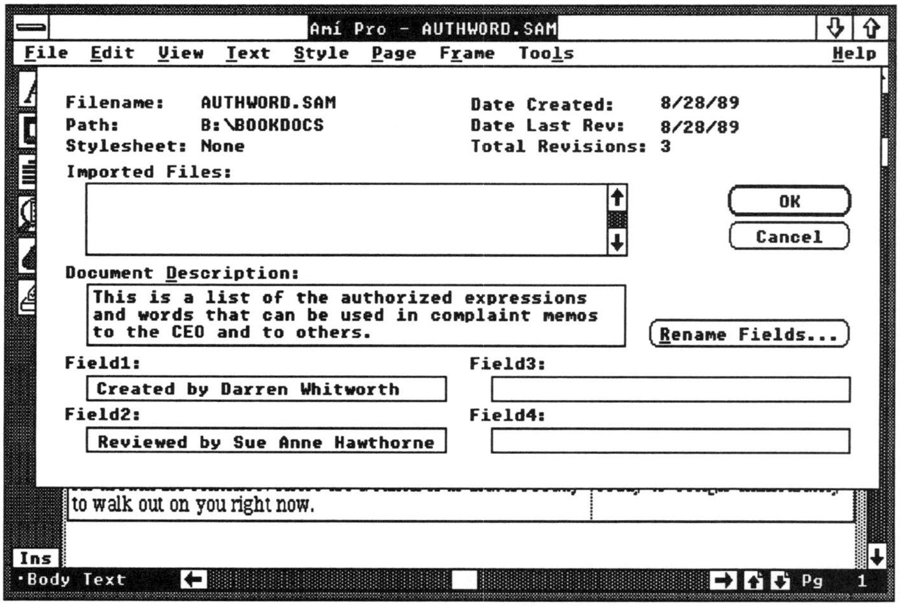

Figure 4-16 Typing information in the Document Description box.

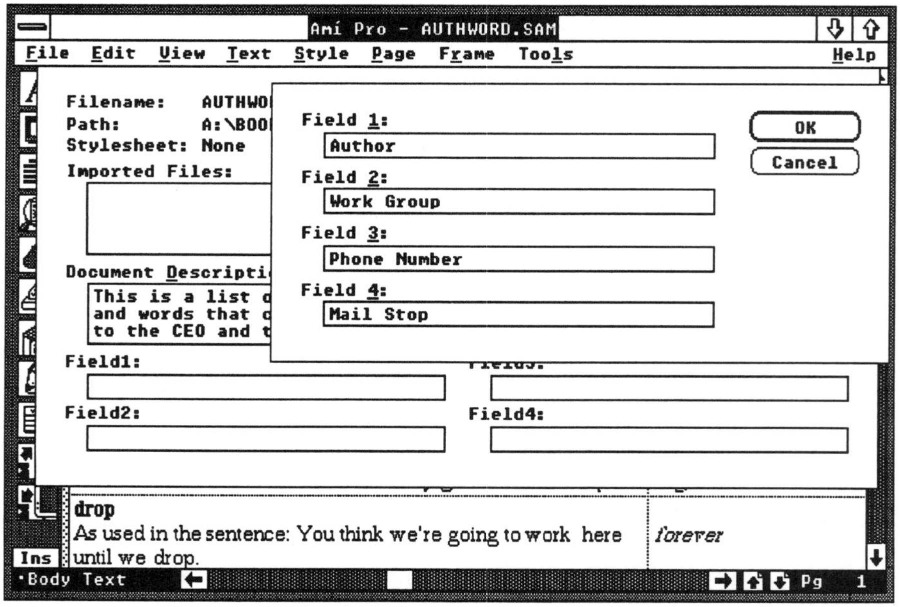

Figure 4-17 Changing the names of fields in the Document Description box.

To add information to the Document Description box:

1. Display the box using one of the procedures described previously.
2. Type information in the Description box and in the field boxes as shown in Figure 4–16.
3. If you want to change any of the four field names, choose the Rename Fields button, type new names for the fields as shown in Figure 4–17, then click OK or press **Enter** to close the Rename Fields dialog box. This changes the names that appear in every document description box.
4. Click OK or press **Enter** to save the document description.

5

Editing Your Amí Professional Files

A document is rarely perfect the first time you type the text. Usually you go back and delete text, add new text, or rearrange the sequence of paragraphs in your file. You might also copy text from another file or work with multiple windows to view different parts of a long file at the same time. This chapter shows you how to do all these tasks. You'll find out more about

- selecting text
- moving around within the document
- cutting, copying and pasting text
- working with multiple documents
- searching for and replacing text, formatting, and styles

SCROLLING THROUGH AN AMÍ PROFESSIONAL FILE

If your Amí Professional file has more text than will fit in the document window, you *scroll* to see all of your file. If you're a mouse user, you'll want to become familiar with clicking on Amí Professional's scroll bars to move through the information in the file. If you like to keep your hands on the keys, you can use the scroll bars as visual guides to tell you where you are in your file.

Scrolling with the Mouse

Figure 5–1 shows how to use the scroll bars. To scroll with the mouse, you use the vertical scroll bar to scroll up or down, or the horizontal scroll bar to scroll right or left (if your text is wider than the window).

To Scroll	Use the Mouse to
One line	Click the arrow in the scroll bar pointing toward the location of the text you want to see. For example, click the down arrow in the scroll bar to see the next line of text at the bottom of the window.
One windowful	Click above or below the scroll box in the vertical scroll bar, or click either side of the scroll box in the horizontal scroll bar toward the location of the text you want to see. For example, click below the scroll box in the vertical scroll bar to see the next windowful of text at the bottom of the window.

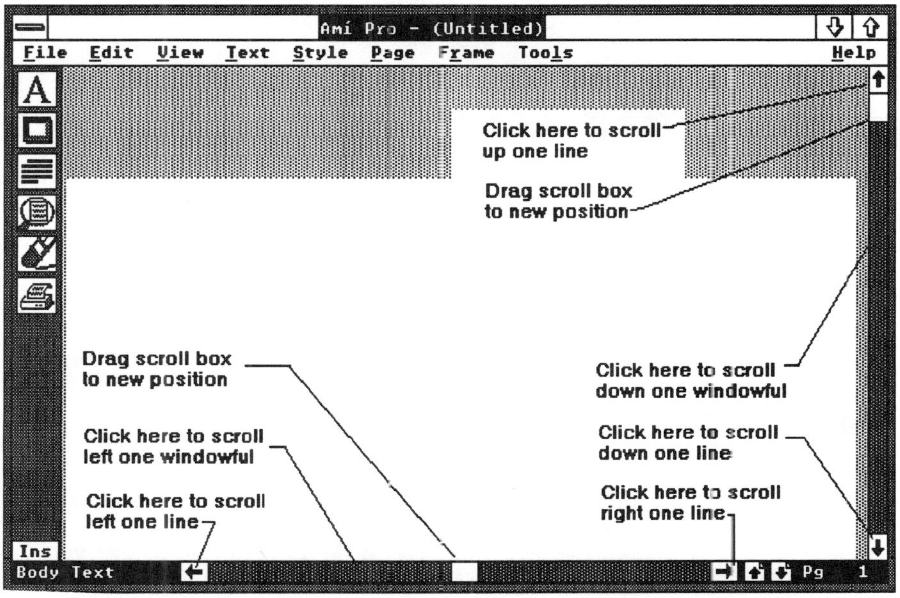

Figure 5–1 Use the scroll bars to move through your file's text using the mouse.

To the next page	Click the next-page icon in the horizontal scroll bar (it looks like a tiny page with a black down arrow on top).
To the previous page	Click the previous-page icon in the horizontal scroll bar (it looks like a tiny page with a black up arrow on top).
To a relative location	Drag the scroll box to a location relative to the text you want to see in the document. For example, drag the scroll box to the middle of the scroll bar to see the middle of your document.

Scrolling with the Keyboard

If you use the keyboard to scroll when the scroll bars are displayed, the scroll boxes move to reflect the position of the text in the window relative to the entire file. For example, if the scroll box is near the bottom of the vertical scroll bar, the text you see in the window is near the end of your file.

Scrolling with keys is the same as moving the cursor with keys. See the following section for more information on using the keyboard to move around in files.

MOVING THE CURSOR

The first step in editing is learning to move the *cursor* (the little straight line that marks where you can type) around in a file. The cursor moves only within text—you can't position a cursor just anywhere on a blank screen.

Moving the Cursor with the Mouse

To move the cursor with the mouse:

1. Place the I-beam mouse pointer where you want the cursor to be in your text.

2. Click the mouse button to set the cursor. The blinking cursor appears. (You may need to move the I-beam pointer to see the cursor.)

Note that the cursor and the I-beam mouse pointer are two different objects, as shown in Figure 5–2—you can move the I-beam pointer by rolling the mouse, but the cursor stays in the same place until you click a new location.

Moving the Cursor with Keys

To move the cursor with keys:

- Use the arrow keys to move short distances or use the keys on the numeric keypad (with NumLock off) as shown in Figure 5–3. Hold down the Ctrl key while you press the number key to get the action listed in italic for each key in the figure.

You can also use these key combinations to move the cursor to other locations:

Use	To Move
CTRL+. (period)	Forward one sentence
CTRL+, (comma)	Back one sentence

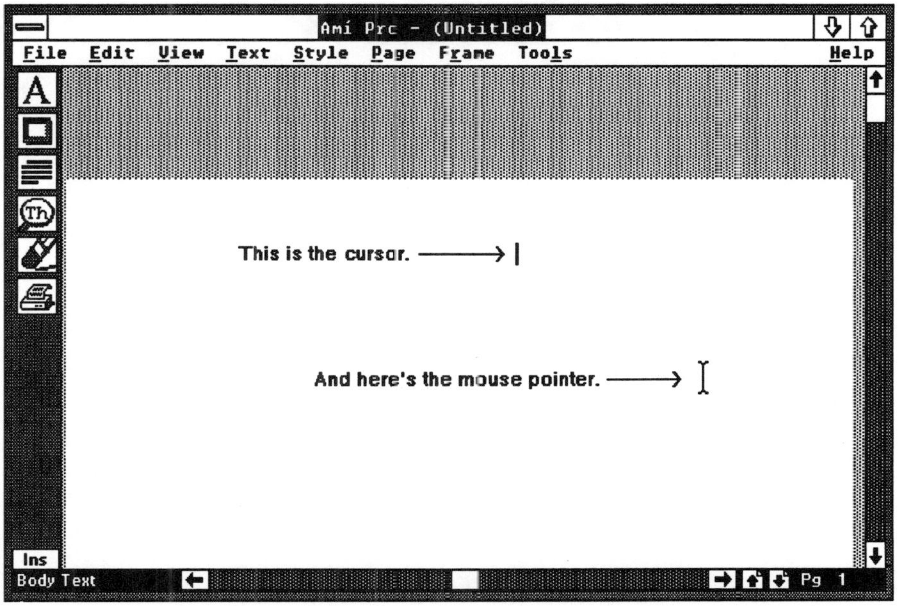

Figure 5–2 The cursor and the mouse pointer are two different objects.

Figure 5-3
You can use the keys on the numeric keypad to move the cursor; press **Ctrl** plus the key to make the moves shown in italic.

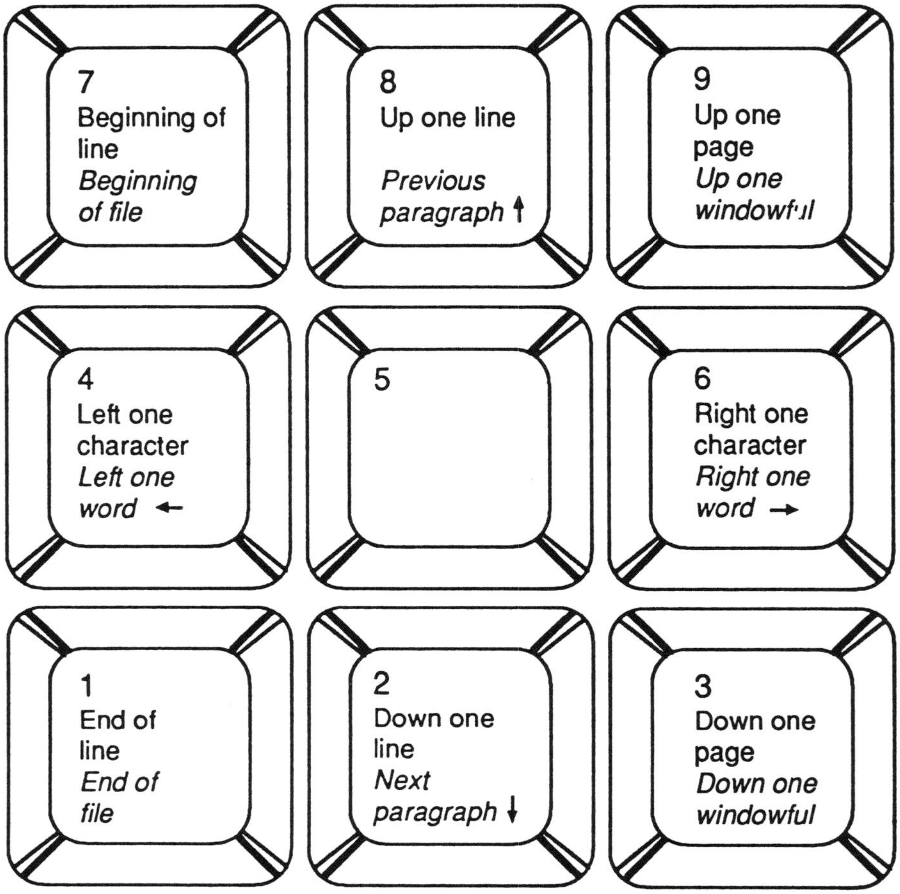

USING THE NUMERIC KEYPAD TO TYPE NUMBERS

You can use the numeric keypad at the right of the keyboard to move the cursor *or* to type numbers, like those on a 10-key calculator. Use the NumLock key to switch between the two uses.

To type numbers:

1. Press the **NumLock** key.

2. Type numbers or symbols on the keypad.

To switch back to using the keypad for movement and commands:

□ Press the **NumLock** key again.

USING COMMANDS TO JUMP TO A NEW LOCATION

Amí Professional has two commands on the Tools menu that jump to new locations:

Command	Description
Tools Go To	Moves to a specific place in a file. You can type a response to jump to a page, frame, note, bookmark, header, footer, tab ruler, footnote, page break, and many other locations. You'll find out more about using Tools Go To in various chapters of this book.
Tools Find & Replace	Searches for the next occurrence of a specific word or phrase. You'll learn more about searching and replacing later in this chapter.

SELECTING: TELLING AMÍ PROFESSIONAL WHERE TO MAKE CHANGES

To change text in Amí Professional:

1. Select the text you want to change. Selecting highlights the text so you can easily see what you've selected, as shown in Figure 5–4. The commands you choose affect that text as long as it's highlighted.
2. Choose a command or use a key combination to change the selected text.

Selecting with the Mouse

Here's the basic procedure to select text with the mouse:

1. Set the cursor at the beginning of the text you want to select.
2. Hold down the left mouse button while you move the mouse pointer to the end of the text you want to select.
3. When all the text you want is highlighted, release the mouse button.
4. Choose a command or press a key combination to change the selected text. If you change your mind while selecting and want to start over

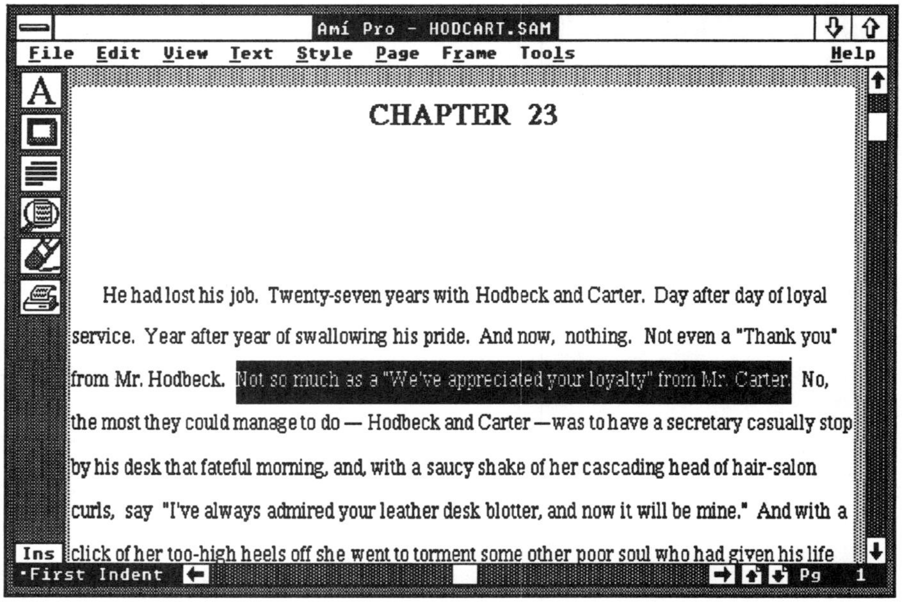

Figure 5-4 Text that has been selected is highlighted.

again, just release the mouse button, then click to remove the highlight and set the cursor in a new location.

Amí Professional accepts many variations in the way you select text with the mouse. The following procedures describe the most useful variations:

- To select one word, double-click the word. This selects the word and the following space (if any).
- To select lines of text, hold down the mouse button and drag the mouse pointer down the left edge of the text until you've selected all the lines you want.
- To select a large amount of text:

    1. Set the cursor at the beginning of the text you want to select.
    2. Move the mouse pointer to the end of the text you want to select, using the scroll bars if necessary.
    3. Hold down the Shift key and click the mouse button to set the end point of the selected text.

Amí Professional highlights the selected text. For example, to select the entire file, position the cursor at the beginning of the file, drag the scroll box to the bottom of the vertical scroll bar to move to the end of the file, then point to the last character in the file, hold down the **Shift** key, and click the left mouse button.

Note: It's important for you to first press and hold down the Shift key, then click the mouse button. If you don't press the Shift key first, clicking the mouse button moves the cursor instead of selecting the text.

Selecting with Keys

Amí Professional has two basic methods you can use to select text with keys. You should choose a command or press a key combination immediately after selecting the text. If you move the cursor instead, Amí Professional removes the highlighting and the text is no longer selected.

To select short pieces of text:

- To select individual characters, hold down the **Shift** key while you move the cursor with the Left or Right arrow keys.
- To select one word, hold down the **Shift** key and press **Ctrl+Right arrow** key or **Ctrl+Left arrow** key.

See Moving the Cursor with Keys earlier in this chapter to see a list of keys that move the cursor.

You can also select longer pieces of text, beginning at the cursor position:

To Select All Text	Press
To the end of the sentence	**Shift+Ctrl–.** (period).
To the beginning of the sentence	**Shift+Ctrl–,** (comma).
To the end of the line	**Shift+End.**
To the beginning of the line	**Shift+Home.**
To the top of the previous page	**Shift+Page Up.**
To the bottom of the present page	**Shift+Page Down.**
To the beginning of the file	**Shift+Ctrl+Home.**
To the end of the file	**Shift+Ctrl+End.**

For information about selecting text in tables, see Chapter 14.

TYPING OVER TEXT

In Amí Professional, text that you type replaces any text you have selected at that time.

You can also use Amí Professional's typeover mode to type new text on top of existing text, just as you would on a typewriter.

To use typeover mode:

1. Press the **Insert** key. Amí Professional displays `Type` in the box in the lower left-hand corner of the screen.

2. Type over the text.

3. Press the **Insert** key again when you want to turn off typeover mode.

DELETING TEXT

In Amí Professional, deleting text means *permanently* erasing the text, so be sure this is what you want to do before you delete text.

Deleting text in Amí Professional is easy:

1. Select the text.

2. Press the **Delete** key to erase the text.

You can reverse a deletion if you choose the Edit Undo command *immediately* after pressing the Delete key.

If you want to delete text and paste it in somewhere else, use the Edit Cut command as described in the following section. If you want to delete text from your file but save it for later use, you can define it as a glossary entry. Then you can use that text again wherever and whenever you want, or delete it at a later time if you decide not to use it. See Chapter 6 for more information.

MOVING TEXT

When you move text, use the Edit Cut and Edit Paste commands. When you use the Edit Cut command to remove text, Amí Professional moves that text to the Windows Clipboard. Text stays in the Clipboard until the next time you copy or "cut" text. The Clipboard always contains the *last* piece of text or the last graphic you copied or cut. The process of using the Clipboard is illustrated in Figure 5-5. As long as the text is in the

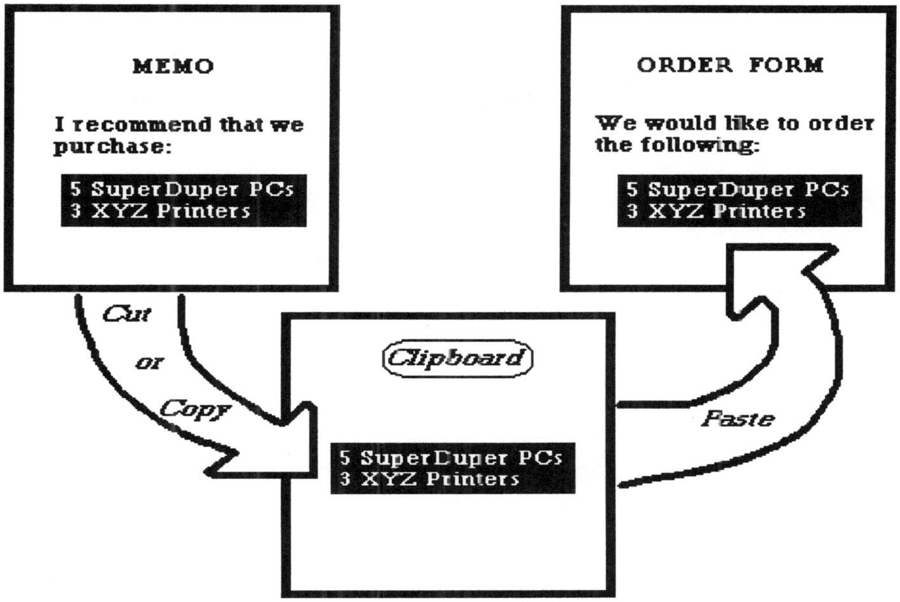

Figure 5-5
The Edit Cut, Edit Copy, and Edit Paste commands use the Clipboard to move text.

Clipboard, you can move the cursor to a new location in the same file or to a different file, then paste in the text. (The last part of this chapter gives more information about working with multiple files.)

To move text:

1. Select the text you want to move.
2. Choose the Edit Cut command or press **Shift+Delete**. Amí Professional removes the selected text from your file and places it in the Clipboard.
3. Place the cursor where you want to insert the text. If you want the inserted text to replace existing text, select the text you want to replace. Otherwise, make sure no text is selected.
4. Choose the Edit Paste command or press **Shift+Insert**. Amí Professional inserts a copy of the text from the Clipboard. If you want to delete text but preserve the information that's in the Clipboard, use the Delete key to erase selected text without placing it in the Clipboard.

COPYING TEXT

To reuse a previously typed phrase, a paragraph, or even a whole file in another location, you can copy that text and paste it in another place without affecting the original text. You can copy text within the same file or to a different file. (See the discussion later in this chapter for more information about working with multiple files.)

To copy text and paste the copy in a new location:

1. Select the text you want to copy.
2. Choose the Edit Copy command or press **Ctrl+Insert**. Amí Professional puts a copy of the selected text in the Clipboard.
3. Place the cursor where you want to insert the copy. If you want the copied text to replace existing text, select the text you want to replace. Otherwise, make sure no text is selected.
4. Choose the Edit Paste command or press **Shift+Insert**. Amí Professional inserts a copy of the text from the Clipboard. As long as the text you want is in the Clipboard, you can use the Edit Paste command to insert a copy as many times as you like. If you paste frequently, it's quicker for you to press the Edit Paste command's shortcut key, **Shift+Insert**, to paste without choosing the command each time from the menu.

If you want to use the same text often, you can save that text as a glossary entry and insert it wherever and whenever you like. See Chapter 6 for more information.

VIEWING THE CONTENTS OF THE CLIPBOARD

As previously mentioned, when you delete or copy text, Amí Professional puts that text in the Clipboard. You can check the Clipboard any time you like.

To view the contents of the Clipboard:

1. Activate the MS-DOS Executive Window and display the Windows directory.
2. Double-click CLIPBRD.EXE or choose the File Run command and type **clipbrd** in the text box, then press **Enter**. Amí Professional opens the Clipboard window to show you the contents of the Clipboard, as shown in Figure 5–6.

To close the Clipboard window:

- Choose the Close command from the Clipboard Control menu or press **Alt+F4**.

Figure 5–6
Displaying the contents of the Clipboard.

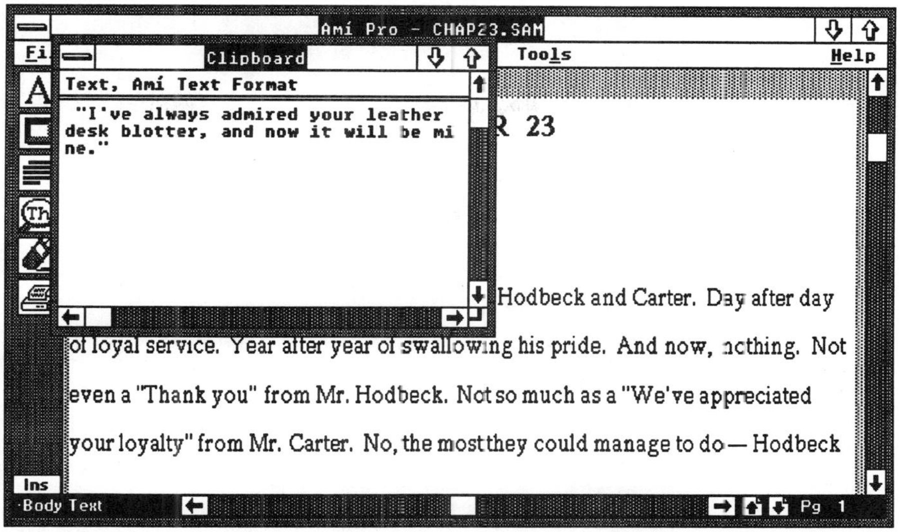

WORKING WITH MULTIPLE DOCUMENT WINDOWS

In addition to copying and moving text within the same document, you can copy or cut text from one file, then use the File Open command to open another file and paste in the text. When you do this, Amí Professional automatically closes the first file, asking you if you want to save any changes, before it opens the next file.

You can also display multiple documents in individual Amí Professional windows to review them simultaneously or to copy or move text from one file to another.

To display another document in another window:

1. Choose the File Open command.

2. Type or select the name of the file you want to open. The list displays the names of files in the active disk drive and directory. To see names of other files, type a drive name or directory names in the text box. For example, to see a list of Amí Professional files in the LETTERS directory on drive A, you would type **a:\letters** in the text box, then press **Enter**. To open a new empty file, type a new name in the text box.

3. Choose the Open Another button. The file opens in a separate Amí window, as shown in Figure 5–7.

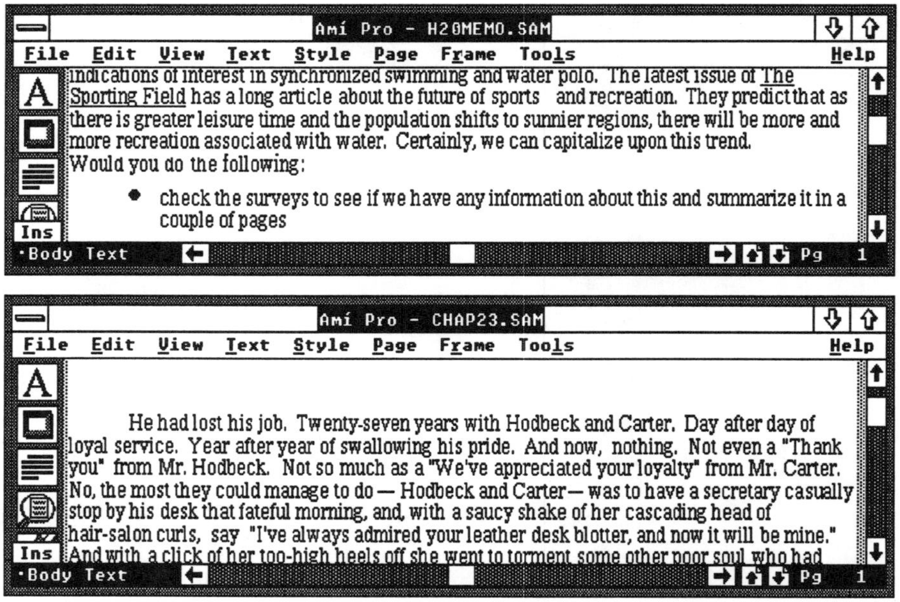

Figure 5-7 You can work with multiple files simultaneously in separate windows with Amí Professional.

Moving from Window to Window

To move the cursor from window to window when you have more than one document displayed on the screen:

- Click the window you want.

or

- Press **Alt+Tab** until the title bar of the window you want is highlighted.

Resizing and Moving Document Windows

Just as you would with any window created using a Microsoft Windows application, you can move and change the size of Amí Professional's document windows. If you're a Windows novice, you can find more details in Appendix A.

To change the size of a window:

- Point to any window border or corner, as shown in Figure 5-8, then drag the window outline to a new size. When you release the mouse button, the window changes to the new size.

Figure 5–8
Changing the size of an Amí Professional window with the mouse.

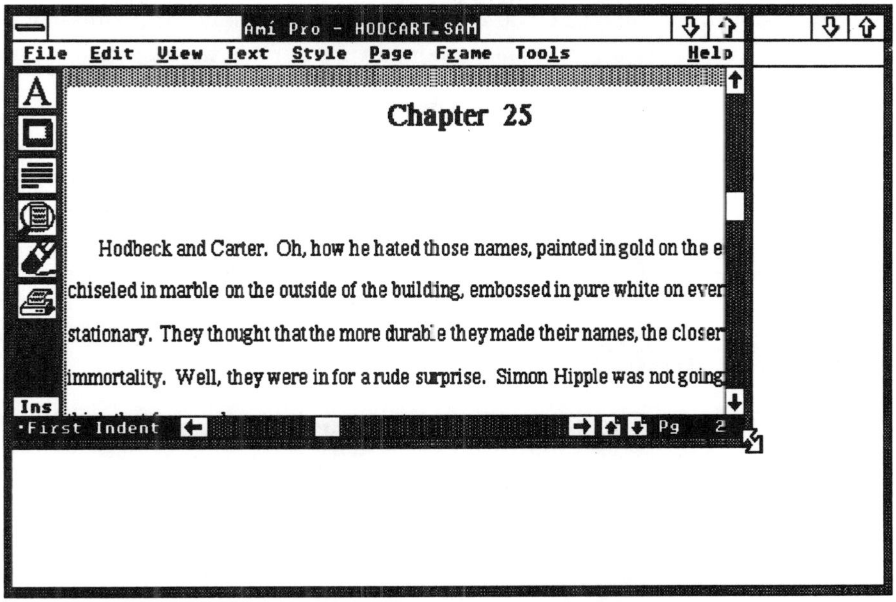

or

- Choose the Size command from the Amí Professional Control menu (**Alt+F8**), then use the arrow keys to change the size of the window's outline. When you press **Enter**, the window changes to the new size.

To move a window:

- Point to the window's title bar, then drag the window outline to a new position. When you release the mouse button, the window moves to the new location.

or

- Choose the Move command from the Amí Professional Control menu (**Alt+F7**), then use the arrow keys to move the window's outline. When you press **Enter**, the window moves to the new location.

You can change the size and location of the Amí windows to suit yourself. For example, Figure 5–9 shows an arrangement in which two Amí Professional documents appear side by side for easy comparison.

Closing Document Windows

No matter how many Amí Professional windows you display on the screen at one time, you close each window the same way:

- Choose the File Exit command or double-click the Control menu icon in the upper left corner of the window.

When you close one window, the remaining windows stay the same size. You may want to change the size or position of windows as described in the previous section or use the Maximize command on the Control menu (Alt, Spacebar, X) to make a window occupy the full screen (a process sometimes called *zooming*).

UNDOING A CHANGE

Everyone knows that "Oh, no!" feeling that you get when you've made a mistake in a word processing file. You've just deleted text you should have kept, moved a phrase to the wrong place, or chosen the wrong command. When this happens to you, don't panic! Amí Professional has made allowances for mistakes, and there is practically nothing you can do in Amí Professional that can't be undone.

If you realize your mistake immediately after you've made it, you can choose Amí Professional's Edit Undo command or click the eraser icon at the left edge of the window. The Edit Undo command can, in most cases, reverse the last action you took. By default, the program "undoes" only the last command, but you can tell Amí Professional how many prior actions

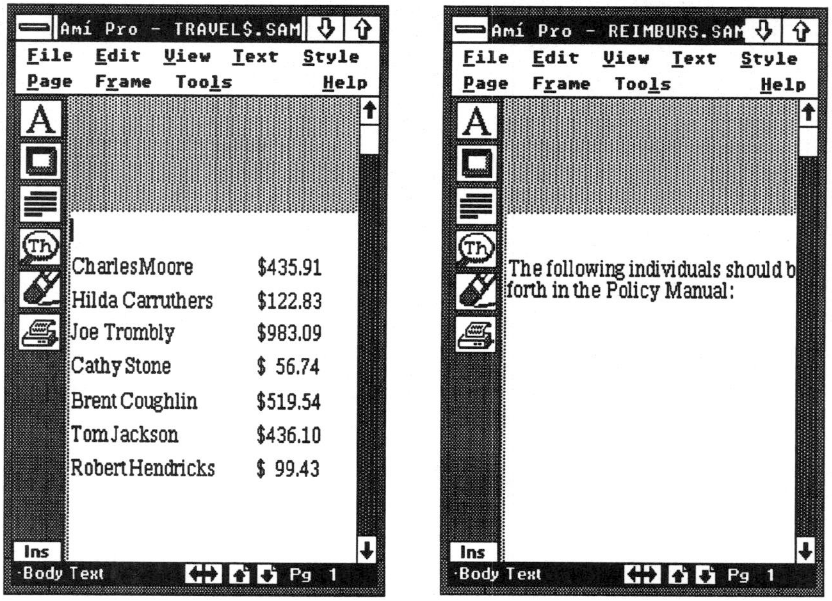

Figure 5-9 Side-by-side Amí Professional windows.

or levels you want to undo in the Edit Defaults dialog box, as shown in Figure 5–10. For example, to set Amí Professional to reverse the last two actions, you could choose the Edit Defaults command, then choose 2 Levels in the dialog box.

If you've just done something that Amí Professional can't undo, the Edit Undo command is dimmed. In that case, you can probably choose a different command to correct the problem.

To undo the last action, do one of the following:

- Click on the eraser icon at the left edge of the screen, as shown in Figure 5–11.

or

- Choose the Edit Undo command.

or

- Press **Alt+Backspace**.

If you've made a disastrous mistake and the Edit Undo command won't work, you can use the File Revert command. You'll lose all the changes you've made since the last time you saved the document, but that outcome may be more desirable than keeping the file in its altered state. You can also use the File Exit command to close your file without saving it.

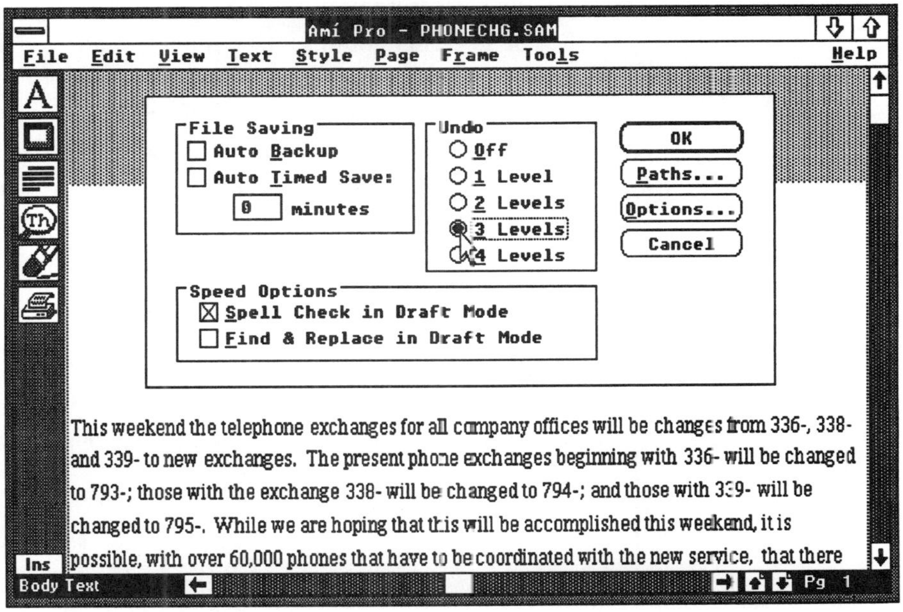

Figure 5–10
Setting Undo levels in the Edit Defaults dialog box.

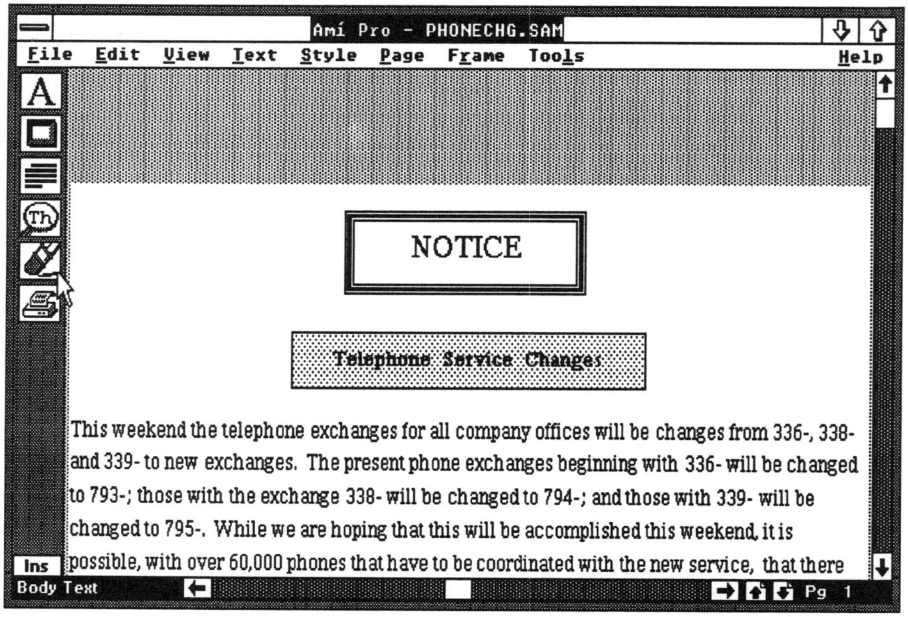

Figure 5-11 Clicking the eraser icon at the left edge of the screen is the same as choosing the Edit Undo command.

FINDING TEXT, FORMATTING, AND STYLES

Amí Professional has a command that can find and/or replace text, formatting, or styles: Tools Find & Replace.

You can use this command to quickly find a word, a phrase, or text formatted with a specific style. Either replace occurrences of the text or styles one by one or replace every occurrence at one time.

By default, Amí Professional searches from the cursor to the end of the file, so you may want to move the cursor before you start a search. You can also tell Amí to begin elsewhere or to reverse the direction of the search with the Options button in the Tools Find & Replace dialog box.

Speed Tip

If you're searching a long document, find and replace operations may seem a little slow. To speed up search and replace operations, you can do this:

1. Choose the Edit Defaults command.
2. Turn on the Find & Replace in Draft Mode option.
3. Click OK or press **Enter**.

When you choose the Find & Replace command in layout mode, this option switches Amí Professional to draft mode, performs the find and replace operations, then switches back to layout mode.

Finding Text

To quickly find text, beginning at the cursor:

1. Choose the Tools Find & Replace command. Amí Professional displays the dialog box shown in Figure 5–12.
2. Type the text you want to find in the Find box. Leave the Replace With box blank. Be sure to type *exactly* the text you want to find—if you type two spaces between words in a phrase, for example, Amí Professional won't find the phrase with just one space between words in your file.

   There is *one* case in which you don't have to type exactly the text you want to find. You can use a question mark (?) to take the place of any character in a word when searching. (For example, you could type **n?w** to find *new* and *now*.)
3. Choose the Find button to begin the search. Amí Professional high-

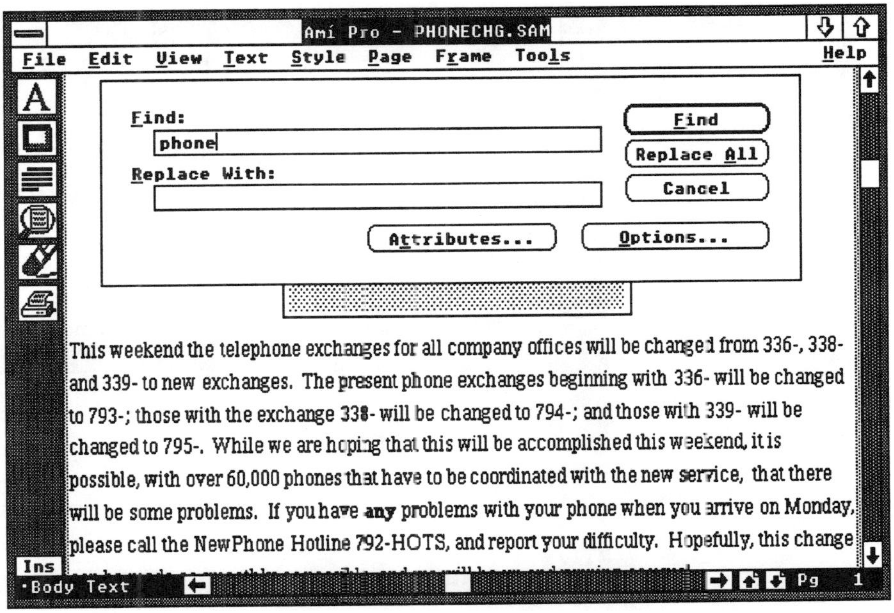

Figure 5–12
Filling in the Tools Find & Replace dialog box to find text.

lights the first occurrence of the text you specified (as shown in Figure 5–13).

4. Choose one of the following options:

   - To return to the document, click on the document or press **Escape**.
   - To find the next occurrence, click the Find Next button or press **Enter**.

Finding Formatting

As well as finding text, you can find formatting such as bold, italic, and underlines. You can find formatting alone (any bold text, for example) or find specific text with that formatting (the word *aardvark* in bold, for example).

To find formatting:

1. Choose the Tools Find & Replace command.
2. To find any text with a certain format, type an asterisk in the Find box. To find specific text that has a certain format, type that text in the Find box. Leave the Replace With box blank.

Figure 5–13
The dialog box displayed when Amí Professional finds a match.

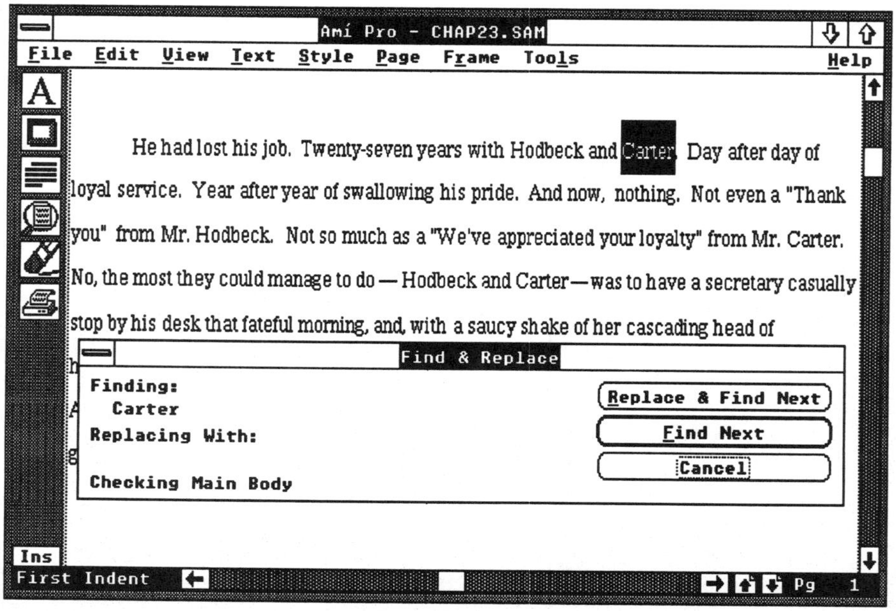

3. Choose the Attributes button to display the dialog box shown in Figure 5–14.
4. Select the formats you want to search for in the Find box, then click OK or press **Enter** to return to the Find & Replace box.
5. Choose the Find button to begin the search. Amí Professional highlights the first occurrence.
6. Choose one of the following options:
   - To return to the document, click on the document or press **Escape**.
   - To find the next occurrence, click the Find Next button or press **Enter**.

Finding Styles

Besides finding text, you can find styles attached to text. To find styles, you must know the name of the style or the function key assigned to it.

To find styles:

1. Choose the Tools Find & Replace command.

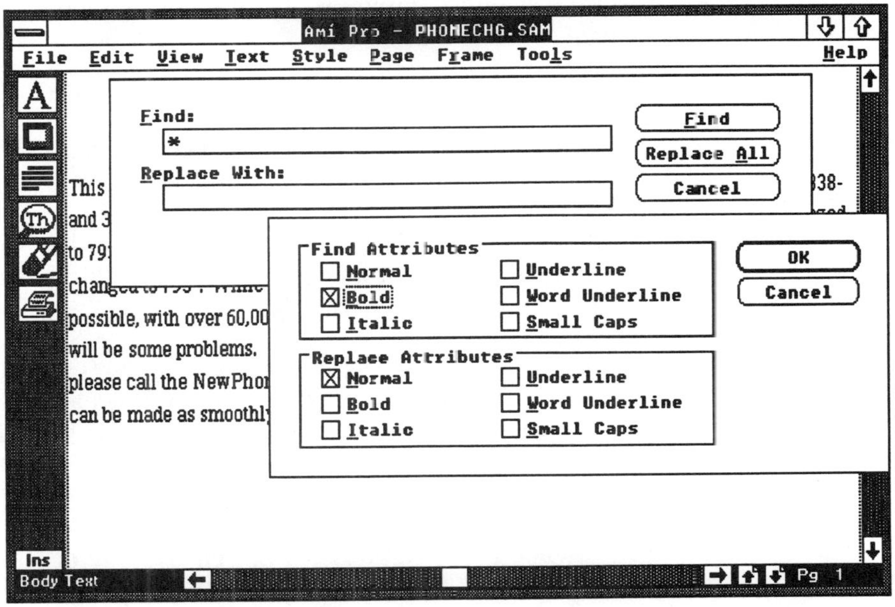

Figure 5–14 Using the Attributes dialog box in the Tools Find & Replace command.

2. In the Find box, type the name of the style you want to find, or press its assigned function key. Leave the Replace With box blank.
3. Choose the Options button to display another dialog box and then choose Style in the Find & Replace box. If you want to change the starting point or the direction of the search, choose a new option from the Range and Direction list, then click OK or press **Enter**.
4. Click the Find button or press **Enter** to begin the search. Amí Professional highlights the first occurrence of the style you specified, or, if it reaches the end of the file before finding an occurrence, Amí Professional displays a message asking you whether to search from the other end of the file.
5. Choose one of the following options:
   - To return to the document, click on the document or press **Escape**.
   - To find the next occurrence, click the Find Next button or press **Enter**.

REPLACING TEXT, FORMATTING, OR STYLES

You can replace existing text, formatting, or styles with new text, formatting, or styles in one easy step. You can ask Amí Professional to make all the changes automatically, or you can approve each change before it's made.

1. Choose the Tools Find & Replace command.
2. Fill in the Find box (as described previously) to tell Amí Professional what to find.
3. Fill in the Replace With box to tell Amí Professional what to replace with, as shown in Figure 5–15. You fill in the Replace With box in the same way as the Find box.
4. If you're replacing formatting, choose the Attributes button, turn on the format options you want to find in the Find box, turn on the format options you want to replace with in the Replace With box, and then click OK or press **Enter**.
5. If you want to narrow the search or change the range or direction, choose the Options button, choose any of the options (described in the next section), then click OK or press **Enter**.

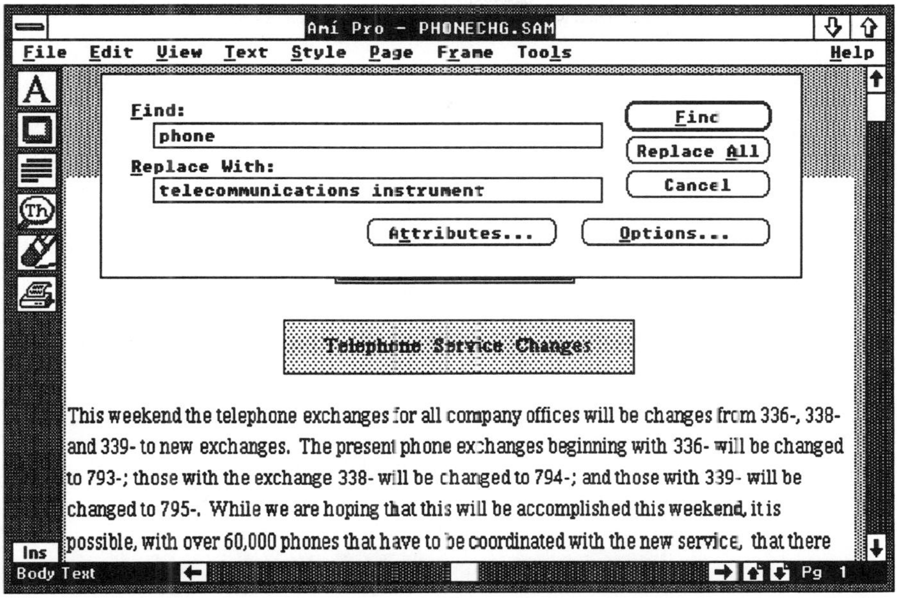

Figure 5–15 Finding and replacing text with the Tools Find & Replace command.

6. Choose one of the following options:

   - If you want Amí Professional to automatically replace all occurrences of the text, choose Replace All. A message appears telling you how many occurrences were found and replaced.

   - If you want to approve each change before it's made, click the Find button or press **Enter** to begin the search. When Amí Professional finds a match, choose from one of the following options:

To	**Do This**
Return to the document	Click on the document or press **Escape**.
Ignore the match and find the next match	Click the Find Next button.
Replace the match and find the next match	Click the Replace & Find Next button.

If you choose Replace All, Amí Professional makes all the replacements automatically and lists the number of replacements in a message box. If this number looks suspiciously high, you can choose the Edit Undo command immediately, or check your replacements. Then, if you've made a mistake, use the Tools Find & Replace command again to reverse the process.

EXAMPLE: Replacing Formatting

Say you've typed all new terms in italic throughout your file to emphasize them, but then you discover that your printer doesn't print italic well. You decide to change from italic to bold. Instead of changing each occurrence individually, you can do this:

1. Choose the Tools Find & Replace command.
2. In the Find box, type an asterisk (*).
3. In the Replace With box, type an asterisk (*).
4. Choose the Attributes button, turn on the Italic option in the Find box, turn on the Bold option in the Replace With box, and then click OK or press **Enter** to close the Attributes dialog box.
5. Choose the Replace All button.

Narrowing Find and Replace Operations

If you want to be more exact in your searches, you can use the Options button and the Attributes button in the Tools Find and Replace dialog box to specify limits to the search, as follows:

1. Choose the Tools Find & Replace command.
2. Type the text you want to find in the Find box.
3. If you want to search only for occurrences of the text that have a specific character format, choose the Attributes button, turn on the format options you want in the Find box, then click OK or press **Enter**.
4. Choose the Options button to display the options (shown in Figure 5–16) and select the options you want. Then click OK or press **Enter**.

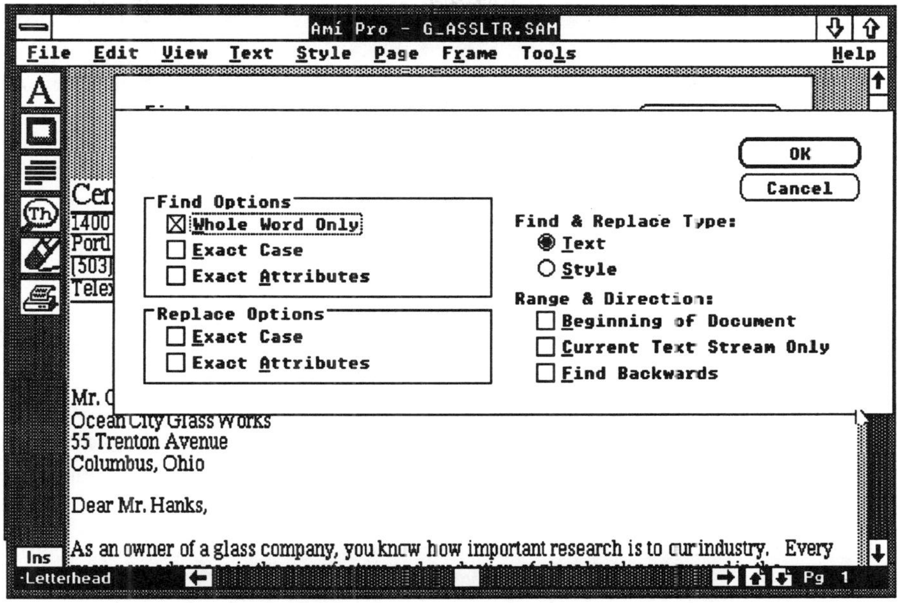

Figure 5–16 The dialog box displayed by the Options button in the Tools Find & Replace dialog box.

Choose	If You Want to
Whole Word Only	Find only a whole word, not part of a word. For example, if you choose this option and you type **ear** in the Find box, Amí Professional will find only the word *ear*; otherwise, the program might find and display matches such as *hear, earth,* or *research*, because they contain the letters you typed.
Exact Case	Pay attention to uppercase and lowercase letters when searching. For example, you might want to find *United* or *UNITED* but not *united.* If you don't choose Exact Case, Amí Professional searches for all cases of the letters you type.
Exact Attributes	Find only occurrences of the text that have the character formatting (such as bold, underline, or italic) that you've specified with the Attributes button.
Beginning of Document	Search from the beginning of the document to the end.

Current Text Stream Only	Search only the part of the document that contains the cursor (for example, a frame, the footnote section, the main body, and so on).
Find Backwards	Search from the cursor to the beginning of the document.

5. Click Find or press **Enter** to begin the search.

Helpful Hint

To enter text faster and with fewer mistakes, substitute a two- or three-character code for long words or phrases that you type often. For example, instead of typing *Hi-Tech Services, Inc.* several times in a memo, just type **hhh**, then use the Tools Find & Replace command later to replace *hhh* with Hi-Tech Services, Inc.

When you choose a code like this, be sure to choose a letter or number combination that doesn't occur other places in your file, such as qq, xx, p9, or any character repeated several times: www,]]], \\\, or %%.

6

Inserting Glossary Items, Dates, Special Characters, and Document Description Fields

This chapter describes how to insert all kinds of special elements into your document. When you have bits of text you want to use over and over again, you can store those items in a glossary, then quickly insert the items whenever you want. You can also insert dates, special ANSI characters, and fields from the Document Description box.

USING GLOSSARIES

Do you have an address, a letterhead, or a picture that you'd like to use over and over again in your documents? With Amí Professional you can save text and graphics as items in a glossary. Using a glossary is like renting a safety deposit box—you can put the items you want to keep in it, then open it up and take out the items any time you like. Almost anything can be kept in a glossary item, from one character to a company logo to several pages of text.

To use a glossary, you'll follow two steps:

1. Create a data file containing the glossary items you want to use.
2. Use the Tools Glossary command to open the data file and insert glossary items in your document.

Creating a Glossary Data File

A glossary data file contains items you want to use again and again. Each item is preceded by a short code name that identifies the item and a separator character, and each item ends with a special end character you choose. (If you're familiar with creating data files for print merge, you'll notice that this procedure is similar.)

You might want to create several different data files: one containing addresses, one containing lists of names, one containing graphics and company logos, and so forth. To create a data file:

1. Use the File New command to open a new empty file.

2. At the top of the file, type the character you want to use between the code name and the item, followed by the character you want to use to end each item. For example, you might type

   %@

   to tell Amí Professional that you're using %s to separate code names from items and @ to end each item.

3. On the second line, type a reminder to yourself about how you're using these special characters. For example, you might type

   CodeName%Item@

   If you don't want to type a reminder like this, press the **Enter** key to insert a blank line after the first line.

4. Type your glossary items, preceding each with a short code name and the separator character you chose. Be sure to make the code name memorable, because you'll need to select it from a list of code names whenever you want to insert the glossary item. For example, you might use initials as code names for someone's address and MEMO for a list of names to send memos to, like this:

   MJM%Michael J. McCollum
   1000 New Deal Avenue
   Dustville, TX 73349-9862@

   MEMO%Sam Wu, Connie Ramirez, Suzanne Beauchamp, Fred MacNamara, Bob Nguyen@

   Indicate the ending of each item with the special end character you specified in the first line. Items can be several lines long (like the two above), so this end character is the only indicator to Amí Professional of where one item ends and the next begins. Figure 6–1 shows items in a sample glossary data file.

5. Use the File Save command to save your data file with a name that

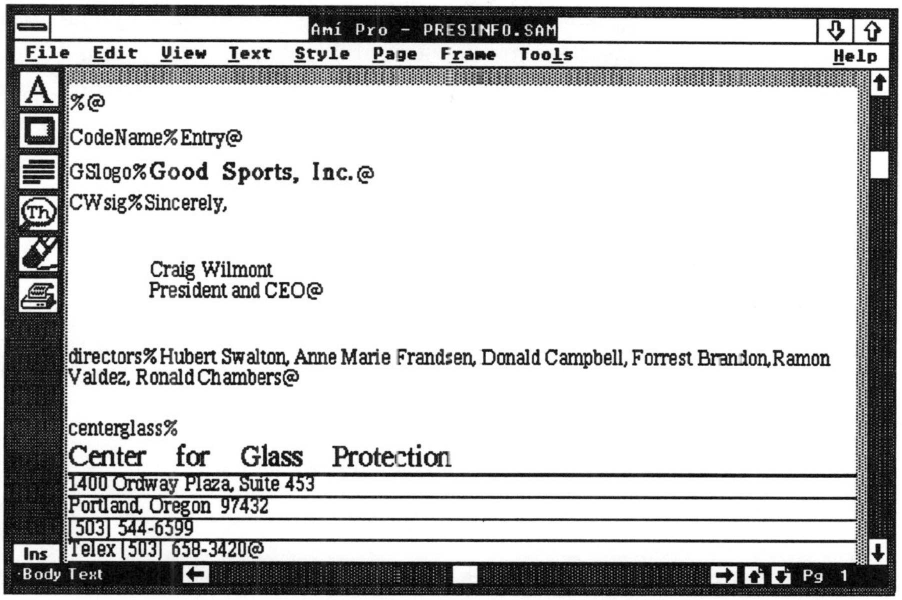

Figure 6–1 A sample glossary data file.

you'll remember as a glossary data file (such as GLOSSARY.SAM, ADDRESS.SAM, or LIST.SAM).

Copying Text to Glossary Data Files

Instead of typing items in the data file as just described, you can use the Windows Clipboard to transfer long sections of text or tables to the data files.

To copy text to a glossary data file:

1. Open the Amí Professional file that contains the text or graphics you want to copy.
2. Select the text.
3. Choose the Edit Copy command.
4. Open the glossary data file you want to paste the copy into.
5. Place the cursor where you want to insert the copy, then choose the Edit Paste command to paste it in.
6. Save the glossary data file.

Note: Copied glossary items retain only the formatting controlled by the Text menu (bold, italic, fonts, and so on). If you want your glossary items to use formats controlled by styles, you'll need to attach styles to those items. See Chapter 9 for more information about styles.

Inserting Glossary Items

Once you've created a data file containing your glossary items as described in the previous section, you can use those items whenever you like with the Tools Glossary command, whose dialog box is shown in Figure 6–2.

To insert a glossary item:

1. Place the cursor where you want to insert the item.
2. Choose the Tools Glossary command.
3. If the list of items you want to use is not displayed in the dialog box, choose the Data File button to display a list of files to choose from, then select the name of the glossary file you want to use and choose OK (or double-click the name of the glossary file).
4. Select the code name of the item you want from the Glossary Items list.

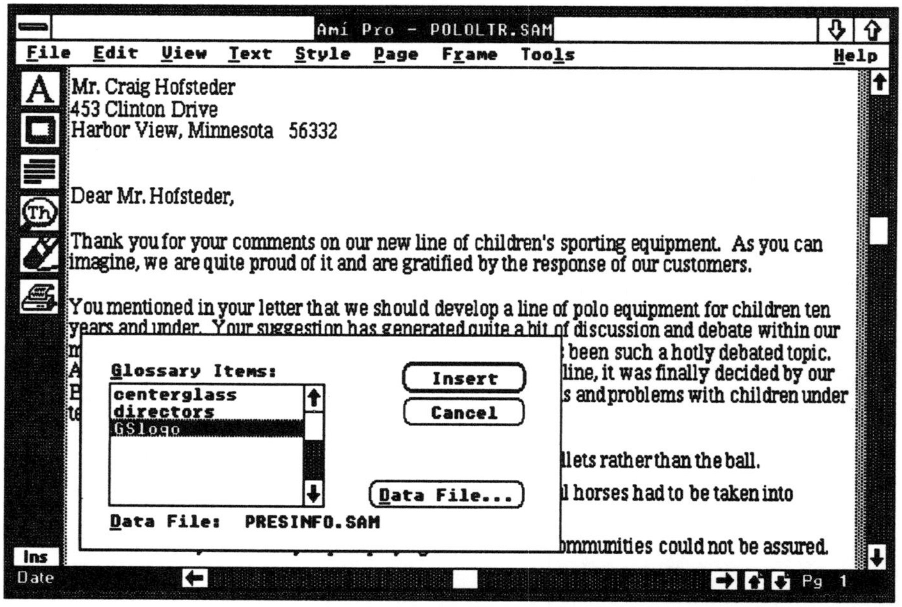

Figure 6–2 Glossary items in the Tools Glossary dialog box.

5. Choose Insert. Amí Professional inserts the glossary item into your document.

Mouse Shortcut

You can also double-click the name of the glossary item in the list to select it, insert it, and close the Tools Glossary dialog box at the same time.

Keyboard Shortcut

If you know the name of the glossary item you want, you can insert it quickly this way:

1. Place the cursor where you want to insert the item.
2. Type the code name of the glossary item, then press **Ctrl+K**. If the program can't find the glossary file, it opens the Tools Glossary dialog box. Otherwise, it immediately inserts the glossary item.

EXAMPLE: Using a Glossary Item

Say you frequently send a memo to the same group of people, so you'd like to save something like the following as a glossary item:

Fred Bianco

Sally Wozinski

Marie Chu Lin

Patrick Macintosh

Here's what you'd do:

1. Type and format the name and address, then select them.
2. Create a data file (DATA.SAM, for example) and put the name and address in it as a glossary item. The file might look like this:

```
%@

LIST%Fred Bianco
Sally Wozinski
Marie Chu Lin
Patrick Macintosh@
```

3. Write your memo. Position the cursor after the TO: heading, choose Tools Glossary, use the Data File button to open the DATA.SAM file (you'll only have to open the file the first time you want to use this item), and double-click on the LIST item to insert the list of names.

INSERTING SPECIAL CHARACTERS

You can add all sorts of characters by typing their special codes. Use either set of special characters:

- the ANSI (American National Standards Institute) character set of 256 characters. The first 128 characters correspond to the letters and symbols on a standard U.S. keyboard. The second set of 128 codes represents special characters such as letters in foreign alphabets, accents, currency symbols, fractions, or other symbols.
- the IBM PC Extended Character Set. However, you can use only the characters that match ANSI characters, because Windows uses the ANSI set.

Use the proper codes from the character set you select. Remember to use the numeric keypad with NumLock turned on. For instance, to make a bullet using the IBM PC Extended Character Set, you would press **Alt+249**. To make the same bullet using the ANSI character set, you would use **Alt+0183**.

To add special characters to an Amí Professional document:

1. Place the insertion point where you want to insert a special character.
2. If necessary, press the **NumLock** key to turn on NumLock.
3. Hold down the Alt key and press either the IBM PC Extended Character Set code or 0 (zero) and the ANSI Character Set code on the numeric keypad for the character you want.

Special characters may look different in different fonts, so if you don't get just what you're expecting, select the special character and change the font.

ADDING DATES AND DOCUMENT DESCRIPTION FIELDS

When you want to add the date or information from the document description to your document, you use the Edit Insert Variable command.

This command tells Amí Professional to get the information from your computer and insert it into your document. You might want to use this information in headers or footers (described in Chapter 15), or to create a cover sheet for your document.

To add a date to your document:

1. Place the cursor where you want to insert the date.
2. Choose the Edit Insert Variable command. Amí Professional displays the dialog box shown in Figure 6-3.
3. Choose one of the following:
   - ◻ To insert today's date, which will remain the same, choose Today's Date.
   - ◻ To insert a date that the program will update every time you open the document, choose System Date.
   - ◻ To insert the date that the file was last revised, choose Date of Last Revision.
4. Choose a format for the date from the Date Style list.
5. Click OK or press **Enter** to insert the date.

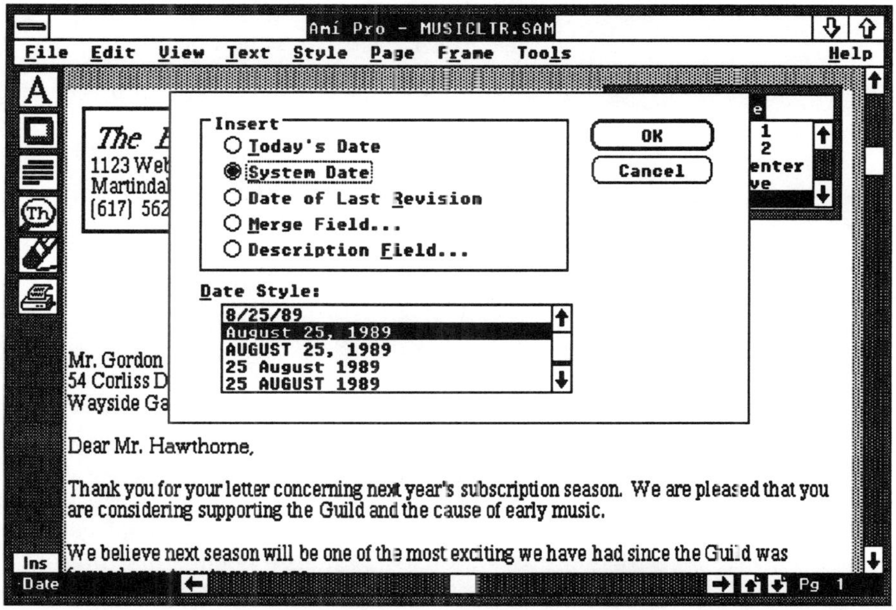

Figure 6-3
Inserting a date for Amí Professional to keep current with the Edit Insert Variable command.

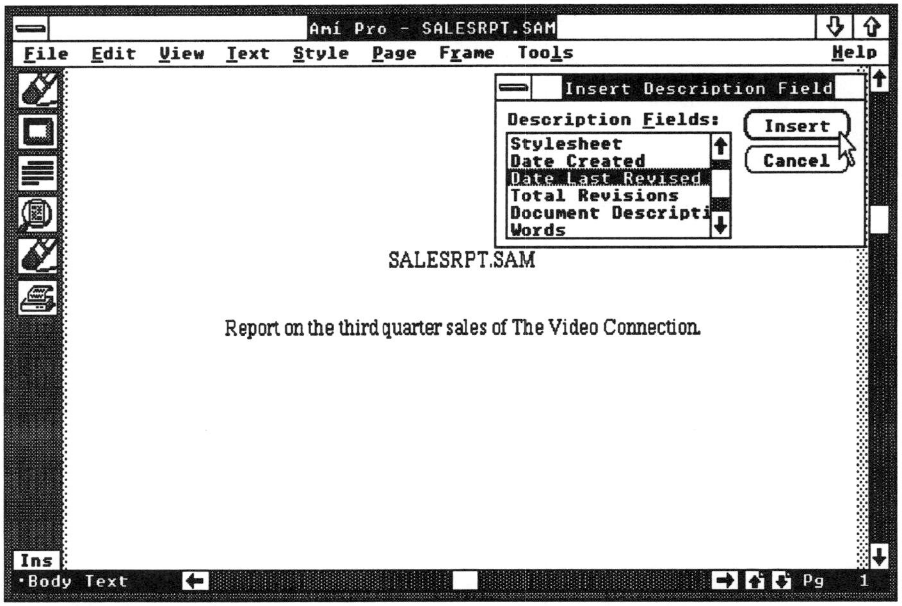

Figure 6-4
Inserting information from the Document Description box.

You can insert information from any field in the Document Description box. This is particularly useful if you've renamed and filled out the four fields with information valuable to you. Of course, you must have filled out the Document Description box already to provide information for Amí Professional to insert. For details about using the Document Description box, see Chapter 4.

To insert information from the document description:

1. Place the cursor where you want to insert the information.
2. Choose the Edit Insert Variable command.
3. Choose the Description Field option.
4. Click OK or press **Enter**. Amí Professional displays another window, as shown in Figure 6-4.
5. Select a description field from the list, then click Insert or press **Enter** to insert it.
6. Move the cursor and repeat step 5 as necessary to insert more fields. When you're done, click the Cancel button or press **Escape** to close the Insert Description Field window.

You may have noticed the Merge Field option in the Edit Insert Variable dialog box—it's used to merge documents to create form letters, address labels, and so forth. See Chapter 17 for more information.

7

Using the Spelling Checker and the Thesaurus

After you finish revising your document, you probably want to check the spelling before you pass the document along to someone else. If you find that you use one word too frequently, you can substitute some synonyms so your writing won't sound too repetitious. This chapter shows you how to do these tasks. It describes

- using Amí Professional's spelling checker
- using the thesaurus

CHECKING SPELLING

When you finish editing a document, you can use Amí Professional's built-in spelling checker to check for typing errors and spelling mistakes. Amí Professional compares words in your document with words in its main dictionary and in a personal dictionary if you create one. Amí Professional also checks for mistakes in capitalization (as in *washington*).

Amí Professional's spelling checker is relatively sophisticated, but it can't do all your work for you. To check spelling, Amí Professional's spelling checker compares each word in your document with words in its dictionaries. If there's a match, Amí Professional assumes that the word is spelled correctly. So if you type *too* when you mean *two*, the spelling checker won't flag an error. It also won't tell you if numbers or single letters surrounded by spaces are wrong, because its dictionaries contain all the letters of the alphabet and all numbers.

Beginning a Spelling Check with No Text Selected

When you have no text selected and you invoke the spelling checker, Amí Professional doesn't begin checking your text right away. The dialog box gives you an opportunity to choose various options and select foreign-language dictionaries (if any) first. Then, when you're ready to begin, you choose the Check Spelling button. See the next discussion for instructions on checking selected text.

To begin a spelling check this way:

1. Move the cursor to where you want the spelling check to begin.
2. Choose the Tools Spelling command. Amí Professional displays the dialog box shown in Figure 7–1.
3. Choose from the following options if desired:

   - If you want to check spelling from the beginning to the end of the document, turn on the Beginning of Document option.

   or

   - If you want to check the spelling only within the part of the document that contains the cursor (main body, frame, header, and so on), turn on the Current Text Stream Only option.

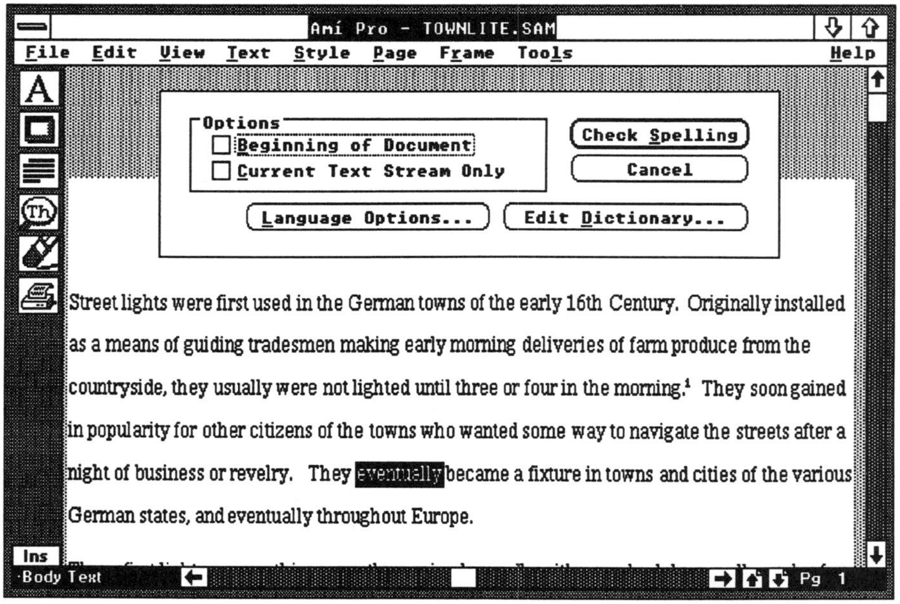

Figure 7–1 Beginning a spelling check of selected text with the Tools Spelling command.

4. Choose the Check Spelling button. If all words in the text match words in the dictionary, Amí Professional displays `Spelling Check Complete:` *n* `Words` in a message box.

   If the program finds a word not in its dictionary, it displays the word in the Spelling dialog box shown in Figure 7–2. See What to Do When Amí Professional Flags a Word for details about how to use this dialog box.

Speed Tip

If you're checking a long document, spelling check operations may seem a little slow. To speed up spelling check operations, you can do this:

1. Choose the Edit Defaults command.
2. Turn on the Spell Check in Draft Mode option.
3. Click OK or press **Enter**.

If you're using layout mode when you choose the Tools Spelling command, this option switches Amí Professional to draft mode, performs the spelling check, then switches back to layout mode.

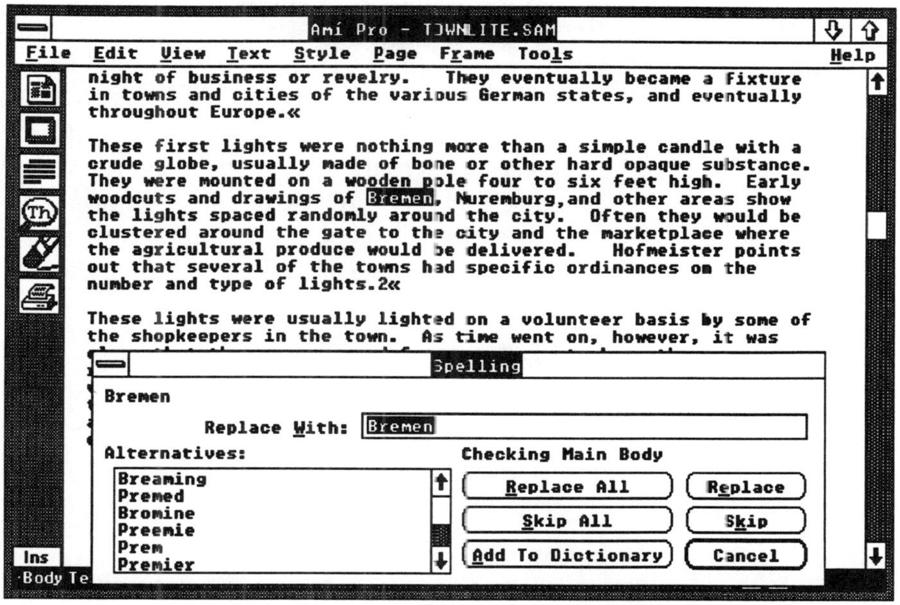

Figure 7–2 The dialog box displayed by Amí Professional when it finds a word not in its dictionary.

Checking the Spelling of Selected Text

You can quickly check the spelling of one word or a block of text by selecting only that text in your document, then choosing the Tools Spelling command. If the selected text is correct, the program displays the message `Spelling Check Complete`. If a word in the selected text is not in the dictionary, the program displays the usual spelling dialog box, whose use is described next.

What to Do When Amí Professional Flags a Word

When Amí Professional encounters a word you have used that is not in its main dictionary or in an open personal dictionary, it displays the unknown word in the upper left corner of the Spelling dialog box, as Figure 7–2 shows. The word may not actually be misspelled—this just means that the word does not match anything in Amí Professional's dictionaries.

When this dialog box appears, you can do any of the following:

- Correct the spelling by typing the appropriate word in the Replace With box and choosing the Replace button (to replace just that one occurrence) or the Replace All button (to replace all occurrences of the same word).
- Use the mouse to select a spelling from the Alternatives list, then choose the Replace or Replace All button. Amí Professional displays a list of alternative spellings in the Alternatives list. If the program can't find any alternatives, it displays a message telling you so. If this happens, or if none of the alternatives are correct, type the correct spelling in the Replace With box, then choose the Replace or Replace All button.
- Ignore the word and continue checking by choosing Skip (to skip just this one occurrence) or Skip All (to skip all occurrences of the same word). Do this when Amí Professional displays names of people or places, or specialized terminology that you don't want to save in a dictionary.
- Add the word to your personal dictionary by choosing the Add To Dictionary button. For example, if your business regularly uses certain terms that aren't in Amí Professional's dictionary, you may want to add them to your personal dictionary so that the spelling checker recognizes them as valid words.

- Cancel the spelling check and return to the document by clicking the Cancel button or pressing the **Escape** key.

> **Helpful Hint**
>
> Because Amí Professional always displays the number of words in a document at the end of a spelling check, you can run the spelling checker to find out how many words your document contains. Just start the spelling checker at the beginning of the document and wait to see the word count displayed when the check is complete.

Editing Your Personal Dictionary

You can't change any of the words that come in Amí Professional's main dictionary, but you can add your own specialized terms to your personal user dictionary so that the program recognizes the vocabulary you use frequently.

You can also type new terms in your own dictionary file instead of waiting to add terms during a spelling check operation. If you find that you've added a misspelled word to your dictionary, you can easily change or delete the word.

To edit your personal dictionary:

1. Choose the Tools Spelling command.
2. Choose the Edit Dictionary button. Amí Professional opens the dictionary file (asking you if you want to save your document first if necessary) and displays the list of words you've added to the dictionary, a sample of which appears in Figure 7–3.
3. Change or delete any incorrect words. Type any new words you want to add.
4. Use the File Save command to save the file.

Using Foreign Language Spelling Checkers

If you're using Amí Professional to create documents in a foreign language, you can choose a foreign-language dictionary. Only one dictionary is included in the Amí Professional package, but you can order a variety of foreign-language dictionaries from Samna Corporation.

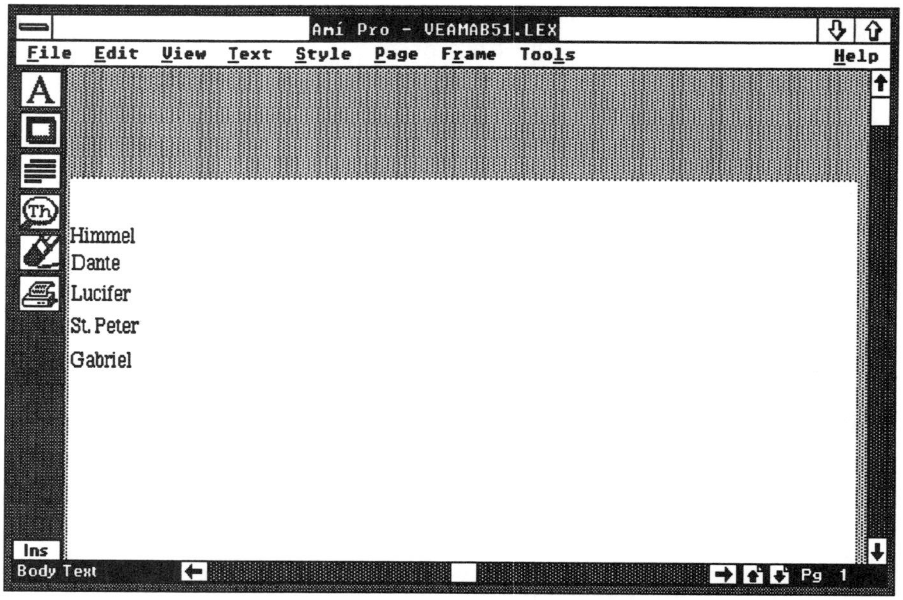

Figure 7-3 Correcting words previously added to your personal dictionary.

If you have more than one dictionary, you can switch dictionaries this way:

1. Choose Tools Spelling.
2. Choose the Language Options button.
3. Select a new language from the list.
4. Click OK or press **Enter**.

USING THE THESAURUS

If you use the same word over and over again in your documents, your writing can become monotonous. To introduce some variety, use the thesaurus to look up synonyms for your most commonly used words.

Looking Up Synonyms for a Word

You can select a word in your document and look up synonyms for it, or you can type a word in the Tools Thesaurus dialog box, then display a list of synonyms. The Thesaurus dialog box also shows definitions for each synonym, so you can choose just the right shade of meaning.

To look up synonyms for a word in your document:

1. Select the word.
2. Make sure you've spelled the selected word correctly. Choose the Tools Thesaurus command. The Thesaurus dialog box appears, containing a list of synonyms for the selected word, such as the one in Figure 7–4. The synonyms will be for the root of the selected word, so they may not exactly match suffixes and so forth. If the word is not in the thesaurus, Amí Professional displays the message `x is not in the thesaurus` at the top of the Thesaurus dialog box.
3. Choose one of the following actions:
   - To replace the selected word with a synonym, use the mouse to select a word from the Synonyms box, then choose Replace.
   - To view definitions for a synonym, select a word from the Meaning Variations box, then read the definitions in the Meaning box.
   - To look up synonyms for a word in the Synonyms box, select the word, then choose Lookup.
   - To go back to the last synonym list that was displayed, choose Previous.
   - To close the Thesaurus dialog box, choose Cancel or press **Escape**.

Figure 7–4
The thesaurus lists synonyms for the selected word.

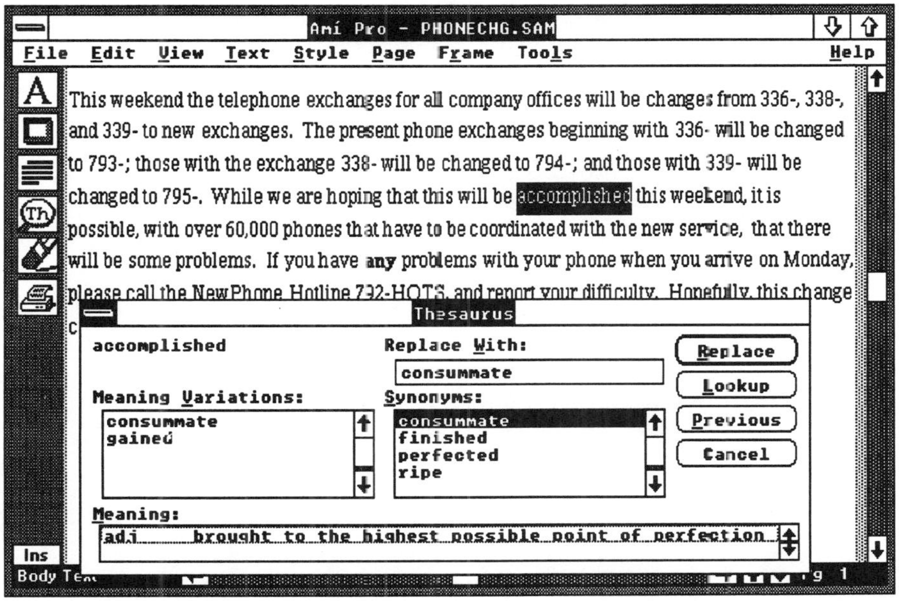

You can select another word in your document without closing the Thesaurus dialog box, then choose Lookup to see synonyms for the new word.

Finding a Synonym for a Word You Type

To type a word in the Thesaurus dialog box and display synonyms for it:

1. Choose the Tools Thesaurus command.
2. Type the word in the Replace With box.
3. Choose Lookup.
4. Repeat steps 2 and 3 to look up more words. When you're finished, click Cancel or press **Escape**.

8

Adding Notes, Footnotes, and Bookmarks

When you want to add information to your document that doesn't clutter up the main text, you can add notes (annotations) or footnotes. This chapter discusses

- how to add, display, and remove notes
- how to add, format, and control the printing of footnotes
- how to mark text with bookmarks and how to jump to bookmarks

ADDING NOTES

When you want to add comments to a file, whether it's writing a reminder to yourself or a comment for someone else to read, you can add notes. These notes won't show up in the printed document.

Adding a note is very simple:

1. Place the cursor where you want to add a note.
2. Choose the Edit Notes command to display the dialog box shown in Figure 8–1.
3. The Insert Note option is already chosen, so click OK or press **Enter**. Amí Professional adds a note marker to the document and displays a "notepad" for you to type text on.
4. Type your note. Amí Professional automatically records the time and

Figure 8–1 Adding notes to a file with the Edit Notes command.

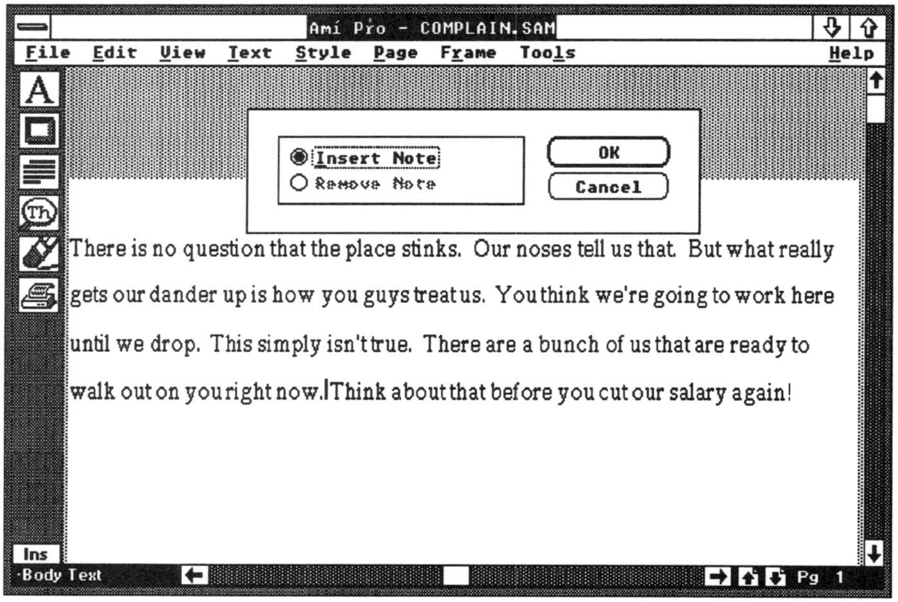

date. If several people will be adding annotations to a file, you might want to include your initials in the note.

5. To get back to your document, click on the document or press **Escape**.

Controlling the Display of Note Markers

You can control whether you see note markers in your document in this way:

1. Choose the View Display Preferences command.
2. Turn the Marks option on or off.
3. Click OK or press **Enter**.

Displaying Notes

You can display a note whenever you want. You can edit notes, copy or cut the text, then paste the note in the document.

To display a note:

1. Double-click the note marker. If you have more than one note in the

same position, the notes will appear "stacked," as shown in Figure 8–2. To read notes behind the first one, click on the edge of the note you want.

2. To close the notes and return to the document, click the document (away from the notes) or press **Escape**.

Jumping to a Note

You can use the Tools Go To command to quickly move the cursor (jump) to the next note:

1. Choose the Tools Go To command.
2. Choose the Next Item option, then select Note from the list, as shown in Figure 8–3.
3. Click Go To or press **Enter**.

Keyboard Shortcut

After you've used the Tools Go To command to jump to one note, you can press **Ctrl+H** to quickly jump to subsequent notes.

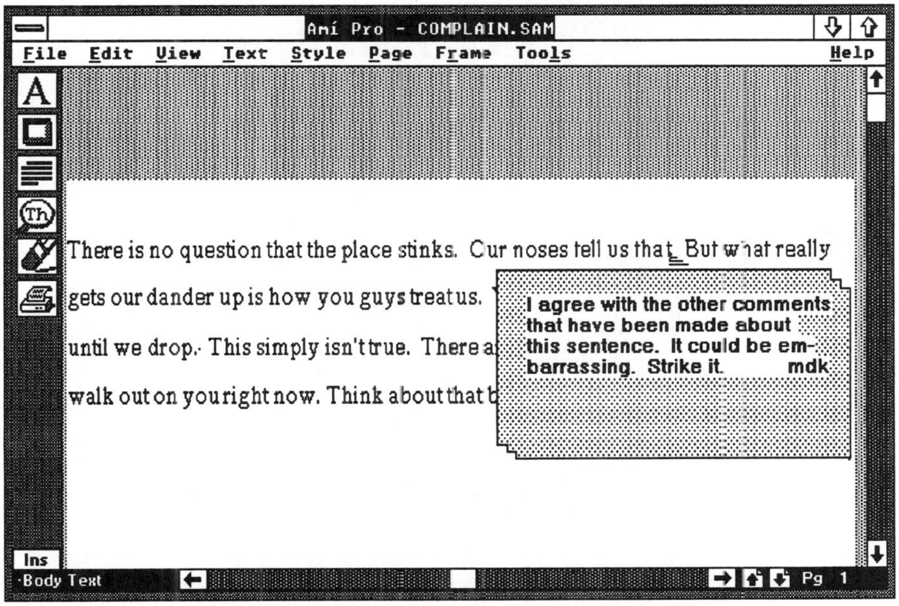

Figure 8–2 Groups of notes at the same location appear "stacked."

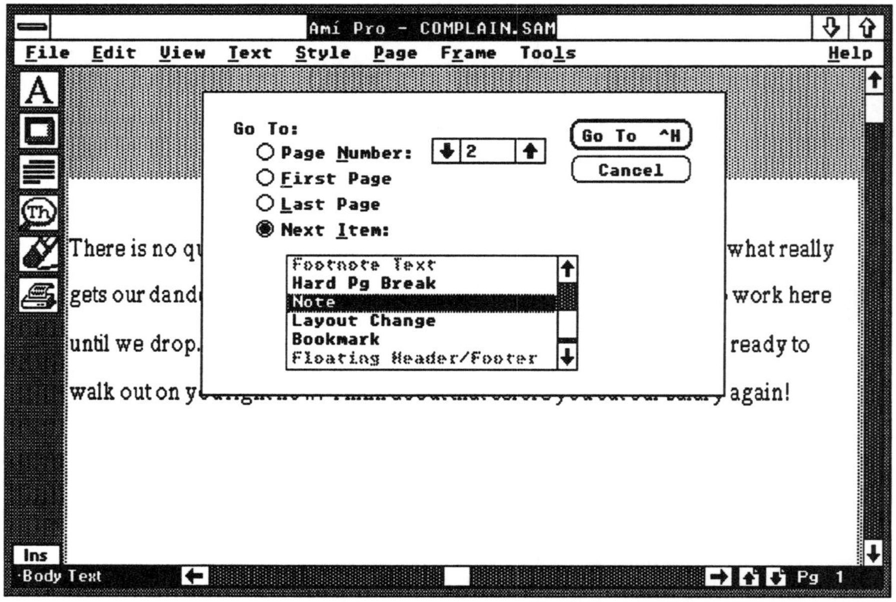

Figure 8–3
Using the Tools Go To command to jump to the next note.

Removing a Note

To remove a note:

1. Place the cursor immediately after the note marker (or on the note itself in a stack of notes) you want to remove.
2. Choose the Edit Notes command.
3. Choose the Remove Note option.
4. Click OK or press **Enter**.

ADDING FOOTNOTES

When you write a document in which you need to explain your sources, you'll want to add footnotes. Amí Professional automatically numbers footnotes. You can choose options to change the footnotes' indents and to control where footnotes are printed. Figure 8–4 shows a document with footnotes at the bottom of the page.

Adding a footnote is easy:

1. Place the cursor where you want to insert a footnote reference number.

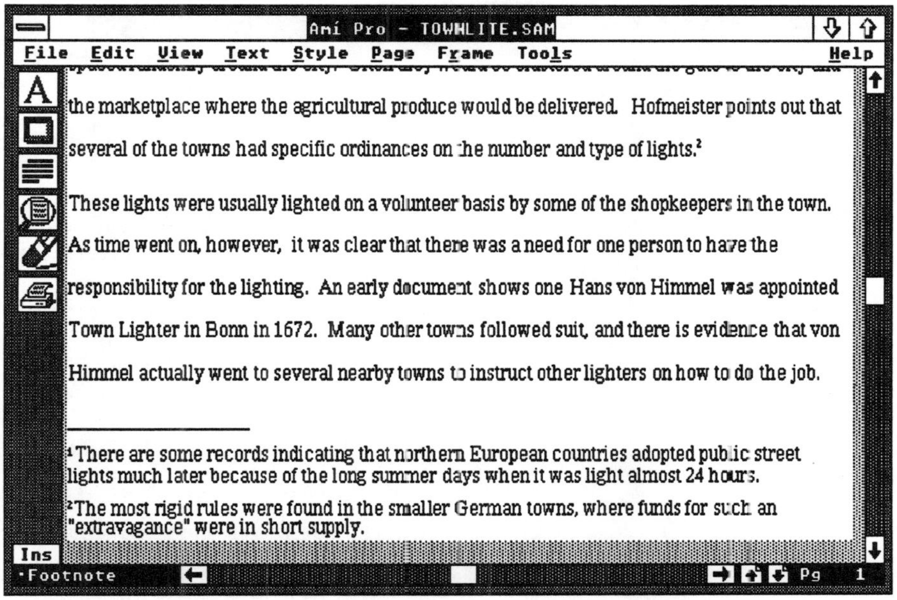

Figure 8-4 A document with footnotes.

2. Choose the Edit Footnotes command.
3. The Insert Footnote option is already chosen, so click OK or press **Enter**. Amí Professional adds a reference number for the footnote and jumps to the bottom of the page so that you can type the footnote text.
4. Type the text for the footnote. You may have to use the enlarged view to see the reference number in the footnote.
5. To get back to the text area of the page, do one of the following:
   - Press **Escape** to go back to the position of the footnote's reference number.

   or

   - Click on the text area above the footnote text, then scroll as necessary.

Choosing Options for Footnotes

All footnotes use the Footnote style, which Amí Professional creates when you insert the first footnote. You can change this style using techniques

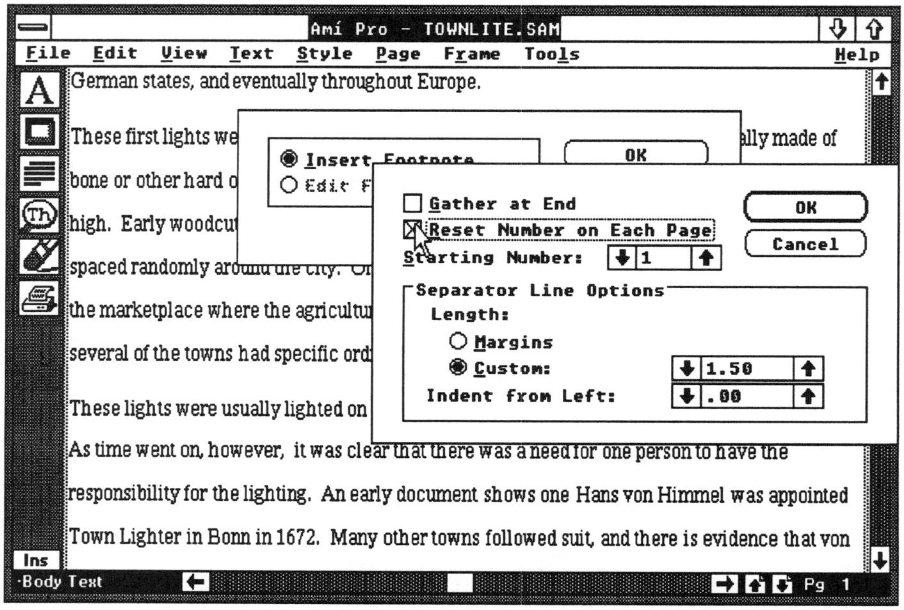

Figure 8–5 Choosing options for footnotes with the Edit Footnotes command.

described in Chapter 9. For example, you might want to change the Footnote style to a different font or size, or set the indents for the footnote paragraphs at different locations.

You can also choose options to control the following aspects of footnotes:

- whether they print at the bottom of each page or at the end of the document
- the length of the line that separates them from the preceding text
- whether they are sequentially numbered throughout the document or their numbers start at 1 on each page

The options you choose affect footnotes throughout your document. Figure 8–5 illustrates the options for controlling footnotes.

To choose options for footnotes:

1. Choose the Edit Footnotes command.
2. Choose the Options button.
3. Choose the following options as desired:

Option	How to Use
Gather at End	Turn on only if you want all footnotes to be printed at the end of the document. Make sure this option is turned off if you want footnotes printed at the bottom of each page.
Reset Number on Each Page	Turn on only if you want footnote numbers to start over again on each page. Make sure this option is off if you want footnotes to be numbered consecutively throughout the document.
Starting Number	If you want to use a different starting number for the first footnote in the document, type or select a new number from this running list.
Separator Line Length	If you want to change the length of the line that separates the footnotes from the text, choose Margins if you want the line to extend from the left margin to the right, or choose Custom and type or select a measurement for the line length in the running list box.
Indent from Left	If you've specified a Custom line length and you also want to indent the separator line from the left margin, type or select a new measurement in the running list box.

4. When you've set all the options you want, click OK or press **Enter**.

Figure 8–6 shows footnotes at the bottom of the page with a three-inch separator line indented ½ inch from the left margin.

Editing Footnotes

To edit the text of a footnote:

1. Select the reference number of the footnote you want to edit.

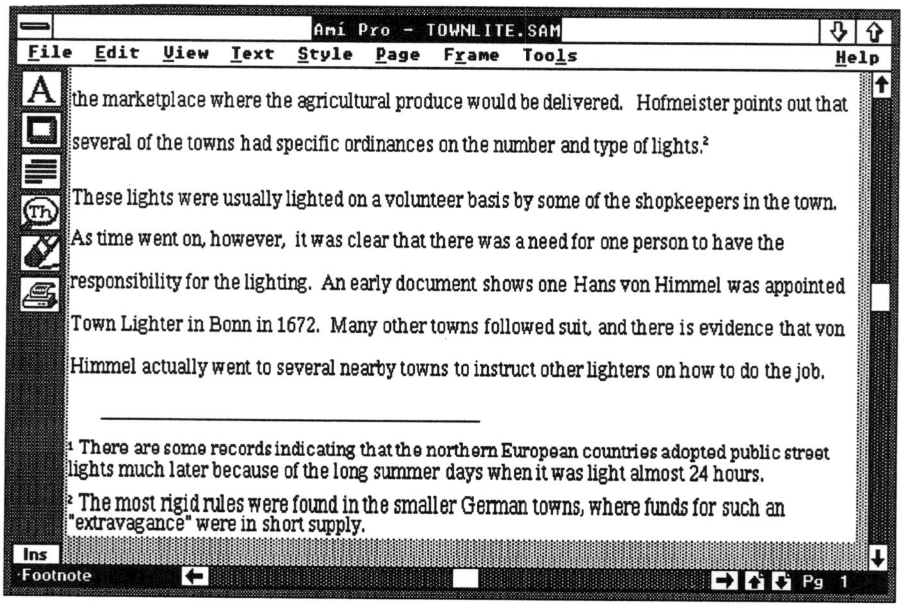

Figure 8–6 Footnotes below a customized separator line.

2. Choose the Edit Footnotes command, choose the Edit Footnote option in the dialog box, then click OK or press **Enter** to jump to the footnote.
3. Edit the footnote text as necessary.

Jumping to the Next Footnote

You can use the Tools Go To command to quickly move the cursor to the next footnote mark or to the text of the next footnote.

To jump to the next footnote:

1. Choose the Tools Go To command.
2. Turn on the Next Item option.
3. Select Footnote Mark or Footnote Text from the list.
4. Click OK or press **Enter**.

Keyboard Shortcut

After you've used the Tools Go To command to jump to a footnote mark or footnote text, you can easily jump to the next item of the same type by pressing **Ctrl+H**.

Removing Footnotes

When you remove a footnote, Amí Professional automatically removes both the reference number and the text, then renumbers the remaining footnotes.

To remove footnotes:

1. Select the reference number of the footnote you want to delete.
2. Press the **Delete** key.
3. When Amí Professional displays a message asking whether it's okay to delete the footnote reference, click Yes or press **Y**.

USING BOOKMARKS FOR EASY REFERENCE

In Amí Professional, bookmarks are not slips of paper you use to mark your place in a manuscript, but they have a similar function. Amí Professional's bookmarks are names that you attach to selected text. For example, you might want to name a section of a report Sales_by_Region or a section of your great American novel Dramatic_Climax. A bookmark can mark anything—it might be a list of illustrations, a picture and its caption, a paragraph, or several pages of text.

Once you've attached a bookmark name to a piece of text or to a picture, you can use the Edit Mark Text command to quickly move the cursor to that spot.

Creating a Bookmark

To create a bookmark, you name a position in the text. A bookmark name can be up to 20 characters long, must begin with a letter, and can contain letters, numbers, spaces, and underscore characters (_). Here are some examples of bookmark names: Epilog, Buying List, Calendar 90, and Mtg Minutes.

Each bookmark name must be unique within a document. If you try to assign a name that's already in use, Amí Professional will display an error message.

To create a bookmark:

1. Place the cursor where you want to attach a name.
2. Choose the Edit Mark Text command.

3. Choose the Bookmark option, then click OK or press **Enter** to close the Edit Mark Text dialog box. Amí Professional displays the dialog box shown in Figure 8–7.

4. Type a name for your bookmark.

5. Choose Add.

That's all there is to it! Don't expect to see any changes in the Amí Professional window—bookmarks are invisible.

Jumping to a Bookmark

You can quickly move the cursor (jump) to the next bookmark in the text or jump to a particular bookmark that you specify.

To jump to the next bookmark:

1. Choose the Tools Go To command.

2. Turn on the Next Item option, then select Bookmark from the list.

3. Click Go To or press **Enter**. Amí Professional moves the cursor to the end of the next section of "bookmarked" text.

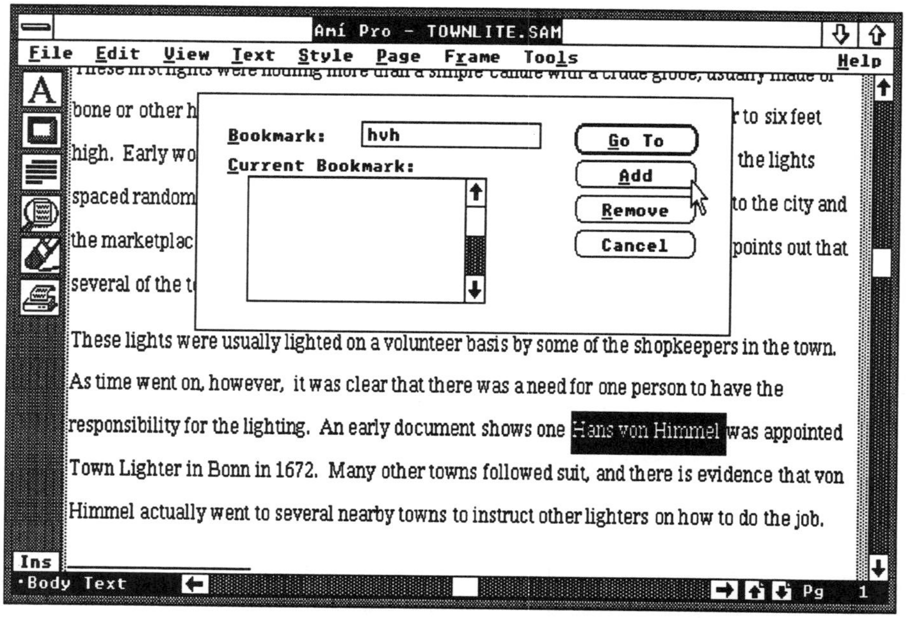

Figure 8–7 Attaching a bookmark name to selected text with the Edit Mark Text command.

Keyboard Shortcut

After you've used the Tools Go To command to jump to a bookmark, you can press **Ctrl+H** to jump to the next bookmark.

To jump to a particular bookmark:

1. Choose the Edit Mark Text command and choose the Bookmark option.
2. Click on OK or press **Enter**. Amí Professional displays a list of bookmarks used in the document, as shown in the box of Figure 8–8.
3. Select a bookmark name from the list.
4. Click Go To or press **Enter**. Amí Professional moves the cursor to the end of the "bookmarked" text.

Deleting Bookmarks

To delete a bookmark:

1. Choose the Edit Mark Text command.

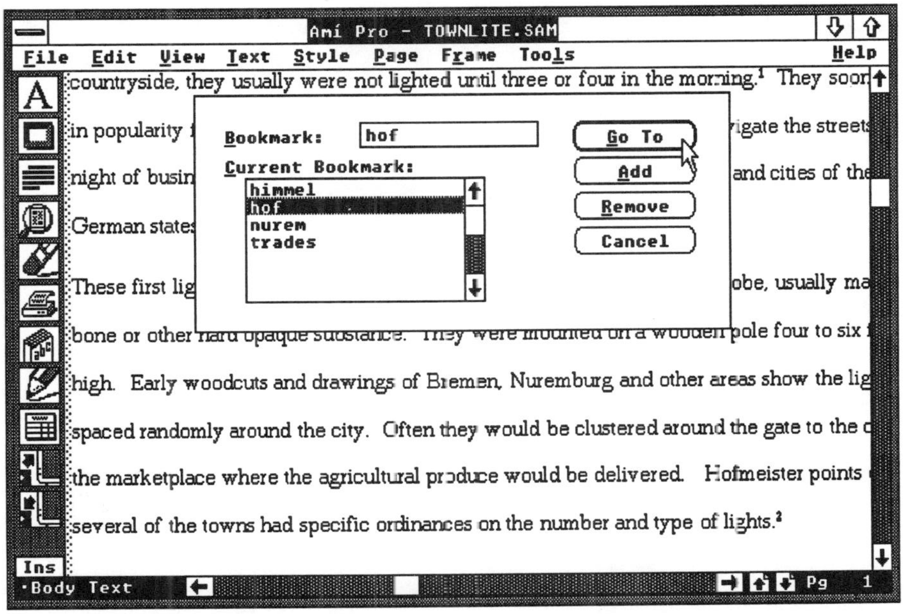

Figure 8–8 Selecting from a list of bookmarks.

2. Choose the Bookmark option, then click OK or press **Enter** to close the Edit Mark Text dialog box.
3. Select the bookmark name you want to delete from this list.
4. Choose Remove.
5. Repeat steps 3 and 4 for all the bookmarks you want to delete.
6. Click OK or press **Enter**.

9

The Essence of Formatting: Using Style Sheets

To control the way text looks in your documents, Amí Professional uses *style sheets,* which are collections of *styles.* Using styles has these advantages:

- When you apply a style, you can apply a multitude of format options in one step to save time.
- You can control format options that are not available through other commands, such as bullets and numbers before the text, lines above and below paragraphs, page break prevention in paragraphs, control of blank space above and below paragraphs, control of the spacing of characters on a line, and formatting for numbers in table cells.
- You can use the same styles over and over again to give your documents a consistent format.
- If you change a style, Amí Professional automatically reformats all text with that style.

INTRODUCTION

What Are Styles?

Styles are named sets of formatting instructions that you can use over and over again. Using a style is simple. Say you want a chapter heading to look like this:

CHAPTER
TWO

The text is bold, the font is New Century Schoolbook, the size is 14 point, and the text is centered and has lines both above and below it. To use this format for all chapter headings, you could save this format as a style named Chapter, then apply the Chapter style to all your chapter heading paragraphs to make them look alike.

All paragraphs in Amí Professional have a style attached to them. If you haven't chosen a special style sheet or applied any styles of your own, all paragraphs have Amí Professional's default style, the Body Text style. You can always view the name of the style attached to a paragraph by selecting the paragraph and checking the name in the lower left corner of the Amí Professional window, as shown in Figure 9–1.

What Are Style Sheets?

Style sheets are special Amí Professional files that contain paragraph styles and page layout formatting. (Page layouts are covered in Chapter 11.) If

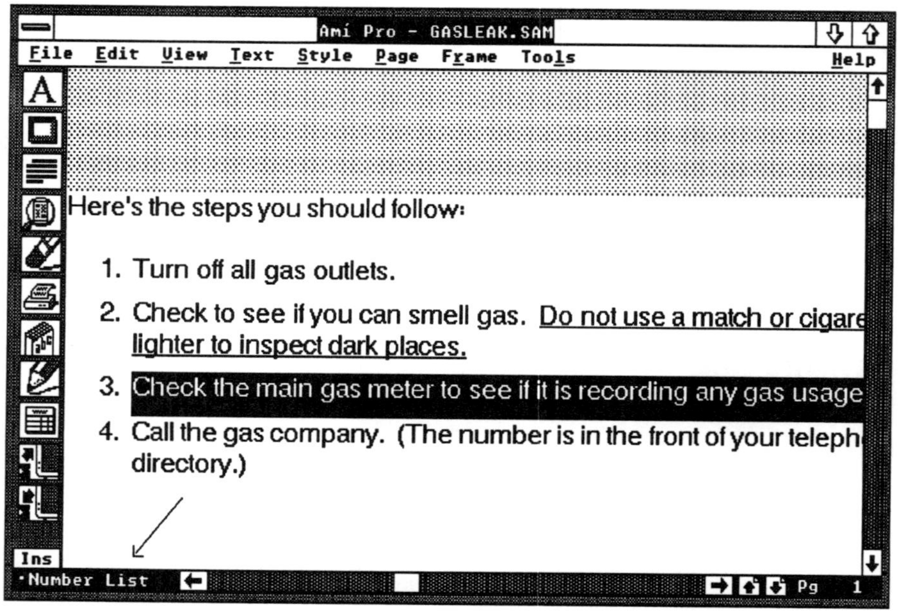

Figure 9–1 The name of the style for the selected paragraph is shown in the lower left corner of the Amí Professional window.

you don't select a style sheet when you create an Amí Professional document, the program automatically assigns the default style sheet, ˜DEFAULT.STY, to your document. All style sheet files end with the .STY extension. Amí Professional comes with a wide variety of style sheets that you can use. For example, Figure 9–2 shows the ˜MEMO5.STY style sheet supplied in the Amí Professional package. You can also modify these provided style sheets or create your own style sheets to meet your needs.

As well as styles, style sheets can also contain boilerplate text—text that you'll use again and again. For example, as Figure 9–2 shows, the ˜MEMO5.STY style sheet contains standard memo headings.

WORKING WITH THE STYLES BOX

When you start Amí Professional without first selecting a file, or if you start a new file without choosing a different style sheet, the styles in the ˜DEFAULT.STY file are listed in the styles box.

The styles box lists both the styles in the document and the styles in the style sheet file. Styles that belong only to the document are listed with bullets in front of their names in the styles box.

The styles box is a separate window, so you can use standard Windows commands and procedures to move it, change its size, or close it, just like any other window. (To activate the styles box with keys, press **Ctrl+Y.**)

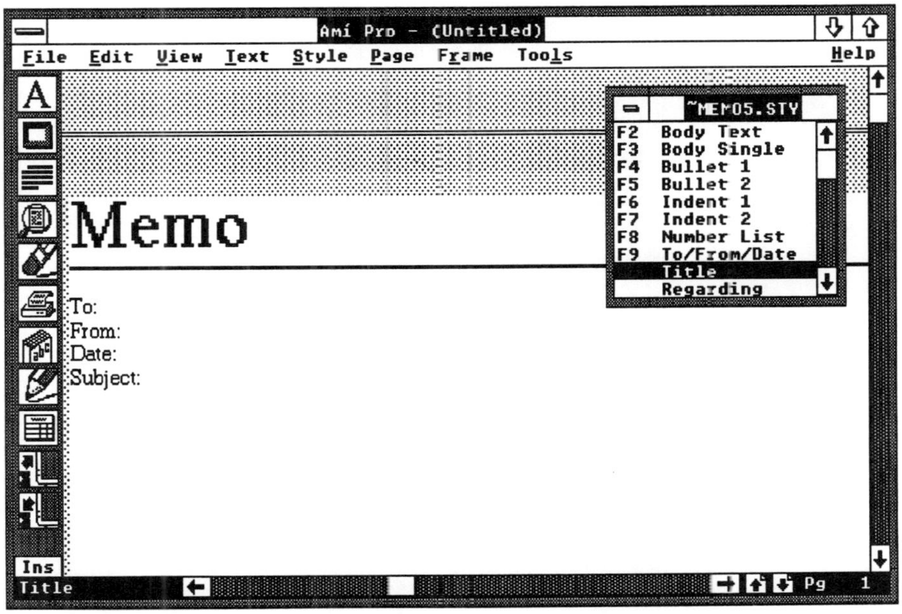

Figure 9–2 The ˜MEMO5.STY style sheet provided with Amí Professional, shown with contents (boilerplate text). Note the names of the styles in the styles box.

If you don't want to concern yourself with using styles or you don't need to see the list of styles on the screen, you can close the styles box and remove it from the Amí Professional window.

To close the styles box:

- Choose the Hide Styles Box command from the Style menu.

  or

- Double-click the style name in the lower left corner of the window.

  or

- Double-click the control menu icon in the upper left corner of the styles box.

If you decide later to open the styles box, just choose the Show Styles Box command again.

Keyboard Shortcut

To quickly hide or display the styles box without choosing a command from a menu:

- Press **Ctrl**+**Z**.

CHECKING A STYLE'S FORMATTING

You can see how a style formats a paragraph in two ways: by applying the style to a paragraph, as explained in the next section; or by checking the style's format in the Modify Style dialog box. Applying a style is the easier way, because you see the results immediately, and you can easily choose Edit Undo or apply the old style to change back. To check the format in the Modify Style dialog box:

1. Click the Modify Style icon (straight lines that look like a paragraph) in the icon bar.

   or

   Choose the Modify Style command from the Style menu.

2. When the dialog box shown in Figure 9–3 appears, click the name of the style you want to check in the style list in the upper left corner of the dialog box.

3. Click various options in the Modify box at the left side of the dialog

Figure 9–3
You can check the formatting of styles in the Modify Style dialog box.

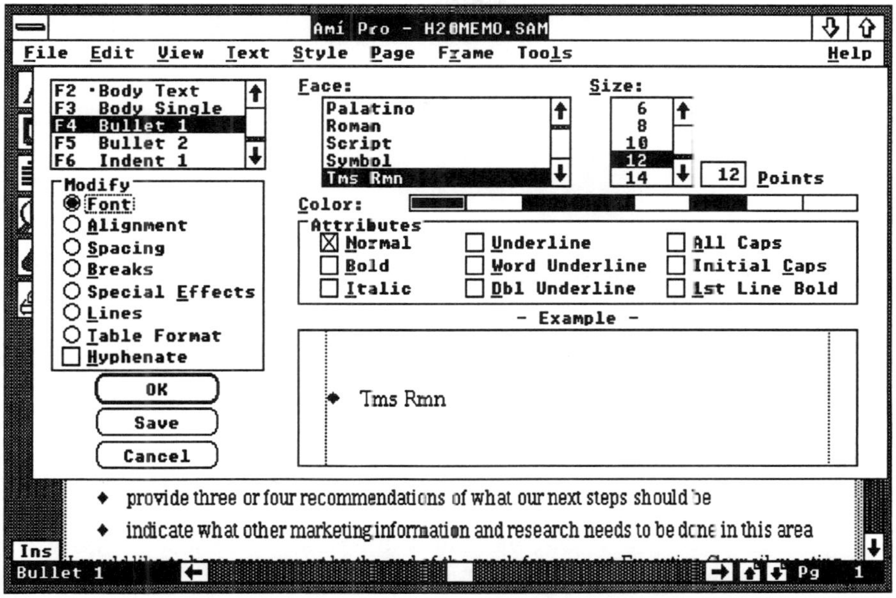

box to see different aspects of the style's formatting. The sample text in the lower right corner of the dialog box shows an example of the formatting in the style.

4. To see the formatting in another style, choose a new style name from the style list in the upper left corner of the dialog box, then repeat step 3.

5. When you're finished checking styles, click Cancel or press **Escape** to close the dialog box.

APPLYING STYLES TO PARAGRAPHS

Applying a new style to a paragraph is easy:

1. Select the paragraph(s) you want to format with the style.

2. Use the mouse to click the style name in the styles box. (Click once—if you double-click, you'll open the Modify Style dialog box.)

   or

   Press the function key listed beside the style name. (If no function key is listed, you can press **Ctrl+Y** to move to the styles box, use

Ctrl+***arrow*** key to highlight the style, then press the **Spacebar** to apply it.)

That's all there is to it! If you don't like the style, you can choose Edit Undo or simply choose another style.

USING A DIFFERENT STYLE SHEET

If you want to use the styles contained in another style sheet, simply open the other style sheet. If a style in the new style sheet has the same name as a style in the previous style sheet, you might see parts of your document change to take on the formatting of the new style. (You can prevent this by saving the styles with the document, as described later in this chapter.)

You can load a different style sheet in two ways:

- Choose a new style sheet in the File New dialog box when you create a new document. You can also load the boilerplate text by choosing the With Contents option.

  or

- Choose the Use Another Style Sheet command from the Style menu, select a new style sheet from the list, then click OK or press **Enter**. Amí Professional opens the new style sheet and displays its styles in the styles box.

Figure 9–4 illustrates choosing another style sheet with the Use Another Style Sheet command.

Amí Professional always looks for style sheet files in the directory specified in the Edit Defaults dialog box, unless you type a different path name in front of the file name when you select a style sheet. By default, this directory is the directory in which you first installed the style sheets. If you want to change the default style sheet directory:

1. Choose Edit Defaults.

2. Choose Paths.

3. Type a new path name in the Style Sheet box, as Figure 9–5 shows.

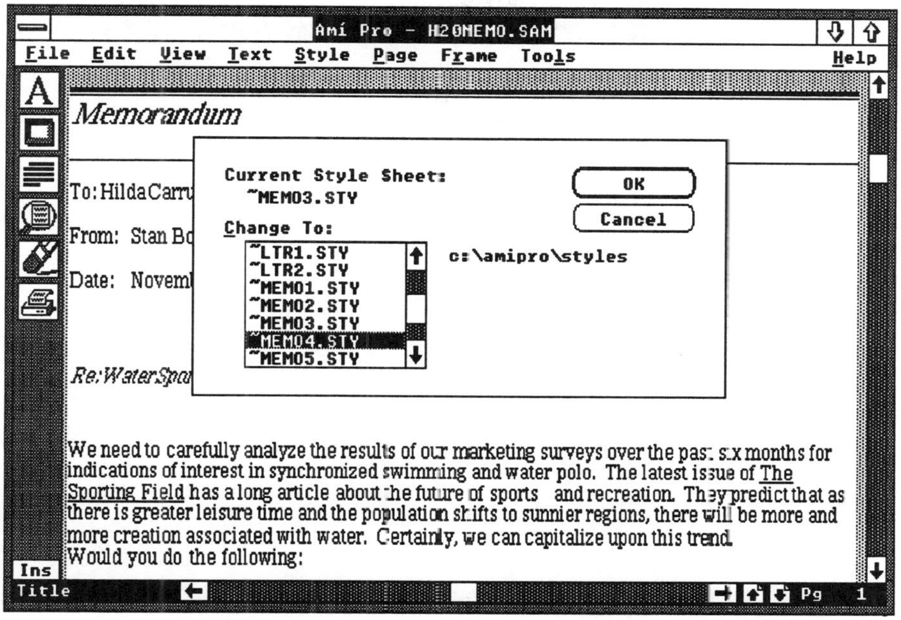

Figure 9-4
Loading a different style sheet with the Use Another Style Sheet command.

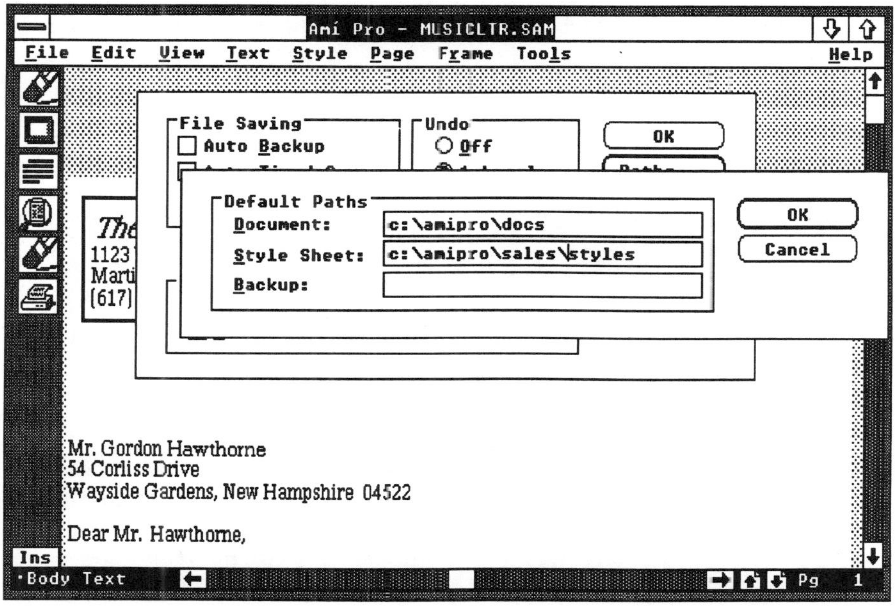

Figure 9-5
Setting a new directory for style sheets with the Edit Defaults command.

EXAMPLE: Using an Existing Amí Professional Style Sheet

Say you want to create a newsletter using Amí Professional's ~NEWSLT1.STY style sheet. Here's what you'd do:

1. Choose File New, select ~NEWSLT1.STY from the list, and click OK or press **Enter**. To use the boilerplate frames contained in the file, click With Contents before you choose OK.
2. When the file opens, click Title in the styles box to select the Title style, then type the title of your newsletter in the frame.
3. Place the cursor in the first column, then press **F6** or click Heading 1 in the styles box to select the Heading 1 style and type the title of your first article.
4. Press **Enter** to begin the first line of the article. The new paragraph automatically takes on the style of the preceding paragraph when you press **Enter**, so press **F2** or click Body Text in the styles box to switch the style to Body Text, a style with an indented first line.
5. Continue to type as many paragraphs of Body Text as you need. The Body Text style is automatically carried on to the next paragraph when you press **Enter**.
6. When you need a bulleted list, press **Enter** to begin a new line, then press **F4** or click Bullet 1 in the styles box to apply the Bullet 1 style to the new line. Amí Professional inserts a bullet and indents the text.

It doesn't matter if you type the text first, then apply the style, or the other way around. Just remember that the cursor must be in the paragraph you want to assign the style to before you apply the style.

CREATING AND CHANGING STYLES

If Amí Professional's supplied styles don't meet your needs, you can always create your own styles or change the existing styles. The only differences between creating a new style and changing an existing one are

- When you create a new style, you give the style a new name. Nothing in your document changes until you apply the new style.
- When you change an existing style, you keep the old name. If par-

agraphs in your document were formatted with the old style, they'll change to match the changes you've made.

Styles you create or change are automatically saved with the document. If you want to use those styles in other documents, you should save the style sheet, as described later in this chapter.

Creating Your Own Styles

To create your own style, you base your new style on an existing style, give it a new name, then make any changes you want:

1. If necessary, load the style sheet that contains the style you want to base your new style on.
2. Choose the Create Style command from the Style menu. Amí Professional displays the dialog box shown in Figure 9–6.
3. Select a style from the list to base your new style on. This means that the new style starts off with the same formatting as the base style. For example, if you're creating a new bullet style, you'll probably want to base your new style on the existing bullet style that's closest to what you want.

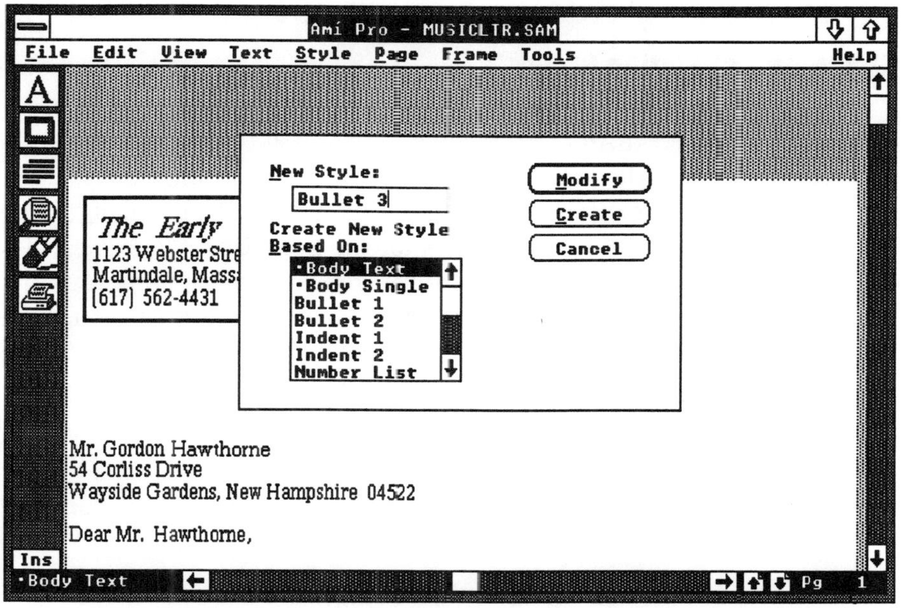

Figure 9–6
Naming a new style in the Create Style dialog box.

4. Type a name for your new style.
5. Do one of the following:
   - If you want to save the style as is, choose the Create button. (This merely gives the existing style another name and saves it with your document.)

   or

   - If you want to change the style, choose the Modify button to display the Modify Style dialog box, choose options in the dialog box to change the style, then choose OK to save the style and close the Modify Style dialog box.

After you create a style, the name of the style appears at the bottom of the list in the styles box. Amí Professional precedes the style name with a bullet to show that the style belongs to the document, not to the style sheet.

New styles you create are automatically saved with the document, not with the style sheet. Because it's attached to the document, the new style always appears in the styles box when you load the document, even if you switch style sheets. If you want to save the new style with the style sheet so you can use it in other documents, you have to move the style from the document to the style sheet, or you can save the modified style sheet. Both methods are explained later in this chapter.

Changing an Existing Style

If Amí Professional's styles don't meet your needs, you can always change them. Keep in mind that when you change an existing style, *all* paragraphs formatted with that style automatically change. For example, to change the indent settings for the Body Text style, you select the Body Text style, change the indent settings, and every paragraph that has the Body Text style in your document changes to match the new settings.

The changes you make to styles are saved with the document, not automatically saved in the style sheet. To save the changes in the style sheet, see instructions for saving a style sheet later in this chapter.

To change an existing style:

1. If necessary, load the style sheet that contains the style you want to change.
2. Do one of the following:

- Click on the Modify Style icon (it looks like lines of text on a page) in the icon bar, as shown by the mouse pointer in Figure 9–7.

or

- Choose the Modify Style command from the Style menu.

3. Select the style you want to change from the list in the upper left corner of the dialog box (for instance, the Body Text style is selected in Figure 9–8).
4. Choose options to change the style until the sample text in the lower right corner of the dialog box looks the way you want it.
5. Choose OK to save the style and close the Modify Style dialog box.

If you want to keep the Modify Styles dialog box open while you change several styles, click the Save button after completing changes to each style, then click the OK button when you're ready to close the dialog box.

Shortcuts

To open the Modify Style dialog box without choosing the command from the Style menu:

- Press **Ctrl**+**A**.

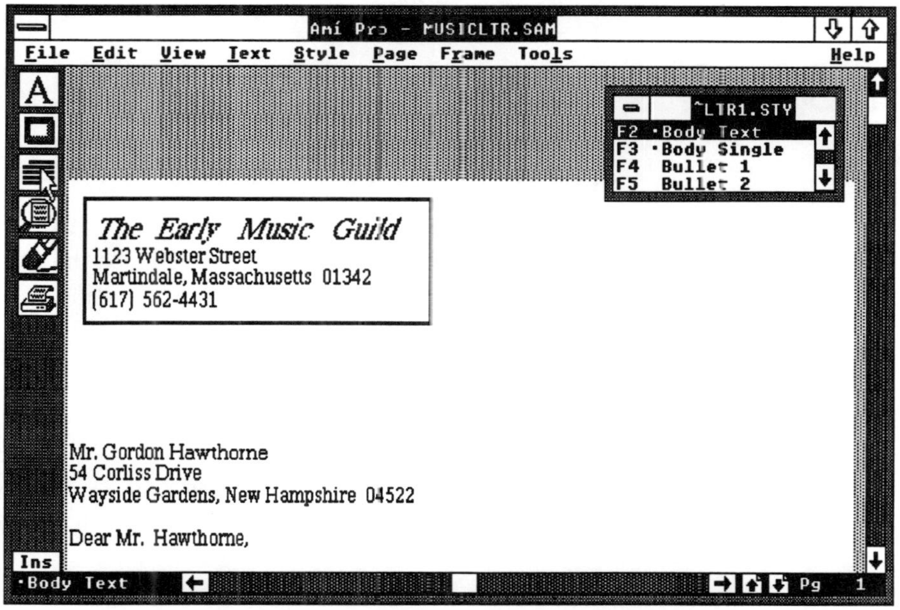

Figure 9–7
You can click the Modify Style icon to display the Modify Style dialog box.

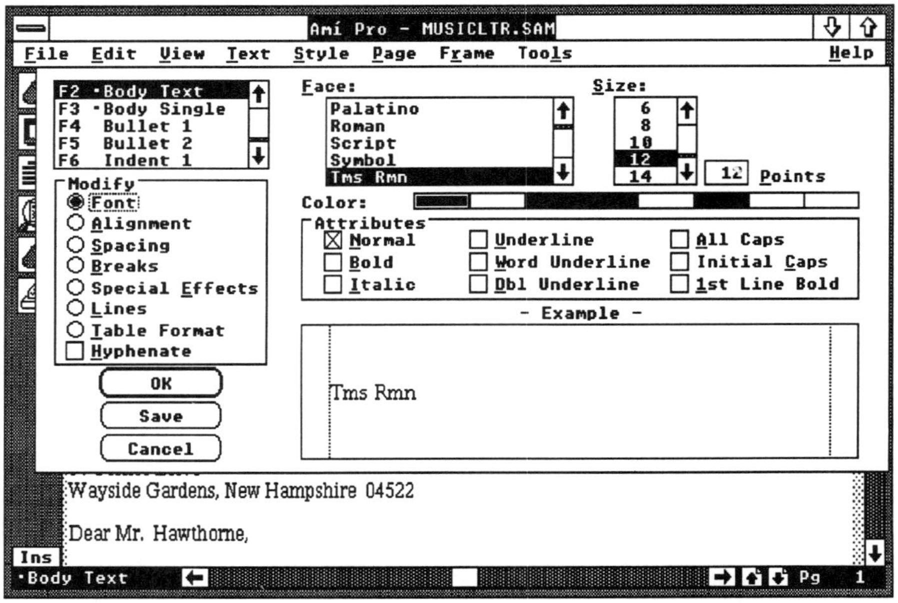

Figure 9-8
You use the Modify Style dialog box to change a style.

To select a style and open the Modify Style dialog box at the same time:

- Double-click the style name in the styles box.

The procedures you use to change a style in the Modify Style dialog box are covered next.

Changing the Font, Point Size, Color, and Character Attributes

To change the font, point size, color, or character attributes (bold, italic, and so on) for a style:

1. In the Modify Style dialog box, choose the Font option in the Modify box. Amí Professional displays the options shown in Figure 9–9.
2. Choose options until the sample text in the lower right corner of the dialog box looks the way you want:

Option	What to Do
Face	Select a new font name. Amí Professional displays only those fonts that are installed for the

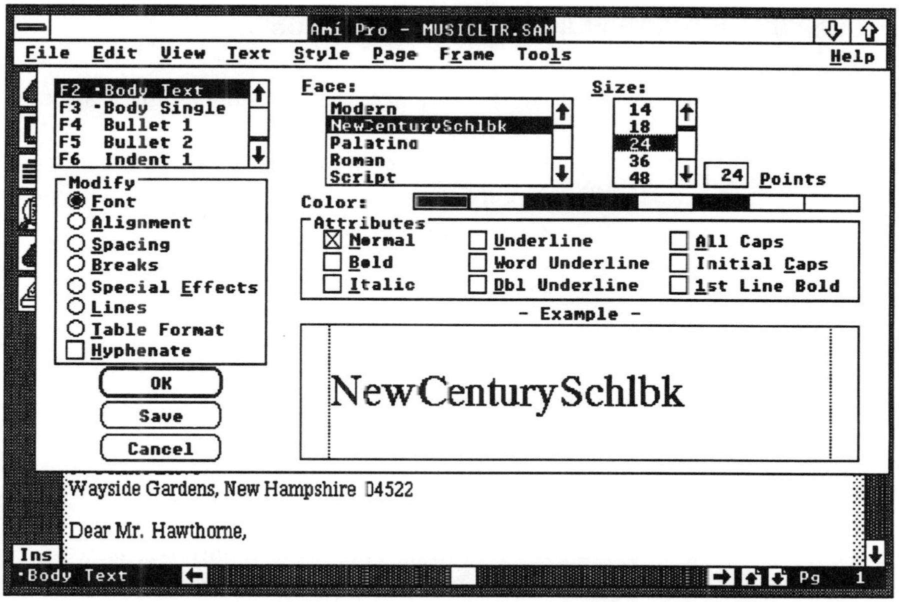

Figure 9–9
Changing the font and point size in the Modify Style dialog box.

current printer. (You may be able to install new ones with the Windows Control Panel.)

Size — Select a new point size from the list or type a new size in the Points box. Point sizes in the list are the point sizes available for that font.

Color — Click on the color you want in the color bar.

Attributes — Choose options to turn them on or off (an X in the check box next to an option indicates that it is "on"). If an attribute is dimmed, you can't use that attribute with the selected font.

Helpful Hint

If you're doing a presentation by displaying Amí Professional text on a screen, you can make your audience focus on important areas of text by creating styles with different text colors, then changing styles with keystrokes to make the colors change. For example, you could create a style with white text and apply it to paragraphs you don't want the audience to see (white text on a white background would be invisible), or you could create a red style and apply it to the point you want your audience to focus on.

Changing Paragraph Alignments or Indents

To change the alignment or indents for a style:

1. In the Modify Style dialog box, choose the Alignment option in the Modify box. Amí Professional displays the alignment and indent options shown in Figure 9–10.

2. Choose options until the sample text in the lower right corner of the dialog box looks the way you want:

Option	What to Do
Alignment	Choose Left, Center, Right, or Justified alignment.
Indention: All	Use only if you want to indent all lines in the paragraph by an equal amount. Type or select a measurement in the running list box. To make the indent apply to both right and left sides of the paragraph, turn on the Both Sides option. To cancel the indent, choose No Indent.

Figure 9–10
Setting the first-line indent for a justified paragraph in the Modify Style dialog box.

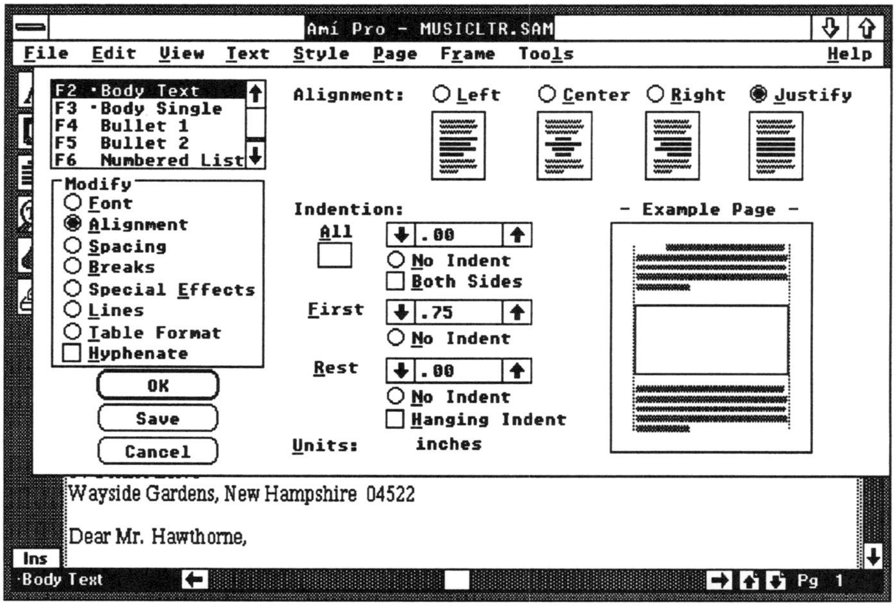

Indention: First	Use only if you want the first line of the paragraph to have a different indent from the rest of the lines. Type or select a measurement in the running list box. To cancel, choose No Indent.
Indention: Rest	Use only to set indent for second and following lines in the paragraph when you set a different first line measurement. Type or select a measurement in the running list box. To cancel, choose No Indent. To create a hanging indent with a first-line tab setting that matches the Rest indent, make sure the measurement in the First Indent box is smaller than the measurement in the Rest box, then turn on the Hanging Indent option.

Figure 9–10 illustrates the selection of a .75 indent for the first line in a justified paragraph. Figure 9–11 illustrates setting a hanging indent in a left-aligned paragraph.

Figure 9–11
Setting a hanging indent in the Modify Style dialog box.

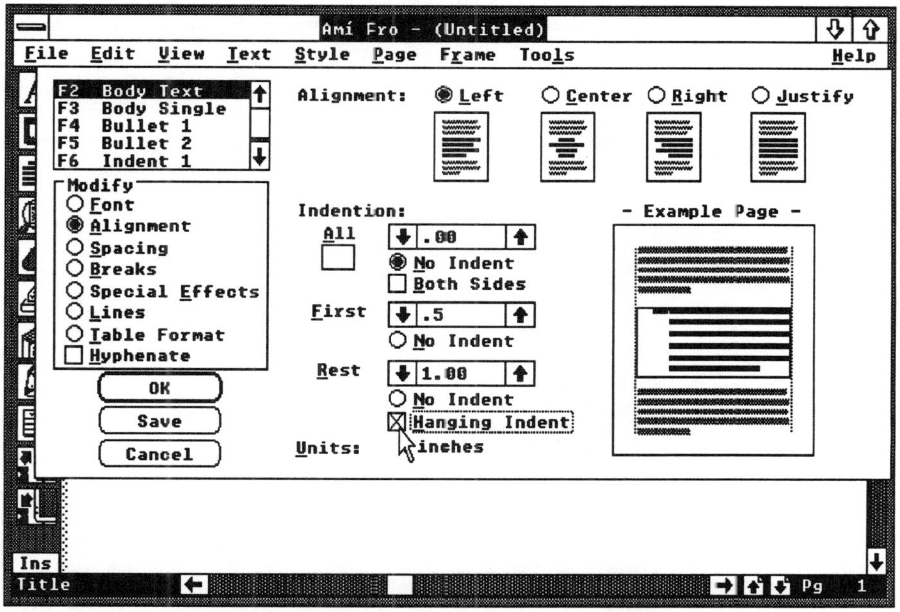

Helpful Hint

If you want to change the indent for only one paragraph in your document (a quotation, for example), you'll probably want to create a new style just for that paragraph.

Changing Spacing of Lines and Characters

To change spacing between lines within paragraphs, the spacing between paragraphs, and the spacing between words on a line:

1. In the Modify Style dialog box, choose the Spacing option in the Modify box.

   Amí Professional displays the spacing options shown in Figure 9–12.

2. Choose options until the sample text in the lower right corner of the dialog box looks the way you want:

Option	What to Do
Line Spacing	Choose Single, 1 1/2, Double, or Custom and type or select a measurement in the running list box.

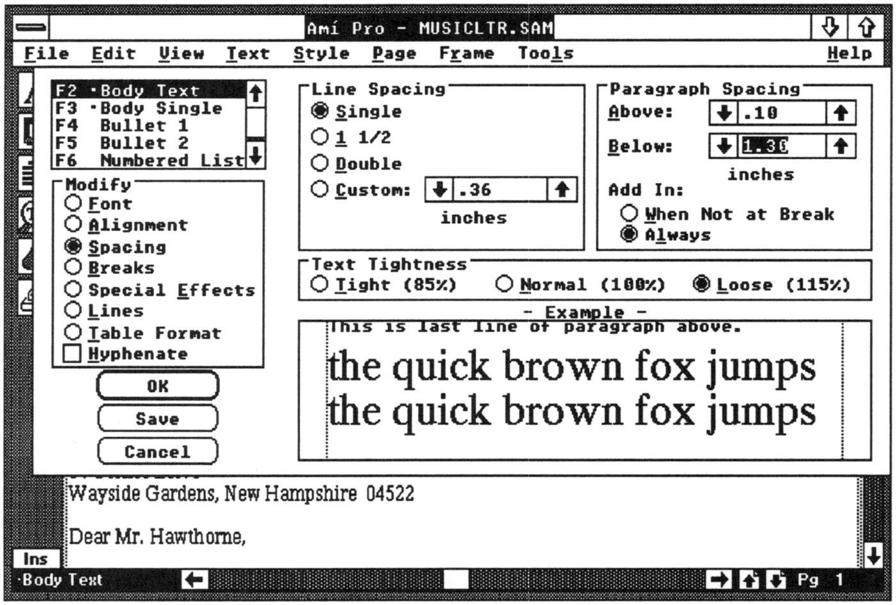

Figure 9–12 Changing the spacing after a paragraph and expanding the space between characters in the Modify Style dialog box.

Paragraph Spacing	Type or select measurements in the Above and Below running list boxes to specify space above and below the paragraph. Below the list boxes, choose When Not at Break to add the space only when a page break does not occur next to the paragraph or choose Always to add the space no matter where a page break occurs.
Line Tightness	Choose Tight to reduce spacing between words to 85% of normal, squeezing more characters on a line; choose Normal for normal spacing; or choose Loose to expand space between words by 15%, putting fewer characters on a line.

The space after a paragraph will be added to the space before the next paragraph. For example, if you add .25 inch of space after one style and the following paragraph style has .25 inch of space before it, the space between the two paragraphs will be .5 inch.

Changing Page Break Control

Sometimes you have a paragraph that absolutely must be kept all on one page or a paragraph that must be kept with the next paragraph in order to make sense. You can control page breaks in paragraphs by changing a style in the Modify Style dialog box.

1. In the Modify Style dialog box, choose the Breaks option in the Modify box at the left. Amí Professional displays the page break options as shown in Figure 9–13.

2. Turn on the options you want:

Option	Description
Page Breaks: Before Paragraph	Forces a page break to occur before the paragraph (useful for chapter title styles and so on)
Page Breaks: After Paragraph	Forces a page break to occur after the paragraph

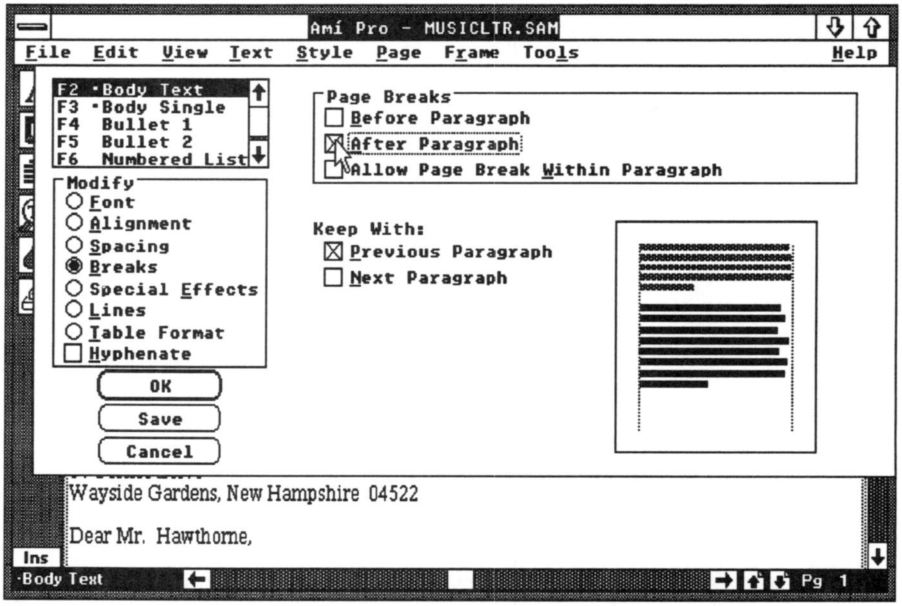

Figure 9–13 Controlling page breaks in a style in the Modify Style dialog box.

Page Breaks: Allow Page Break Within Paragraph	If turned on, allows page breaks to occur within the paragraph. If turned off, keeps all the lines in the paragraph on the same page (if a page break would naturally occur within the paragraph, Amí Professional forces the page to break before the paragraph)
Keep With: Previous Paragraph	Keeps the paragraph on the same page with the previous paragraph (if a page break would naturally occur within either paragraph or between the paragraphs, Amí Professional forces the page to break before the first paragraph)
Keep With: Next Paragraph	Keeps the paragraph on the same page with the following paragraph (if a page break would naturally occur within the first paragraph or between the paragraphs, Amí Professional forces the page to break before the first paragraph)

When you choose an option, the sample text in the lower right corner of the dialog box changes to show how page breaks will occur in paragraphs.

For more information about controlling pagination, see Chapter 16.

Changing Bullets, Numbers, and Special Effects Before List or Outline Text

To format styles that control the look of text in bulleted lists, in numbered steps, or in outlines, you can use the Special Effects option of the Modify Style dialog box. When you choose Special Effects, Amí Professional displays the options shown on the right side of Figure 9–14.

Adding or Changing Bullets

To add or change bullets for the selected style:

1. In the Modify Style dialog box, choose the Special Effects option in the Modify box at the left.
2. Choose the Insert Bullet button.
3. Choose a bullet type from the list, as shown in Figure 9–15, then click OK or press **Enter** to close the Bullets box. Amí Professional puts a somewhat confusing number code in the box at the top of the

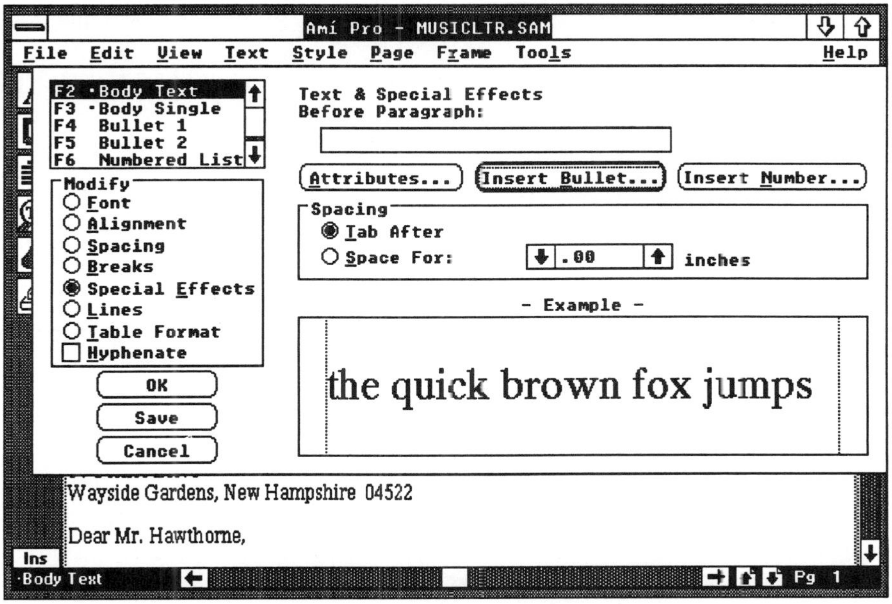

Figure 9–14 Special Effects options in the Modify Style dialog box.

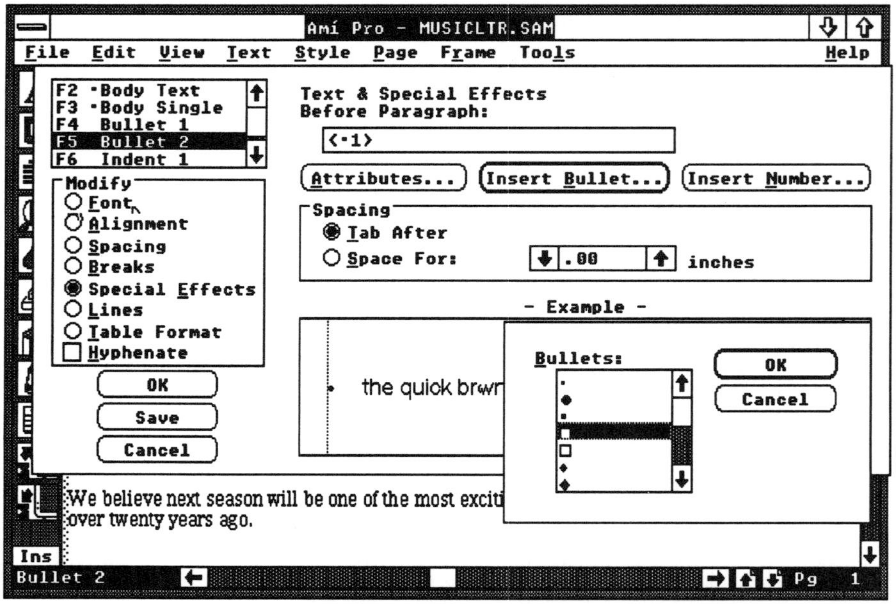

Figure 9–15
Adding bullets in the Modify Style dialog box.

dialog—ignore this and look at the sample in the lower right corner to see your bullet.

4. If you want to add blank space after the bullet character, turn on Tab After in the Spacing box to put a tab character after the bullet, or turn on Space For and type a measurement for the amount of space between the beginning of the bullet and the following text.

To delete a bullet from a style, delete the codes from the top box.

Adding or Changing Numbers

To add or change numbers for the selected style:

1. In the Modify Style dialog box, choose the Special Effects option in the Modify box at the left.
2. Choose the Insert Number button to display the dialog box shown in Figure 9–16.
3. Choose a number type from the Number Styles box.
4. If you want Amí Professional to recognize the selected style as part of an outline, choose the level you want in the Numbering Options box. For example, to set levels for traditional outline styles (I, A, 1, a, and so on), you'd select I in the Number Style box and Outline

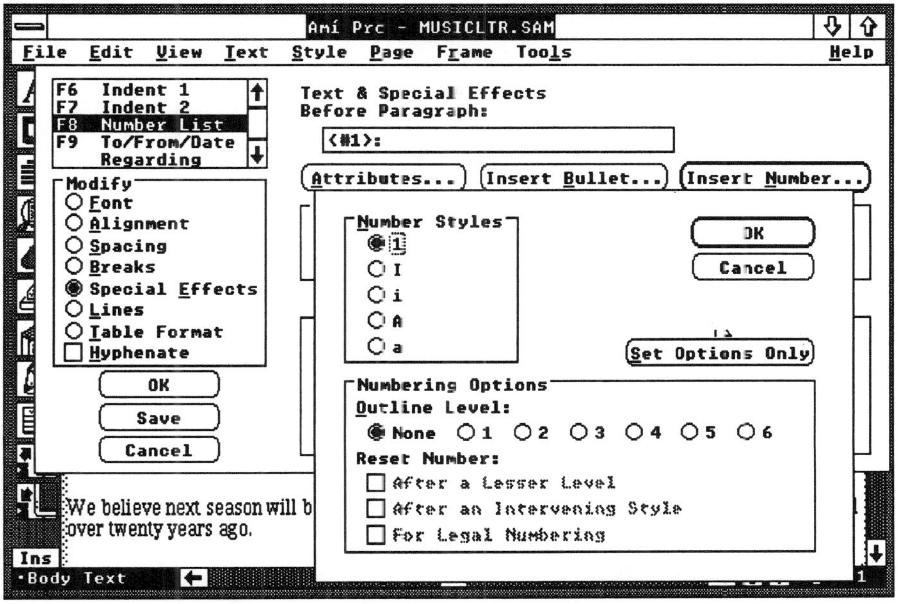

Figure 9–16 Adding numbers to paragraphs in the Modify Style dialog box.

Level 1 in the Numbering Options box for the first-level style; select A and Outline Level 2 for the second-level style; select 1 and Outline Level 3 for the third-level style; select a and Outline Level 4 for the fourth-level style; and so on. It's not as complex as it sounds—see Chapter 18 for more examples.

5. Click OK or press **Enter** to close the Numbers box.

6. If you want punctuation (such as a period) to appear after your number, add that punctuation after the number code in the top box (for example, <#1>.).

7. If you want to add blank space after the number character, turn on Tab After in the Spacing box to put a tab character after the number, or turn on Space For and type a measurement for the amount of space between the beginning of the number and the following text.

To delete a number from a style, delete the codes from the top box.

You can learn more about numbering paragraphs and numbering lines in Chapter 18.

Adding or Changing Special Text

If you don't want to use a bullet from the Bullets list or a number or outline format, you can also specify your own text or special character to insert before text in the selected style. For example, you might choose to put **Note:** before the following text.

To specify your own text or special characters for the selected style:

1. In the Modify Style dialog box, choose the Special Effects option in the Modify box at the left.

2. In the Before Paragraph box, type the text or special character you want to precede the normal text of the paragraph. For example, you might type **Note:**.

3. To format the text you type in some special way, choose the Attributes button to display the dialog box shown in Figure 9–17.

4. Turn on options in the Special Effects Attributes box to format the special text the way you want, then click OK or press **Enter** to close the box.

5. If you want to add blank space after the text you've specified, turn on Tab After in the Spacing box to put a tab character after the text or turn on Space For and type a measurement for the amount of space between the beginning of the special text and the following paragraph text.

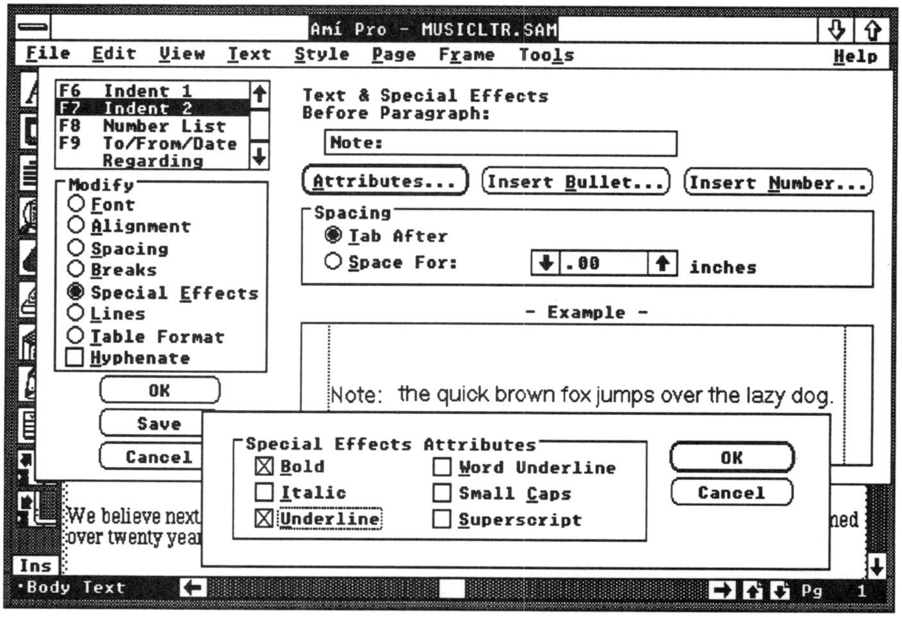

Figure 9–17 Adding specially formatted characters before paragraphs in the Modify Style dialog box.

Changing Lines Above and Below Paragraphs

You can draw lines of different lengths, line thicknesses, and colors above and below a paragraph.

1. In the Modify Style dialog box, choose the Lines option in the Modify box at the left. Amí Professional displays the line formatting options shown in Figure 9–18.

2. Turn on the options you want:

Option	What to Do
Line Above	Turn on if you want a line above the paragraph. Then choose options for this line: choose a line thickness from the Line Style list; type or select a measurement for spacing between the text and the line in the Spacing running list box; choose a Length: Text (line will be as long as the first line of the paragraph), Margins (line extends from margin to margin), or choose Other, then type or select a measurement in the running list box; click on a color in the color bar.

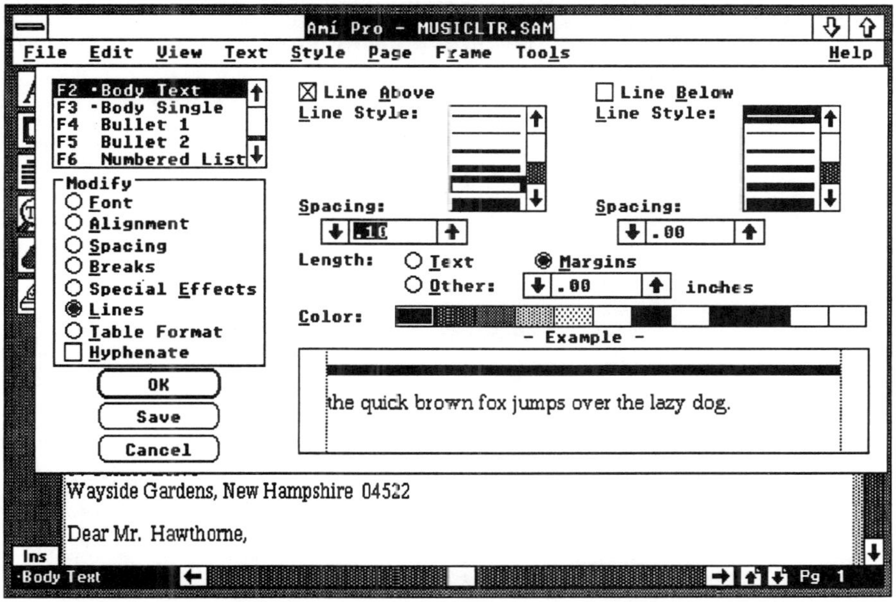

Figure 9–18 Adding a thick line that extends from margin to margin .10 inch above the paragraph in the Modify Style box.

Line Below	Turn on if you want a line below the paragraph. Then choose options for this line: choose a line thickness from the Line Style list; type or select a measurement for spacing between the text and the line in the Spacing running list box; choose a Length: Text (line will be as long as the last line of the paragraph), Margins (line extends from margin to margin), or choose Other, then type or select a measurement in the running list box; click on a color in the color bar.

Figure 9–18 illustrates adding a line .10 inch above the paragraph.

Changing Table Format

The text in a table cell can use the same style as other paragraphs in your document or can have a unique style all its own. Use the following procedures to modify only those styles that you'll use in table cells. For more information about setting up tables, see Chapter 14.

To change a selected table style:

1. In the Modify Style dialog box, choose the Table Format option in the Modify box. Amí Professional displays the table format options shown in Figure 9–19.

2. Change options until the sample number in the box at the lower right corner of the dialog box looks the way you want:

Option	**What to Do**
Cell Format	Choose General to work with text; Fixed Decimal to work with numbers having a fixed number of decimal places; Currency to work with numbers preceded with currency symbols; or Percent to work with percentages.
Numeric Format	If desired, change the number of decimal places you want to display in the No. Decimal Places box or type a new symbol in the Decimal Symbol box. If you want to use a separator between thousands and hundreds, turn on the Thousands Separator option and type the separator character you want in the following box.

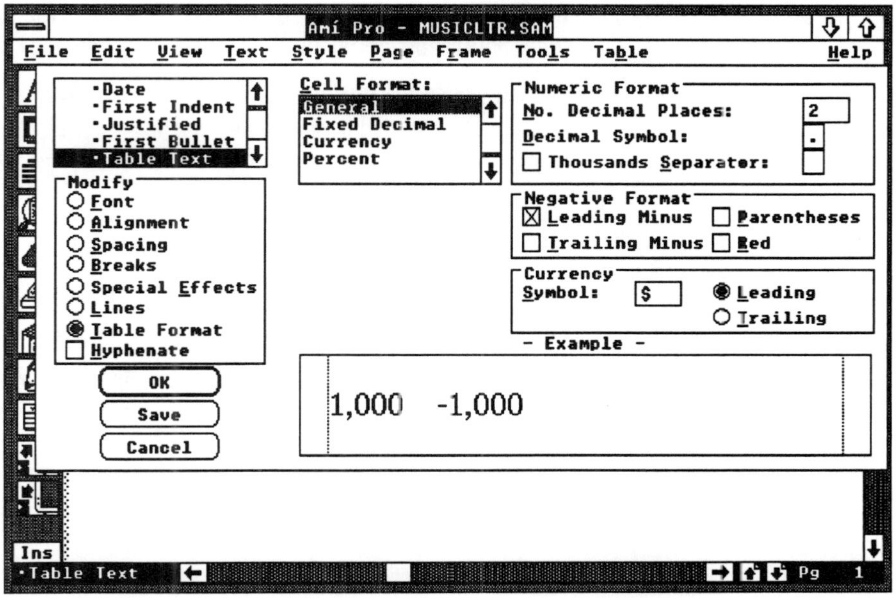

Figure 9–19 Changing a table style in the Modify Style dialog box to show numbers with no thousands separator and two decimal places.

Negative Format	Choose the format in which you want to display negative numbers: Leading Minus, −2; Parentheses, (2); Trailing Minus, 2−; or Red (color on screen).
Currency Symbol	If desired, type a new currency character in the Symbol box, then choose Leading to make the character precede the number ($25) or choose Trailing to make the character follow the number (25FF).

EXAMPLE: Creating a Style Sheet

Say you want to create a special style sheet just for your book on poetry. You've looked at all the styles in the provided style sheets and decided you could start with ~DEFAULT.STY and alter the Indent 2 style (to format poems) and the Bold & Center style (for chapter titles) to meet your needs. Here's how you might go about it:

1. Choose File New, select ~DEFAULT.STY from the list, and click OK.
2. Choose Create Style from the Style menu, type **Poem** in the text box, select Indent 2 to base your new style on, then click the Modify button to open the Modify Style dialog box.
3. Change the style to have an italic font, a 1.75-inch indent on both sides, and

1 1/2 spacing, then click OK to save the new style. You've created the Poem style, and it appears at the bottom of the styles box list.

4. Choose Create Style from the Style menu, type **Title** in the text box, select Bold & Center to base your new style on, then click the Modify button to open the Modify Style dialog box.
5. Change the style to have a line above and below it at .15 inch, then click OK to save the new style. Now you've created a new Title style.
6. Choose the Save As A New Style Sheet command from the Style menu, type **POETRY.STY** in the text box, then click OK to save your new style sheet.

It's easy to create your own style sheets like this. You can also modify Amí Professional's existing style sheets, then save them by typing the same name in the Save As A New Style Sheet dialog box. And you can put boilerplate text such as logos and headings in a style sheet, then save it with the With Contents option in the dialog box. You can use your customized style sheets over and over again.

Changing Hyphenation Options

If your paragraphs are left-aligned or right-aligned and you think one margin looks too "ragged," you can change paragraph styles in two ways to help smooth out the margin. You can

- justify the paragraph
- hyphenate words to help fill the lines

To justify paragraphs (make the left and right sides even), Amí Professional adds enough spaces between words to fill up the lines. This can put big gaps in your text and make your pages look as though they're filled with "holes." You can fill these "holes" by using a combination of justified paragraphs and hyphenated words.

You may also choose to keep left or right alignment, but use hyphenation to make the other margin less ragged. See how adding even one hyphen makes the right side of a paragraph more even in the following example:

She could hear the intruder coming up the winding
staircase, creeping as silently as possible. From
her cramped position behind the heavy mahogany
door, Angelina could see his shadow, barely
visible in the gloom, approaching her bedroom. He
clutched a revolver in his hand.

She could hear the intruder coming up the winding staircase, creeping as silently as possible. From her cramped position behind the heavy mahogany door, Angelina could see his shadow, barely visible in the gloom, approaching her bedroom. He clutched a revolver in his hand.

For more information on changing the alignment in styles, see Changing Paragraph Alignments or Indents earlier in this chapter.

You can always press the hyphen key to add a hyphen to a word, but if you later add text or change margins or indents, the hyphen remains in the word even though the word may no longer be at the end of a line. A safer way to hyphenate is to let the program put hyphens in paragraphs throughout your document. Amí Professional inserts "optional hyphens" that are removed if the word is later relocated. This also saves you the trouble of using a dictionary to determine where to break a word.

You can see hyphens only in layout mode. When you turn on hyphenation, the rules Amí Professional follows are

- hyphenating words near the ends of lines (within the *hot zone* specified with the Edit Defaults command), but not hyphenating more than two consecutive lines (this prevents "stacking" of hyphens on pages)
- preventing hyphenation of words that contain numerals or words separated by a required space

Hyphenation is a style option, so you can change styles to make them automatically hyphenate words in specific paragraphs, or you can select all the paragraphs in your document at once and then use the Modify Style command to turn on hyphenation. To have Amí Professional hyphenate all appropriate words automatically:

1. Select the paragraphs you want to hyphenate in your document or select the style you want to add hyphenation to in the styles box.
2. Choose the Style Modify Style command.
3. Turn on the Hyphenate option in the Modify box.
4. Click OK or press **Enter**.

When hyphenation is in effect, Amí Professional inserts hyphens in appropriate words within the *hot zone,* which is a certain number of characters from the right margin. By default, the hot zone is five characters from the margin, but you can change the hot zone measurement for all styles in this way:

1. Choose the Edit Defaults command.
2. Choose the Options button.
3. Type a new number in the Hyphenation Hot-Zone box.
4. Click OK or press **Enter**.

Hyphenation remains on until you turn it off. If you want to insert an optional hyphen into a word that Amí Professional didn't hyphenate, press **Ctrl**+- (hyphen).

SAVING A STYLE SHEET

If you change styles or create new styles, Amí Professional saves those styles with your document, not with the style sheet. To reuse those styles in other documents, save the modified style sheet. If you want to save both the previous style sheet and the modified style sheet, give the modified style sheet a new name to leave the original style sheet file unchanged.

To save a style sheet:

1. Choose the Save As A New Style Sheet command from the Style menu.
2. Do one of the following:
   - To save your changes as a completely new style sheet, type a new name for your style sheet.

   or

   - To save your changes in an existing style sheet (changing the style sheet), type the name of the open style sheet file.
3. If you want to save the text, frames, or graphics in your document along with all the styles, turn on the With Contents option.
4. Click OK or press **Enter**. If you typed the name of an existing style sheet to save the changes in that style sheet, Amí Professional asks whether you want to overwrite the style sheet. Click Yes or press **Y** to overwrite the old style sheet file with your changes or press **N** if you've typed the name of an existing file by accident.

Figure 9–20 illustrates saving a style sheet.

Amí Professional always saves style sheet files in the directory specified in the Edit Defaults dialog box, unless you type a different path name in front of the file name when you save the file. The directory is normally

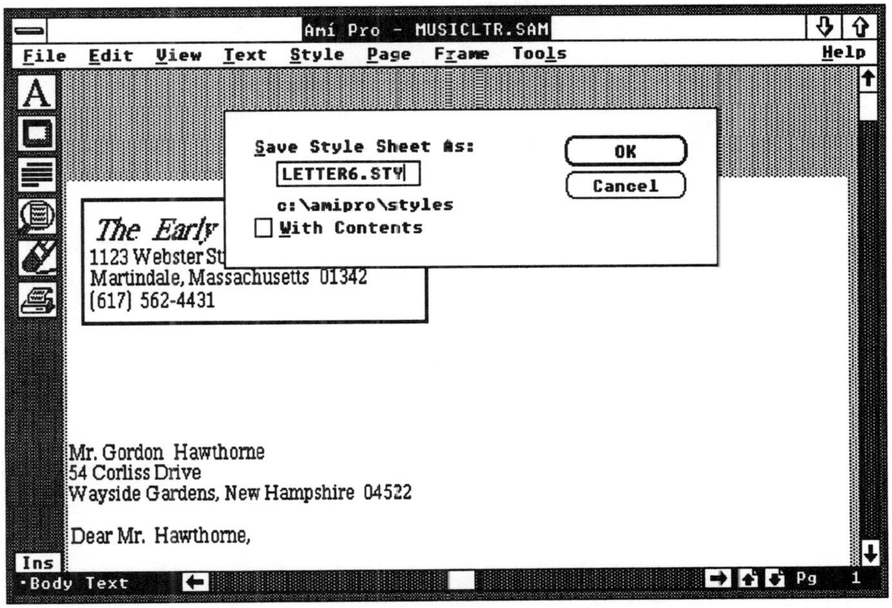

Figure 9–20 Saving a new style sheet with the Save As A New Style Sheet command.

the one you copied style sheet files to when you first installed Amí Professional. If you want to change the default directory, use the Paths button in the Edit Defaults dialog box to change the path.

MOVING STYLES BETWEEN DOCUMENTS AND STYLE SHEETS

Unless you save the style sheet as described in the previous section, modified styles and new styles are saved with your document, which means they can only be used when that document is open. If you want to use those styles in other documents, you can move those styles to the style sheet. Then all documents based on that style sheet can use the style.

If you want to base your document on one style sheet but also use a few styles from another, you can move the few styles from a style sheet into your document, then open a different style sheet to make the rest of the styles available.

You can use the Style Management command to move styles from a document to a style sheet, or from a style sheet to a document file. If the styles box says NONE.STY (which happens if you choose the Keep Format with Document option while you save), you'll have to save the style sheet with another name before you can move any styles to it. (See the instructions earlier for saving a style sheet.) When you move a style to or from an existing style sheet, the modified style sheet is automatically saved.

To move styles:

1. Load the document and the style sheet you want to use.
2. Choose the Style Management command from the Style menu. Amí Professional displays the dialog box shown in Figure 9–21.
3. Choose either of the following:
   - To move a style from the style sheet to the document, select the style from the Style Sheet list, then choose the Move button with "arrows" pointing toward the Document list (<<). You might want to do this so that you can keep both the styles and the text in one file.

   or

   - To move a style from the document to the style sheet, select the style from the Document list, then choose the Move button with "arrows" pointing toward the Style Sheet list (>>). You might want to do this so that you can use the style in other documents.
4. Click OK or press **Enter** to save the new assignments.

Helpful Hint

If you want to move a style from one style sheet to another, you can use the Style Management command to move the style from the first style sheet

Figure 9–21
Using the Style Management dialog box.

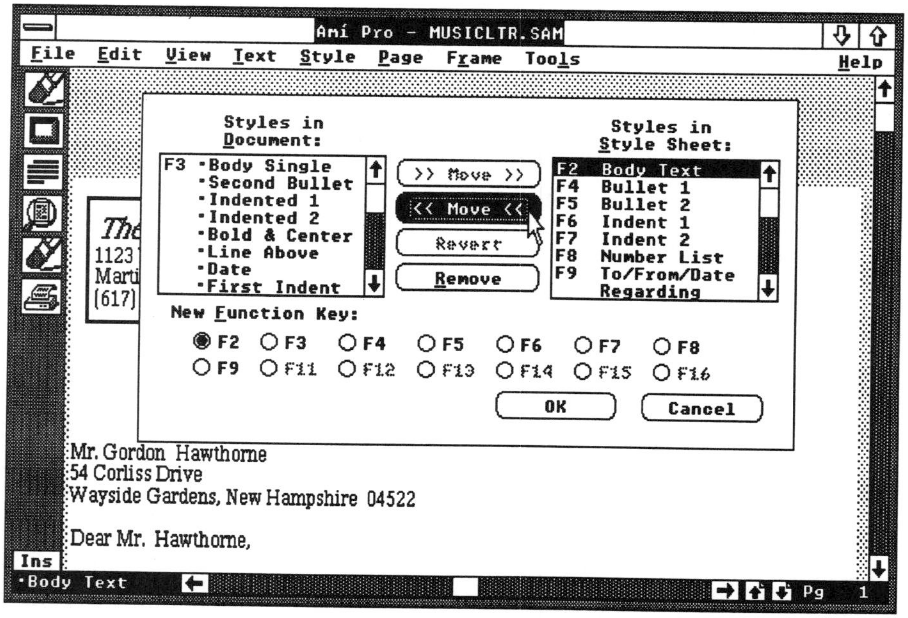

to a document. Use the Use Another Style Sheet command to open the second style sheet, then use the Style Management command to move the style from the document to the second style sheet.

DELETING STYLES

If you've added a style to a style sheet by accident or you no longer use an old style, you can delete it this way:

1. Open the document or load the style sheet containing the style you want to delete. You can open a document at the same time—deleting a style won't change the document unless paragraphs in the document have the style attached.
2. Choose the Style Management command from the Style menu.
3. Select the style name you want to delete from the list.
4. Choose the Remove button.
5. Click OK or press **Enter** to save the modified style sheet.

If you delete a style used by paragraphs in your document, those paragraphs will assume the Body Text style.

When you delete a style from an existing style sheet, the modified style sheet is automatically saved.

ASSIGNING NEW FUNCTION KEYS TO STYLES

Amí Professional automatically assigns a function key to a new style, provided that a key is available. However, you can change the key assignments this way:

1. Load the document or style sheet containing the style.
2. Choose the Style Management command from the Style menu.
3. Select the style name from the list.
4. Choose a new function key below. If you select a key used by another style, the program will swap function key assignments.
5. Click OK or press **Enter** to save the new key assignments. You'll see the key name appear beside the style name in the styles box.

Helpful Hint

You'll be able to switch from style sheet to style sheet more easily if you always assign the same function key to similar styles. For example, you might always use F2 for a Body Text style, the style you'll use for most of the paragraphs in your document.

10

Adding Formatting in Addition to Styles

There will be times when you want to change only one or two aspects of a paragraph, but you won't want to change the style throughout your document. For example, you might want to change the font or formatting for only one word within a paragraph. Changing the font in the style would not only change the entire paragraph but would also change other paragraphs that use the same style. To add formatting without using styles, you use commands from the Text menu or shortcut key combinations.

Commands on the Text menu take precedence over the formatting controlled by the style. In other words, if the style specifies roman (not italic) text, but you select Italic from the Text menu, the text will become italic even though it uses a roman style.

This chapter discusses the formatting that you can add to text on top of styles. The chapter includes

- information about fonts and point sizes
- adding a variety of attributes to format characters
- changing alignment and line spacing within paragraphs

Amí Professional uses the term *text attributes,* which includes character formatting. This section focuses primarily on how to format individual characters.

APPLYING CHARACTER FORMATS

Figure 10–1 shows all the formats you can add to characters with the Text menu commands. (We say "to characters" because you can use these

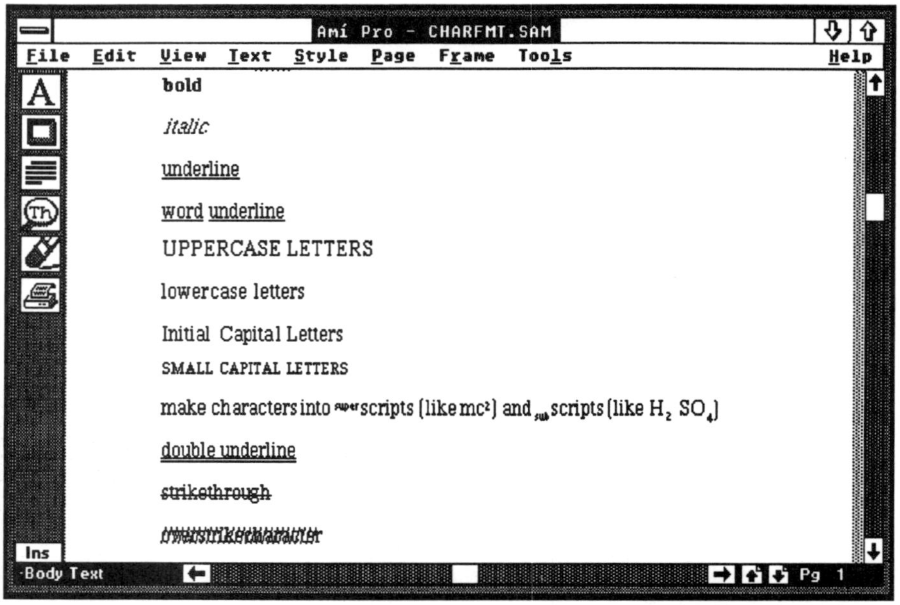

Figure 10-1 Character formatting you can add with the Text menu.

options to format one character or an entire document—the commands you choose affect only those characters that are selected at the time.) You can

- give characters the following formats: bold, italic, single (continuous) underline, word (not spaces) underline, double underline, strikethrough, small capitals, initial capitals, uppercase or lowercase.
- make characters into superscripts and subscripts.
- change fonts and sizes.

If you have a color monitor, you can also change the color of your text. This changes the color of the text only on your screen—the file won't print out in color unless your printer can produce multiple colors.

All of the commands on the Text menu (shown in Figure 10-2) except Alignment and Spacing format characters.

As you can see from Figure 10-2, a few of the commands—those with ellipses—display dialog boxes with more options you can choose. The other commands on the Text menu are *toggles*: You choose them (toggle them on) to assign the format to selected text, and you choose them again (toggle them off) to remove the format. When a toggle command is in effect for selected text, a check mark appears next to the command on the menu. (Dialog box options with check boxes next to them are also toggles, as explained in Chapter 2.)

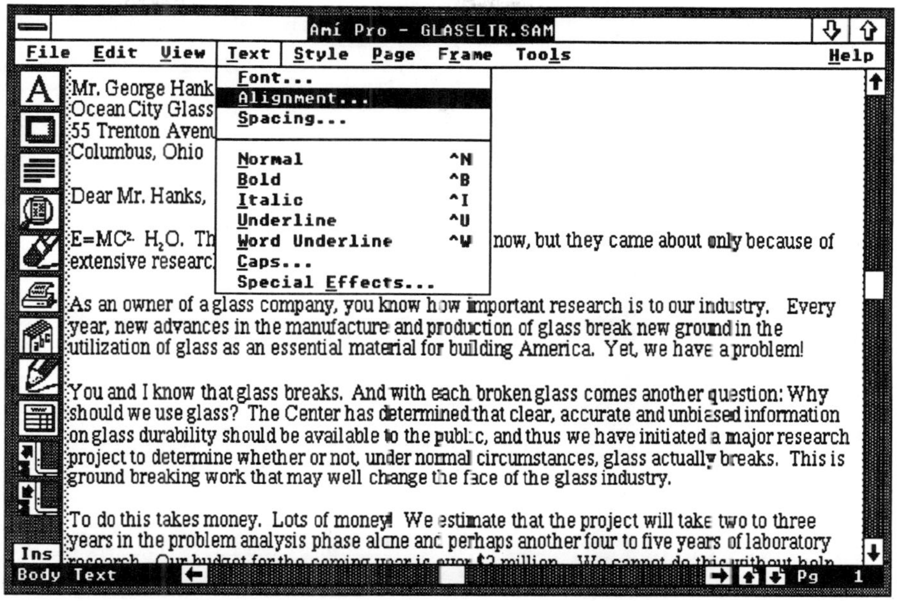

Figure 10–2 Commands on the Text menu. Those with ellipses display dialog boxes with more options; the other commands take effect immediately.

To format characters using the Text menu:

1. Select the characters you want to format.
2. Choose a command from the Text menu.

   If the command is a toggle command, it will take effect immediately. If the command displays a dialog box, choose options in the dialog box, then click OK or press **Enter**.

You can apply many different character formats to the same selected text. Figure 10–3 illustrates changing the font and point size of selected text. Figure 10–4 illustrates making a number into a superscript. Superscripts and subscripts are automatically formatted in a smaller point size but use the same font as the rest of the paragraph. If you want them to use a different font, you can use the Text Font command and choose a new font from the list.

Keyboard Shortcuts

You can use the following key combinations to quickly format selected text without choosing commands from the Text menu:

Normal (removes character formats applied to styles)	**Ctrl+N**

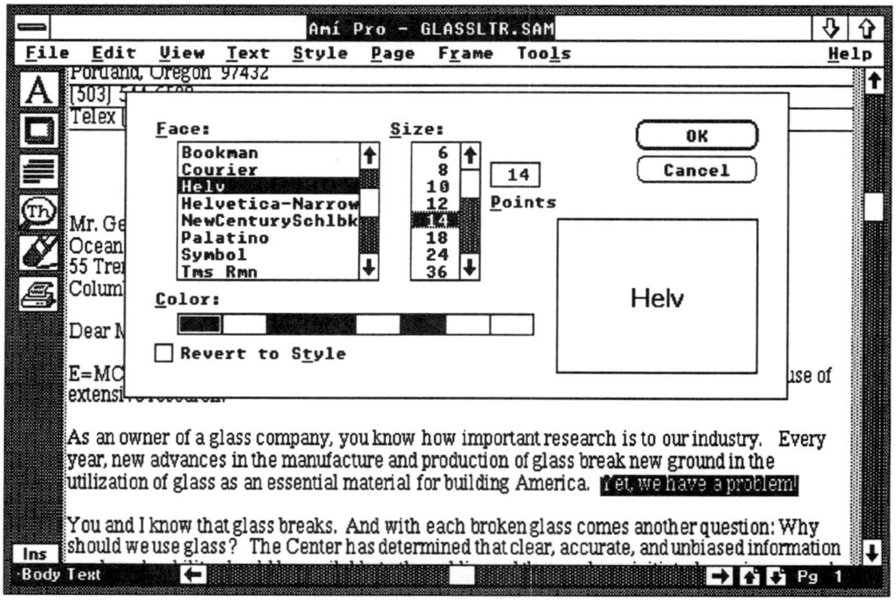

Figure 10-3 Assigning a new font and point size to selected text with the Text Font command.

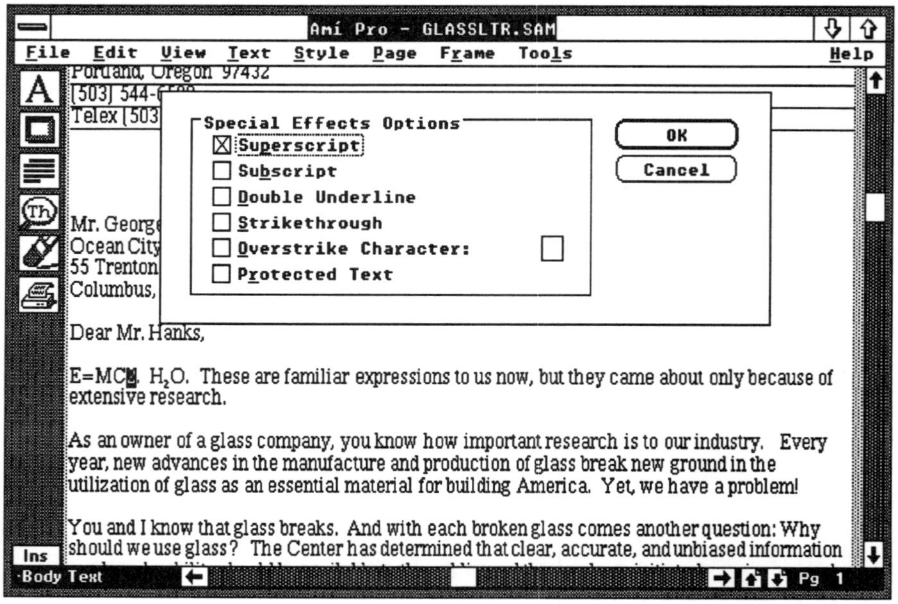

Figure 10-4 Changing a selected number into a superscript with the Text Special Effects command.

Bold	**Ctrl+B**
Italic	**Ctrl+I**
Underline	**Ctrl+U**
Word Underline	**Ctrl+W**

About Fonts and Point Sizes

Fonts are families of characters that share a style—one that's very straight and simple, for example, for a Helvetica font, or very curvy and ornate for an Old English font. Figure 10–5 shows a few samples of fonts.

Fonts come in different sizes, which are measured in points. A *point* is roughly 1/72 of an inch. Because the sizes available for one font often are different from another's, you should always select a font in the Text Font dialog box before you select the point size for that font. You can also type a new point size in the Points box.

Note: When you choose a small point size, the selected text may be replaced by shading. Don't panic! Your text isn't gone—it's just too small for Amí Professional to display on the screen. If you switch to enlarged view, you can see the characters in proportion to one another. Even if you see only shading on the screen, the printed document will look fine.

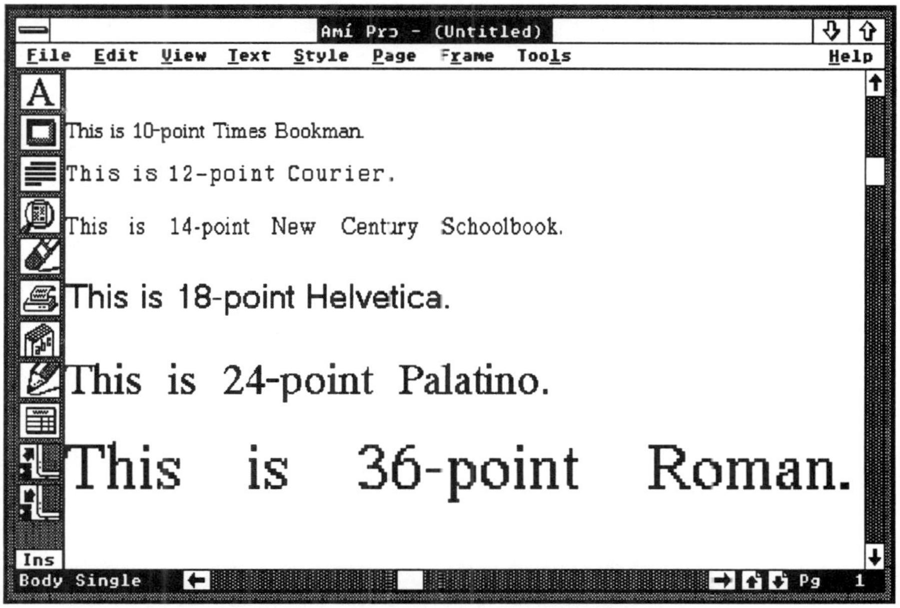

Figure 10–5
With Amí Professional you can select from a variety of fonts and point sizes. *(Point sizes reduced here.)*

EXAMPLE: Formatting Characters

Important Sale

17th century French *armoire.* Antique furniture and other collectibles.

Call 689-6207.

To format text like this:

1. Select *Important Sale.*
2. Choose the Text Font command and select the Helvetica® font from the Font list. (If this font isn't available on your printer, choose another font.)
3. Select 14 from the Points box.
4. Click OK or press **Enter**.
5. Choose Text Special Effects and turn on the Double Underline option.
6. Select *armoire.*
7. Press **Ctrl**+**I** to make the word italic.
8. Select *Call 689-6207.*
9. Press **Ctrl**+**B** to make the text bold.

Changing the Color of Text

If you have a color monitor, you'll want to take advantage of Amí Professional's capability to format text in color. However, unless your printer can print in different colors, text will always print in black, no matter what color it is on the screen.

To change the color of text on the screen:

1. Select the text you want to assign a color to.
2. Choose the Text Font command.
3. Select a color from the color bar, as illustrated in Figure 10–6.

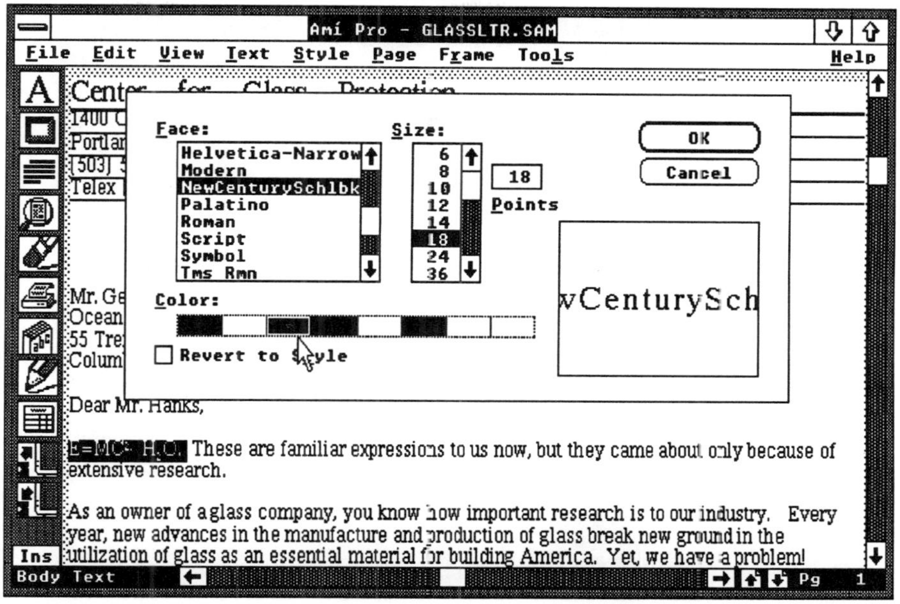

Figure 10–6
Changing the color of selected text on the screen with the Text Font command.

4. Click OK or press **Enter**.
5. Move the cursor to remove the highlight and see the color.

Helpful Hint

You can specify character formats before you type by choosing the format options with no text selected—this applies the format to the cursor, and any text typed afterward will have that format. For example, if you're a speed typist, the fastest way to format characters is to enter the formats as you type, as in

You are the **greatest**.

Here you press **Ctrl+I** (for italic), type **you**, press **Ctrl+N** (for normal text), type **are the**, press **Ctrl+B** (for bold), type **greatest**, press **Ctrl+N**, then type the period.

CHANGING THE ALIGNMENT OF PARAGRAPHS

If you want to change the alignment of a paragraph, you can use the Text Alignment command.

Figure 10–7 shows how these different paragraph alignments work. Paragraphs are aligned between indents, if any, or between margins if

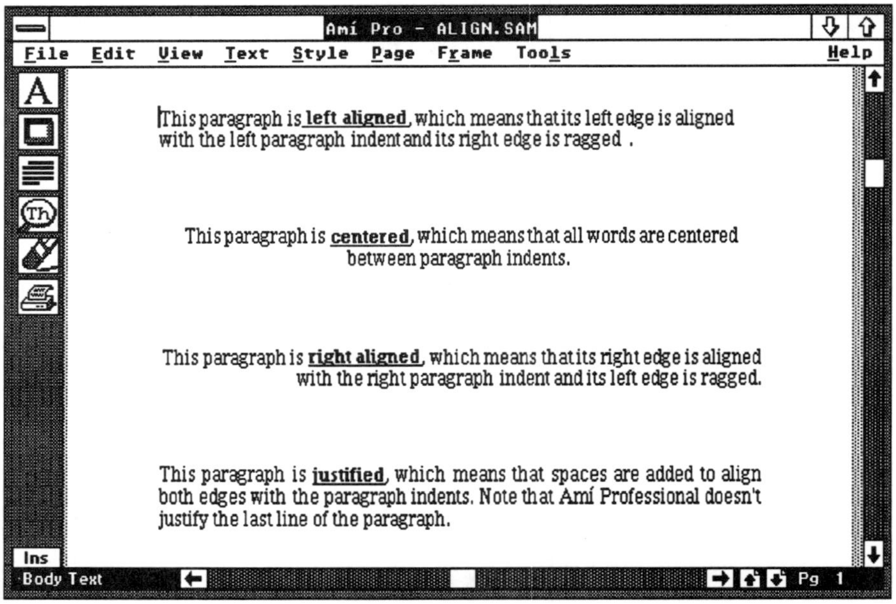

Figure 10-7 Amí Professional has four different types of paragraph alignments you can apply with the Text Alignment command.

you haven't assigned indents to the style with the Modify Style command (described in Chapter 9).

To align paragraphs with the Text Alignment command:

1. Select the paragraphs.
2. Choose the Text Alignment command.
3. Choose an option in the dialog box.
4. Click OK or press **Enter**.

Keyboard Shortcuts

You can use the following key combinations to align paragraphs without choosing commands:

Press	To
Ctrl+L	Align text with left indent.
Ctrl+C	Center text.
Ctrl+R	Align text with right indent.
Ctrl+J	Justify text.

CHANGING LINE SPACING WITHIN PARAGRAPHS

You may want to change the line spacing for part or all of your document. You can use the Text Spacing command to specify the exact spacing you want between lines in a paragraph (as shown in Figure 10–8), or choose between single, double, and 1 1/2 line spacing. This is especially useful when you want to change line spacing temporarily (for example, to print out a double-spaced copy for editing).

To change line spacing in paragraphs with the Text Spacing command:

1. Select the paragraphs.
2. Choose the Text Spacing command.
3. Do one of the following:
   - ☐ Choose among the Single, Double, or 1 1/2 Spacing options.

   or

   - ☐ To specify your own measurement, choose the Custom option, then select a measurement from the running list box or type a measurement in the text box.
4. Click OK or press **Enter**.

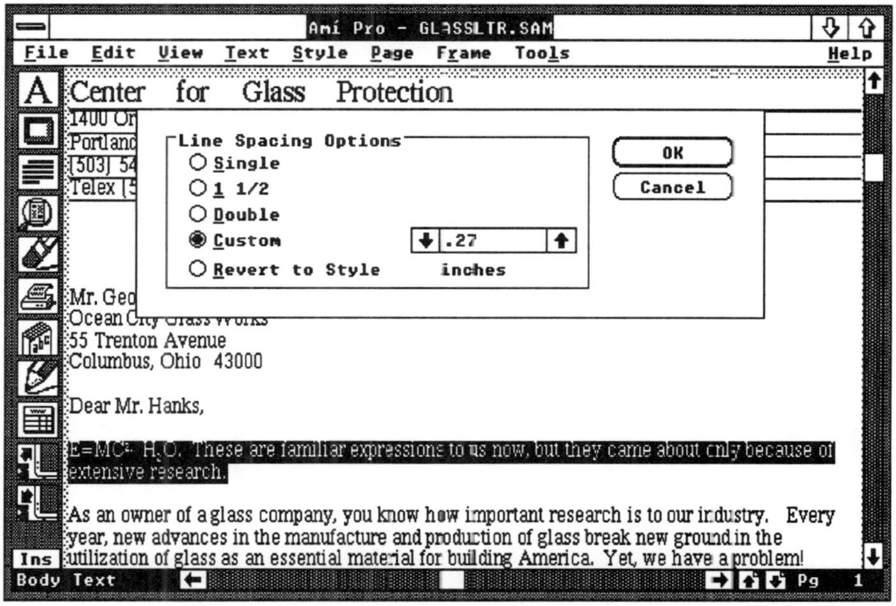

Figure 10–8 You can type a precise line spacing measurement in the Text Spacing dialog box.

REMOVING FORMATTING APPLIED ON TOP OF STYLES

The formatting you apply on top of styles overrides the style, so you can't just apply the style again to get back the original format. If you've applied a number of formats from the Text menu or with key combinations and you want to get your text back to the original style, here's how:

1. Select the text you want to remove additional formats from.
2. Press **Ctrl+N** to remove all added formats or do any of the following to remove selected fonts:
   - If you've applied character formats such as bold, italic, underline, superscripts or subscripts, and so on (all those options at the bottom of the Text menu), choose the same options again to remove them.
   - If you've changed the spacing, choose the Text Line Spacing command and turn on the Revert to Style option.
   - If you've changed the alignment, choose the Text Alignment command and select the original alignment. (If you can't remember what that was, you'll have to do this first: Choose the Modify Style command from the Style menu, select the style from the list in the upper left corner, choose the Alignment option, and note which alignment is displayed for the style.)

11

Changing the Page Layout

This chapter deals with several options that affect the entire page's look: paper size, width of margins, number of text columns, lines around the outside of the page, and so forth. These options are part of a *page layout* in Amí Professional, which is part of the style sheet you're using for your document. The page layout settings in a style sheet control

- top, bottom, left, and right margins
- whether margins are mirrored on facing pages
- number of columns of text and space between them
- tab settings
- page size and orientation
- border lines around pages and lines between columns
- tabs and margin settings for headers and footers

You can read about tab types and settings in Chapter 14; check Chapter 15 for details about headers and footers. The rest of the page layout settings are covered in this chapter.

Your document can include several different page layouts. For example, you might want one page to use a single column of text and subsequent pages to have two columns of text, or you might want to use lines to border the pages only in one section. To achieve these formats, you insert new page layouts wherever you want the format to change, then change the options to whatever you want. Later, this chapter gives more information about using a variety of page layouts in one document.

CHANGING PAGE SIZE

Normally you use the same page size throughout a document. Most style sheets are set up for the standard 8½ × 11-inch pages, printed in portrait (vertical) orientation. If you're using a different size of paper, you need to let the program know so it can display and print pages correctly.

To tell Amí Professional to use a different page size or orientation:

1. Choose the Page Modify Layout command.
2. Choose the Page Settings option in the Modify box. Amí Professional displays the dialog box shown in Figure 11–1.
3. Type new measurements in the Custom boxes (the left box is width, the right is length) and choose a new orientation if necessary.
4. Click OK or press **Enter**.

The Page Modify Layout command controls the way pages are displayed on the screen. The File Printer Setup command tells Amí Professional the size of the printed pages.

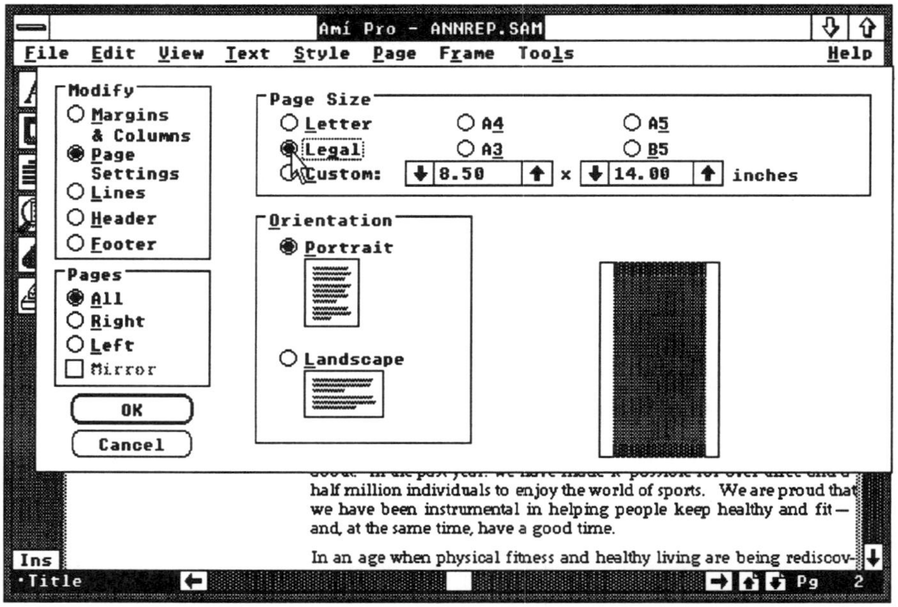

Figure 11–1 Choosing a new page size in the Page Modify Layout dialog box.

Helpful Hint

If you want to format your documents for a small page size but print them on a bigger page, you can set the Page Modify Layout dialog box to the dimensions of the smaller page. Then print on the larger page using the Print Crop Marks option in the File Print Options dialog box so you'll know where to trim your pages.

CHANGING MARGINS

Margins are the white spaces between your text and the edges of your page. Most style sheets use the following margins by default:

Top	1″
Bottom	1″
Right	1″
Left	1″

If you need to allow space for binding pages in a notebook or cover, make your inside margin larger than the outside margin, as shown in Figure 11–2. If your pages will be printed double-sided, you need to have large inside margins on the left side of right (odd-numbered) pages and

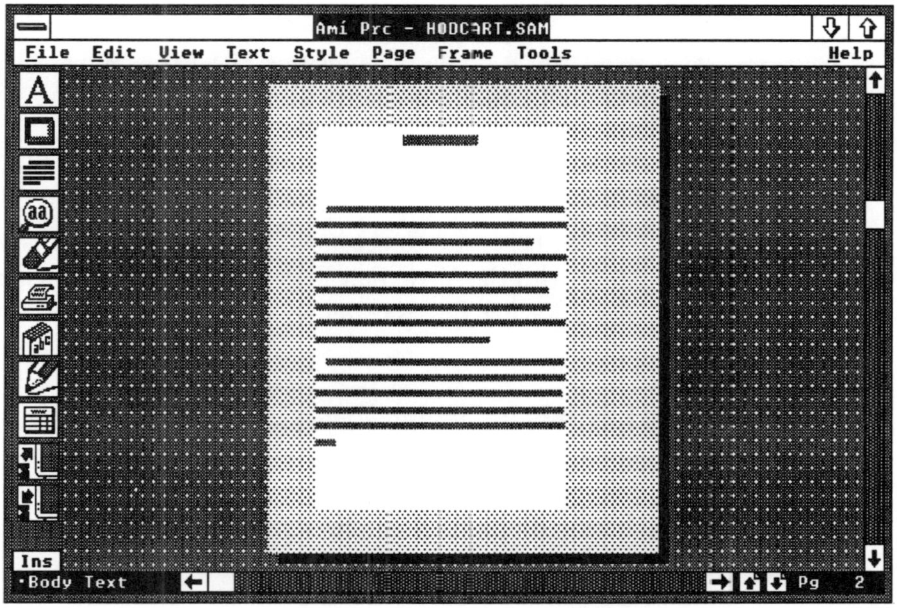

Figure 11–2 A page with a large inside margin for binding.

on the right side of left (even-numbered) pages. You can accomplish this layout by setting up the right page and telling Amí Professional to "mirror" the margins on facing pages, as described in the next discussion.

You always change margins the same way, no matter which view or mode you're using to display the text on the screen.

When you change margins, it affects every page in your document (or in that layout section, if you're using more than one page layout), even though you can only see one or two pages at a time. If you want one page to have more white space around the text than other pages, you have to indent the paragraphs on that page or put that page in a separate layout section.

To change the margins:

1. Choose the Page Modify Layout command.
2. If necessary, choose the Margins & Columns option in the Modify box.
3. In the Pages box, choose All to set the same margins for all pages, Right to set margins for right (odd-numbered) pages, or Left to set margins for left (even-numbered) pages.
4. In the Left, Right, Top, and Bottom running list boxes, type a new number or use the mouse to select a new measurement. You can also use the mouse to drag margin markers in the ruler at the top of the dialog box to change the left and right margins, as shown in Figure 11–3.

   The sample document in the lower right corner of the dialog box changes to reflect the new margins.

5. Repeat steps 3 and 4 as necessary to set more margins, then click OK or press **Enter**.

The best way to see how your margins look is to switch to full-page view with the View Full Page command or to facing-pages view with the View Facing Pages command.

Creating Mirrored Layouts on Facing Pages

If your document will be printed double-sided (on both the fronts and backs of pages), you may want to format your pages so that the margins mirror each other. This is especially useful if you want to set a large inside margin to reserve space for binding. Compare Figures 11–4 and 11–5 to

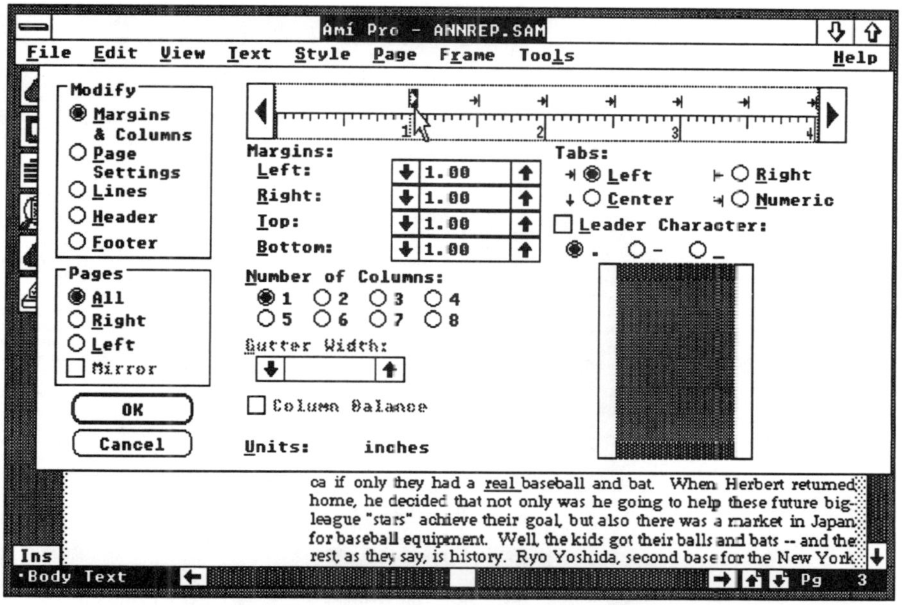

Figure 11-3
Changing the left margin by dragging the ruler margin marker in the Page Modify Layout dialog box.

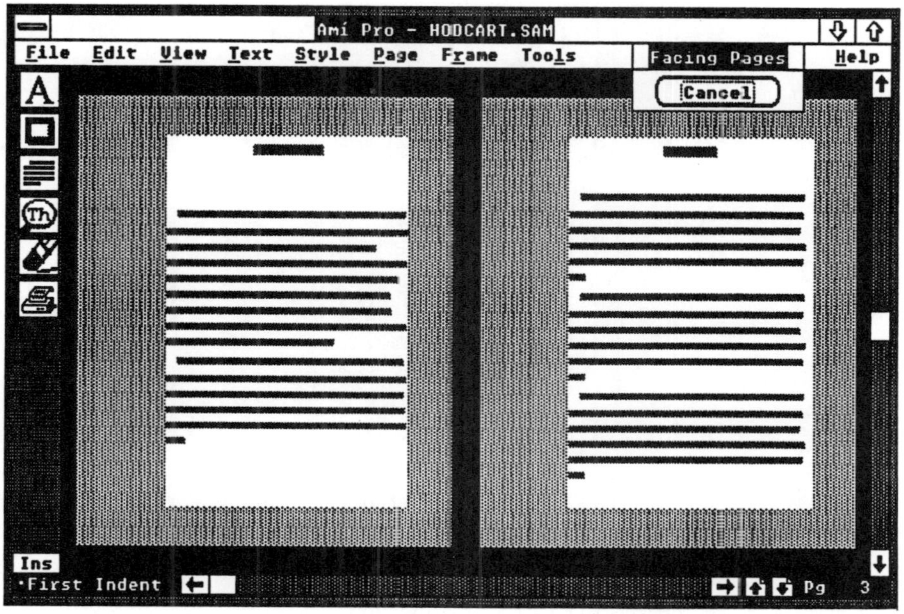

Figure 11-4
Regular pages with a two-inch left margin and a one-inch right margin.

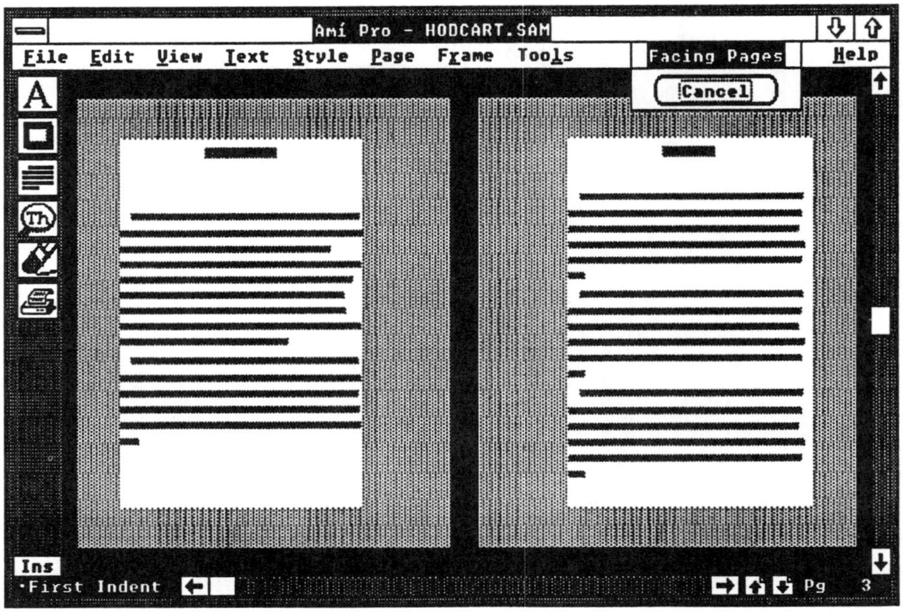

Figure 11-5 Mirrored pages with a two-inch inside margin and a one-inch outside margin.

see the difference between regular pages with uneven margins (as in Figure 11–4) and pages with mirrored margins (in Figure 11–5).

If you want to create different headers or different page number positions for even and odd pages, you create different right and left headers and footers as described in Chapter 15.

To make margins mirror each other on facing pages:

1. Choose the Page Modify Layout command.
2. If necessary, choose the Margins and Columns option in the Modify box.
3. Select Right in the Pages box.
4. Set the margins in the Left, Right, Top, or Bottom running list boxes to set up the right page, making sure to choose a measurement for the large inside margin in the Left box.
5. Turn on the Mirror option in the Pages box. Amí Professional automatically sets up the facing (left) pages for you by reversing the Right and Left margin measurements. (If you want to check this, choose Left in the Pages box.)
6. Click OK or press **Enter**.

Note: Amí Professional always makes even-numbered pages left pages and odd-numbered pages right pages, so page 1 of your document may have no facing page.

USING MULTIPLE COLUMNS

When you want to format your text into columns and rows, use tables (described in Chapter 14). When you want to format your text into multiple flowing columns, like a newspaper, use the procedures described in this section.

You might want to place only certain parts of your document in multiple columns. If you want to have different numbers of columns on the same page—one wide column centered above two narrower ones, for example—you should put part of the text in a frame. To switch the number of columns when you begin a new page, you can insert new page layout instructions where you want the layout to change. See Chapter 12 for more information about frames. Later, this chapter gives more information about using different page layouts in the same document. Figure 11–6 shows two pages from a document in which the left page (three-column format) has one page layout and the right page (one-column format) has another.

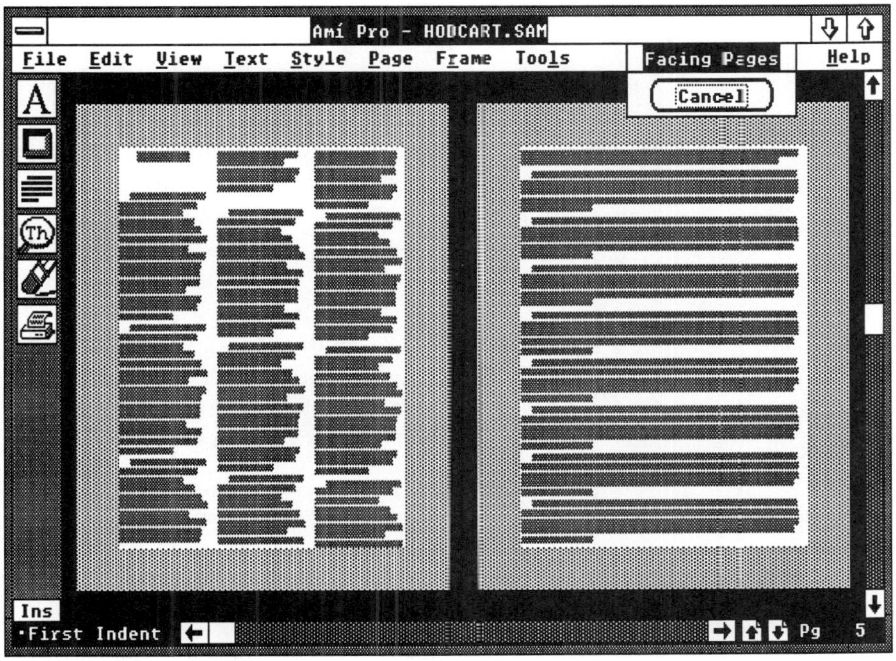

Figure 11–6 You can use different page layout sections to change the number of columns within a document (shown in facing-pages view).

When you want to change the number of columns throughout the page layout area containing the cursor (except for those areas within frames):

1. Choose the Page Modify Layout command.
2. Choose a new number of columns in the Number of Columns section of the dialog box.
3. If you want to change the amount of space between columns, type or select a new measurement in the Gutter Width running list. If you want to change the unit of measurement, click on the word after `Units:` until you see the unit you want.
4. If you want all columns to be the same length (instead of having the last column possibly run shorter than others), turn on the Column Balance option.
5. Click OK or press **Enter**. You can also add or remove vertical lines between columns or around the page with the Lines option, as described in the next section.

ADDING LINES TO PAGES

You can add lines (often called *rules*) to your pages to create distinctive page layouts. You can add lines to any side or to all sides of a page and choose from different line thicknesses or different colors. If you're using more than one column of text in your layout, you can also choose to add vertical lines between columns. Figure 11–7 shows a page in which lines have been added to frame the entire page, box rules surround items like the title and the "sidebar" on the right, and vertical lines separate the columns.

To add lines to pages:

1. Choose the Page Modify Layout command.
2. Choose the Lines option in the Modify box. Amí Professional displays the options shown in Figure 11–8.
3. Choose options to specify where to add border lines in the Around Page box: All (all four sides), Left, Right, Top, or Bottom. If you don't want any lines around the page edges, make sure all these options are turned off.
4. If you added border lines, select a line thickness from the top Style

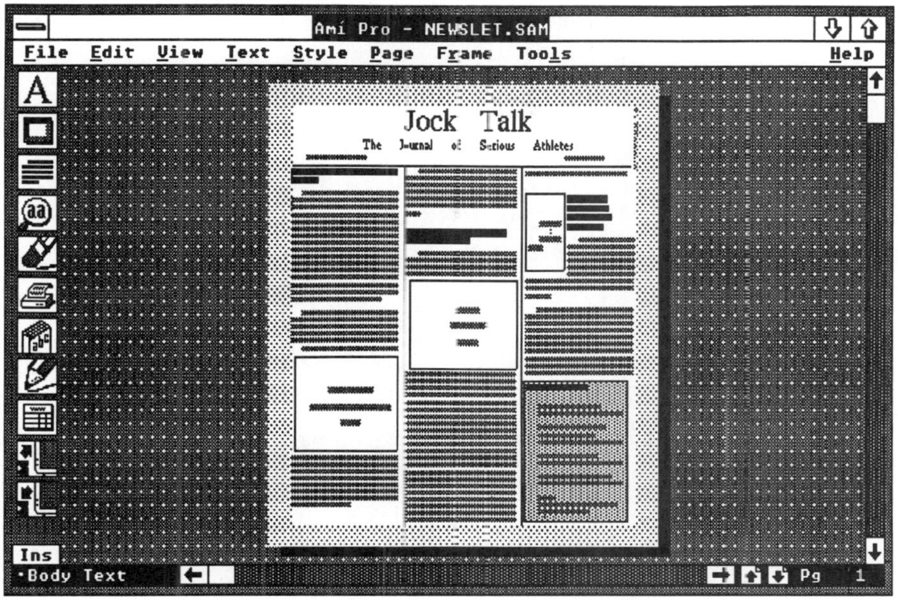

Figure 11-7
A page layout with border lines, box rules, and vertical lines between columns.

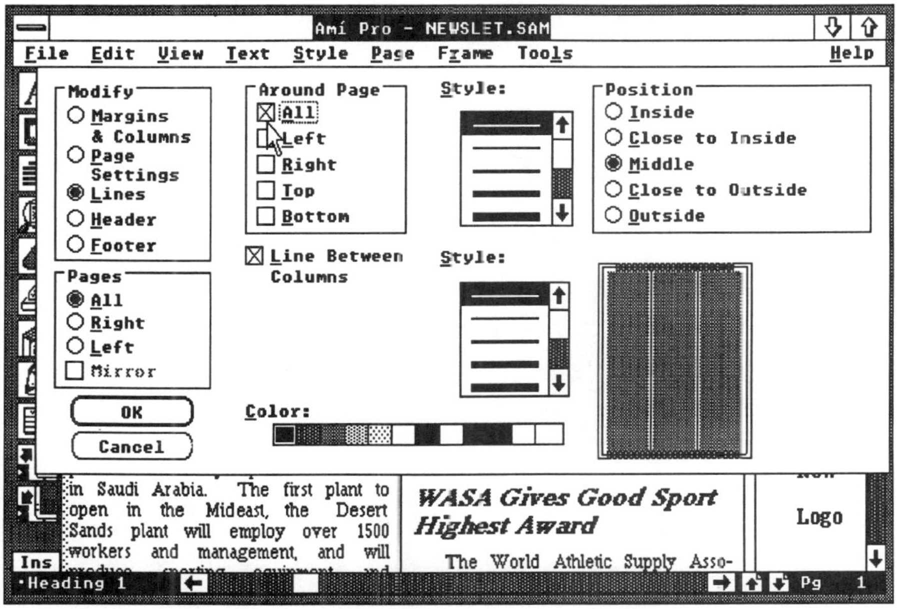

Figure 11-8
Adding lines to a page layout with the Page Modify Layout command.

list, select an option in the Position box to specify the position of the lines within the margins, and select a color from the color bar.

5. If you have more than one column of text and you want to add lines between columns, turn on the Line Between Columns option, then select a line thickness from the bottom Style box and a color from the color bar. If you don't want lines between columns, make sure this option is turned off.
6. When the sample page in the lower right corner of the dialog box looks the way you want, click OK or press **Enter**.

USING MORE THAN ONE PAGE LAYOUT IN YOUR DOCUMENT

When you want to use a different page layout for part of your document, you'll need to insert new layout instructions wherever you want margins, columns, or any other page layout option to change. If you don't insert new instructions, Amí Professional uses the same layout settings (controlled by the style sheet) throughout the document. You'll place the cursor where you want to begin a new page layout, then use the Page Insert/Remove Layout command to change the settings for the following text. Keep in mind that Amí Professional begins to use the new layout settings at the cursor position, continuing to use them until the program encounters other page layout instructions in your document.

Helpful Hint

Every time you use the Page Insert/Remove Layout command to change the page layout for part of a document, Amí Professional shifts the text to begin a new page. If you want to use different layouts on the same page, place text inside of frames, as described in Chapter 12.

Changing the Page Layout for a Section

To begin a new page layout within a document:

1. Place the cursor where you want to change layout settings. For example, to switch from a one-column layout to a two-column layout, place the cursor immediately after the one column of text. The cursor must be within the main body of the document—if it's in the margins or in a frame, the Insert/Remove Layout command won't be available.

2. Choose the Page Insert/Remove Layout command.
3. The Insert New Layout option is already selected, so just click OK or press **Enter**.

   Amí Professional shifts any subsequent text to a new page and displays the Page Modify Layout dialog box so you can change settings.
4. Choose new layout options as described previously in this chapter, then click OK or press **Enter**. (For example, you might change the margins or the number of columns.) Amí Professional attaches an invisible set of layout instructions to this position.

Removing a Page Layout

If you change your mind and you decide that you don't want to use different page layout options for part of your document, you can remove the page layout instructions and make the following text take on the page layout settings of the previous section.

To remove a set of page layout instructions:

1. Move the cursor into the layout section you want to change.
2. Choose the Page Insert/Remove Layout command.
3. Choose the Remove Current Layout option.
4. Click OK or press **Enter**.

Note: If the Remove Current Layout and Change to Standard Layout options are grayed out in the Page Insert/Remove Layout dialog box, the cursor is in a section that uses the standard settings controlled by the style sheet.

Returning a Layout Section to the Standard Settings

You can return a page layout section to the standard layout controlled by the style sheet this way:

1. Move the cursor into the section whose page layout you want to change.
2. Choose the Page Insert/Remove Layout command.
3. Choose the Change to Standard Layout option.

4. Click OK or press **Enter**.

   Amí Professional changes the following text back to the standard settings controlled by the style sheet.

The previous instructions tell you how to change a section back to the standard layout settings. There may be times, however, when you want to leave the previous section alone, but begin a new page layout section using the default layout in the style sheet. In this case, you use the Page Insert/ Remove Layout command to create a new page layout section. When the Modify Layout dialog box appears, you can change options back to the standard settings, or you can click OK, then use the Page Insert/Remove Layout command again and choose the Change to Standard Layout option.

12

Using Frames to Position Text and Graphics

When you want to fix the position of a block of text or a graphic on a page, you use a *frame*. Although you can do some tasks by pressing keys, it's much easier to use a mouse to work with frames. In this chapter, you'll see how to

- insert frames
- change the size and position of frames
- import graphics from other programs into frames
- type and format text in frames
- make frames transparent or opaque for special effects
- flow text around frames
- layer and group frames

You can also draw your own graphics in frames and create sophisticated charts, using Amí Professional's drawing and charting tools. You'll learn about these tools in the next chapter.

WHAT'S A FRAME?

In Amí Professional, a frame isn't necessarily a visible outline—it's just a rectangular area that stays where you put it. Frames can have thin or thick lines surrounding them, or no visible borders at all. Frames can contain text or graphics, but the same frame cannot contain both (unless you "draw" the text with a drawing tool, as explained in Chapter 13). However, because you can have many frames on a page and frames can overlap, the layout possibilities are endless. Take a look at Figures 12–1 through 12–3, which show various uses of frames for headlines or mastheads, graphics, and sidebars.

Imported graphics, drawings, and charts put inside a frame become objects separate from the frame. Just as you can move your furniture around and change the arrangement inside your house, you can change and rearrange objects (imported graphics, drawings, or charts) within a frame. The only exception to this rule of thumb is text, which always stays in the same position within the frame (unless you add spaces or change the alignment).

ADDING A FRAME

To use frames, you must be using layout mode, so, if necessary, choose the View Layout Mode command to switch to layout mode before you use the following procedure.

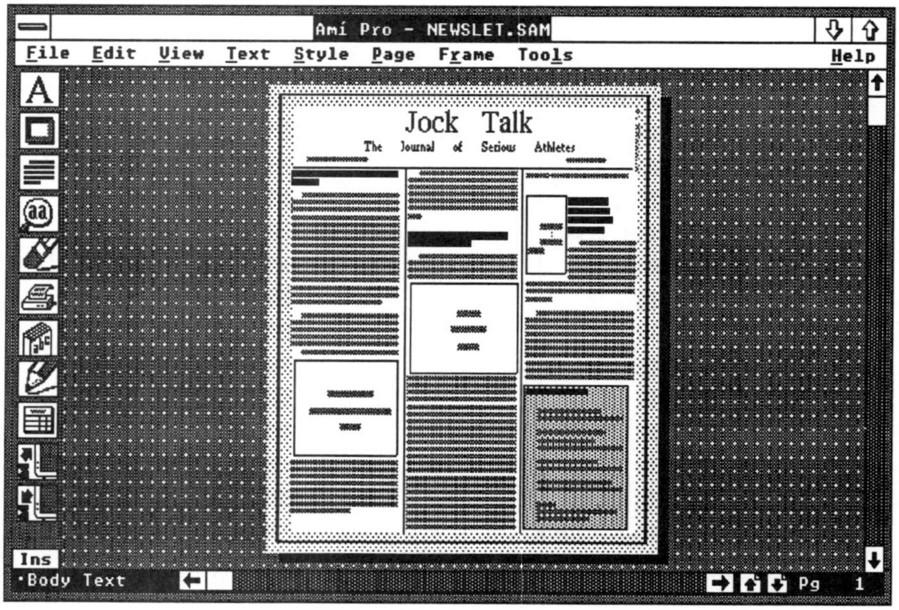

Figure 12-1
A frame can position one wide paragraph over several columns of text.

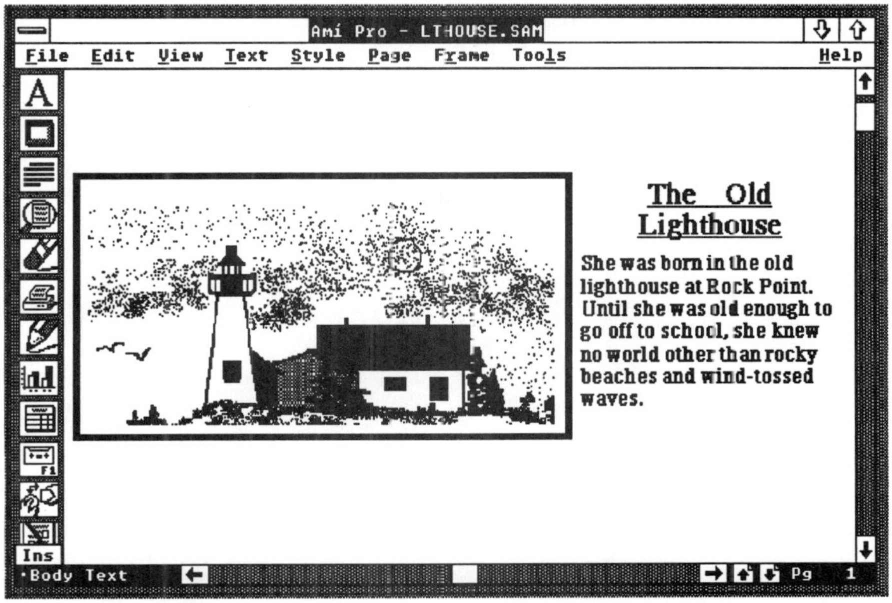

Figure 12-2
Graphics are always enclosed in frames.

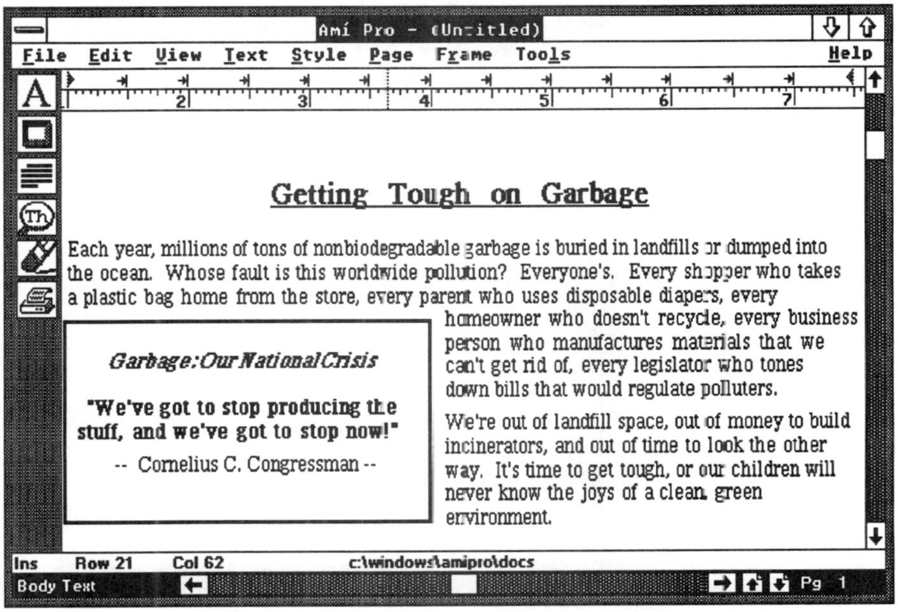

Figure 12-3
You can use frames to create sidebars—framed insets around which the surrounding text flows.

To add a frame:

1. Do one of the following to turn the mouse pointer into a frame as shown in Figure 12–4:

   - Click on the frame icon in the sidebar to the left of the document window.

   or

   - Choose the Add a Frame command from the Frame menu.

2. Move the frame pointer to where you want one corner of the frame, then hold down the left mouse button, drag the frame outline until it's the size you want, then release the button to draw the frame. Figure 12–5 illustrates dragging a frame.

Don't worry if the frame is not quite the right size or in the perfect position—you can always change that later.

To add a frame using the keyboard:

1. Choose the Frame Add a Frame command. The pointer becomes a frame icon.

2. Use an arrow key to move the frame icon to the position on your

Figure 12–4 Clicking on the frame icon turns the mouse pointer into a frame.

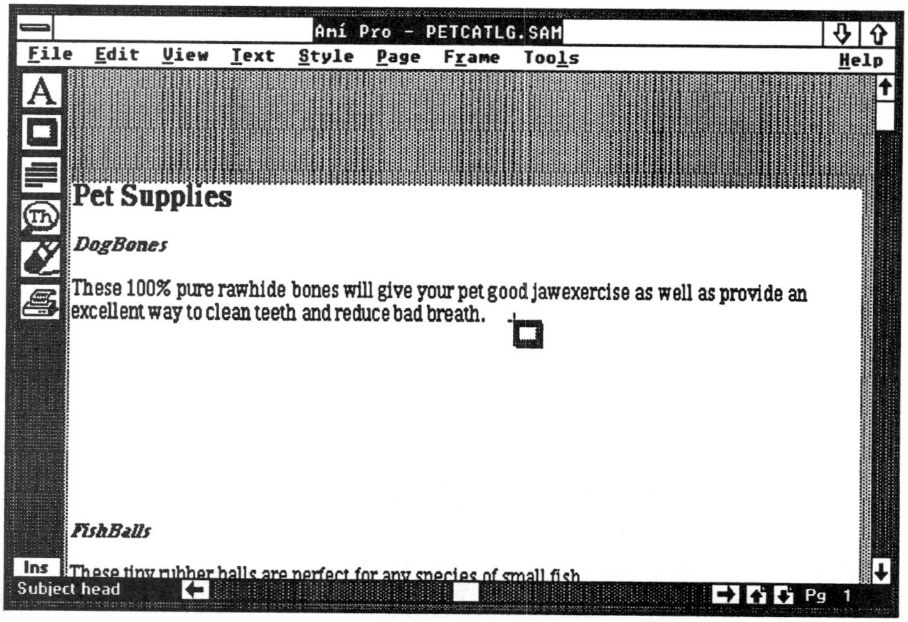

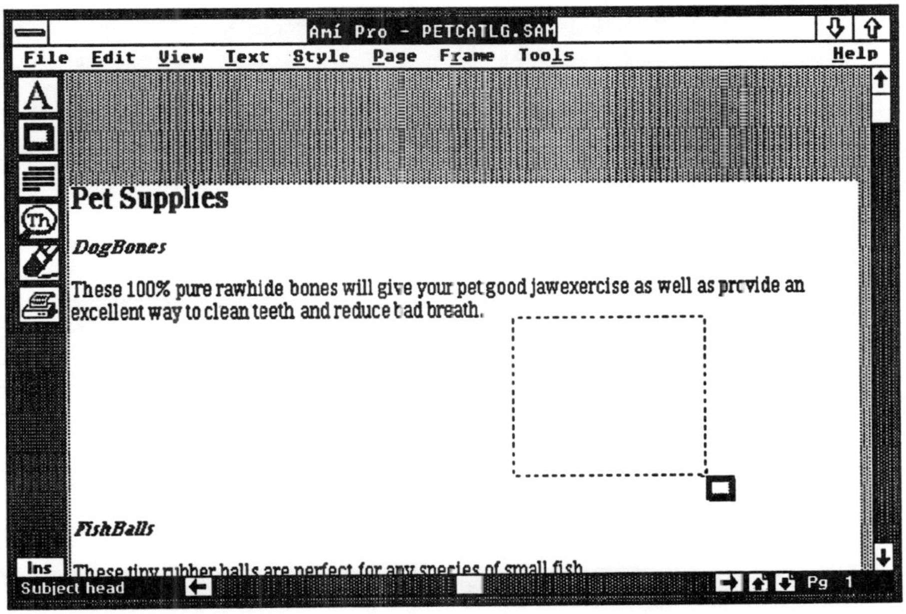

Figure 12–5
Adding a frame with the mouse.

page where you want the frame to begin. You can move the frame icon in larger increments by pressing **Ctrl+*arrow*** key.

3. Hold down the **Spacebar** and use the arrow keys or **Ctrl+*arrow*** to move the frame icon to another corner of the frame.

4. Release the keys. Black "handles" appear to show the frame is selected.

SELECTING A FRAME

Before you can change the size or position of a frame or put anything into a frame, you must select it. To select a frame with a mouse:

□ Click anywhere in the frame.

When a frame is selected, small square, black "handles" appear around the frame, as shown in Figure 12–6.

To select a frame using the keyboard:

1. Press **Ctrl+G** to display the Tools Go To dialog box.

2. Press **Tab** until the focus moves to the list box, then use the arrow keys to move the highlight to Frame. If Frame is already selected,

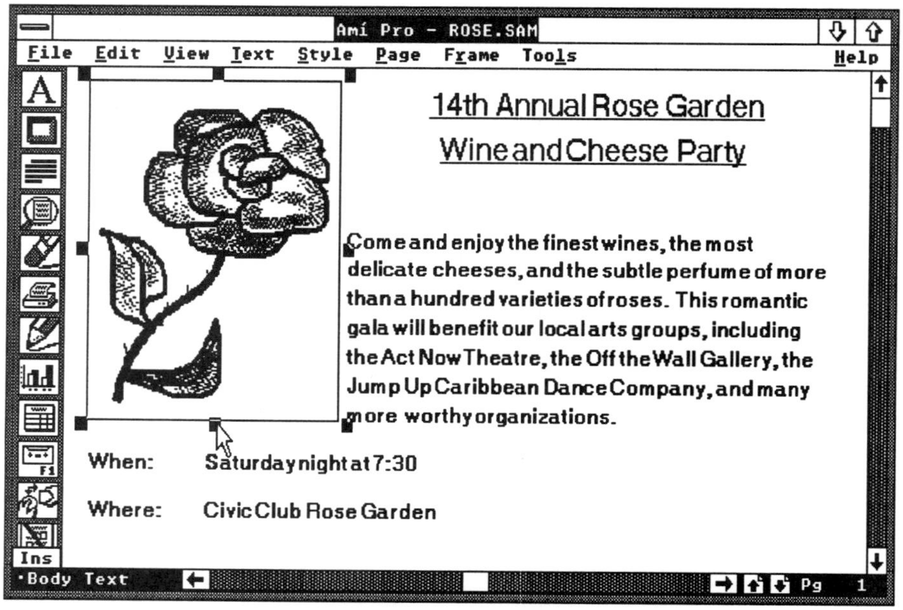

Figure 12-6 Small square "handles" appear around a selected frame.

press the **Down arrow** key to move the highlight off, then press the **Up arrow** key to move it back.

3. Press **Enter** to select the first frame. The cursor appears as an I-beam when it is outside the frame, but changes to an arrow when it is moved to one of the handles of the frame.

4. To select a different frame, press **Ctrl+H** until the correct frame is selected.

MOVING A FRAME

To move a frame (with its contents) on the same page with a mouse:

1. Select the frame.

2. Drag the frame outline to a new position, as shown in Figure 12-7.

To move a frame on the same page using the keyboard:

1. Select the frame as described in Selecting a Frame.

2. Use the arrow keys to position the cursor inside the frame.

3. Hold down the **Spacebar** and use an arrow key to move the frame

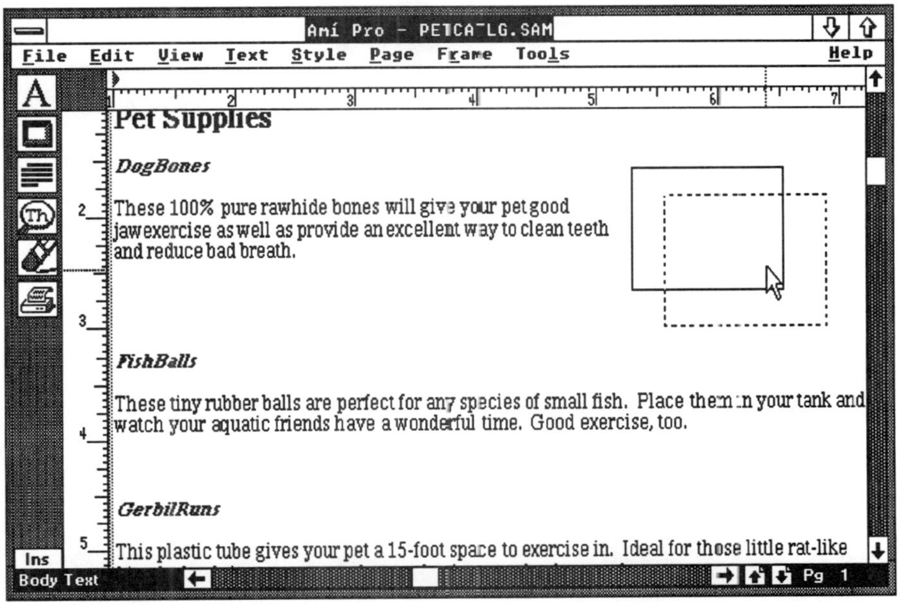

Figure 12-7 Changing the position of a frame with the mouse (shown in enlarged view with the tab ruler and vertical rulers displayed).

to a new position. Using **Ctrl+*arrow*** key while holding down the **Spacebar** moves the frame in larger increments.

4. Release the keys when the frame is in the position you wish.

Helpful Hints

To precisely position a frame, use the View Enlarged command to switch to enlarged view, use the View Display Preferences command to display the vertical ruler, and use the View Tab Ruler command to display the horizontal ruler.

When frames overlap, you might want to select more than one at a time to move them as a group. To move multiple frames:

1. Hold down the **Shift** key while you click on all the frames you want to move.

2. Continue to hold down the Shift key while you drag the frames to a new position on the page.

You can also "group" frames to make them automatically move together. Grouping is described later in this chapter.

To move a frame to a different page:

1. Select the frame.
2. Choose the Edit Cut command.
3. Move the cursor to the new page.
4. Choose the Edit Paste command to insert the frame.

You can also use the Edit Copy command instead of the Edit Cut command in step 2 to copy a frame to a new page.

CHANGING THE SIZE OF A FRAME

To change the size of a frame:

1. Select the frame.
2. Point to the square handle on the side of the frame you want to move or point to a corner handle to move two sides of the frame at once.
3. Hold down the left mouse button and drag the frame to a new size, as shown in Figure 12–8.

To change the size of a frame using the keyboard:

1. Select the frame as described in Selecting a Frame.

Figure 12–8 Changing the size of a frame with the mouse.

2. Using the arrow keys, position the I cursor over the handles that you want to resize. The I-beam becomes an arrow pointer.

3. Hold down the **Spacebar** to select the handle and use the arrow keys to resize the frame. Using **Ctrl+*arrow*** while holding down the **Spacebar** resizes the frame in larger increments. A rectangle of dashes indicates the new size of the frame as you resize it.

4. Release the keys when the frame is the size you wish.

WORKING WITH GRAPHICS IN FRAMES

Whenever you want to put a graphic in your document, you must add a frame to your document first. Then you can put a graphic into the frame in any of three ways:

- Use Amí Professional's drawing or charting tools to create your own graphics.
- Use the Clipboard to copy and paste a graphic created by any Windows graphics program.
- Use the File Import/Export command to import a file from another program.

You can read more about drawing and charting in Chapter 13. Using the Clipboard and details about the File Import/Export command are covered in this chapter.

Whatever you put into a frame becomes a separate object that you can move, resize, and make other changes to within the frame. You don't need to worry about getting the size of an imported graphic perfect the first time; you can crop and scale it at any time, using the procedures described later in this chapter. You can import the following types of formatted files, listed here by their file extensions:

.PCX	PC Paintbrush®
.TIF	Scanned images
.PIC	Lotus 1-2-3 graphics
.EPS	Encapsulated PostScript
.WMF	Windows metafiles

Using the Clipboard to Copy a Windows Graphic

To use the Clipboard to import a graphic created by a Windows graphic program, such as Microsoft® Windows Paint:

1. Open the graphics file.
2. Select the part of the graphic you want to copy to your document.
3. Use the Edit Copy command to copy the graphic to the Clipboard.
4. Open the Amí Professional file.
5. Select the frame you want to place the graphic in.
6. Use the Edit Paste command to insert the graphic. Figure 12–9 shows a Microsoft Windows Paint graphic pasted into an Amí Professional document.

Importing a Non-Windows Graphic

To import a graphic file created by a non-Windows program:

1. Select the frame you want to put the graphic in.

Figure 12–9 A Microsoft Windows Paint graphic pasted into an Amí Professional document.

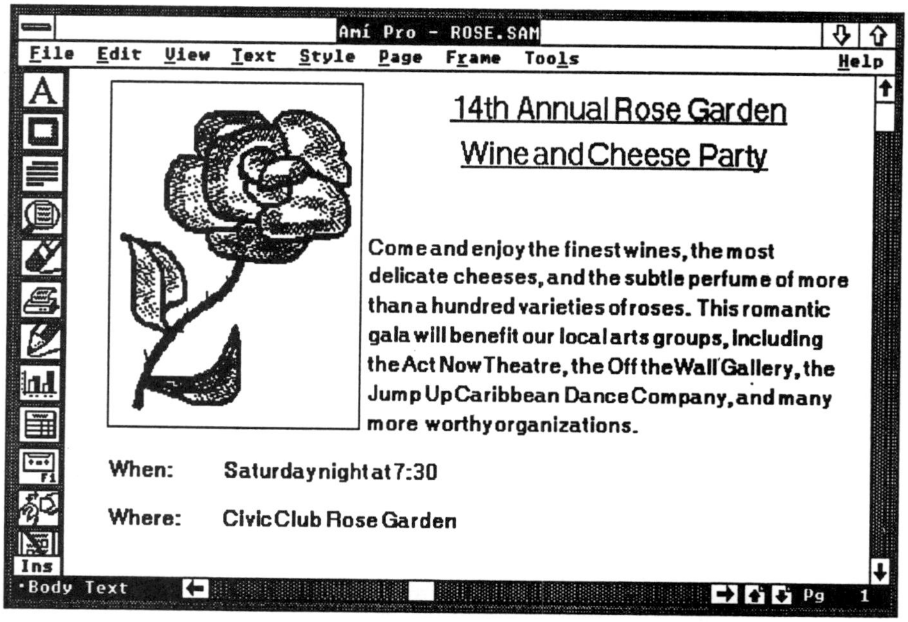

2. Choose the File Import/Export command. Amí Professional displays the dialog box shown in Figure 12–10.
3. Select the file's current format from the list box.
4. Select the name of the file from the list. The list displays the names of files in the active disk drive and directory. To see names of other files, you may need to type a drive name, directory name(s), or file name indicators in the text box. For example, to see a list of files with *.PCX extensions in the PBRUSH directory on drive A, you would type **a:\pbrush*.pcx** in the text box, then press **Enter**.
5. If you want to insert a copy of the graphic that isn't linked to the original file, turn on the Copy Image option. This option stores a copy of the graphic in an image file with the name of your document and an extension beginning with .G followed by a number (MINE.G00, for example). If you don't choose this option, Amí Professional links your document to the original graphics file and will automatically update the graphic if you change the original file.
6. Click OK or press **Enter**.

Scaling a Graphic

When you *scale* a graphic, you change the size of the graphic, not the size of the frame.

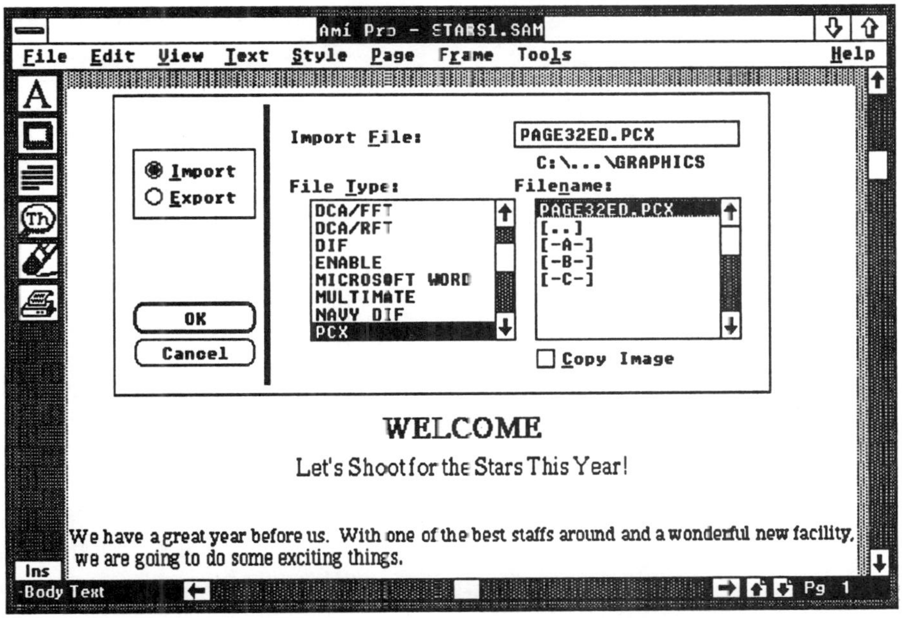

Figure 12–10 Importing a graphic file with the File Import/Export command.

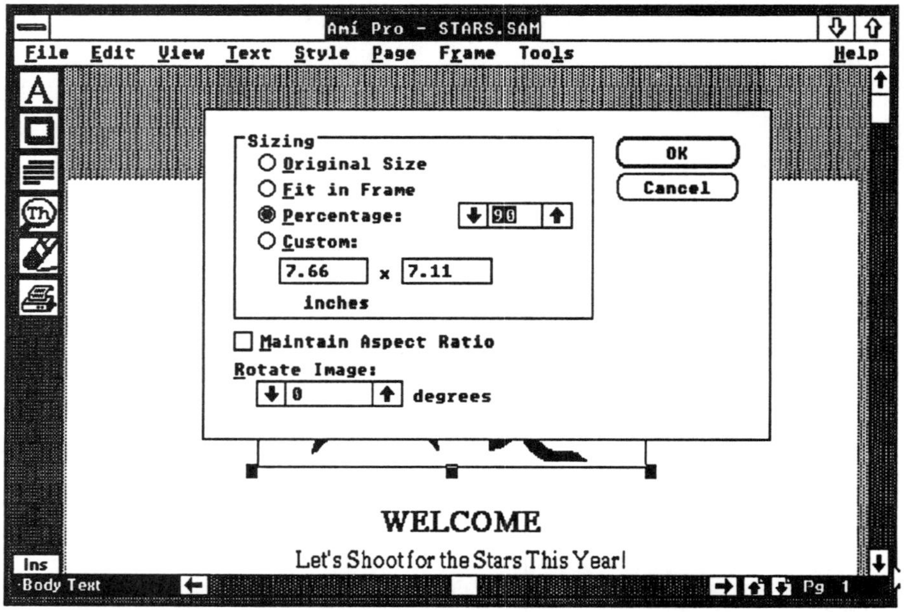

Figure 12-11 Scaling a graphic with the Frame Graphics Scaling command.

To scale a graphic:

1. Double-click on the graphic within the frame to select it. The handles around the frame turn gray and the mouse pointer becomes a hand.
2. Choose the Frame Graphics Scaling command. Amí Professional displays the dialog box shown in Figure 12–11.
3. Do one of the following:

   - To return the graphic to its original size, turn on the Original Size option.

   or

   - To make the graphic fit the dimensions of the frame, choose the Fit in Frame option.

   or

   - To scale the graphic to a specific percentage of the original, turn on the Percentage option, then type or select a new percentage number in the running list. For example, if you want the imported graphic to be half the size of the original, type **50** here. This is an easy way to experiment with different sizes.

   or

- To specify the dimensions for the graphic, choose the Custom option and type the dimensions you want in the boxes. (The left box is for width; the right box is for height.)

  Note: If you want to maintain the original proportions of the graphic while changing its size, turn on the Maintain Aspect Ratio option.

4. Click OK or press **Enter**.

Moving a Graphic in a Frame

If the graphic is in the wrong position within the frame, you can move it in this way:

1. Double-click the graphic within the frame. The handles around the frame turn gray, and the mouse pointer becomes a hand.
2. Point to the center of the graphic, then hold down the left mouse button and drag the graphic to a new position. Figure 12–12 illustrates moving a graphic within a frame.

To move a graphic image in a frame using the keyboard:

1. Select the frame as described in Selecting a Frame.

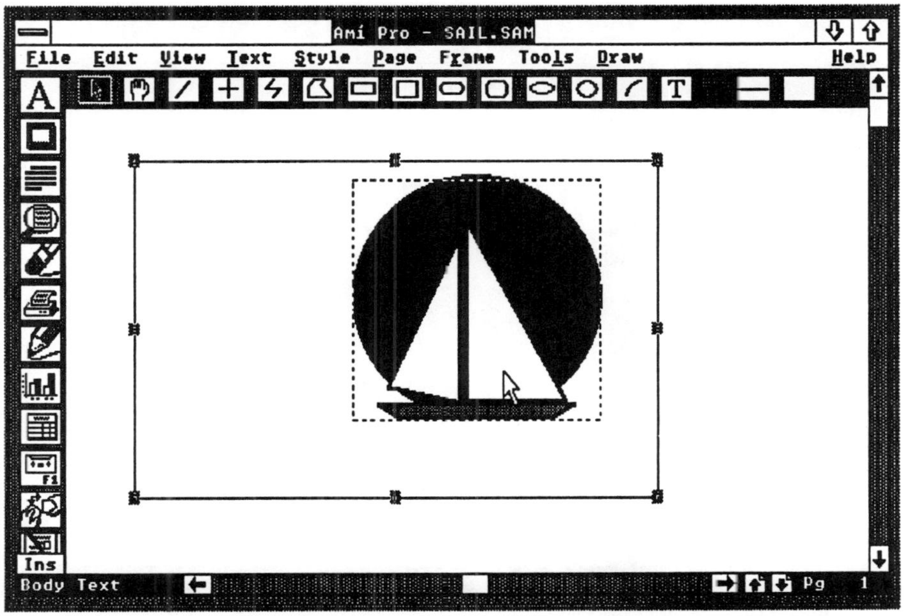

Figure 12–12
Moving a graphic within a frame.

2. Press **Enter**. The handles become gray and the cursor becomes a hand.
3. Use the arrow keys to move the graphic image within the frame. Using **Ctrl+*arrow*** key moves the hand in larger increments.
4. Press **Escape** twice when you are finished to remove the frame selection.

Cropping a Graphic

If there is too much white space around the graphic or if you want to cut off parts of the graphic, you can crop the image by changing the size of the surrounding frame, as shown in Figure 12–13. Instructions for changing the size of a frame appear earlier in this chapter.

Helpful Hint

If you want to use only a portion of a graphic, you can move the graphic in the frame to display only the portion you want, then scale the graphic by typing a percentage (like **300%**) using the Frame Graphics Scaling command. For instance, if you want to use an enlarged graphic of the state of Florida, which is part of a map of the United States, you could move the graphic in

Figure 12–13 Cropping a graphic by reducing the size of the frame.

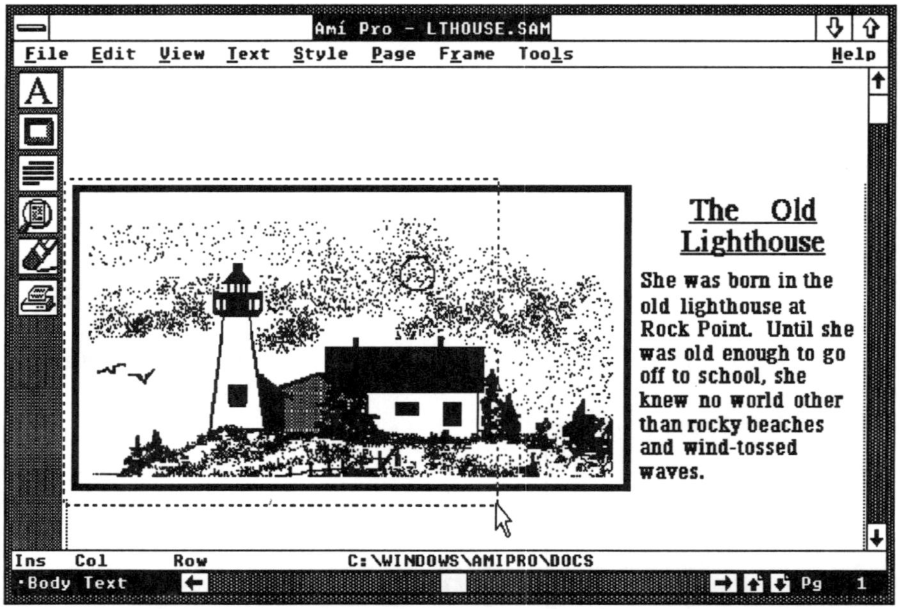

the frame until Florida is displayed, then scale the graphic to 300% (or whatever size you wish).

Rotating a Graphic

You can rotate a graphic within its frame in this way:

1. Double-click the graphic within the frame. The handles around the graphic turn gray.
2. Choose the Frame Graphics Scaling command.
3. Type or select a number of degrees in the Rotate Image running list box. For example, to turn the image upside down, type **180**. To return the image to its original orientation, type 0 (zero).
4. Click OK or press **Enter**.

Note: You can only rotate bit-mapped graphics (those made up of dots, as opposed to vector graphics such as those created by Amí Professional).

Enhancing Scanned Images

As you import a scanned image into your Amí Professional document, you may want to change the shades of gray or change the contrast of the image with the Frame Image Processing command. This command is available only when a gray-scale scanned image is selected. Here's how it works:

1. Select the graphic within the frame.
2. Choose the Frame Image Processing command.
3. Choose one of the following options:

Option	**Description**
Enhance Edges	Defines the edges of an object more clearly.
Smooth Image	Turn on to smooth out jagged lines.
Invert Image	Turn on to create a reverse image by changing white to black and black to white.

Brightness and Contrast sliders	Use the mouse to move the white square within the slider bar to change the brightness or contrast. You'll see the image change in the lower right corner of the dialog box.

4. Click OK or press **Enter** to save the changed graphic, or click Restore to return the image to its original state.

Deleting a Graphic from a Frame

If you want to delete a graphic but keep the frame:

1. Double-click the graphic within the frame. The handles around the graphic turn gray and the mouse pointer becomes a hand.
2. Press the **Delete** key.

To do the same using only keys, use the procedure in Moving a Graphic in a Frame, but press **Delete** in step 3. You can also use the Cut, Copy, and Paste commands from the Edit menu to delete, copy, and paste a graphic.

WORKING WITH TEXT IN A FRAME

You can place text in a frame to create special effects such as one column of text over two, sidebars, insets, tables that text wraps around, and so forth. Another common use of framed text is to add a caption to a graphic, as shown in Figure 12–14. Remember: You can't have both text and graphics in the same frame unless you add the text with a drawing tool.

Typing or Editing Text in a Frame

To type or edit text in a frame:

1. Double-click an empty frame or one containing text. The frame handles change from black to gray and a cursor appears in the upper left corner of the frame.

   or

   Select an empty frame or one containing text, as described in Se-

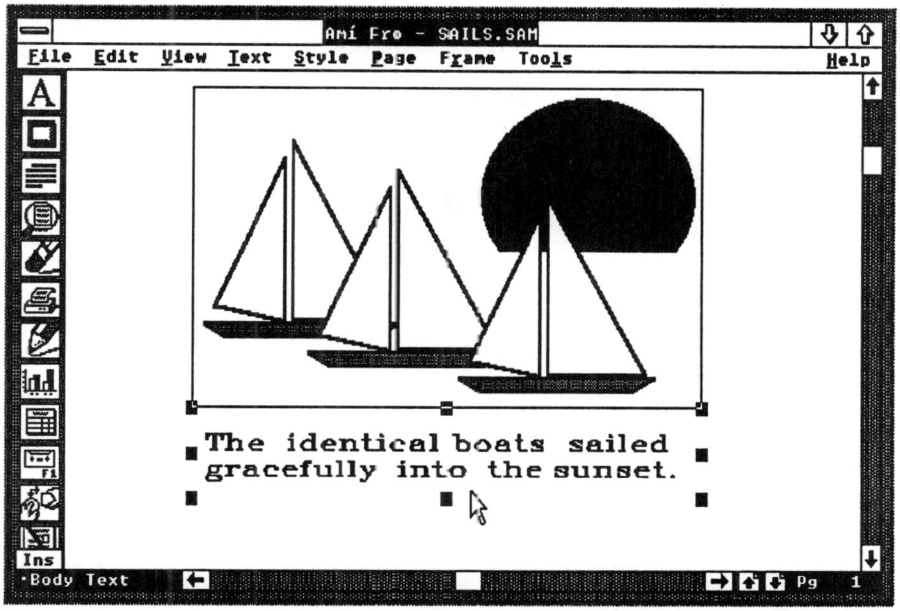

Figure 12-14 The caption for this graphic is in a separate frame beneath the graphic frame.

lecting a Frame, then press **Enter**. The handles become gray and the pointer becomes an insertion point.

2. Type the new text, or select and edit existing text just as you would outside of a frame.
3. When you're through typing in the frame, click outside of the frame or press **Escape** twice.

If you type more text than can fit in the frame, you'll have to enlarge the frame to display all of the text.

Using Styles Inside of Frames

Amí Professional automatically formats new text with the last style used outside of the frame. You can choose a different style and use all the normal commands to edit and format the text in a frame.

Checking Spelling Inside of Frames

You can check the spelling of text inside frames this way:

1. Double-click the frame to move the cursor inside the frame.

2. Choose the Tools Spelling command. (If you're using the Spell Check in Draft Mode option, the frame disappears during the spelling check.)

Changing the Position of Text in a Frame

Unlike graphics, you can only change the position of text within a frame (by using blank lines, tabs, indents, alignments, or styles). You can also make the frame larger or smaller around the text and move the frame to a new position until the text is exactly where you want it.

Changing Tabs and Number of Columns

For the text inside a frame, you can choose tab and column settings that are different from those of surrounding text.

To change the tabs or columns for text in a frame:

1. Select the frame.
2. Choose the Frame Layout command from the Frame menu.
3. Choose the Columns & Tabs option in the Modify box. Amí Professional displays the options shown in Figure 12–15. (This option is dimmed if you select a frame that does not contain text.)
4. Choose from the following options until the sample text in the lower right corner looks the way you want:

Option	How to Use
Number of Columns	Choose a new number if you want more than one flowing column of text.
Column Balance	Available only when you've chosen two or more columns. Turn on only if you want all columns to be the same length in the frame.
Gutter Width	Available only when you've chosen two or more columns. If you want to specify a new measurement for white space between columns, type or select that measurement in the running list box.

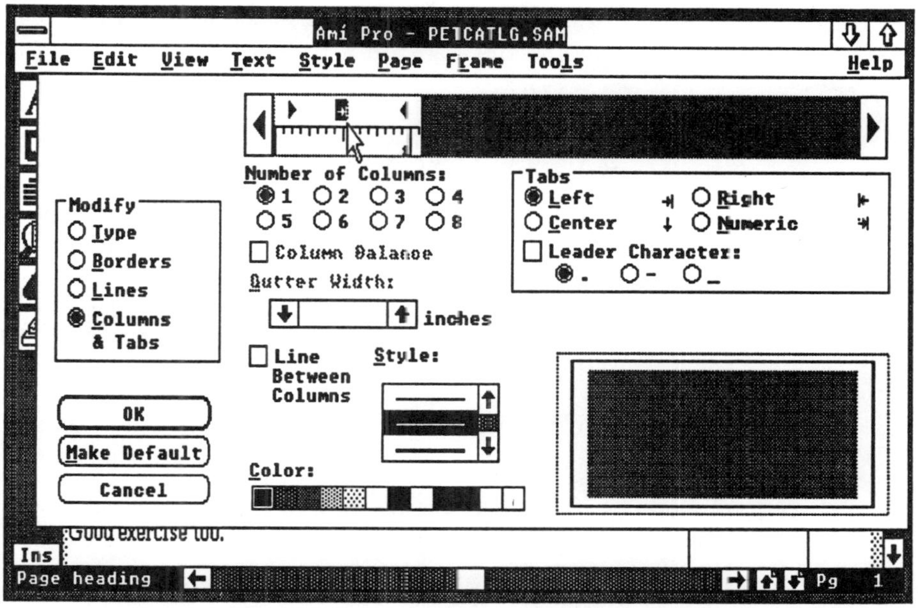

Figure 12–15
Setting tabs in a frame with the Frame Layout command.

Line Between Columns	Available only when you've chosen two or more columns. Turn on only if you want to draw a vertical line between columns, then select a line thickness from the Style list and a line color from the color bar.
Tabs	If you want to set tabs, choose the tab type you want in the Tabs box, turn on the Leader Character option, and choose a character if you want to fill the tab space with characters, then click in the ruler to set the tab position. Figure 12–15 illustrates setting tabs in a frame.

5. Click OK or press **Enter**.

CONTROLLING WHITE SPACE AROUND THE TEXT OR GRAPHIC IN A FRAME

If the text wrapping around a frame looks too close to or too far away from the text or graphic inside the frame, you might want to change the amount of white space inside the frame.

To change the amount of space between the text or graphic inside a frame and the edges of a frame:

1. Select the frame.
2. Choose the Frame Layout command.
3. Choose the Borders option in the Modify box. Amí Professional displays the options shown in Figure 12–16.
4. Type or select new measurements in the Left, Right, Top, or Bottom running list boxes to change the amount of white space inside the frame.
5. If you want to use a measurement other than inches, click the measurement after Units until you see the unit of measurement you want.
6. When the sample box in the lower right corner looks the way you want, click OK or press **Enter**.

Helpful Hint

The Borders option in the Frame Layout dialog box controls how much space lies between the frame contents and the surrounding text. The Lines option controls where lines appear within the border space. So if you want .10 inch space between framed text and frame lines and .10 inch space between

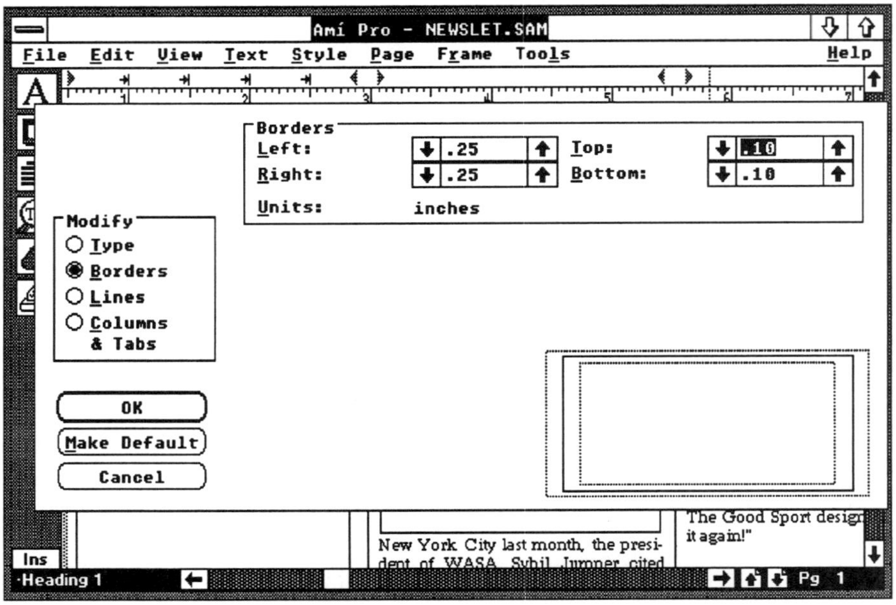

Figure 12–16 Adding more white space around a paragraph in a frame with the Frame Layout command.

frame lines and surrounding text, set the Border spacing to .20 inch and set the Lines to the Middle position.

CHANGING LINES AROUND FRAMES AND SHADING WITHIN FRAMES

You can choose whether to place lines around the outside of frames. You might want to delete lines to make the edges of the frame invisible, or change line thickness or color for different effects. You can also choose to shade ("screen") the background of a frame to make that section of the page really stand out, as shown in Figure 12–17.

To change lines around a frame or shading within a frame:

1. Select the frame.
2. Choose the Frame Layout command.
3. Choose the Lines option in the Modify box. Amí Professional displays the options shown in Figure 12–18.
4. Turn on options to specify where you want to add lines in the Line box. For example, to add lines on the top and bottom of the frame, turn on the Top and Bottom check boxes.
5. Select a line thickness from the Style box.

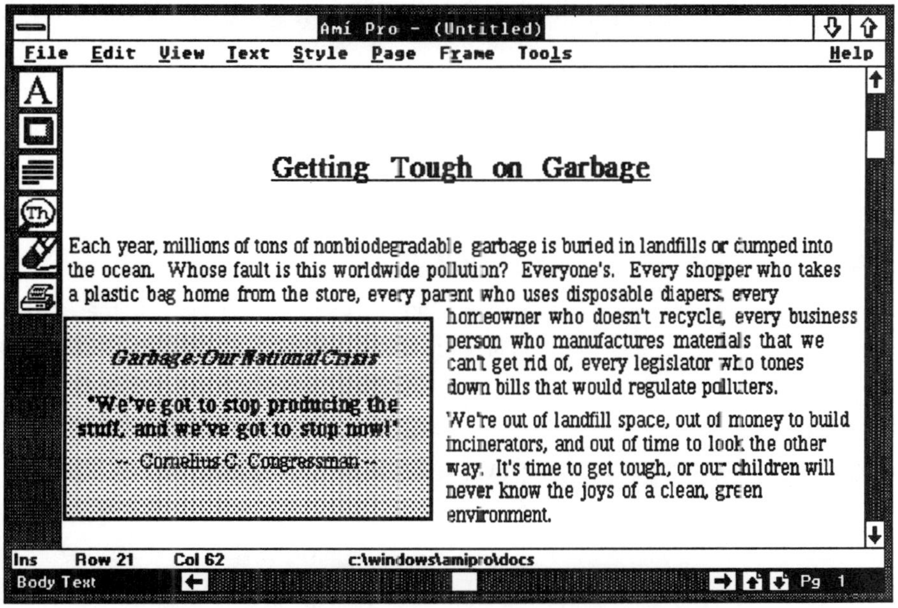

Figure 12–17 Background shading in a frame makes a section of a page stand out.

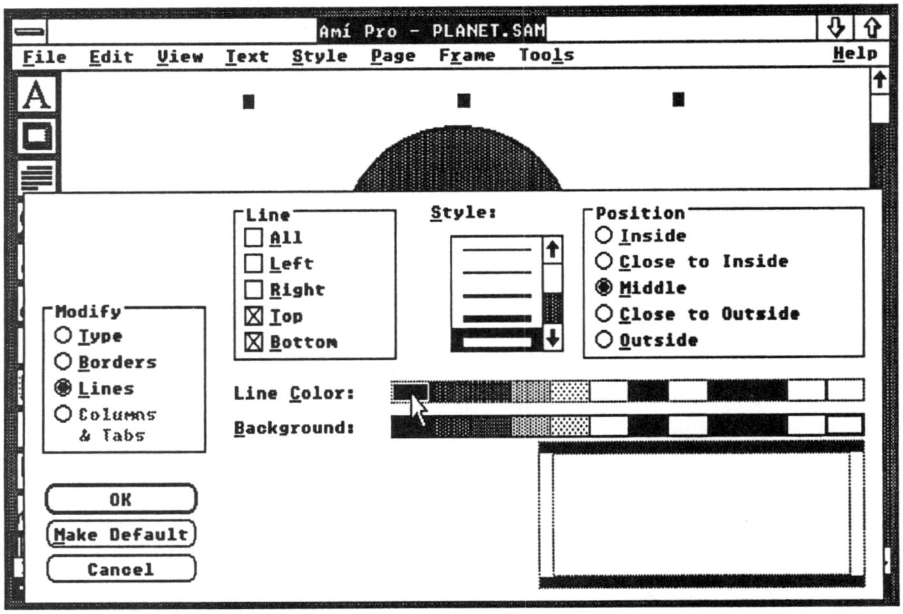

Figure 12–18 Adding thick lines to the top and bottom of a frame with the Frame Layout command.

6. Choose a position in the Position box to determine how close the line(s) will be to the edge of the frame.
7. Choose a line color from the Line Color bar.
8. If you want to change the background of the frame, choose a shading pattern from the Background bar. If you want text or graphics behind to show through, see Layering Frames for Special Effects later in this chapter.
9. When the sample text in the lower right corner looks the way you want, click OK or press **Enter**. Figure 12–18 illustrates adding lines to a frame.

Helpful Hint

To make an opaque background within a frame extend completely to lines surrounding the frame, select Lines in the Frame Layout box and set the position to Inside.

CONTROLLING TEXT WRAPPING AROUND A FRAME

To change the way text wraps around a frame:

1. Select the frame.

2. Choose the Frame Layout command.

3. Choose one of the options in the Text Wrap Around box:

Option	Description
Wrap Around	Text wraps on both sides of the frame if there's sufficient room.
No Wrap Around	Text flows behind the frame. If the frame is opaque, this may hide part of the text.
No Wrap Beside	Text doesn't wrap on either side of the frame but appears only above and below the frame.

4. Click OK or press **Enter**.

Helpful Hint

If you want all the frames you add to have certain characteristics (for example, No Wrap Around frames with large top and bottom borders and no lines), you can choose these options and then click the Make Default box. Each time you add a new frame, it will have these characteristics.

LOCKING FRAMES IN PLACE AND REPEATING FRAMES

You can position a frame on a page by moving it as described earlier in this chapter. You can lock a frame in its current position even after text or paging changes, make it stay with the previous paragraph if the paragraph moves, or copy the frame and its position to other pages in your document.

To choose positioning options for a frame:

1. Select the frame.

2. Choose the Frame Layout command.

3. Choose one of the following options in the Position box:

Option	Description
Where Placed	The frame remains in its current position on the page, no matter now much text is added or deleted around it.

With Para Above — Automatically makes frame No Wrap Beside. This option causes the frame to stay with the paragraph above it. If a page break normally occurs before or within that paragraph, both the paragraph and the frame will be shifted to the next page. When this option is in effect, you can move the frame only horizontally within the column.

Repeat All Pages — The frame appears in the same position on all pages of the document until the next layout.

Repeat Right/Left — The frame appears on every other page of the document until the next layout. If you inserted the frame on an even-numbered (left) page, the frame will repeat on every even-numbered page; if you inserted it on an odd-numbered page, the frame will repeat on every odd-numbered (right) page.

4. Click OK or press **Enter**. Figure 12–19 shows a document with a frame (the logo) repeated in the same position on every page.

Figure 12–19 A document with a frame in the same position on every page (shown in facing-pages view).

LAYERING FRAMES FOR SPECIAL EFFECTS

If you want to combine text and graphics, as shown in Figure 12–20, or to create a shaded, shadowed, or overlapping effect, as shown in Figures 12–21 and 12–22, you can layer frames by moving one on top of another. To move a frame, use the procedure described earlier in this chapter. To control whether text or graphics beneath a frame show through or are blocked by the frame, do this:

1. Select the frame on top.
2. Choose the Frame Layout command.
3. Choose the Transparent option to let text or graphics behind show through the frame, or choose the Opaque option to block out anything behind the frame.

CONTROLLING THE POSITION OF OVERLAPPING FRAMES

When you want to layer frames, sometimes you have no choice but to drag one frame on top of another, although you might really want the top frame

Figure 12–20
Text appears on top of a graphic when you put a transparent text frame on top of a graphics frame.

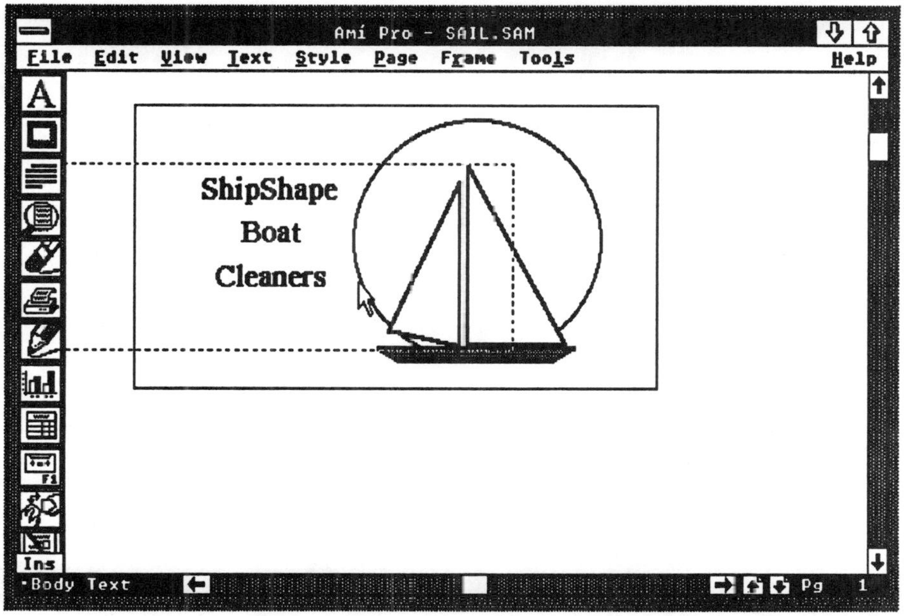

Figure 12–21
Graphics appear to overlap when you put opaque frames on top of each other.

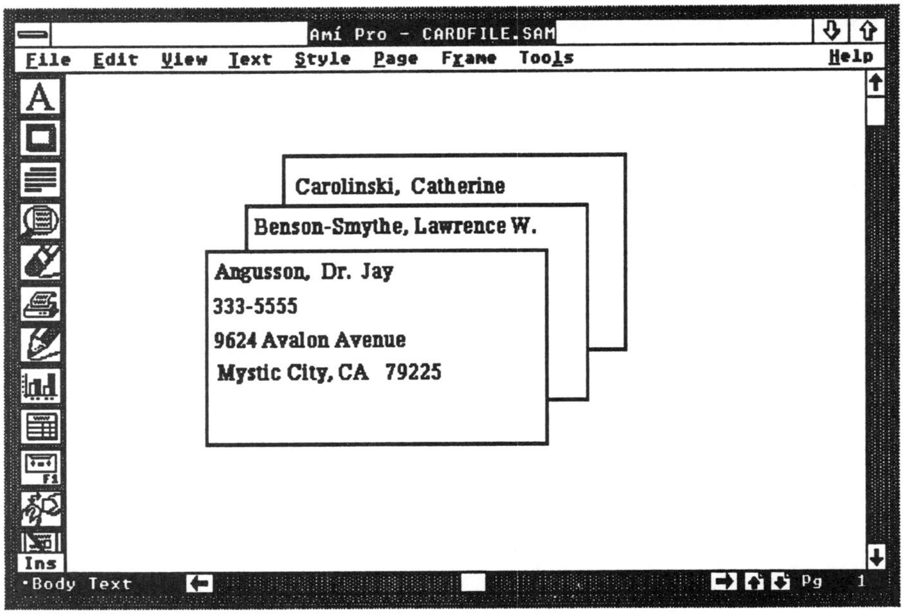

Figure 12–22
You can add a shadow-box effect by positioning an opaque frame on top of a shaded frame.

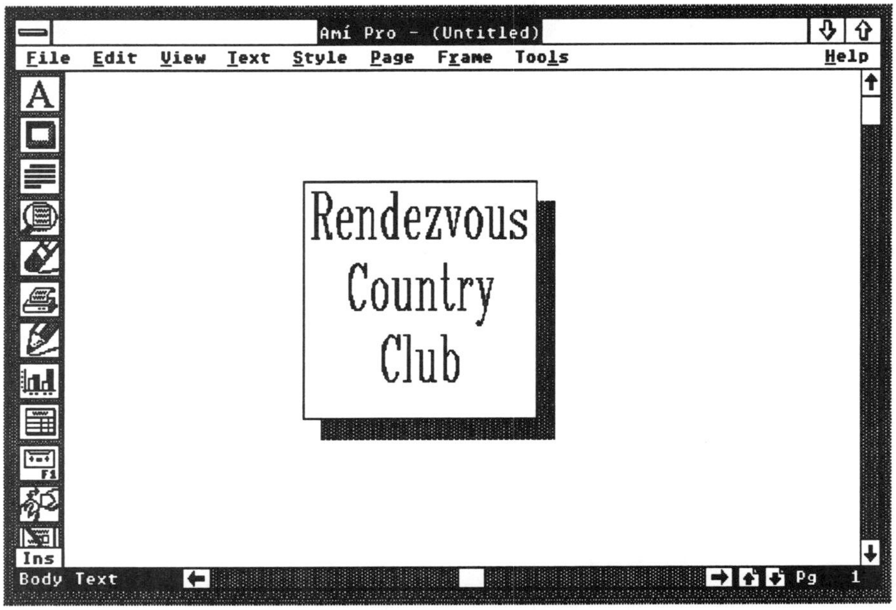

behind the other. No problem! You can control which overlapping frame is on top this way:

1. Click the frame.
2. Choose the Frame Send to Back command to move the frame into the background, or choose the Frame Bring to Front command to move the frame to the foreground.

GROUPING FRAMES TO KEEP THEM TOGETHER

When you have several frames that you want to keep together, you *group* them. Grouping makes the frames move together as one unit. For example, if you added a text frame below a graphic as a caption or positioned one frame on top of another for a shadow-box effect, you want to make sure that if you change the position of one frame, the other moves along with it.

To group frames:

1. Hold down the **Shift** key and click on all the frames you want to group. You'll see handles appear around each frame as you click it.
2. Choose the Group Frames command from the Frame menu. Handles appear around the entire group.

If you're ever in doubt about whether a frame belongs to a group, just select the frame and pull down the Frame menu. If the Group Frames command has a check mark next to it, the selected frame is part of a group. As long as frames are grouped, you can't change only one frame in the group. If you want to do that, you ungroup the frames first, make the change, then group the frames again.

To ungroup frames:

1. Click any frame in the group. Handles appear around the entire group.
2. Choose the Group Frames command from the Frame menu. Now the frames no longer are linked, so you can reposition or otherwise change any individual frame.

13

Drawing and Charting

Chapter 12 showed how to add frames to your document, import graphics into frames, add text to frames, and change the position and size of frames. In this chapter, you'll learn how to use Amí Professional's powerful drawing and charting tools to create your own graphics within frames.

To use the drawing and charting tools, you must have inserted a frame and must be working in layout mode. To draw, you must use a mouse.

CREATING YOUR OWN DRAWINGS

To create your own drawings:

1. Select the frame you want to draw in. (The frame must be empty, or it must contain a chart or drawing.)
2. Choose the Frame Drawing command.

   Amí Professional adds a Draw menu and displays the drawing tools in an icon bar at the top of the screen, as shown in Figure 13–1.
3. To draw, click on the tool you want to use, then use the mouse pointer to draw in the frame. You can get more information about what the different drawing tools do in the next section. Figure 13–2 illustrates drawing in a frame.
4. When you're finished drawing, click outside the frame or press **Escape**.

Figure 13–1
Names of the Amí Professional drawing tools displayed in the icon bar.

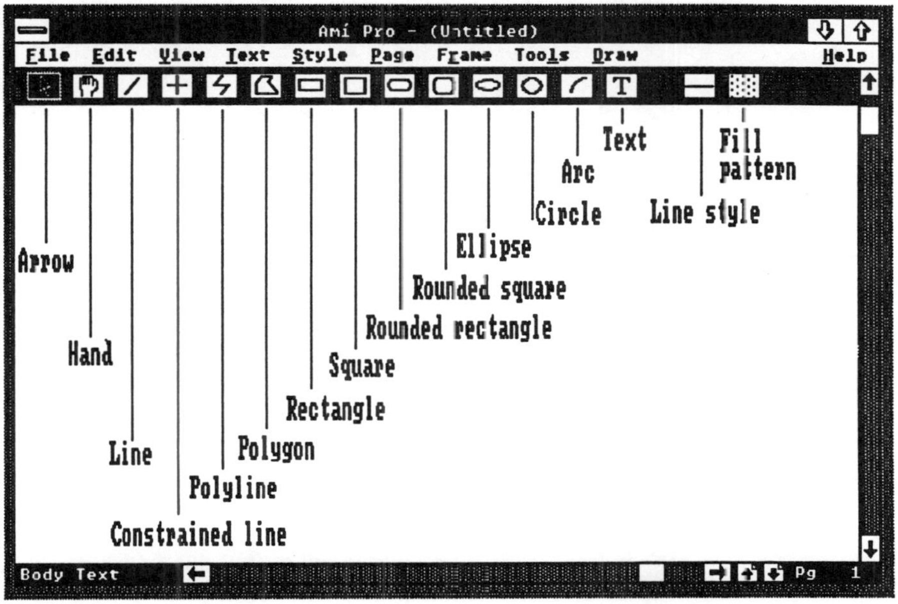

Figure 13–2
Drawing in a frame.

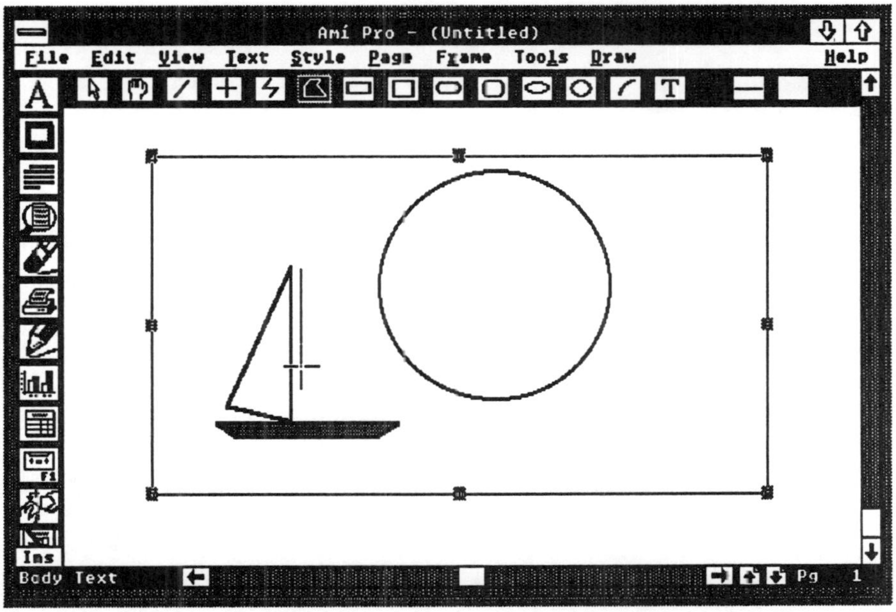

Clicking outside the frame makes the Draw menu and drawing tools disappear. To make them appear again, just double-click the frame.

Helpful Hints

Make the frame bigger so that you'll have blank spots to click inside the frame as well as outside. You can always change the size of the frame later when you're through working on the drawing.

Be sure to click a newly inserted empty frame only once when you want to select the frame before you choose the Frame Drawing command. If you double-click an empty frame you've just inserted, Amí Professional assumes you want to add text to the frame, so the frame handles become gray and the Drawing command is not available on the Frame menu. Once you've selected the frame and chosen the Frame Drawing command, Amí Professional associates that frame with drawing (whether or not you've drawn anything in it). From then on, you can double-click the frame and Amí Professional automatically displays the drawing tools for your use.

Using the Drawing Tools

Here's what the drawing tools do:

Tool	Description
Arrow	Selects an object or a group of objects. Point to the object you want and click.
Hand	Moves the entire drawing within the frame.
Line	Draws a straight line. Hold down the mouse button and drag.
Constrained Line (cross)	Draws a horizontal, vertical, or 45-degree line. Hold down the mouse button and drag.
Polyline (zigzag)	Draws connecting lines. Hold down the mouse button and drag first line, then release button, point and click to draw line from end point to mouse pointer.

Polygon	Draws a complete object made of lines you connect. Hold down the mouse button and drag first line, then release button, point and click to draw line from end point to mouse pointer. To complete the object, point to beginning point and click, or choose a new tool and let Amí Professional complete the object for you.
Rectangle	Draws a rectangle. Point to where you want one corner to appear, hold down mouse button, and drag.
Square	Draws a square. Point to where you want one corner of square to appear, hold down mouse button, and drag.
Rounded Rectangle	Draws a rectangle with rounded corners. Point to where you want one corner to appear, then hold down mouse button and drag.
Rounded Square	Draws a square with rounded corners. Point to where you want one corner to appear, hold down mouse button, and drag.
Ellipse	Draws an ellipse. Point to where you want one edge of ellipse to appear, hold down mouse button, and drag.
Circle	Draws a circle. Point to where you want one edge of the circle to appear, hold down the mouse button, and drag.
Arc	Draws an arc. Point to one end of line, then drag to other end. To change direction of curve, see Moving Objects later in this chapter.
Text	Types text. Double-click to display dialog box so you can choose new font, size, or color; click drawing once to set the position and type the text in the dialog box that appears.

Line Style box	Displays current line style. Double-click to display dialog box so you can choose new line thickness and color.
Pattern box	Displays current fill pattern. Double-click to display dialog box so you can choose a new pattern and color.

Selecting an Object You've Drawn

Each line or shape that you draw in a frame is an independent object that you can select, drag to a new position, change colors, patterns, and line styles, resize, cut, or copy. Just as in working with text outside of frames, the first step in changing an object is to select it.

To select an object:

- If the frame is already selected and the drawing tools are displayed, click the arrow tool, then click the object. Otherwise, double-click the frame first, then click the arrow tool and object.

Black square "handles" appear around a selected object, as shown in Figure 13-3.

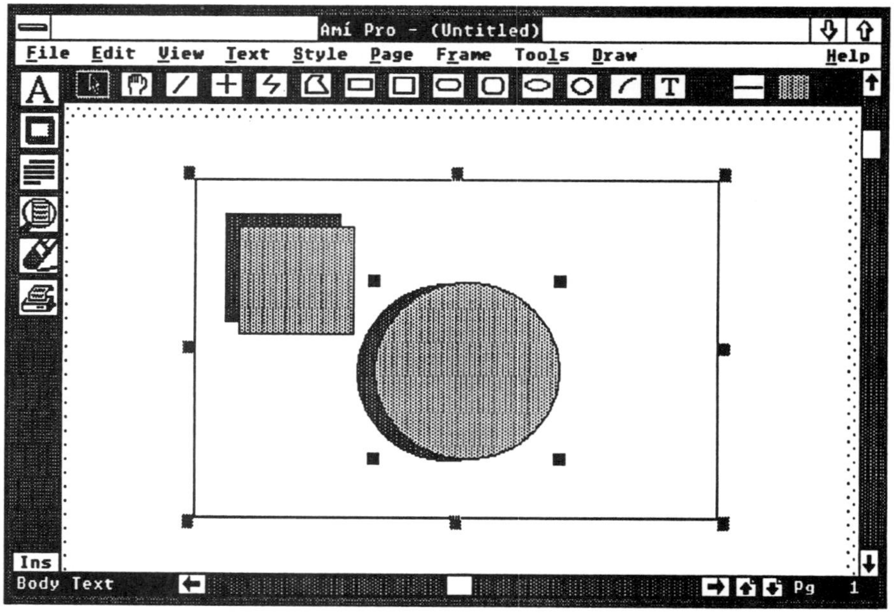

Figure 13-3 When you select an object in a drawing, handles appear around it.

To select more than one object in the drawing:

- Click the first object, then hold down the **Shift** key and click others.

or

- Choose the arrow tool, position the arrow pointer where you want one corner of a selection rectangle to be, then hold down the left mouse button and drag out the selection rectangle. All objects within the rectangle are selected.

To select all objects in the drawing:

- Choose the Draw Select All command.

Changing Line Style, Colors, or Fill Patterns

When you draw an object, Amí Professional outlines the object using the current line style, which appears in the line style box.

To change the line thickness or color:

1. Double-click the line style box.

   or

   Choose the Draw Line Style command.

   Amí Professional displays the dialog box shown in Figure 13–4.

2. Select a new line thickness from the list, select a color from the color bar, then click OK or press **Enter**.

You can fill any object you draw with solid colors or colored patterns. The current pattern appears in the fill pattern box.

To change the fill pattern or color:

1. Double-click the fill pattern box.

   or

   Choose the Draw Fill Pattern command.

2. Select a new pattern from the Fill Pattern list, scrolling as necessary. Select Solid if you want a solid color or Transparent if you don't want a pattern or color.

3. To set colors, select the foreground color from the color bar to color the pattern, then select the background color to color the background of the object. By combining foreground and background colors and

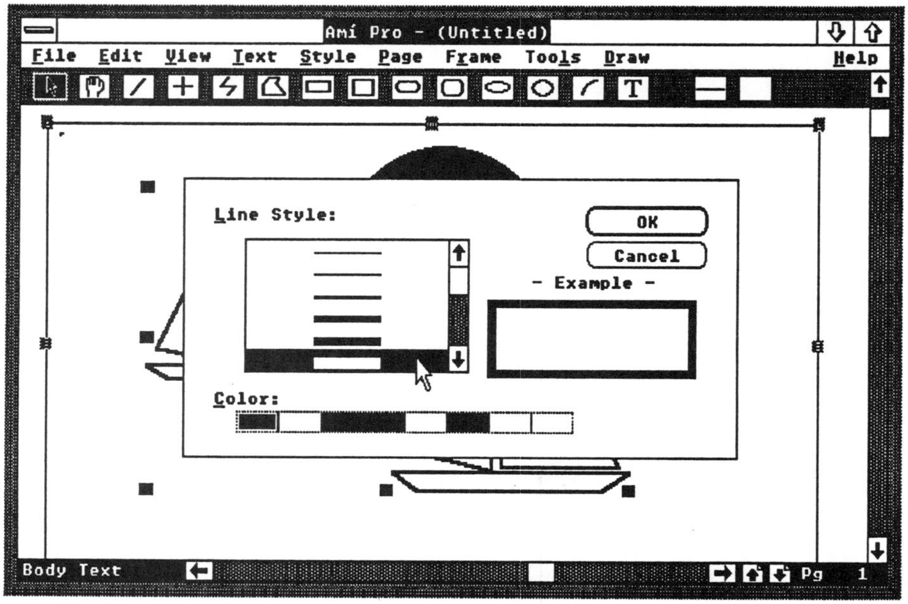

Figure 13–4 Choosing a new line style.

choosing different patterns, you can create a wide variety of colors. Figure 13–5 illustrates setting a new color and fill pattern.

4. Click OK or press **Enter**. Amí Professional uses the line style and fill pattern to draw all new objects.

If you want to apply a new line style or fill pattern to an object you've already drawn:

1. Click on the object to select it. Square handles should appear around the object.
2. Choose the Draw Apply Line & Fill command.

Moving Objects

To move objects:

1. Select the object(s).
2. Hold down the left mouse button and drag to a new position.

If you've used the arc tool to draw an arc and you want to flip it, reversing the direction of its curve:

1. Select the arc.

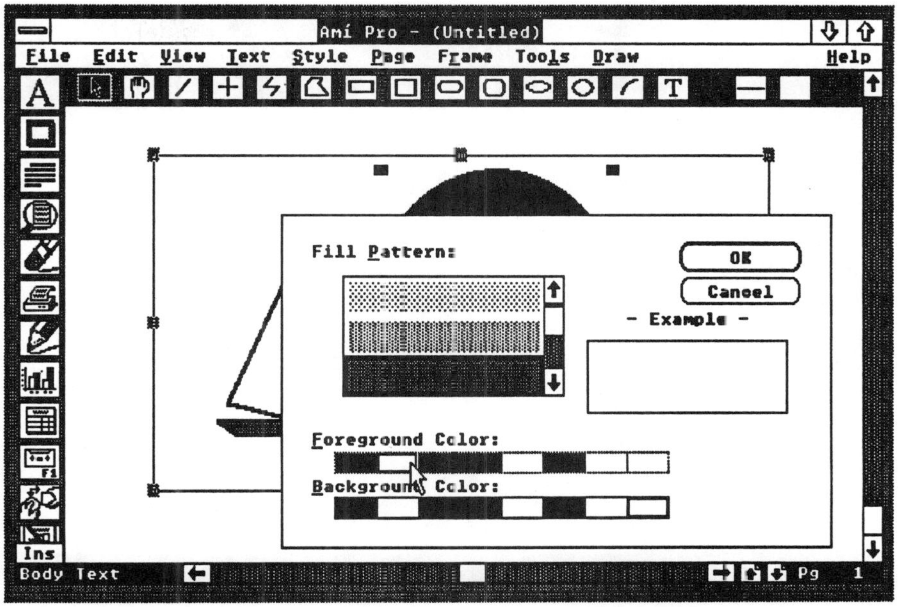

Figure 13–5 Choosing a new fill pattern and color.

2. Point to one of the middle handles (not a corner handle) and double-click the left mouse button.

Using a Grid

If you want your objects to line up in some way, you can use a grid to align your objects. You can make the grid display invisible or visible. Once you've chosen a grid format, Amí Professional displays it every time you draw until you turn the grid off or change it.

To add or remove a grid:

1. Choose the Draw Grid Settings command. Amí Professional displays the dialog box shown in Figure 13–6.

2. Choose a Fine, Medium, or Coarse grid in the Grid Settings box; choose None if you want to remove a grid.

3. If you want to display grid lines, choose Dotted Lines or Dots at Intersect in the Grid Line box. If you choose a grid in the Grid Settings box but don't display grid lines, the grid is still there—it's just invisible.

4. Click OK or press **Enter**.

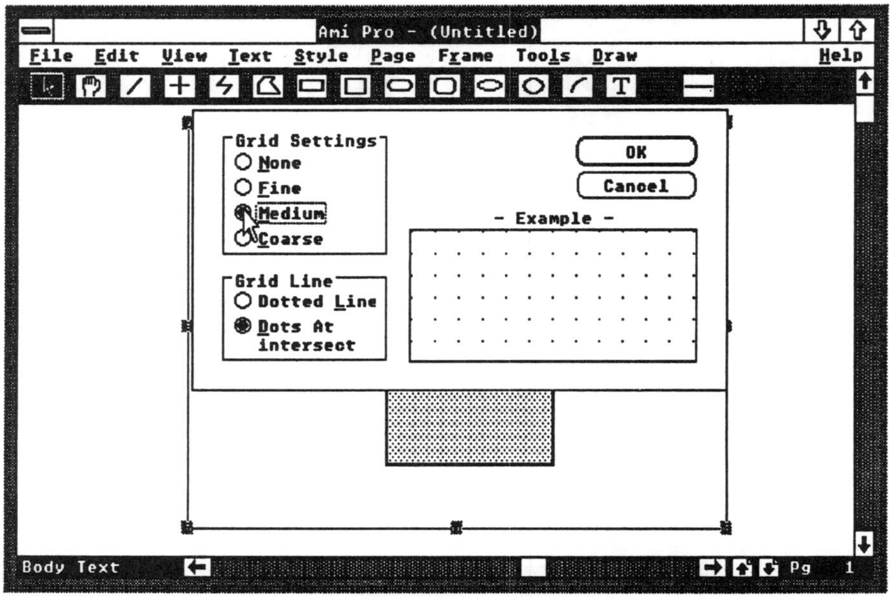

Figure 13–6 Turning on a grid.

To confine objects to grid lines:

□ Choose the Draw Snap To command.

This command aligns all new objects you draw with grid lines. If you move objects when the Draw Snap To command is on, the objects are confined to moving along grid lines. To allow objects to move freely, choose the Draw Snap To command again to turn the feature off.

Adding Text to a Drawing

When you add text to a drawing, it becomes a separate object that you can move around or group with other objects. To add text to your drawing:

1. Double-click the Text tool icon (the T in the icon bar) to display the dialog box shown in Figure 13–7.
2. Select a face (font), point size, or color. If you select a stroke screen font (such as Roman, Modern, or Script), you can also use the Rotate button to rotate the font if you like. Each click rotates the text 45 degrees.
3. When the example looks the way you want, click OK or press **Enter** to save the font settings.

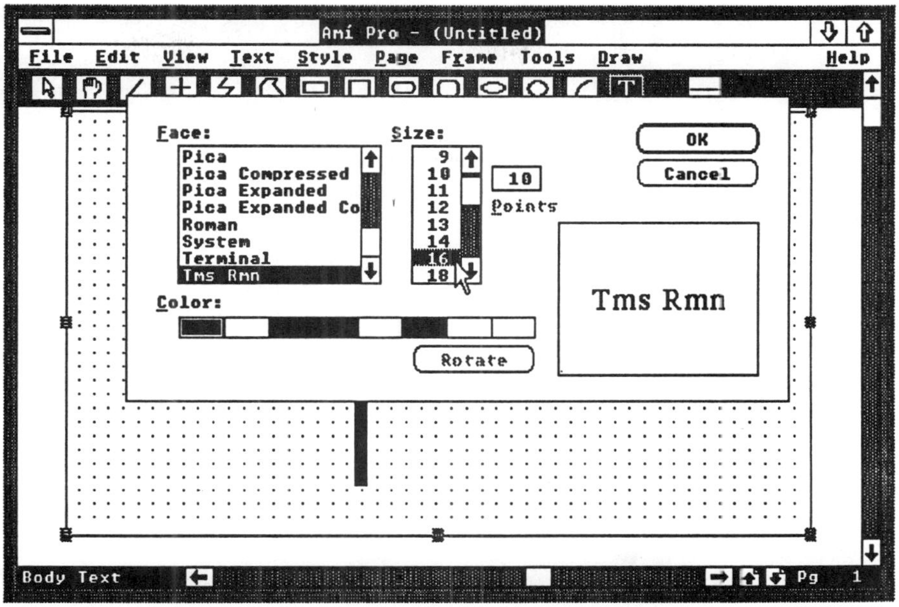

Figure 13–7 Selecting a new typeface (font) and point size for text in a drawing.

4. Click the position where you want the text to begin. A dialog box like the one in Figure 13–8 appears.

5. Type the text in the dialog box, then press **Enter** to add the text to the drawing.

If you want to continue to use the same font settings to add text in different locations, you can just click the text tool once, then skip to step 4 in this procedure.

Editing Text

If the text you added isn't in quite the right spot, remember that the text is an object now, so you can move it. Just click on the arrow tool, then point to the center of the text and drag it wherever you want.

If the text is not spelled correctly or you want to add or delete characters:

1. Click the text tool (the T in the icon bar) if necessary.

2. Position the mouse pointer on top of the text, then press and hold the left mouse button until the text dialog box appears.

3. Edit the text in the dialog box as necessary, then click OK or press **Enter**.

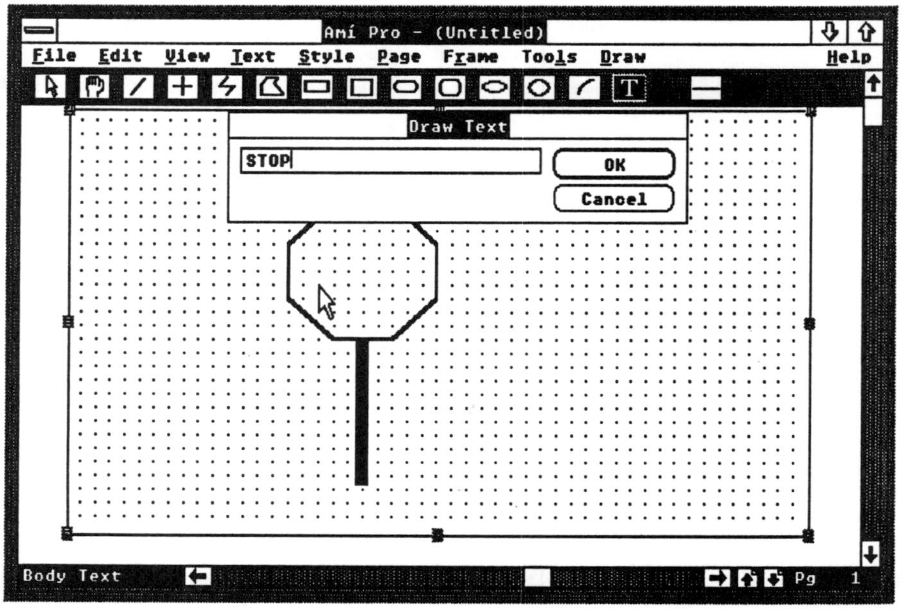

Figure 13-8 Adding text to a drawing.

If you want to change the font type, point size, or color of the text, or rotate the text, do this:

1. Select the text with the arrow tool.
2. Choose the Text Font command.
3. In the dialog box, choose a new font, point size, or color.
4. If you chose a stroke screen font (such as Roman, Modern, or Script) in the list, you can click the Rotate button to rotate the font. Each click rotates the text 45 degrees.
5. When the example looks the way you want, click OK or press **Enter** to redraw the text.

Layering Objects

Because each shape you draw is a separate object in the frame, you can layer objects by dragging one on top of another. Say, for example, you've drawn an orange sun in one area, and in another spot you've drawn a sailboat. You can drag the sailboat on top of the sun, making it look like the boat is sailing into the sunset. If the boat is too big in comparison to the sun, you can always make the boat smaller or make the sun bigger by resizing them, as explained in the next discussion. To make sure the two objects would always stay together, you could group them, as explained later in this chapter.

You can determine which objects appear on top with the Bring to Front and Send to Back commands on the Draw menu. So, if it's more convenient to drag the sun on top of the sailboat, you could just select the sun and choose the Send to Back command to put the sun behind the sailboat. Figure 13–9 shows layered objects.

Changing the Size of Objects

Changing the size of an object is similar to changing the size of a frame or of an imported graphic.

To change the size of an object:

1. Select the object. Black handles appear around it.
2. Point to a handle, hold down the left mouse button, and drag the outline to a new size.
3. When you release the mouse button, Amí Professional draws the object in the new size. Figure 13–10 illustrates changing the size of a drawn object.

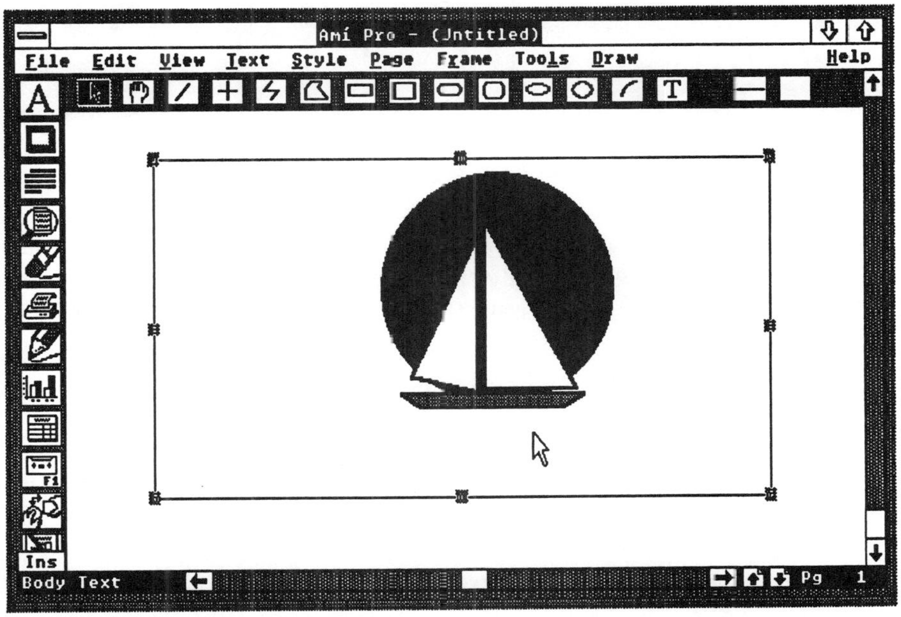

Figure 13–9
You can layer objects in Amí Professional's drawings. This drawing shows three grouped objects (two sails and the boat) on top of another object (the sun).

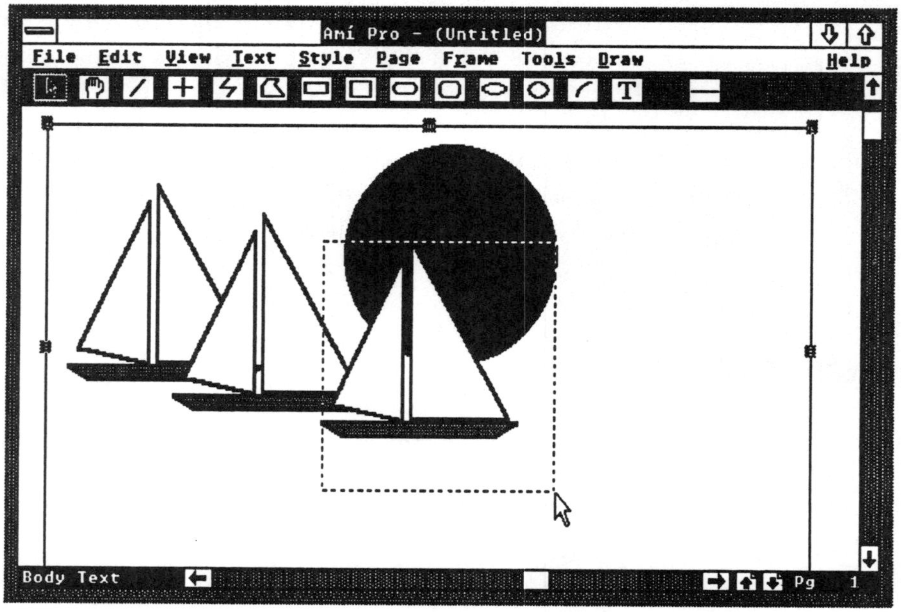

Figure 13-10 Changing the size of a drawn object.

Helpful Hint

Although you can use the mouse to enlarge and shrink text as just described, the results may not be satisfactory. To enlarge or shrink text, it's usually better to select the original text, then use the Text Font command to choose a new point size.

Grouping Objects

Because each shape that you draw in a frame is a separate object, sometimes you'll need to draw several shapes to create a complete object. For example, to draw a sailboat, you might need to make the sail and the boat two separate shapes with two different fill patterns. However, you obviously want to keep these two objects together, so you'll want to group them. Grouping links objects—as long as they're grouped, they move together and change size together, remaining proportional to each other.

To group objects:

1. Hold down the **Shift** key and click on all the objects you want to group. You'll see handles appear around each object as you click it, as shown in Figure 13-11.

   or

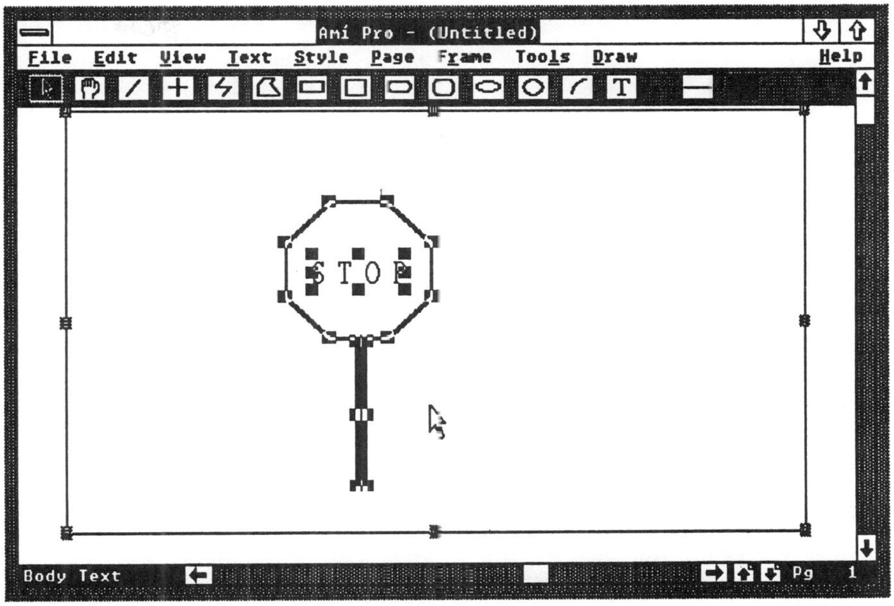

Figure 13-11 Selecting objects in preparation for grouping them.

Click the arrow tool, then hold down the mouse button and drag out a selection rectangle around the objects you want to select.

or

If you want to group all the objects in the drawing, choose the Draw Select All command.

2. Choose the Draw Group command. The handles around individual objects will disappear, and handles will appear around the entire group.

If you later decide to change or move one object in a group, you have to ungroup the objects first. You can regroup them again, if necessary. The Group command on the Draw menu is a toggle command, so to ungroup objects, just select the group, then choose the Group command again.

Cutting, Copying, and Pasting Objects

You can use the Cut, Copy, and Paste commands on the Edit menu to delete, copy, or insert objects into your drawing. This is especially handy when you want to copy or move a shape or a group of shapes from one frame to another. You can also use the Delete key to erase an object without putting it into the Clipboard.

To cut, copy, or paste objects:

1. Select the object(s).
2. Choose the Cut or Copy command from the Edit menu.
3. Move the cursor to a new place or to a different frame, then choose the Paste command to insert the object(s).

Changing the Size or Position of the Entire Drawing

You can move or change the size of the drawing within the frame. This isn't the same as moving or changing the size of a frame, which is described in Chapter 12.

To move the drawing:

1. Click the Hand tool.
2. Position the mouse pointer on the drawing, hold down the left mouse button, and drag the drawing around in the frame, as shown in Figure 13–12.

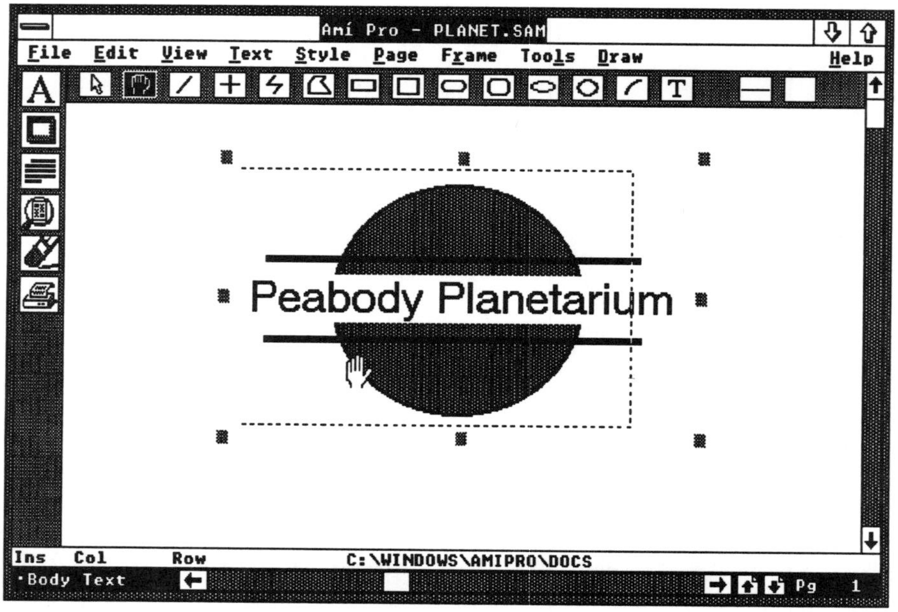

Figure 13–12 Moving a drawing in a frame.

To change the size of the drawing:

1. Choose the Frame Graphics Scaling command.
2. Choose options in the dialog box, then click OK or press **Enter**.

Changing the size of a graphic is described in more detail in Chapter 12.

Saving a Drawing in a Separate File

You might want to save your drawing in a file by itself as well as with your document. Once you save a drawing in a separate file, you can reuse it for different documents. You can also draw symbols, save them as drawings, then use them in symbol charts.

To save a drawing in a separate file:

1. Select the drawing frame.
2. Choose the File Save As Drawing command.
3. Type a new file name for your drawing in the dialog box. You can omit a file extension, letting Amí Professional add it for you, or you can add the .SDW extension (the only extension Amí Professional recognizes for drawing files).
4. Click OK or press **Enter** to save the drawing.

Using Existing Drawings in Frames

Amí Professional comes with a variety of drawings, all of which are saved in files with .SDW extensions. You can insert these drawings (as well as any drawings you've saved) into frames, then modify them until you have just the result you want.

You can even put several drawings together in the same frame to create a more elaborate drawing. For example, if you've saved a city silhouette in one drawing and saved a harbor scene in another, you could put the city in the background of the harbor by putting both drawings in the same frame. Here's how it works:

1. Select the frame to which you want to add a drawing. (If there's no drawing in the frame yet, next choose the Frame Drawing command to let the program know you want to attach a drawing to the frame.)

2. Choose the File Append Drawing command.
3. In the dialog box, select the name of the drawing (.SDW) file you want to put into the frame, then click OK or press **Enter**. If necessary, type or edit the path name in the text box, press **Enter** to display a new list, then select the file you want. For example, if you wanted to switch from the \AMIPRO\DOCS directory (where Amí Professional normally looks for documents) to the \AMIPRO directory (where Amí Professional probably installed the drawing files), you would change \AMIPRO\DOCS*.SDW to \AMIPRO*.SDW.
4. Repeat steps 2 and 3 to add all the drawings you want to the frame.
5. Reposition, resize, delete, and add objects within the frame until you have the effect you want.

Helpful Hints

If you add a drawing, change the size of a drawn object, or paste an object into a frame, sooner or later you're bound to see not a drawing, but gray rectangles or weird-looking scribbles. This is known as *greeking,* and it happens when the frame is too small to display the object or drawing or when the object is too small for Amí Professional to display. You can make the frame bigger. You might also try using the Frame Graphics Scaling command to make the drawing fit in the frame or to choose a new percentage of the original size. If it prints out all right but you need to see it on the screen, use enlarged view.

CREATING CHARTS

When you want to add a chart to your document, you don't have to go to another program to do it. You can create many types of charts using Amí Professional. Figure 13–13 shows side-by-side frames containing two types of charts created from the same data.

Entering Data for a Chart

You can enter the data for a chart in two ways: by copying it from an Amí Professional document or from another Windows application to the Windows Clipboard, or by typing the data in the Charting Data window. Generally speaking, it's easier to copy the data to the Clipboard. You can

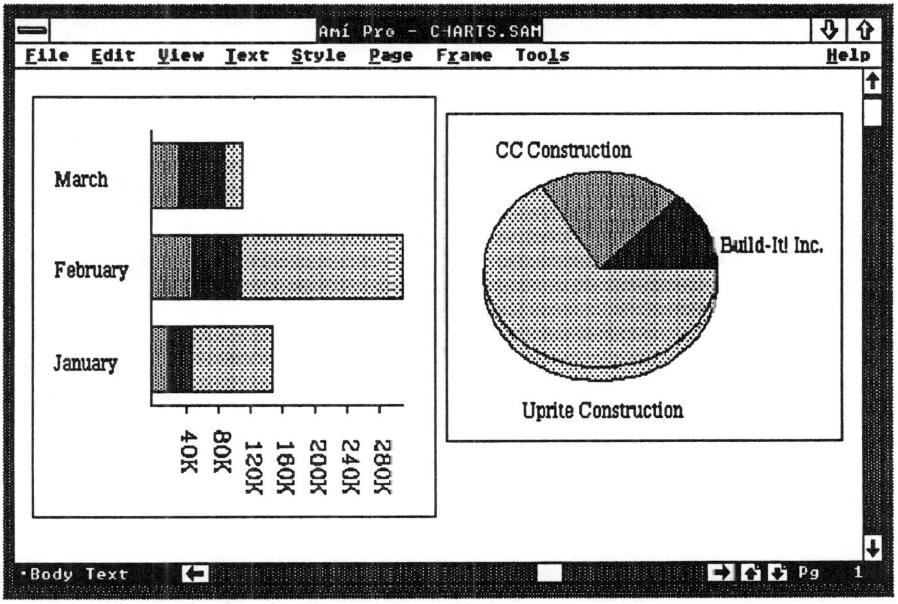

Figure 13–13 A bar chart and a 3-D pie chart.

always use the Charting Data window to modify the data later if you need to. The data must conform to the following rules:

- The data can consist of no more than 16 columns and 16 rows.
- The data must not contain negative numbers.
- Data items must be separated by one or more spaces or by tabs. (Amí Professional automatically uses tabs to separate data copied from Microsoft Excel.)
- If you want to label the data in the chart, put the labels in the first row or column.

Following are some examples of data formats that work well with Amí Professional charting. For example, to compare the expenses for the first quarter of two different years in a column chart, you might use data in this format:

January	February	March
$12,000	$13,500	$15,000
$15,500	$14,500	$17,900

A pie chart displays only one data set (one column or row of numbers).

To compare percentages of spending in a pie chart, you might organize data like this:

Marketing	66,000
Development	80,590
Manufacturing	15,000

The following format works for any type of chart except a pie chart (and can be adapted for a pie chart with the Flip Data option):

Lions	Cheetahs	Hyenas
79	45	65

Creating a Chart by Copying Data to the Clipboard

When you copy data to the Clipboard for an Amí Professional chart, you can either type the data in a document, then copy or cut it, or copy data by selecting data in another Windows application such as Excel. The copied data loses its formatting (bold, underlining, italic, and so on) when the data is used for charting.

To create a chart by copying the data to the Windows Clipboard:

1. Do one of the following:
   - Type the data you want to put in a chart, separating the columns with tabs or spaces, then select the data.

   or

   - Select the data in another Windows application (for example, select up to 16 rows and columns in Microsoft Excel).
2. Choose the Edit Copy command to make a copy or choose the Edit Cut command to delete the data and put it in the Clipboard. Then switch to Amí Professional if necessary.
3. In your Amí Professional document, select the frame you want to draw a chart in. (If necessary, add a frame first—all charts must be in a frame.)
4. Choose the Frame Charting command. Amí Professional displays the dialog box shown in Figure 13–14. The sample charts in the dialog box change when you choose options, so you can see what your chart will look like before creating it.
5. Choose a chart type: Column, Line, Pie, Bar, Axis, or Symbol. Amí Professional displays pictures of variations of that type. (If chart types

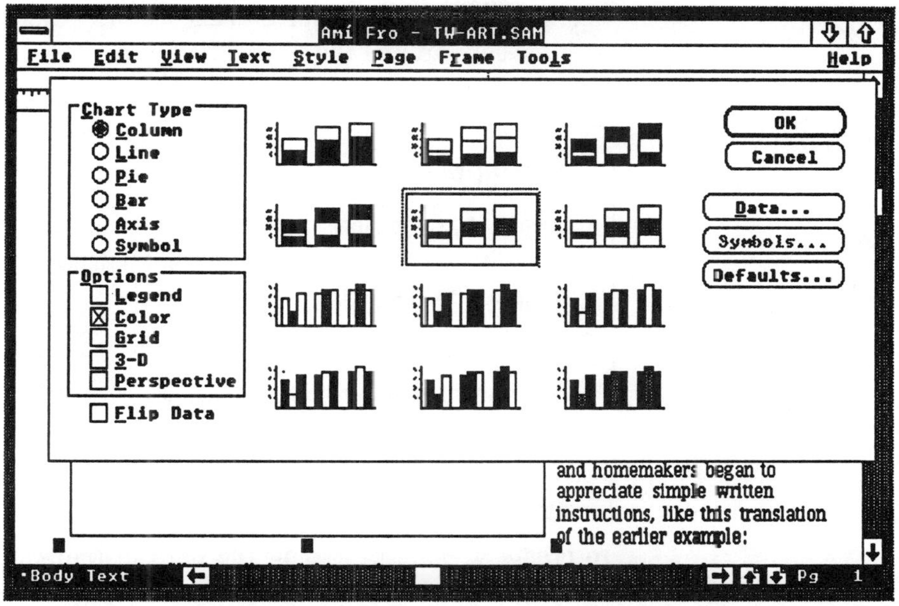

Figure 13-14 The Frame Charting dialog box.

are grayed, there's no data in the Clipboard. In that case, choose Cancel to close the dialog box, then go back and copy the data.)

6. Choose from the following options in the Options box:

Option	**Description**
Legend	Adds a legend box.
Color	Draws charts in color. When Color is turned off, charts are drawn in black and white using different patterns.
Grid	Adds a grid to the background of the chart.
3-D	Makes charts look three dimensional by adding depth to chart shapes.
Perspective	Makes charts look three dimensional by displaying all chart shapes as originating from the same distant point.

Amí Professional redraws the chart pictures as necessary to reflect your choices.

7. Click one of the pictures to choose the variation you want. An outline appears around the picture.

8. Choose OK or press **Enter** to draw the chart.

> **Helpful Hint**
>
> If chart data and labels don't come out quite right, the data may not be in the order Amí Professional expects. Many times you can do the following to quickly fix the problem:
>
> 1. Choose the Frame Charting command again.
> 2. Turn on the Flip Data option.
> 3. Click OK to redraw the chart.

Creating a Chart by Entering Data in the Data Window

To create a chart by typing the data in the Amí Professional Charting Data window:

1. In your Amí Professional document, select the frame you want to draw a chart in. (If necessary, add a frame first—all charts must be in a frame.)

2. Choose the Frame Charting command. Amí Professional displays the dialog box shown in Figure 13–14, but the chart types will be grayed.

3. Click the Data button. Amí Professional opens the data window.

4. Type the data as shown in Figure 13–15, separating items with spaces *(not tabs)* and pressing the **Down arrow** key *(not the Enter key)* at the end of each row. Then click OK to return to the Charting dialog box.

5. Choose a chart type: Column, Line, Pie, Bar, Axis, or Symbol. Amí Professional displays pictures of variations of that type.

6. Choose from the following options in the Options box:

Option	**Description**
Legend	Adds a legend box.
Color	Draws charts in color. When Color is turned off, charts are drawn in black and white using different patterns.
Grid	Adds a grid to the background of the chart.

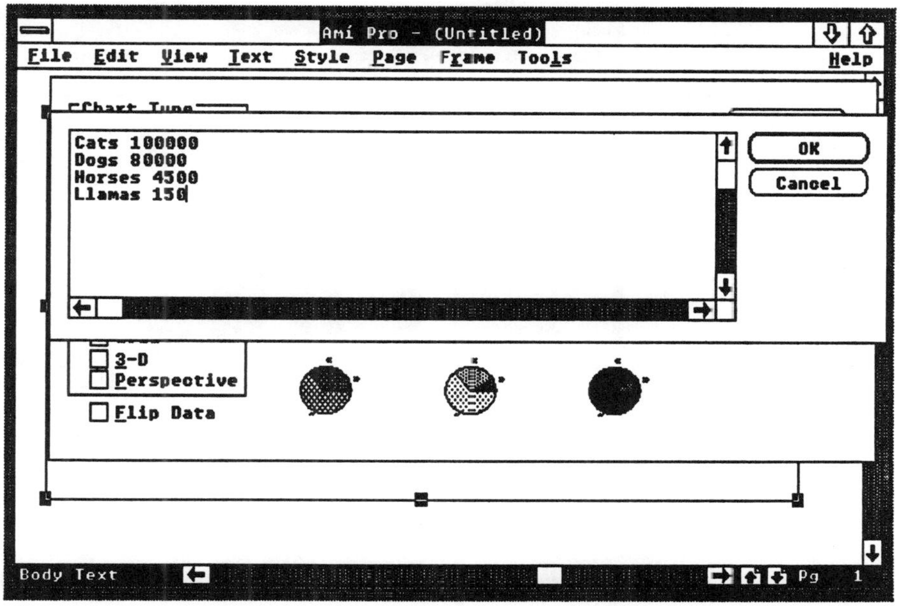

Figure 13–15 Typing data in the Charting Data window. You must press the Spacebar to separate items and press the Down arrow key to move down to the next row.

3-D	Makes charts look three dimensional by adding depth to chart shapes.
Perspective	Makes charts look three dimensional by displaying all chart shapes as originating from the same distant point.

7. Click one of the pictures to choose the variation you want. An outline appears around the picture.

8. Choose OK or press **Enter** to draw the chart.

Adding Text and Lines to a Chart

You can use the drawing tools to add text and lines to a chart. Figure 13–16 shows a chart to which a title and callouts have been added with the drawing tools. You can also put text in separate frames and position them on top of the chart frame—this enables you to use special formatting that you can't apply to text you draw with the drawing tool. See Creating Your Own Drawings earlier in this chapter for more information about drawing tools, and see Chapter 12 for more information about working with text in separate frames.

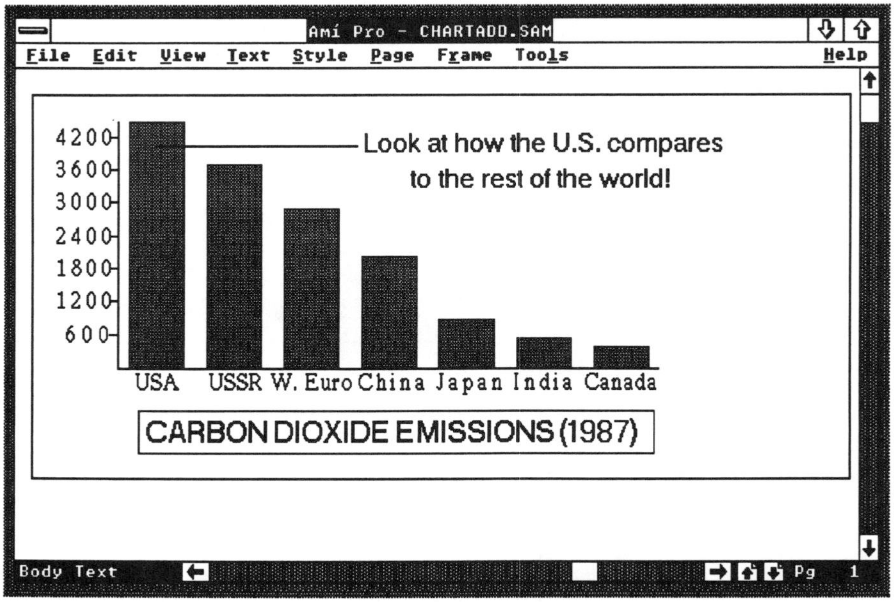

Figure 13-16
A chart with a title and a callout added with the drawing tools.

Speed Tip

You can quickly display the drawing tools this way:

- Double-click the chart.

Editing Chart Data

If you need to make extensive changes to chart data, you may find it easier to delete the chart, work on the data in your document, then create a new chart. However, if you just need to add a new row or column or change a figure, you can easily edit the chart data this way:

1. Select the frame.
2. Choose the Frame Charting command.
3. Click the Data button.
4. Make changes to the data in the window, pressing the **Spacebar** in between items and pressing the **Down arrow** key to move down to the next row.
5. Click OK to save the changes and return to the Charting dialog box.

6. Choose any other options you want, then click OK or press **Enter** to draw the chart.

Helpful Hint

Be sure to click the frame only once when you want to select the chart before you choose the Frame Charting commands. If you double-click the frame, the frame handles become gray, the drawing tools appear, and the Charting command becomes unavailable on the Frame menu.

Changing the Size of a Chart

To change the size of a chart within a frame:

1. Select the frame containing the chart.
2. Choose the Graphics Scaling command.
3. Type or select a new percentage in the running list box, or choose other options to change the size. For example, if you wanted to make the chart 75 percent of the original size (25 percent smaller, in other words), you'd type 75 in the running list box.
4. Click OK or press **Enter**.

Moving a Chart Within a Frame

To move a chart within the frame:

1. Double-click the frame containing the chart. Amí Professional adds the drawing tools and the Draw menu to the screen.
2. Select the Hand tool.
3. Position the hand pointer over the chart, then hold down the left mouse button and drag the chart to a new position in the frame.

Changing Parts of a Chart

Just as in a drawing, each part of a chart is a separate object that you can move and change with the drawing tools and commands. For example, you could drag a section of a pie chart out of the circle to create an exploded pie chart, as shown in Figure 13–17, or you could change the pattern or color of a chart section to make it stand out.

To change any part of a chart:

1. If the drawing tools are not displayed, double-click the frame containing the chart. Amí Professional adds the drawing tools and the Draw menu to the screen.

2. Click the part of the chart you want to change (for example, a column, a pie slice, or a label) to display handles around the selected part. (If objects are small and close together, it may be difficult to select the object you want. Try switching to enlarged view, then use the arrow drawing tool to drag a selection rectangle around the part.)

3. Use the drawing tools and Draw menu commands to change the selection as desired. You might want to choose a new color, pattern, or line style. To move a part, select the arrow tool, position it over the part, then drag the part to a new position.

Choosing New Colors, Patterns, or Line Thicknesses for Data Sets

Although Amí Professional offers several choices of colors, patterns, and line thicknesses for your charts, you can also assign your own favorite

Figure 13–17 Creating an exploded pie chart by dragging a section of a chart to a new position.

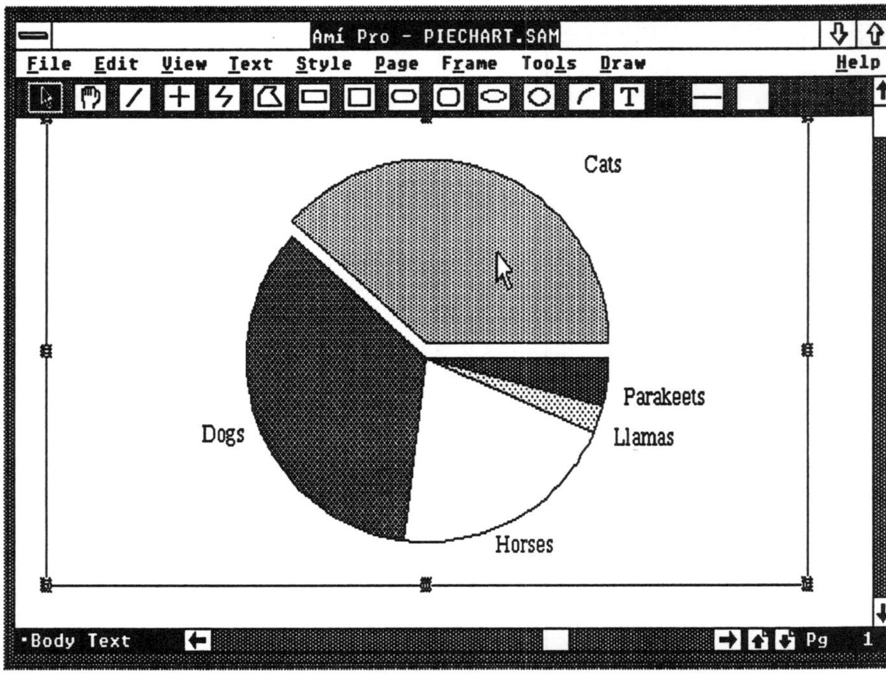

options to data sets in a few selected charts—usually, the topmost and next-to-the-last chart variations in the first column of the Frame Charting dialog box, but this varies depending on chart type. Here's how:

1. Click the frame once to select it. (If you accidentally double-click the frame, click outside of the frame to make the drawing tools disappear, then click the frame once to select it.)

2. Choose Frame Charting. Be sure that the topmost or next-to-the-last chart in the first column of variations is selected.

3. Click the Defaults button in the dialog box to display a new dialog box.

4. Click the number representing the data set you want to set colors or line styles for. For example, to set options for the first column of figures (the first data set) in a chart, click 1 at the left of the dialog box.

5. Click the Color button to display the dialog box shown in Figure 13–18, then change the patterns and colors and click OK.

6. Click the Line button to display a new dialog box, then choose a new line thickness and color and click OK.

Figure 13–18
Changing the default colors for the first data set in a chart.

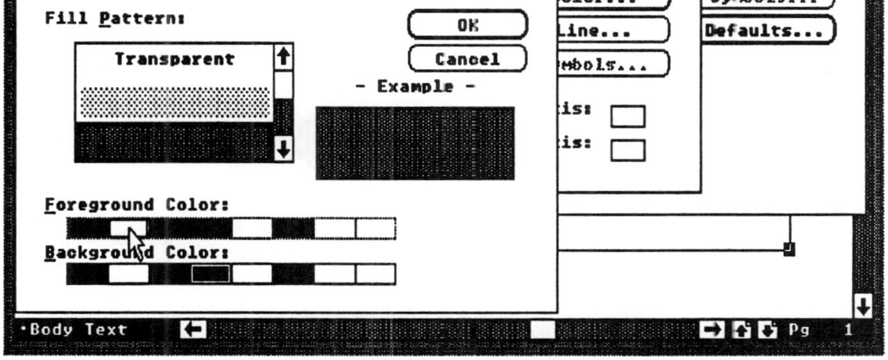

7. Repeat steps 4 through 6 as desired to set colors for all your data sets.
8. If you want to set a new color or line weight for the X axis line, click the X Axis box in the lower right corner, click the Line button and choose the options you want in the dialog box, then click OK.
9. If you want to set a new color or line weight for the Y axis line, click the Y Axis box in the lower right corner, click the Line button and choose the options you want in the dialog box, then click OK.
10. Click OK or press **Enter**.

Choosing New Symbols for Axis or Symbol Charts

When you choose an axis chart or a symbol chart, you can choose from a number of variations. The Amí Professional package contains over 100 drawing files from which you can use symbols, or you can draw and save your own symbols for reuse. For example, if you're charting sales of radial tires, you could draw a tire, save the drawing, then use the tire as the symbol in a symbol chart, stacking up tires to graphically demonstrate how many were sold. For more information about creating and saving drawings, see the first part of this chapter.

Note: If you want to create your own drawing to use as a symbol in a chart, choose the Graphics Sizing command and use the Fit in Frame option to resize the drawing before you save it and import it into a chart.

To choose a different symbol for an axis or symbol chart:

1. Select the frame.
2. Choose Frame Charting and select an Axis or Symbol chart type if necessary.
3. Click the Symbols button in the dialog box. Amí Professional displays the dialog box shown in Figure 13–19.
4. Click the number representing the data set you want to choose a new symbol for. For example, to choose a symbol for the first column of figures (the first data set) in a chart, click 1 at the left of the dialog box.
5. Click the Symbols button to display another dialog box, type or select the name of the drawing file that contains the symbol you want to use, then click OK. If you want your symbols to be in color, you must draw them originally in color.

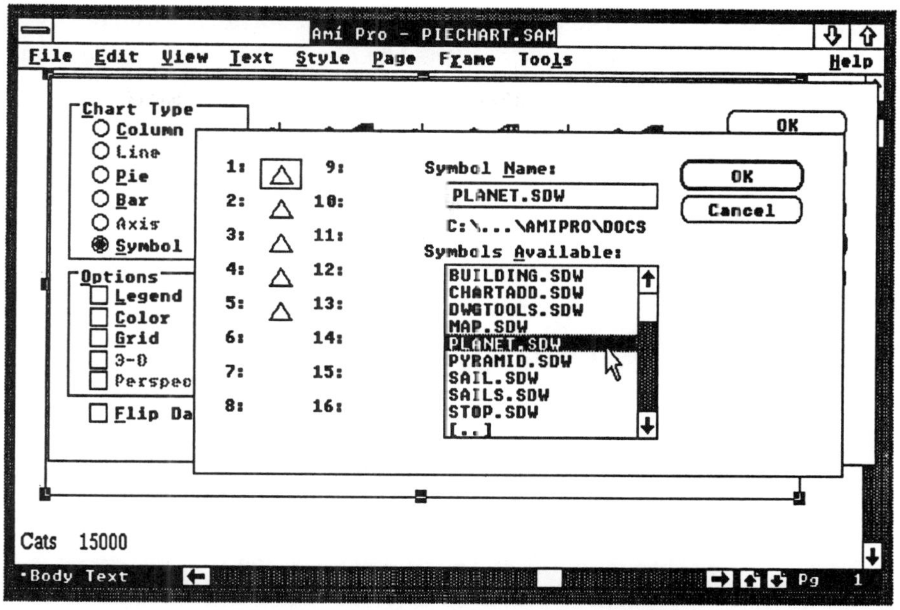

Figure 13-19 Choosing a drawing file to use as a symbol in a symbol chart.

6. Repeat steps 4 and 5 to specify new symbols for more data sets as necessary, then choose OK or press **Enter** to draw the new chart.

Using a Linked Chart from Another Windows File

You can use Dynamic Data Exchange (DDE) to paste in a chart linked to another Windows application such as Microsoft Excel. Linking enables you to update information in your document when the data in the other file changes. You might want to create a report in Amí Professional that includes a chart linked to an Excel file, for example, so you could easily update the information in your report when the Excel file changes.

One advantage of linking chart data rather than simply copying a chart is that your chart will appear in color. However, there is a disadvantage to linking, too. To update a linked chart, both Amí Professional and the original charting application must be open, so linking requires a lot of memory.

Creating the Link

To create a DDE link, you copy the other program's data to the Clipboard, then use the Amí Professional Edit Paste Link command to insert the data into a frame. The other Windows application must support DDE for this process to work; if the Edit Paste Link command is grayed after you've copied data to the Clipboard, the other application doesn't support DDE.

To paste in a linked chart:

1. Open the other Windows file and display the chart.

2. Copy the chart to the Clipboard.

3. Start Amí Professional and open the file you want to paste the information into.

4. Select the frame, then choose the Edit Paste Link command to paste in the data and create the DDE link.

Amí Professional updates linked information when you open the document. If the other application isn't running at the time, you'll see a message asking if it's okay to start that program to get the latest information from the original file. You may decide later either to deactivate the link so that it updates only when you say so or to remove the link altogether.

Managing Linked Charts

If you used the Edit Paste Link command as just described, Amí Professional saves the path name to the information you pasted in, creating a link from your document file to the original file that contained the information. The program uses the path name to find the original file, so if you change the file's location, Amí Professional won't be able to find the other file. If you want to check whether there's linked information in a file, deactivate or break a link, or update linked information, you can use the File Links command this way:

1. Choose the File Links command.

2. In the dialog box, select the link (the name of the original application and path name to the linked file) that you want to affect. (If the list is blank, there are no files linked to the active document.)

3. Click one of the following buttons:

Click	**To**
Update	Update the link, using the path name to get the latest information from the original file. This option is normally used with "deactivated" (nonautomatic) links.

Deactivate	Keep track of the path to the original file, but update the link only when you want to (using the Update button in this dialog box).
Unlink	Destroy the link and erase the path name from the dialog box. This option frees the space taken up by the link information.

4. Repeat steps 2 and 3 to change more links as necessary. When you're ready to close the dialog box, click Cancel.

14

Tabs and Tables

When you want to format text in columns and rows, you have two choices: you can set tabs or create a table. This chapter shows you how to do both.

SETTING TABS

Using tabs used to be the only way to format text in rows and columns in word-processing programs. It was always a painful process to set them up and even worse to edit tabular material. Amí Professional's table feature now makes column-and-row formatting quick and easy. You can learn more about tables in Using Tables later in this chapter.

Although tables are now the easiest way to create rows and columns, there are still times when you'll want to use a tab setting. For example, you can always press the **Tab** key to quickly indent a line of text. You can also use tabs to set positions for text in headers or footers.

There are four types of tabs, as shown in Figure 14–1: left-aligned tabs, right-aligned tabs, centered tabs, and numeric tabs, which align numbers on their decimal points.

The space before a tab is normally just blank, but you can also fill the space with *leader characters.* Leader characters can be periods, hyphens, or underscore characters. Figure 14–2 shows a list in which the page numbers are positioned with a right-aligned tab and preceded by period leader characters.

Figure 14–1
Types of tabs.

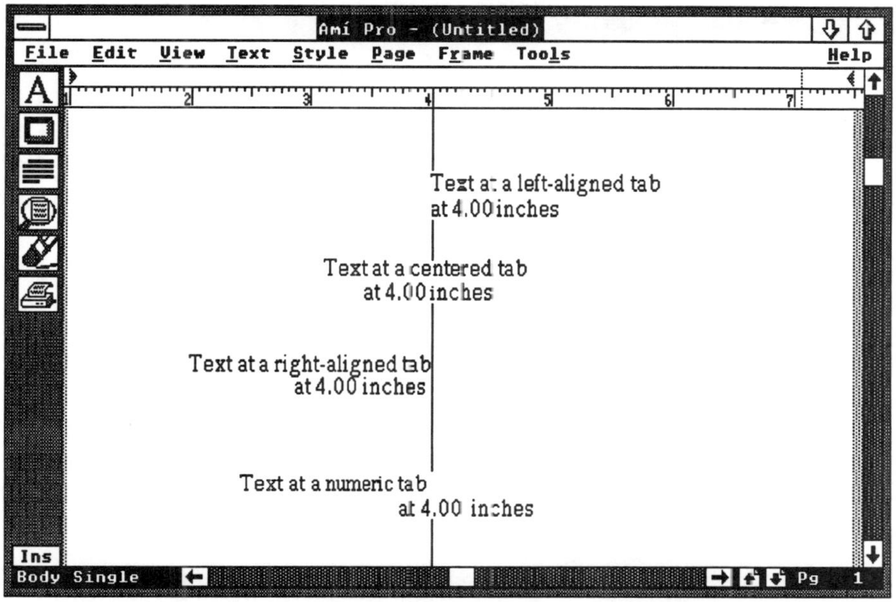

Figure 14–2
The page numbers in this list are positioned by a right-aligned tab and preceded by period leader characters.

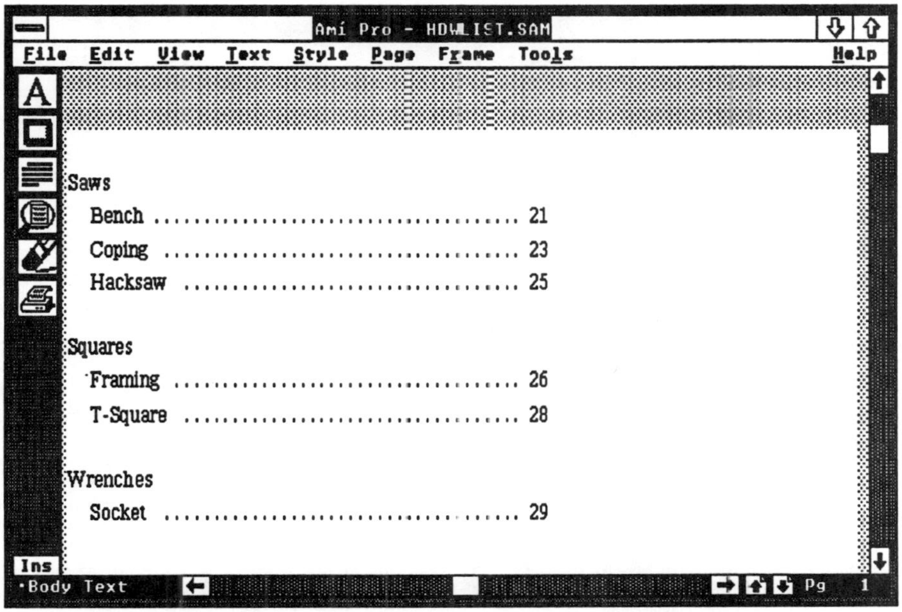

Changing the Tab Settings for the Entire Document

In each style sheet, Amí Professional maintains a list of default tab settings. In most style sheets, these tab settings are spaced every ½ inch across the page, so every time you press the Tab key, the cursor jumps ½ inch to the next setting. Most of the time you'll want to leave these tab settings alone.

If you want to change the tab settings in the style sheet, thus affecting the entire document (and any other documents based on the same style sheet), here's what you do:

1. Choose the Page Modify Layout command. Amí Professional displays the dialog box shown in Figure 14–3. Note the tiny down-pointing arrow above the three-inch mark in the ruler at the top of the dialog box. This arrow stands for a centered tab set at that position.
2. Do any of the following:
   - If you want to delete a tab setting from the ruler, click the tab icon to select it, then press the **Delete** key.
   - If you want to move a tab setting on the ruler, point to the tab icon, hold down the mouse button, and drag it to a new position.
   - If you want to set a new tab, choose the type of tab you want

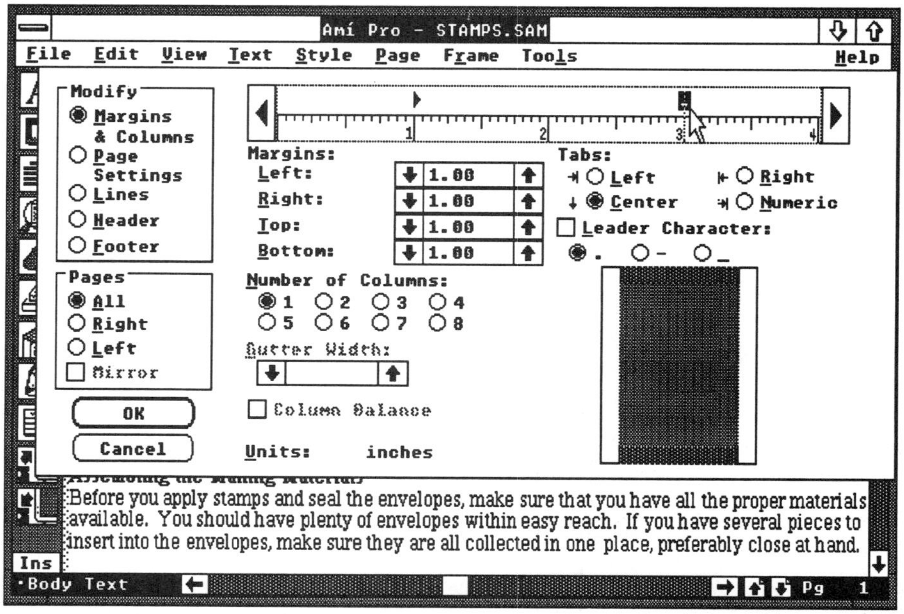

Figure 14–3 Setting a centered tab in the Page Modify Layout dialog box.

under Tabs at the right of the dialog box, then point to the position in the ruler where you want the tab setting and click. A tab icon for that type of tab appears in the ruler.

- If you want a leader character to precede a tab, turn on the Leader Character check box and choose a leader character below, then choose the tab type, point to the position in the ruler where you want the tab setting, and click. A tab icon topped by a small black square representing the leader character appears in the ruler.

3. When all the tab settings in the ruler look the way you want, click OK or press **Enter**.

At any time, you can display a ruler that shows you the tab settings for the paragraph containing the cursor in your document. To display a tab ruler:

- Choose the View Show Tab Ruler command. Amí Professional displays a tab ruler at the top of the screen, as shown in Figure 14–4.

When you want to hide the tab ruler again:

- Choose the View Hide Tab Ruler command.

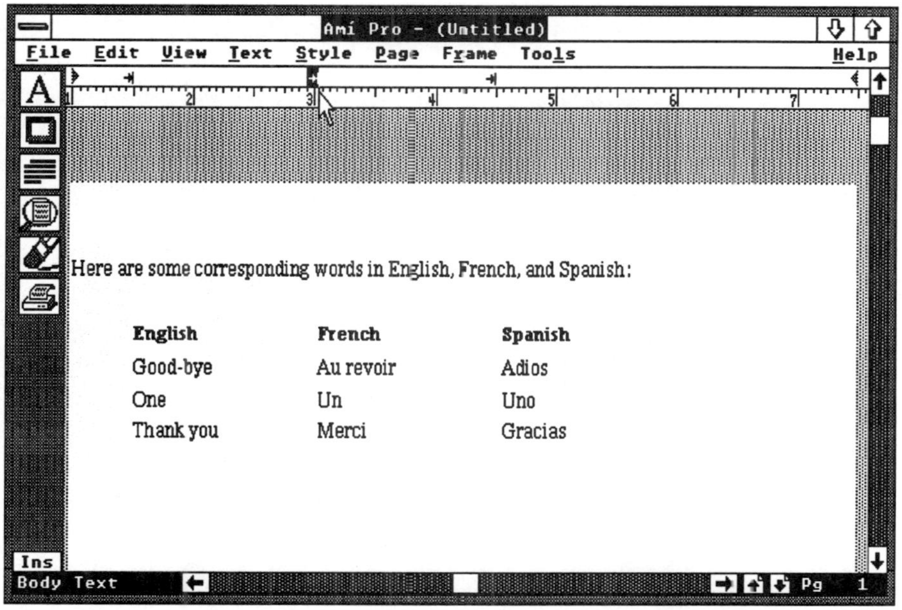

Figure 14–4 You can display the tab ruler to see the tab settings in effect.

Speed Tips

To select multiple tabs in the ruler in the Page Modify Layout dialog box or in an inserted tab ruler, hold down the **Shift** key while you click on the tab icons. When all the tab icons you want are highlighted, you can continue to hold down the **Shift** key and move them as a group in the ruler, or you can release the Shift key and press the **Delete** key to delete them all at once.

To select and delete all of the tabs in a tab ruler, click on the tab ruler, press **A** to highlight all the tab icons, then press the **Delete** key to remove them all at once.

Changing Tab Settings for Part of a Document

When you want to change tab settings in part of a document, you can insert a tab ruler to control a portion of the document. An inserted tab ruler controls the positioning of tabs for all following text until Amí Professional encounters the next tab ruler.

To work with inserted tab rulers, you must be using layout mode, and you should have the Marks option turned on in the View Display Preferences dialog box so you can see the ruler markers.

To insert a tab ruler that controls tab settings in subsequent text:

1. Place the cursor at the beginning of the text that you want to change tab settings in.

2. Choose the Page Tab Ruler command.

3. Choose Insert Tab Ruler, then click OK or press **Enter** to insert the tab ruler. Amí Professional inserts a marker for a tab ruler, as shown in Figure 14–5. (You must have turned on the Marks option in the View Display Preferences dialog box to see the marker.)

4. To display the ruler for that marker and change settings, position the cursor after the marker, then choose the View Show Tab Ruler command (if the ruler is not already displayed at the top of the window).

5. Do any of the following:

   - If you want to delete a tab setting from the ruler, click the tab icon to select it, then press the **Delete** key.

   - If you want to move a tab setting on the ruler, point to the tab icon, hold down the mouse button, and drag it to a new position.

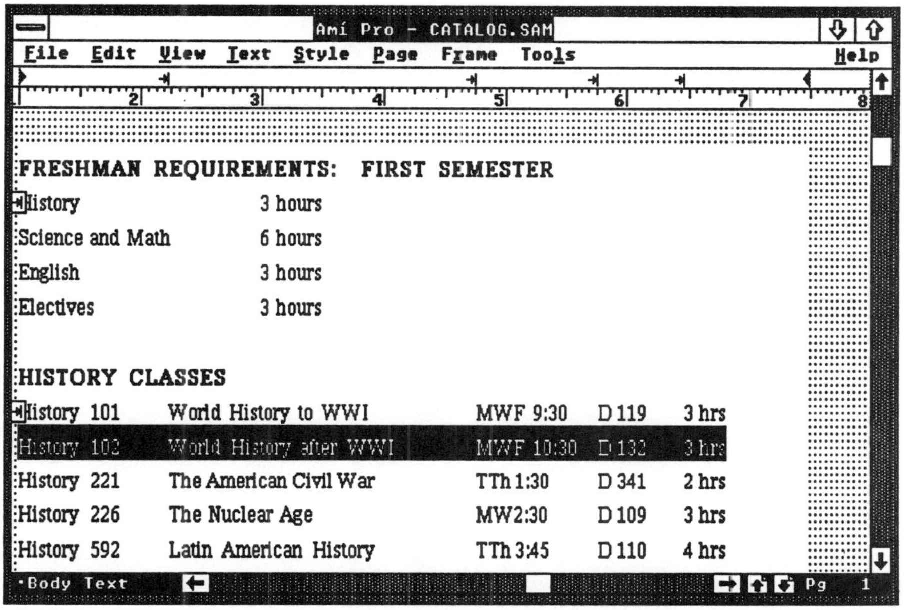

Figure 14–5 Markers indicating inserted tab rulers.

- If you want to set a new tab, click the position on the ruler where you want the tab, then press a key for the tab type you want:

For	Press This Letter Key
Left-aligned tab	**L**
Centered tab	**C**
Right-aligned tab	**R**
Numeric tab	**N**

  A tab icon for that tab type appears in the ruler.

- If you want to set a new tab preceded by a period leader character, click the position on the ruler where you want the tab, then press **Shift** plus a letter key for the tab type you want:

For	Press
Left-aligned tab with period leader	**Shift+L**.
Centered tab with period leader	**Shift+C**.
Right-aligned tab with period leader	**Shift+R**.
Numeric tab with period leader	**Shift+N**.

A tab icon for that tab type, topped by a small black square representing a period, appears in the ruler. A period is the only leader character allowed in inserted tab rulers.

6. To return to the document and save the new settings, click outside of the ruler.

Text with tabs in the paragraphs below the ruler changes to match the new settings. These settings stay in effect until you insert a new tab ruler and change the settings. When you move the cursor into a paragraph, the ruler at the top of the screen changes to show the tab settings for that paragraph.

To change tabs in part of a document back to the settings controlled by the style sheet:

1. Insert a tab ruler.
2. Move the cursor into the paragraph following the ruler marker.
3. Choose the Page Tab Ruler command.
4. Select the Reset to Page Layout Settings option.
5. Click OK or press **Enter**.

To delete a tab ruler:

1. Move the cursor into the paragraph following the tab ruler marker.
2. Choose the Page Tab Ruler command.
3. Select the Remove Tab Ruler option.
4. Click OK or press **Enter**.

The paragraphs below the deleted ruler take on the tab settings for the ruler above them (if any).

Helpful Hint

If you'd like to use the same inserted tab rulers in several places in your document, you can copy the tab settings displayed in the ruler by clicking in the ruler, choosing the Edit Copy command, moving the cursor to the position where you want to insert the settings, and choosing Edit Paste. Amí Professional inserts a copy of the tab ruler at that location. This is a handy way to insert tab rulers that turn on and turn off settings for portions of text throughout your document.

USING TABLES

When you want to arrange a lot of text in rows and columns, you need to create a table. You may be used to thinking of tables as rows and columns of numbers, but in Amí Professional, you can put almost anything into a table *cell* (the intersection of a row and a column), and each cell in a table can have a different format. You can make rows and columns different sizes, connect (merge) cells to create wide cells over narrow ones or tall cells beside stacked cells, and select from many other options. You can use tables to create interesting page layouts as well as use them to do spreadsheet-type functions. See Figures 14–6 through 14–8 for examples of tables.

Putting Tables in Frames

If you want to anchor a table in a certain location or flow text around a table, you can put the table into a frame, then move the frame wherever you like. (If you do not put a table in a frame, it will always be positioned at the left margin.) Putting a table into a frame also helps you to control the height of rows in the table, an option that is not available in tables outside of frames. Frames are discussed in Chapter 12.

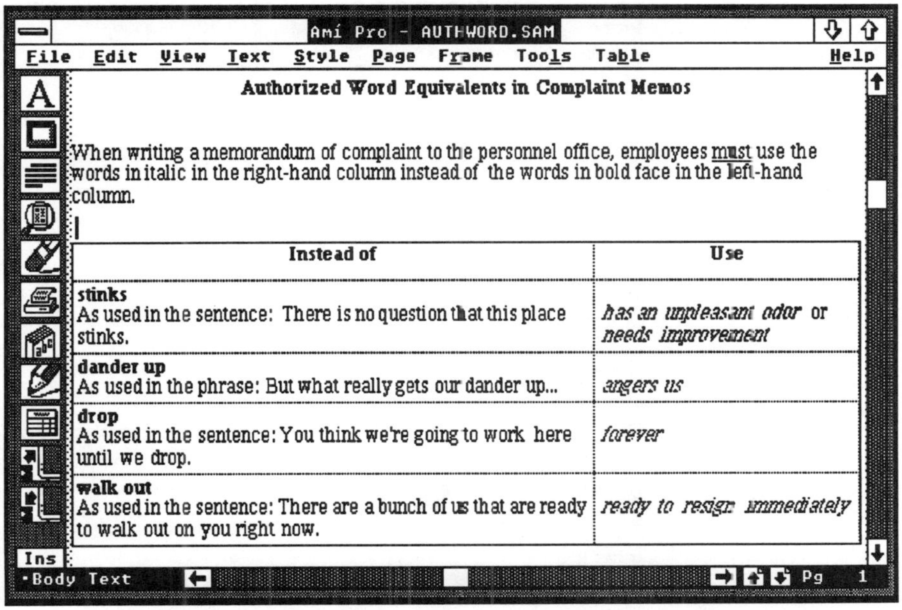

Figure 14–6
You can use tables to put paragraphs side by side.

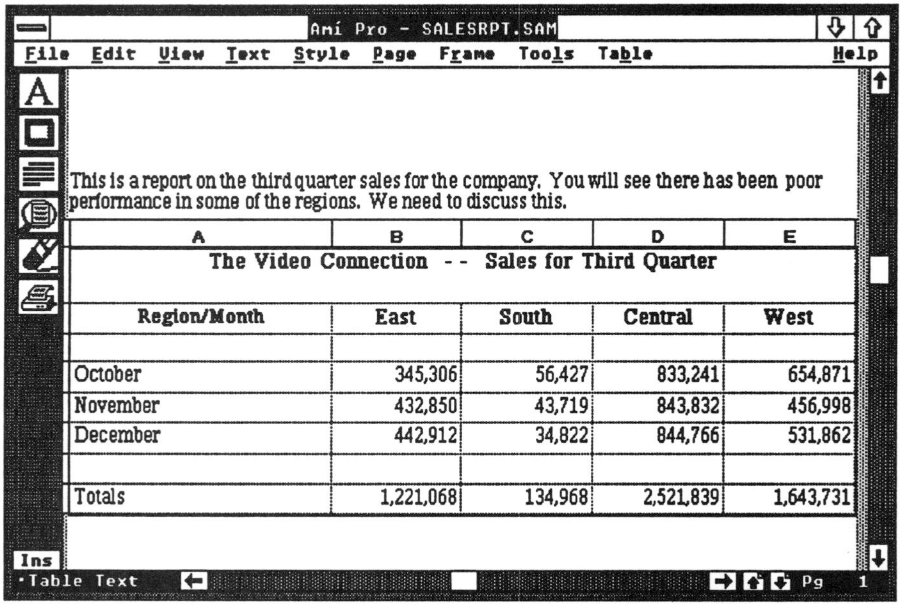

Figure 14-7 You can create calculating spreadsheets in tables.

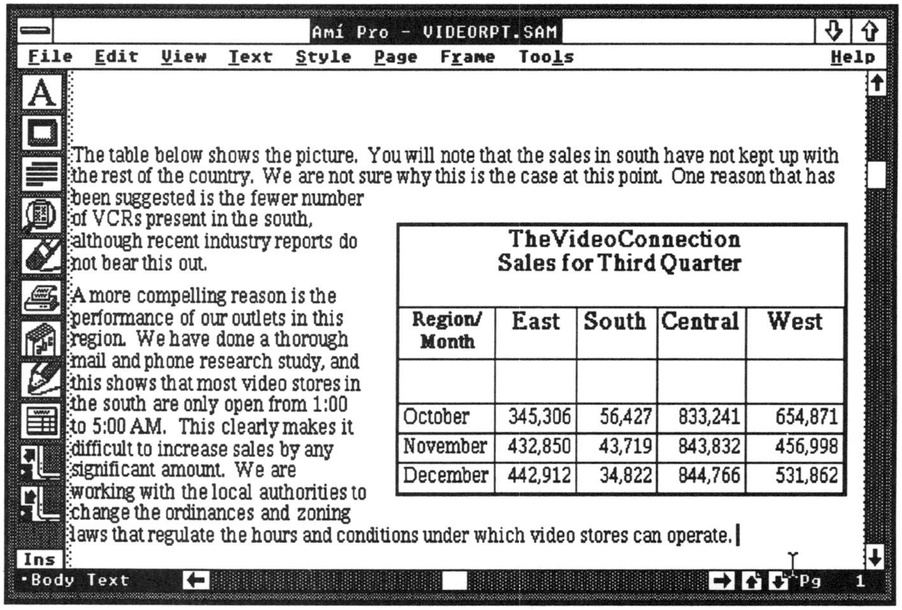

Figure 14-8 You can put tables in frames so text will flow around them.

Inserting a Table

To insert a table:

1. Select the frame (click once) or place the cursor where you want to insert a table. If you want to see the table gridlines or row and column headings, turn on these options in the View Display Preferences command.
2. Choose the Tools Tables command. Amí Professional displays the dialog box shown in Figure 14–9.
3. Type the number of rows and columns you want.
4. If you want to specify layout options, choose the Layout . . . button to display the dialog box shown in Figure 14–10, then change options as necessary. Ways to change the layout are described in more detail in Changing the Layout later in this chapter. You can always change a table's layout, so you may not want to concern yourself with its finer points when you first insert a table.
5. Choose OK or press **Enter** to insert the table.

Amí Professional inserts a blank table, as shown in Figure 14–11, and adds a Table menu to the window. Now you're ready to add the text.

Figure 14–9
Inserting a table with the Tools Tables dialog box.

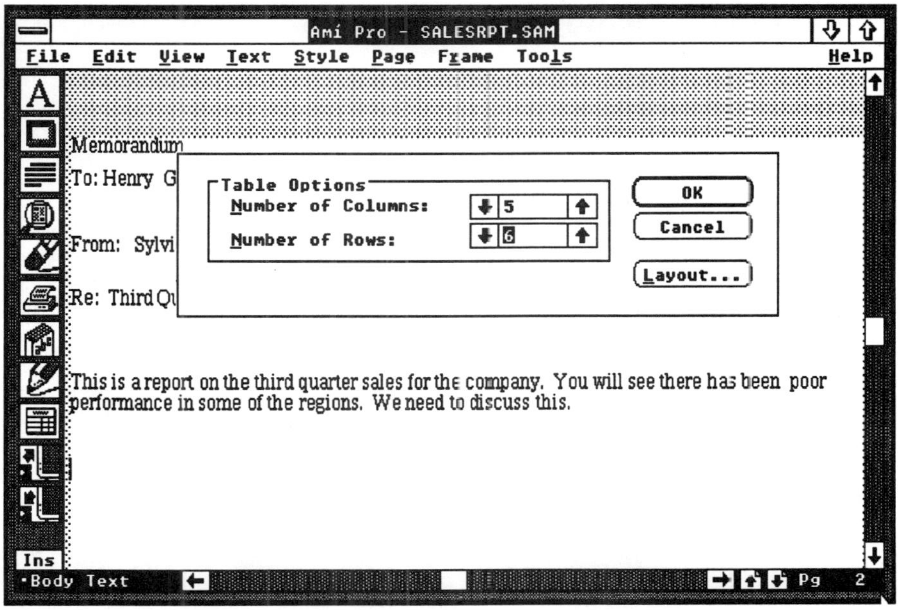

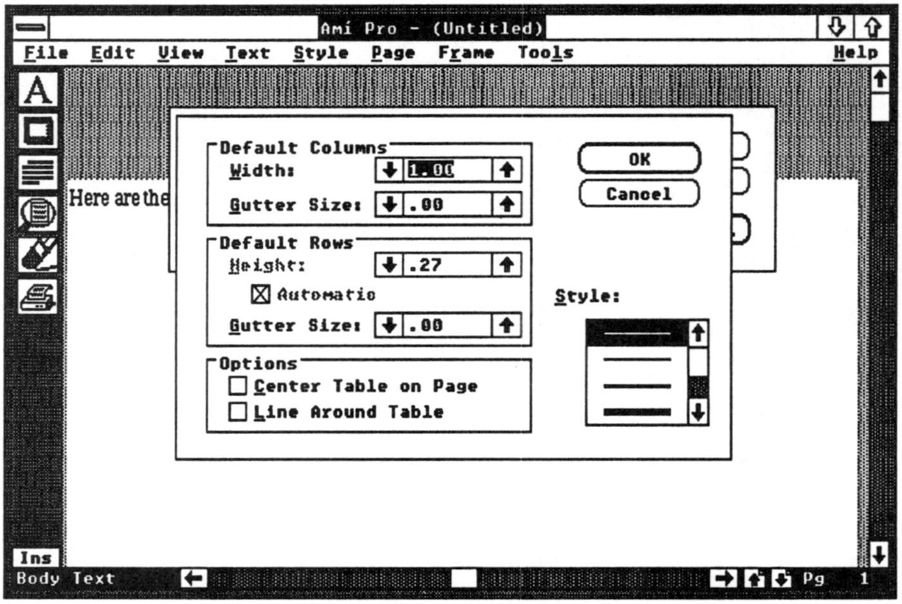

Figure 14-10 Specifying layout options using the Layout option in the Tools Tables command.

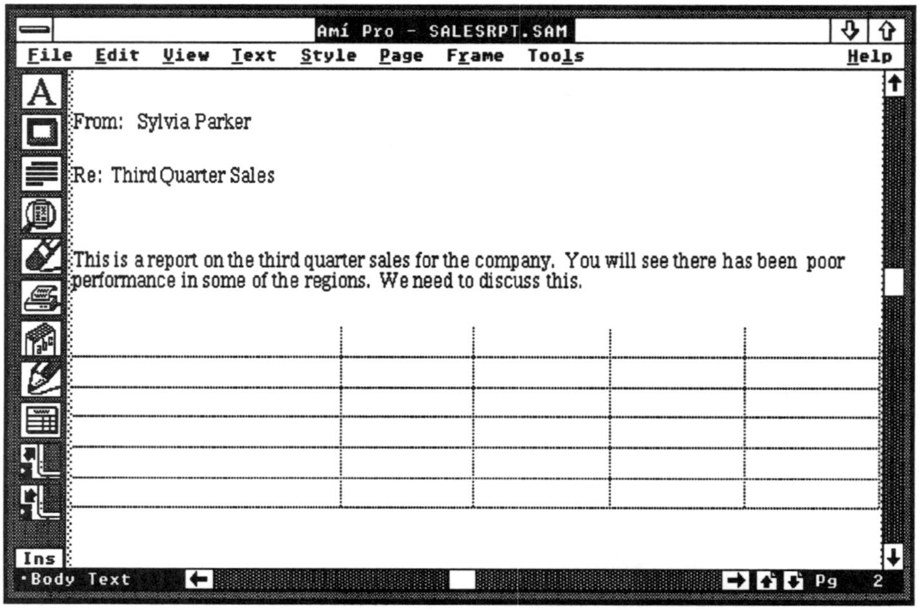

Figure 14-11 A blank table.

Helpful Hint

When you create a table with the Tool Tables command and only use the Table Options dialog box, the first column of the table you create will automatically be twice the width of the other columns (when you have more than two columns). If you want all columns to be the same width, choose the Layout . . . button, choose OK or press **Enter**, and then type in the number of columns and rows you want in the Table Options dialog box.

Entering Data in Table Cells

To add words or numbers to table cells, you can choose from three methods.

- Type the data in each cell.
- Paste the data into the table from the Windows Clipboard.
- Import the data from another file with the File Import/Export command.

Typing the Data

In a table cell, just type characters as you would outside of a table. You can put several paragraphs of text in the same cell if you like. Text wraps within the cell at its right margin, and the heights of the rows adjust as you add text.

To move from cell to cell:

- Click the cell you want.

  or

- Press the **Tab** key or **Ctrl+Right arrow** to move to the next cell, or press **Shift+Tab** or **Ctrl+Left arrow** to move to the previous cell.

Figure 14–12 illustrates entering text in a cell.

Helpful Hint

If you have a lot of data to enter, you may find it faster to type the data outside of the table in draft mode, using a tab to separate columns and pressing **Enter** at the end of each row. Then cut and paste the data into the table.

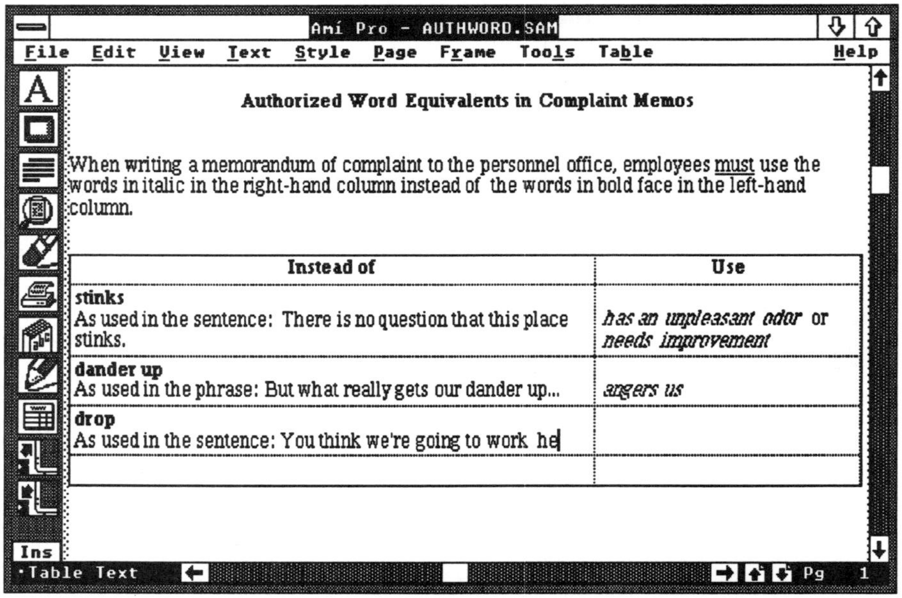

Figure 14-12 Entering text in table cells.

Pasting in Data from the Windows Clipboard

If the data you want to place in your table is part of a file generated by a Windows application, you can copy data to the Clipboard and paste it into your Amí Professional table.

If you're copying data from a spreadsheet and the table is not in a frame, the spreadsheet cells transfer automatically and Amí Professional adds rows and columns as needed, provided there's enough space on the page. If you're copying other types of data, you may need to convert the separator characters (often called *delimiters*) so that only tabs separate columns and only carriage returns (entered by pressing the Enter key) end each row (these are the only characters Amí Professional accepts as separators for table data). You'll also need to put at least as many rows and columns in your table as there are in the data, especially if your table is in a frame.

When Amí Professional reads data from the Clipboard, it treats tab and return characters as signals. When it encounters a tab character, the program places the cursor in the next column and starts inserting the text that follows the tab character. When the program encounters a return character (created by pressing Enter—sometimes called a *paragraph mark* in other applications), the program places the cursor in the next row and starts inserting the text that follows the return character.

If you want more than one paragraph in a cell, you may need to convert returns to a code (such as @@@) before copying the block to the Clipboard. Once you insert the coded data into the table, change the code characters back into returns. Or you might want to add tabs and returns at appropriate places before copying to the Clipboard to tell the program how to place the text in the table.

To enter data from another file generated by a Windows application:

1. Open the file containing the data you want to copy.

2. Select the data.

3. Use the Edit Copy command to copy it to the Windows Clipboard.

4. Open the Amí Professional document and place the cursor in the upper left corner of the block of table cells into which you want to insert the copied data.

5. Choose the Edit Paste command to insert the data. If the copied data didn't end up exactly how you wanted it, you can always cut data from one cell and paste it into another to rearrange it.

You can also link data in tables to other Windows files that support Dynamic Data Exchange (DDE)—see Linking Table Data to Another Windows File later in this chapter for more information.

Importing Data with the File Import/Export Command

If you want to insert data from a non-Windows file, such as from Lotus 1-2-3, you can use the Import/Export command to put the information into a table.

If you're copying data from a spreadsheet, the spreadsheet cells transfer automatically. If you're copying other types of data, you may need to convert the separator characters (delimiters) so that only tabs separate columns and only carriage return characters (entered by pressing the Enter key) end each row. The tab and carriage return are the only characters Amí Professional will accept as separators for table data. Make sure you have enough rows and columns in your table to hold the data.

To enter data from another file using the Import/Export command:

1. Place the cursor in the upper left cell of the block of cells into which you want to insert the imported data.

2. Choose the File Import/Export command.

3. Select the file type from the list and type or select the file name as necessary in the dialog box, then click OK or press **Enter**. A dialog box may appear to ask whether you want to import the entire file or specify a range.

4. Respond as necessary to any dialog boxes that appear.

If the imported text ends up all in one cell, you can cut text from one cell and paste it into another. And although Amí Professional ends the display of information in one cell at the bottom of the page, all of the imported information is in the cell, and you'll see hidden portions appear as you move text out of the cell to make room.

Editing and Formatting Text in Tables

All of Amí Professional's editing and formatting commands are available in table cells. You can select, copy, cut, and paste text, and format words and paragraphs almost any way you like. You can even add nonprinting notes with the Edit Notes command.

To move around in a table, you can use the mouse to click on any cell or use the following keys:

To Move	Press
To the next cell	**Tab** or **Ctrl+Right arrow**.
To the previous cell	**Shift+Tab** or **Ctrl+Left arrow**.
Up a row	**Ctrl+Up arrow**.
Down a row	**Ctrl+Down arrow**.
To the beginning of the text in a cell	**Home**.
To the first cell in the row	**Home, Home**.
To the end of the text in a cell	**End**.
To the last cell in the row	**End, End**.
To the first cell in a table	**Ctrl+Home**.
To the last cell in a table	**Ctrl+End**.
To leave a table	**Ctrl+Down** or **Up arrow**.

Selecting in Tables

You can select table cells to affect all of the text within the cells or to change the shading or lines around the cells. When the cursor is anywhere within a table, you can also choose options that affect the entire table.

To select a single table cell:

- Click the cell or use the **Tab** key to move the cursor into the cell.

To select a group of cells:

- If you can see all of the cells you want to select, hold down the left mouse button and drag the pointer over the cells; or you can hold down the **Shift** key and the **Ctrl** key while you use the arrow keys to highlight the cells.

  or

- If you're using the mouse and you must scroll to see all of the cells you want to select, click in one cell to set the cursor at the corner of a block you want to select, then move the mouse pointer diagonally to the other corner of the block (scrolling if necessary), hold down the **Shift** key, and click the mouse button in the opposite corner of the block. (Be sure to hold down the Shift key *before* you click the mouse button to select the cells: otherwise, you'll just move the cursor.)

You can also select text within a table cell using the same methods you'd use outside of tables.

Formatting Text in Table Cells

You can use all of Amí Professional's commands to add bold, italic, underlines, indents, and other formatting to text in table cells. You can also change table styles to specify the alignment of text in cells. For example, if you're using numbers, you might want to change the Table Text style to a Fixed Decimal format, which gives all numbers the same number of decimal points. With this approach you can align the text on the right so that all the numbers line up on their decimal points. (**Note:** If any text—even a space—accompanies a number in a cell, the number will be formatted as text, not as a number.) See Chapter 9 for more information about changing styles.

Displaying or Hiding Gridlines

The dotted lines around the individual cells in a table are called *gridlines.* These gridlines help you as you enter text in a table—they won't print. If you want lines to print around cells, you can add them as described in Adding Lines or Shading later in this chapter. You can also control whether gridlines appear on the screen this way:

1. Choose the View Display Preferences command.
2. Turn on the Table Gridlines option to display gridlines, or turn it off to hide them.
3. Click OK or press **Enter**. This option remains in effect until you change it again. Figure 14–13 shows a table displayed on the screen without gridlines.

Changing the Layout of a Table

When you first insert a table using the Tools Tables command, you can use the Layout button to specify the default size for rows and columns, whether the table is left-aligned or centered between the margins, and whether a table has a line (*box rule*) around it. You can change these options any time using the Table Layout command on the Table menu. To change these layout options:

1. If you're in the process of creating a table, click the Layout button in the Tools Tables dialog box.

   or

   If you're changing the format of an existing table, move the cursor

Figure 14–13 A table displayed without gridlines around individual cells.

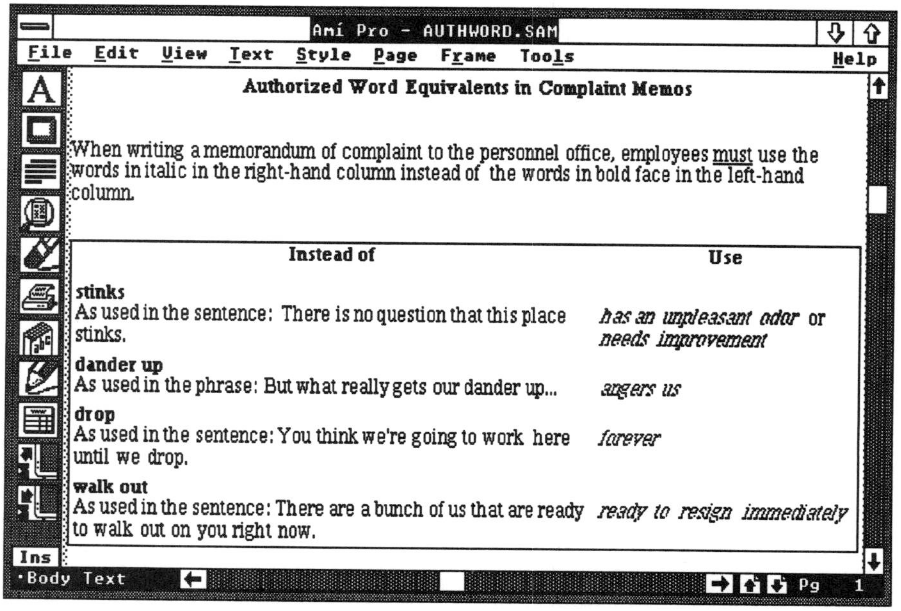

to any part of the table, then choose the Table Layout command from the Table menu.

Amí Professional displays the dialog box shown in Figure 14–14.

2. Choose from the following options in the dialog box to affect the entire table.

Option	Description
Default Columns: Width	Type or select a new measurement in the running list box.
Default Columns: Gutter Size	If you want white space at the left side of each column, type or select a new measurement in the running list box.
Default Rows: Height	Type or select a new measurement in the running list box. This option is available only if the table is in a frame.
Automatic	This option is always on unless the table is in a frame. In a frame, turn option on if you want Amí Professional to determine the height of each row as text is added and subtracted from the cells; otherwise, type a measurement in the Height box.

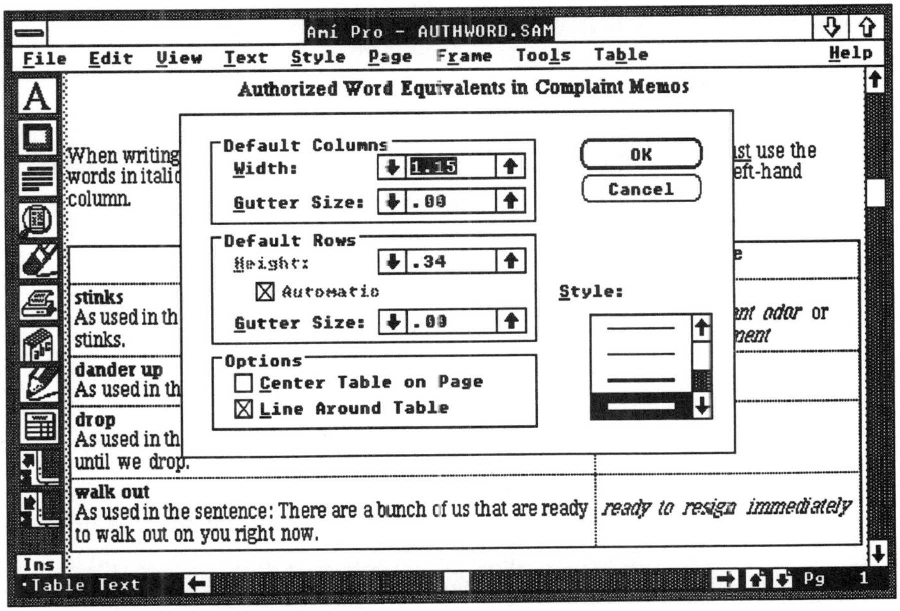

Figure 14–14 Changing the width of all columns and adding a thick line around a table.

Default Rows: Gutter Size	If you want to change the amount of white space at the bottom of each row, type or select a new measurement in the running list box.
Options: Center Table on Page	Turn on if you want to center the table horizontally on the page.
Options: Line Around Table	Turn on if you want to draw a line around the outside of the table on the page, then choose a line thickness from the Style list. Turn off if you don't want a line around the table.
Style list	Choose a line thickness. Available only when you've turned on the Line Around Table option.

3. Click OK or press **Enter**.

The Table Layout dialog box sets the default options for a table, but all cells in a table don't need to be the same size. You can always change the size of individual columns or rows and gutter widths as described next, and add a variety of lines around cells as described later in this chapter.

Changing the Size of Rows or Columns

You can change the width of columns using the mouse or a command. If your table is in a frame and you've typed a measurement in the Default Rows: Height box, you can also change the height of rows this way. The Automatic check box in the Table Layout dialog box must be turned off.

To change the width of a column (or the height of a row, if the table meets the conditions specified above) using the mouse:

1. Place the mouse pointer on top of the cell gridline you want to move. For example, place the mouse pointer on the gridline at the right of a cell to change the width of the column. The pointer becomes a four-headed arrow. (Within a highlighted area, this arrow looks like a cross.)

2. Hold down the left mouse button and drag the gridline to the new position, as shown in Figure 14–15. When you release the mouse button, Amí Professional redraws the table.

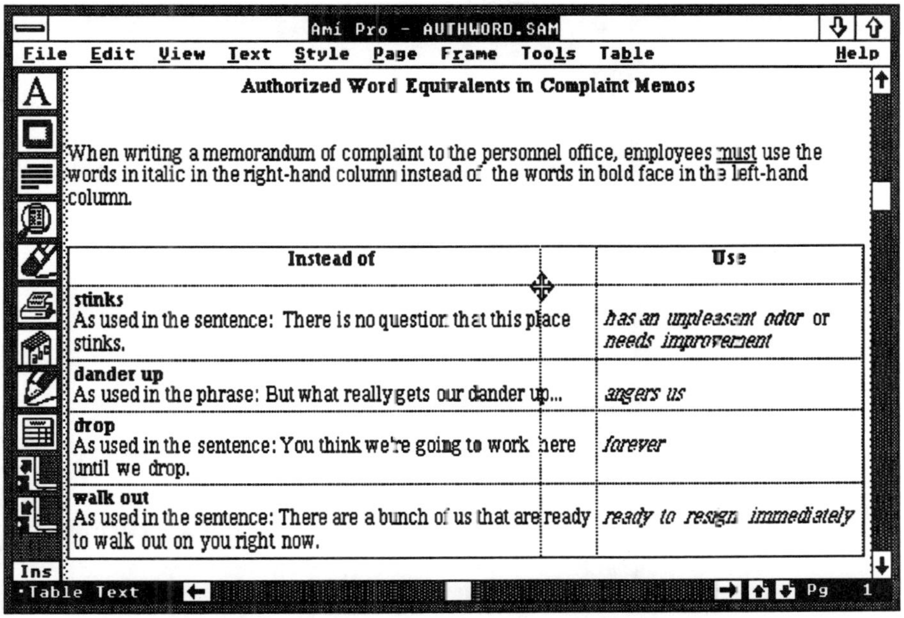

Figure 14–15 Dragging a gridline to change the width of a column.

3. Repeat steps 1 and 2 until all columns (and rows, if appropriate) are the size you want.

To change the size of columns (or rows, if the table is in a frame and has a set row height) with a command:

1. To select one column or row, move the cursor into any cell in the column or row you want to affect.

   or

   To select several columns or rows, highlight them using the methods described under Selecting in Tables earlier in this chapter.

2. Choose the Table Column/Row Size command. Amí Professional displays the dialog box shown in Figure 14–16.

3. Choose from the following options in the dialog box.

Option	Description
Columns: Width	Type or select a new width measurement in the running list box.
Columns: Gutter Size	If you want to change the amount of white space at the left side of each cell, type or select a new measurement in the running list box.

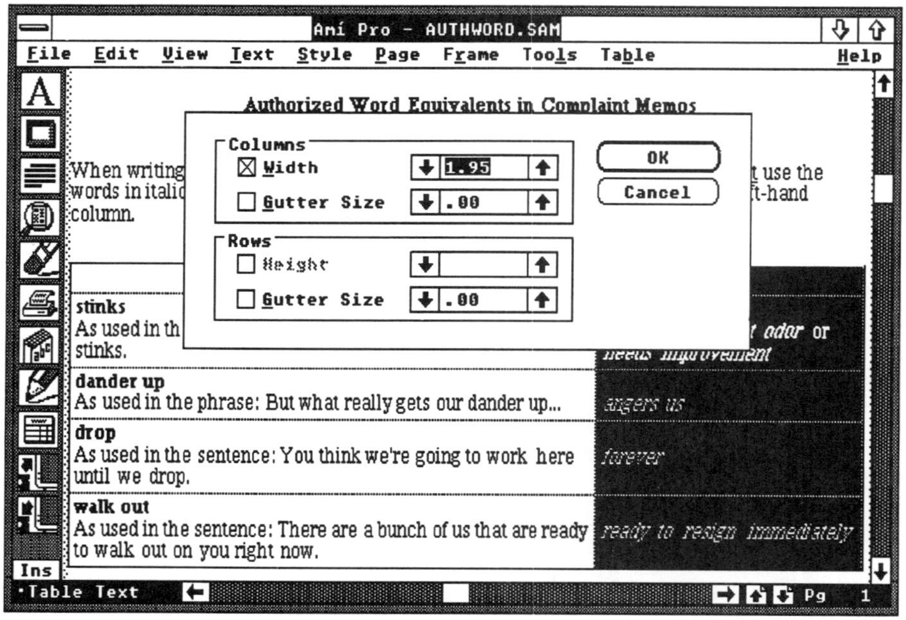

Figure 14–16 Changing the column width of a selected column.

Rows: Height	Type or select a new measurement in the running list box. This option is available only when the table is in a frame.
Rows: Gutter Size	If you want to change the amount of white space at the bottom of the rows, type or select a new measurement in the running list box.

4. Click OK or press **Enter**. Amí Professional redraws the table using the new measurements.

Adding or Deleting Columns or Rows

After you create your table, you may find that you need to add more data, or that you don't have enough data to fill out all the rows and columns in the table. No sweat—you can easily insert or delete columns or rows.

If there's enough space between margins or edges of a frame, you can use the following procedure to add columns or rows either before or after the cursor. When there's not enough space, an option may be grayed in the dialog box; you'll have to reduce the size of the rows or columns in your table or increase the text area (by decreasing the margins) or increase the size of the frame.

1. Move the cursor into the column or row before or after you want to insert new columns or rows.
2. Choose the Table Insert Column/Row command. Amí Professional displays the dialog box shown in Figure 14–17.
3. If you want to insert columns, select Columns in the Insert box, type the number of columns you want to insert in the Number to Insert box, and choose Before or After from the Position box to add the columns in front of or behind the column containing the cursor.

   or

   If you want to insert rows, select Rows in the Insert box, type the number of rows you want to insert in the Number to Insert box, then choose Before or After from the Position box to add the rows on top of or below the row containing the cursor.
4. Click OK or press **Enter** to add the new cells to the table.

To delete columns or rows:

1. Select the columns or rows you want to delete. If you want to delete

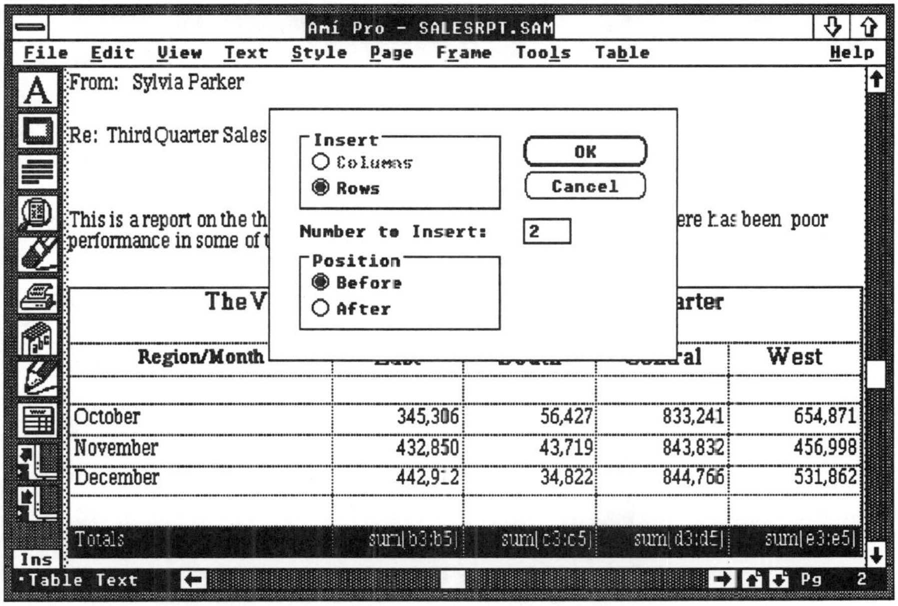

Figure 14–17 Adding two rows before a selected row with the Table Insert Row/ Column command.

a single column or row, you can simply move the cursor to any cell in that column or row.

2. Choose the Table Delete Row/Column command.
3. If you want to delete columns, choose Delete Column.

   or

   If you want to delete rows, choose Delete Row.
4. Click OK or press **Enter**. Amí Professional displays a message to ensure that this is what you really want to do.
5. Click Yes or press **Y** to delete the cells and redraw the table.

Connecting Table Cells

If you want row or column headings in your table, you may want to have one cell that's as wide as or as high as two or more cells adjacent to it. Figure 14–18 shows a table whose heading in the top row spans five columns. To create large cells, you just connect (merge) cells to create one large cell this way:

1. Select the cells you want to merge into one larger cell.

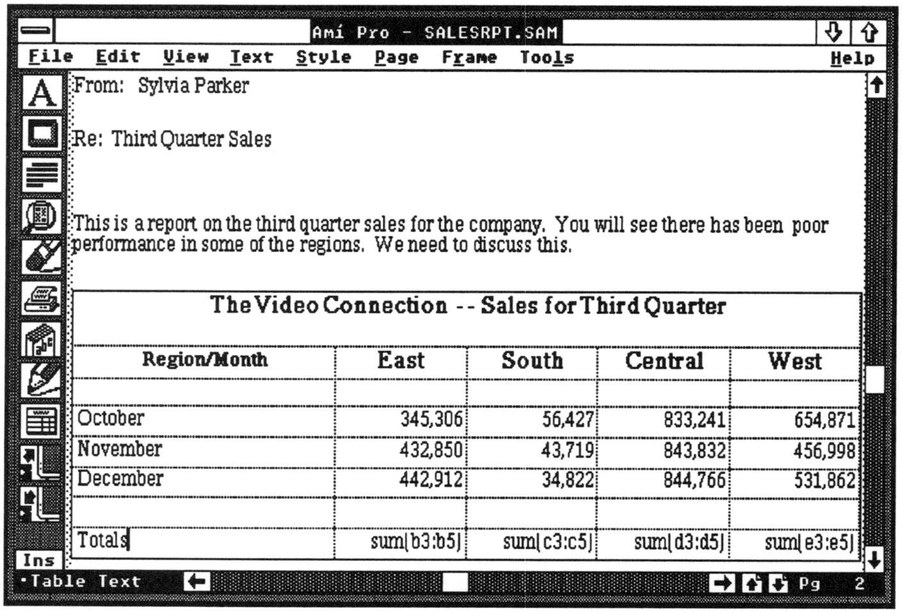

Figure 14–18 A table with a column heading created by merging cells.

2. Choose the Table Connect command. Amí Professional erases the boundary lines between the selected cells to create one large cell. The Table Connect command is a toggle command. When it's active, a check mark appears beside Connect on the menu. To reverse the action and redraw the boundary lines in a large cell, just select the cell, then choose the Table Connect command again.

Speed Tip

If you use the Table Connect command often, you may want to place Amí Professional's table connect icon in the icon bar. Then you simply select the cells you want to connect and click the table connect icon. For more information about adding icons, see Chapter 21.

Adding Lines and Shading

You can add a variety of lines and background shading to highlight individual table cells or to format the entire table. Figure 14–19 shows tables that have a variety of line and shading formats.

To add or change lines and shading for table cells:

1. Select the cells in which you want to change lines or shading.

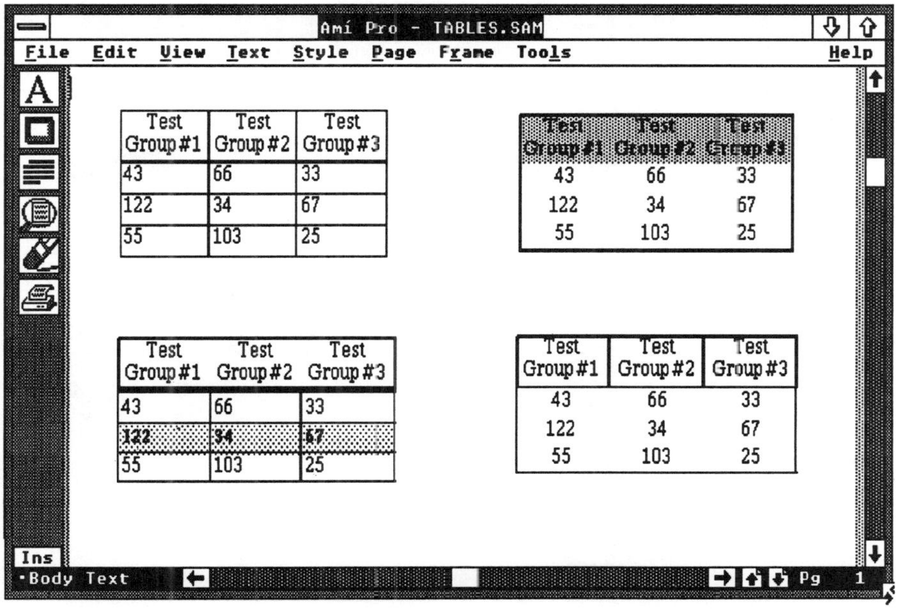

Figure 14–19 Tables with a variety of lines and shading.

2. Choose the Table Lines/Shades command. Amí Professional displays the dialog box shown in Figure 14–20.

3. Choose from the following options in the dialog box:

Options	Description
All Sides	Turn option on if you want to add lines around the outside of each cell in the selected block of cells. If you have selected only one cell, this option has the same effect as Outline. If you've selected a block of cells, this option draws a box around the block.
Left	Turn option on if you want to add a line to the left side of each selected cell.
Right	Turn option on if you want to add a line to the right side of each selected cell.
Top	Turn option on if you want to add a line to the top of each selected cell.
Bottom	Turn option on if you want to add a line to the bottom of each selected cell.

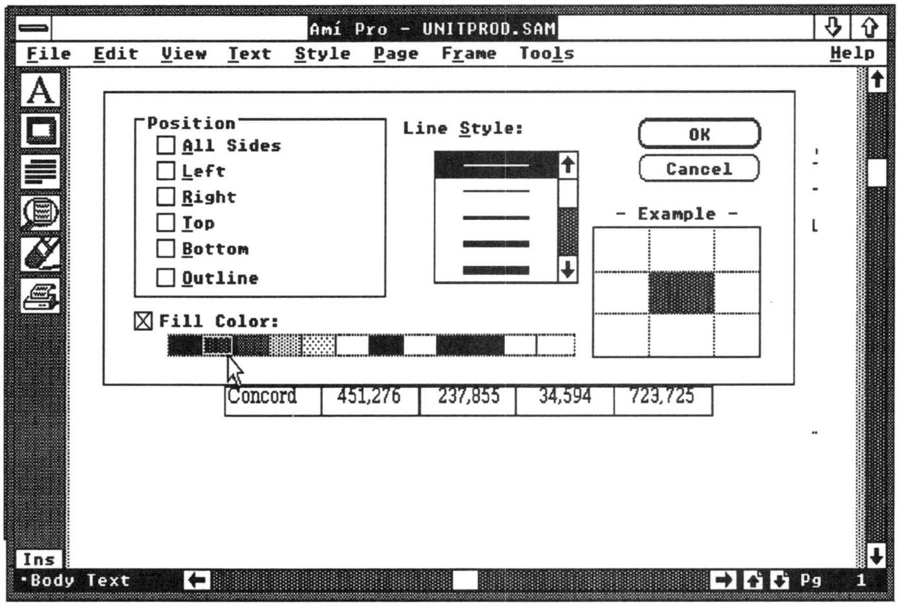

Figure 14–20 Adding shading to a selected cell.

Outline	Turn option on if you want to draw lines all around each selected cell.
Line Style	Choose a line thickness for the lines you specified.
Fill Color	Turn option on if you want to shade the background of the selected cells, then choose a color and pattern from the color bar beneath.

4. When the example in the lower right corner of the dialog box looks the way you want, click OK or press **Enter** to redraw the table.

Adding Leader Characters

You might want to create a table in which connecting lines or dots link columns of data to show their relationship. Figure 14–21 shows such a table. These connecting characters are called *leader characters.* Leader characters fill the space in each cell that is not occupied by text.

To add leader characters to table cells:

1. Select the cells you want to add leader characters to.

2. Choose the Table Leaders command.

Figure 14–21
A table in which leader characters connect related columns of information.

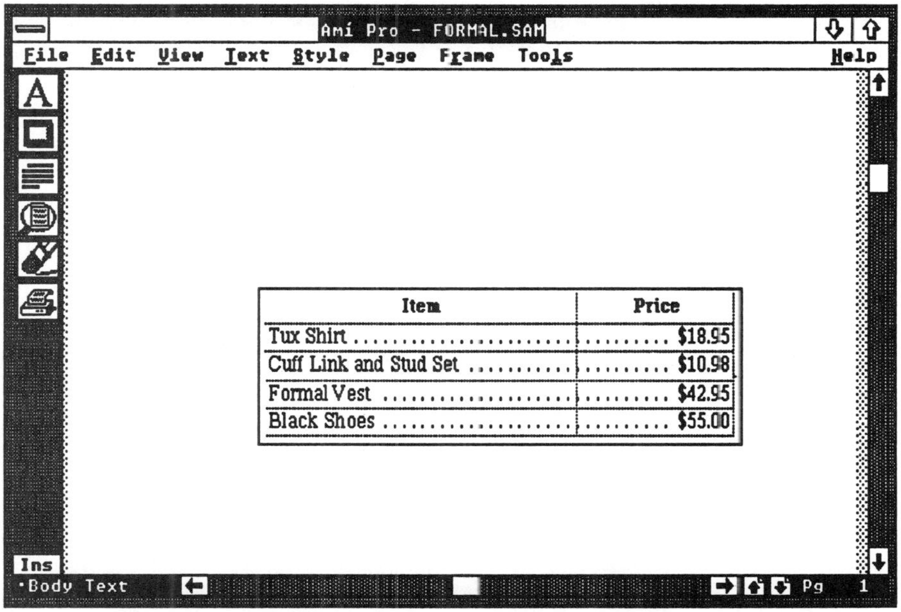

3. Choose the type of leaders you want.

4. Click OK or press **Enter**.

Calculating in Tables

Although Amí Professional isn't a spreadsheet program, you easily use it to add spreadsheet-type tables to your document. You can even perform mathematical calculations and sum rows or columns using cell references, just as in a spreadsheet program.

Summing the Numbers in a Row or Column

One of the most common calculation tasks people want to do is to sum the numbers in a row or column. Amí Professional has a special Quick Add command that sums the numbers and pastes the results in the cell containing the cursor. Here's how to use it:

1. Move the cursor into an empty cell to the right of cells you want to sum in a row or beneath cells you want to sum in a column.

2. Choose the Table Quick Add command.

3. Choose Add Column to add all the numbers in the column or choose Add Row to add all the numbers in the row. (If the Add Column option is grayed, the cursor isn't beneath column data; if the Add Row option is grayed, the cursor isn't to the right of row data.)

4. Click OK or press **Enter**. Amí Professional pastes the result into the cell. If you later change numbers in the summed area, click the cell containing the sum to update the total.

Basic Calculations

You can use the following operators to set up mathematical formulas in table cells: + (addition), − (subtraction), * (multiplication), / (division), % (percentage). Use parentheses to group operations, like you would in any standard mathematical calculation. As examples of using the operators, you could type any of the following formulas to display the answer 10:

3+7 16−6 2*5 300/30 20−50% (2+3)*2

To add calculations to a cell or change a formula already in a cell:

1. Move the cursor to the cell in which you want to perform a calculation.

2. Choose the Table Edit Formula command. Amí Professional displays the dialog box shown in Figure 14–22.

3. In the Formula box, type a formula for the calculation you want to perform. You can type numbers or cell references, specifying the mathematical operation by typing the characters shown in the Operators box.

4. Click OK or press **Enter**. Amí Professional displays the result of the calculation.

Calculating with Cell References

To refer to cells in formulas, Amí Professional uses letters for the columns and numbers for the rows, starting at the upper left corner of the table. So the cell in the upper left corner is A1, the next cell to the right is A2, the first cell in the next row is B1, and so forth.

To help you keep track of the cell references for a table, you can choose the View Display Preferences command and turn on either or both of two options:

- the Status Bar option, which displays a status bar (shown at the bottom in Figure 14–23) that always lists the row number and column letter of the cell containing the cursor.

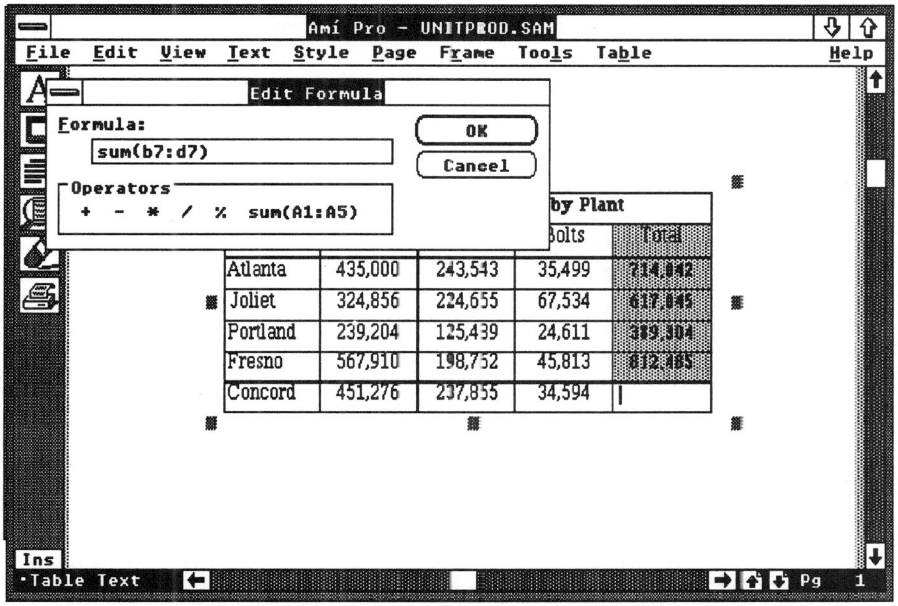

Figure 14–22
Typing a formula in the Table Edit Formula dialog box to do a calculation in a table cell.

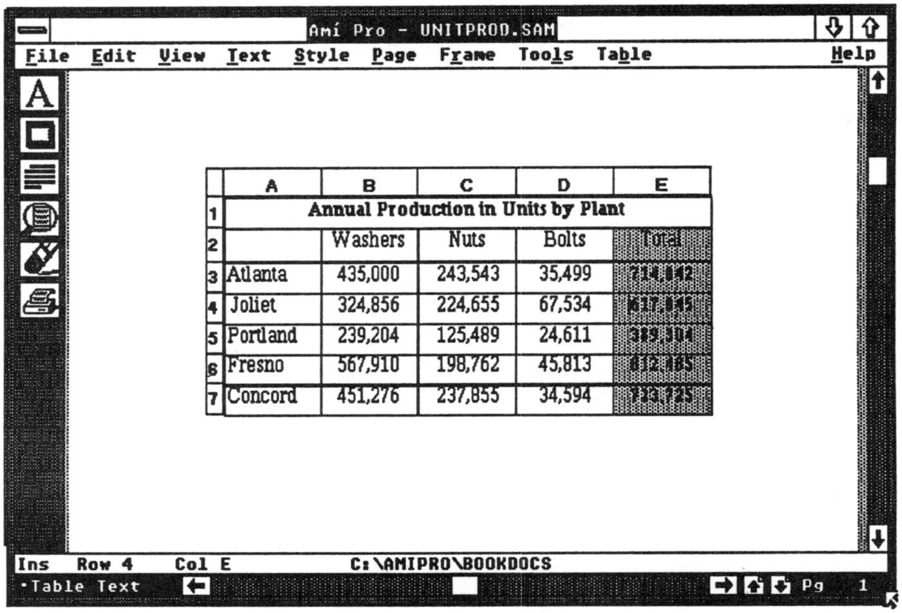

Figure 14–23 To make it easier to use cell references in a table, you can display the status bar and nonprinting row and column headings.

- the Table Row/Column Headings option, which displays row and column headings, as shown in Figure 14–23. These labels won't print, even though they show on the screen (you may need to scroll to see them).

These settings remain in effect until you turn them off, so if you've turned on the Table Row/Column Headings, you'll see them in every table you display until you use the View Display Preferences command to turn them off.

To calculate, you can use cell references instead of specific numbers: A1+B2 to add the values in cells A1 and B2, or A10*C10 to multiply the value in cell A10 by the value in cell C10, for example. To sum cells in a range, type the word **sum** followed by the cell range in parentheses, like this formula that displays the sum of the numbers in A12 through Z10:

sum(A12:Z10)

Figure 14–22 shows a formula using cell references.

Dealing with Unexpected Results of Calculations

Following are several surprises that might result from calculations:

Problem: If Amí Professional can't find a cell you've referenced in a formula, it may display REF in that cell or display a message saying it can't understand the formula.

Solution: Check your formula to ensure that your cell references are correct and that data exists in the referenced cells. As you add new rows or columns, Amí Professional changes references to adapt to your changes. For example, if you typed B1 in a formula, then added a column in front of the original column B, Amí Professional would update your formula to read C1. To ensure that your formula always references a specific cell no matter what other changes might be made to a table, type dollar signs in front of the cell reference. For example, B1 will *always* reference cell B1, no matter how many rows or columns might be added to a table after you enter the formula.

Problem: If the contents of a cell can't fit within the cell, Amí Professional displays asterisks (***) in the cell.

Solution: Widen the column enough to display the cell contents.

Problem: The cell contents are displayed in a narrow column instead of side by side, so they're unreadable. This happens when columns are narrow and row height is automatic. The program is using wordwrap to display the information.

Solution: Widen the column enough to display the cell contents in a readable form.

Deleting a Table

To delete a whole table:

1. Select the entire table.
2. Choose the Table Delete Row/Column command.
3. Click OK.

Linking Table Data to Another Windows File

If your computer has a lot of memory, you can use Dynamic Data Exchange (DDE) to paste in data from and to link that data to another Windows application, such as Microsoft Excel. Linking enables you to update the information in your document when the data in the other file changes. You might want to create a report in Amí Professional that includes a table containing linked data from an Excel spreadsheet, for example, so you could easily update the information in your report when the Excel file changes.

Creating the Link

To create a DDE link, you copy the data to the Clipboard, then use the Amí Professional Edit Paste Link command to insert the data into a table. The other Windows application must support DDE for this process to work. If the Edit Paste Link command is grayed, the other application doesn't support DDE. Make sure your table has enough rows and columns to hold the data.

To copy and link data to your document using DDE:

1. Open the other Windows file that contains the data you want to copy.
2. Select the data, then use the Edit Copy command to copy it to the Clipboard.
3. Start Amí Professional and open the file you want to paste the information into.
4. Select the table cell that you want to be the upper left corner of the block of cells you're inserting.
5. Choose the Edit Paste Link command to insert the copied data and create the DDE link.

Amí Professional updates linked information when you open the document. If the other application isn't running at the time you update, you see a message asking whether it's okay to start the other program to get the latest information from the original file. You may decide later to deactivate the link so that it updates only when you say so, or to remove the link altogether.

Managing Linked Table Data

If you used the Edit Paste Link command as described previously, Amí Professional saves the path name to the information you pasted in, creating a link from your document file to the original file that contained the information. The program uses the path name to find the original file, so if you change the file's location, Amí Professional won't find the other file. If you want to check whether there's linked information in a file, deactivate or break a link, or update linked information, you can use the File Links command this way:

1. Choose the File Links command.

2. In the dialog box, select the link (the name of the original application and path name to the linked file) that you want to affect. (If the list is blank, there are no files linked to the active document.)

3. Click one of the following buttons:

Click	**To**
Update	Update the link, using the path name to get the latest information from the original file. This option is normally used with "deactivated" (nonautomatic) links.
De-activate	Keep track of the path to the original file, but update the link only when you want to (using the Update button in this dialog box).
Unlink	Destroy the link and erase the path name from the dialog box. This option frees up the space taken up by the link information.

4. Repeat steps 2 and 3 to change more links as necessary. When you're ready to close the dialog box, click Cancel.

Converting a Table to Regular Text

To place the data from a table into another place in your document:

1. Select the entire table.

2. Choose the Edit Copy command to copy the data in the cells or choose the Edit Cut command to delete the data.

3. Place the cursor where you want to insert the data.

4. Choose the Edit Paste command. Amí Professional inserts the data, placing tabs between columns and carriage returns at the ends of the rows. If you have leader characters in your table, they will not be copied. You will need to add leader characters to your tab settings.

5. Delete the table if necessary as described in Deleting a Table earlier in this chapter.

15

Adding Headers, Footers, and Page Numbers

You can add page numbers alone to a document, or you can add other text at the top or bottom of the document to create a header or footer. This chapter shows how to add and format page numbers, headers, and footers.

ADDING PAGE NUMBERS

You can add page numbers by themselves to your document, or you can include page numbers in a header or footer that repeats on every page. The Page Numbering command controls the number type and starting page, and Amí Professional automatically increments the numbers as you add pages.

Whenever you want to add page numbers:

1. Move the cursor to where you want the page number to appear (usually in the top or bottom margin). You may have to add a tab character if you don't want the page number to appear at the left margin.

2. Choose the Page Numbering command from the Page menu. Amí Professional displays the dialog box shown in Figure 15–1.

3. Select the number style you want from the Style box. (Select 1 to get 1, 2, 3, and so on; I to get I, II, III, and so on; i to get i, ii, iii, and so on; A to get A, B, C, and so on; a to get a, b, c, and so on.)

4. If you want page numbers to start on a page other than 1, turn on

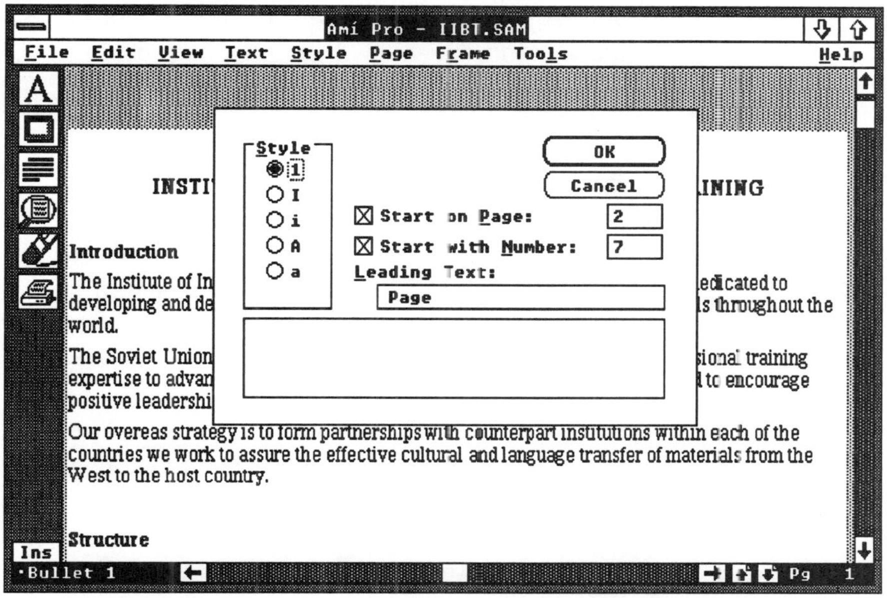

Figure 15–1
Adding page numbers with the Page Numbering command.

the Start on Page option and type the page number in the following text box.

5. If you want to start with a page number other than 1, turn on the Start with Number option and type the page number in the following text box.

6. If the page number is not part of a header or footer, but you want text to appear before the page number, type that text in the Leading Text box. For example, you might want to type the word *Page* followed by a space, or type a chapter number and a dash to get a double number like 3–1. Text you type in this box will also appear in tables of contents and indexes.

7. Click OK or press **Enter**.

Figure 15–1 illustrates adding the word *Page* followed by a space and the page number in the top margin.

When you type anything in the top or bottom margins, Amí Professional automatically uses the tab and margin settings specified for headers and footers in the page layout. You can change these settings to put the page number precisely where you want. For example, you might want to put a tab character before the page number and set a right-aligned tab at the right margin to align the page number with the right margin in a header.

You might also want to set a centered tab in a footer to move the page number to the center of the bottom margin.

ADDING HEADERS OR FOOTERS

When you want to print text at the top of each page, you add a header (also known as a *running head*), as shown in the upper right corner of Figure 15–2. When you want to print text at the bottom of each page, you add a footer (also known as a *running foot*), as shown at the bottom of Figure 15–3.

In Amí Professional, you can have two types of headers and footers: *fixed* and *floating*. Fixed headers and footers appear on every page of your document and are placed in top or bottom page margins. When you use fixed headers and footers, you can have only one header or footer per layout. To have different headers or footers for right (odd-numbered) or left (even-numbered) pages or for different sections of your document, you use a floating header or footer. You can also mix floating headers or footers and fixed headers or footers. For example, you might want headers to change from page to page (floating headers), but want the same footer on every page (fixed footer).

Figure 15–2
A header shown in working view.

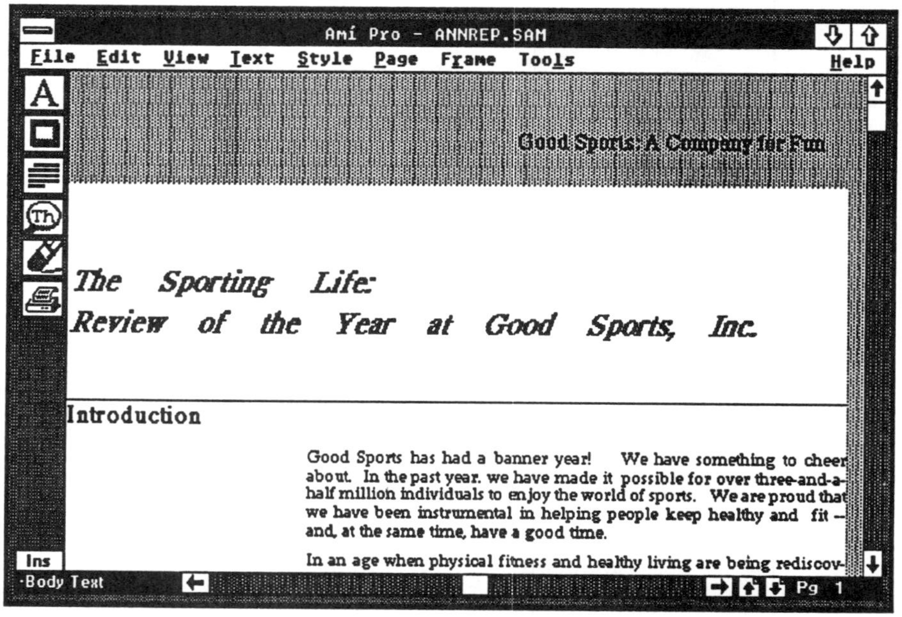

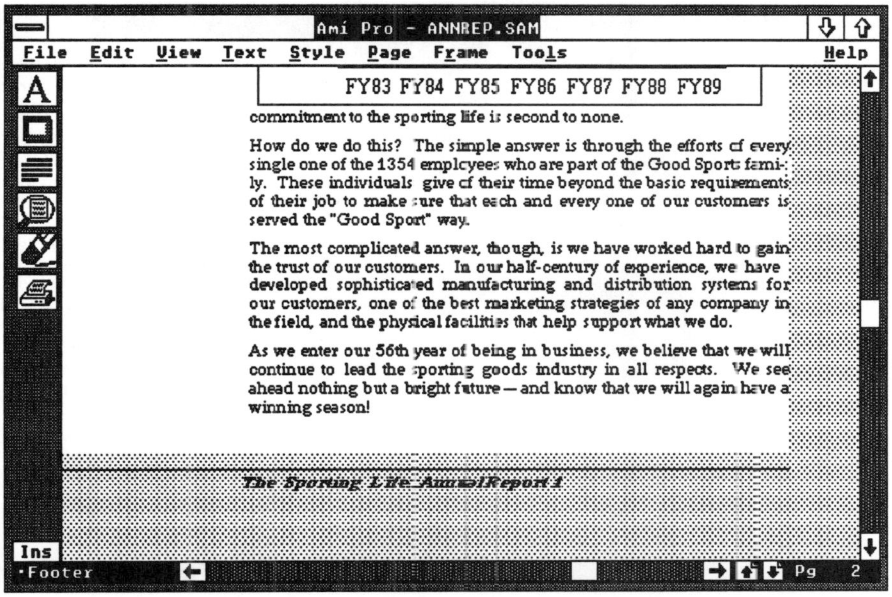

Figure 15–3
A footer shown in working view.

Creating a Fixed Header or Footer

To add a fixed header or footer to appear on each page of the document:

1. Click the top margin to add a header or click the bottom margin to add a footer. Figure 15–4 illustrates adding a fixed footer to a document.

2. Type and format the text for the header or footer.

3. If you want to add a page number to the header or footer, use the Page Numbering command as described earlier in the chapter.

4. If you want to add a date that Amí Professional will update automatically when you print the document, choose the Edit Insert Variable command, choose the System Date option, select a date format from the list, then click OK or press **Enter**. (You can get more information about using variables in Chapter 6.)

Creating Floating Headers and Footers

When you want different headers or footers for different pages of your document, you use floating headers or floating footers. For example, in-

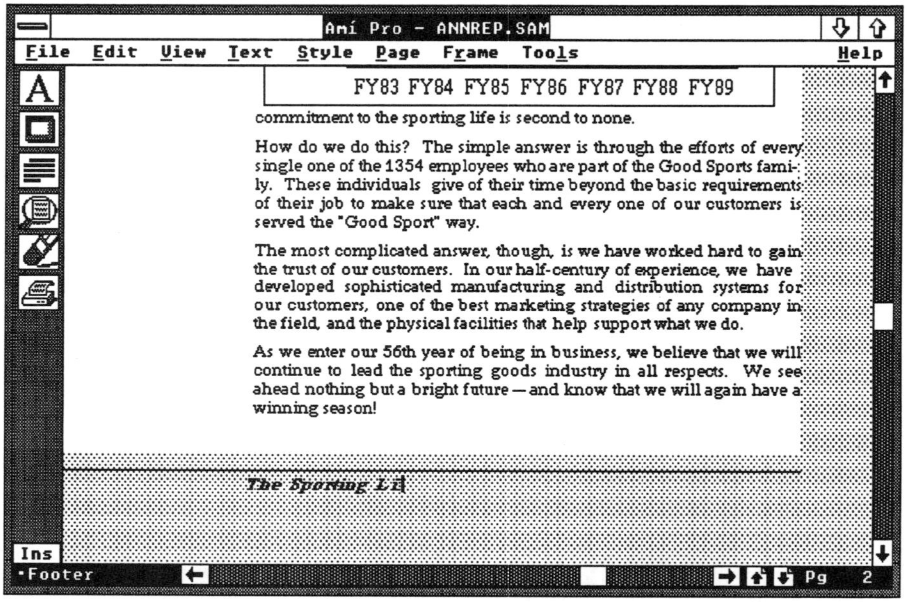

Figure 15–4 Adding a fixed footer to a document.

stead of having the same header and footer on each page, you may want to put the company name in the header on all left (even-numbered) pages and put the document title in the header on all right (odd-numbered) pages. Although you can't read the text in Figure 15–5, you can see that the headers and footers are different on the facing pages.

Floating headers or footers appear on the pages you specify (right, left, or all pages) until Amí Professional encounters a subsequent floating header or footer. Floating headers or footers are attached to text, so they move with that text if it shifts to a new page. When Amí Professional reaches the top of a page and begins its formatting for that page, it uses whatever header or footer is in effect in the first paragraph. If it encounters a new marker further down on the page, it begins the new header or footer on the next page. You can use one header or footer for one section, then use another one for the next section, and so on throughout the document.

Helpful Hint

If you want a header or footer to appear on every page of your document except for the first page, put the text in a floating header or floating footer on the second page.

Here's an example of using floating headers: If you're writing a feasibility study that has three sections—Background, Description of Study,

Figure 15–5
Amí Professional can create different headers and footers for left and right pages.

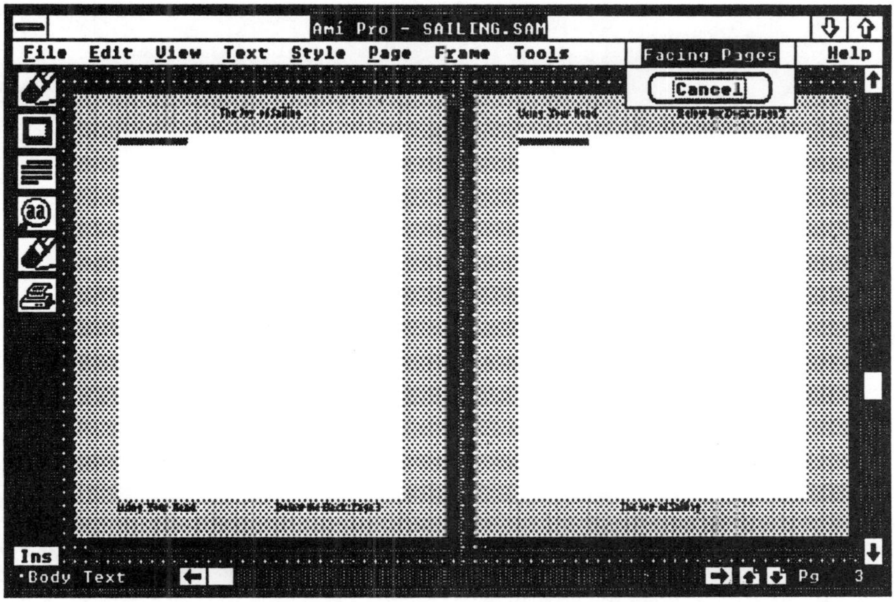

and Recommendations—you might put the company name in a floating header that appears on even-numbered pages throughout the document, put the title *Background* in the floating header on right pages throughout that section, *Description of Study* on right pages throughout that section, and *Recommendations* on right pages throughout that section. You could use a fixed footer to add the page number at the bottom of every page.

Helpful Hint

To avoid changes in page breaks that could throw off your headers or footers, it's a good idea to wait until your document is nearly finished before adding floating headers and footers.

To create a floating header or footer:

1. Select a word or two where you want to add a header or footer. You might want to select text at the top of the page, or if you want to make sure the header or footer remains with a specific heading in your document, select that heading.
2. Choose the Page Floating Header/Footer command. Amí Professional displays the dialog box shown in Figure 15–6.
3. Choose the Floating Header option to add text at the top of the page or choose the Floating Footer option to add text at the bottom.

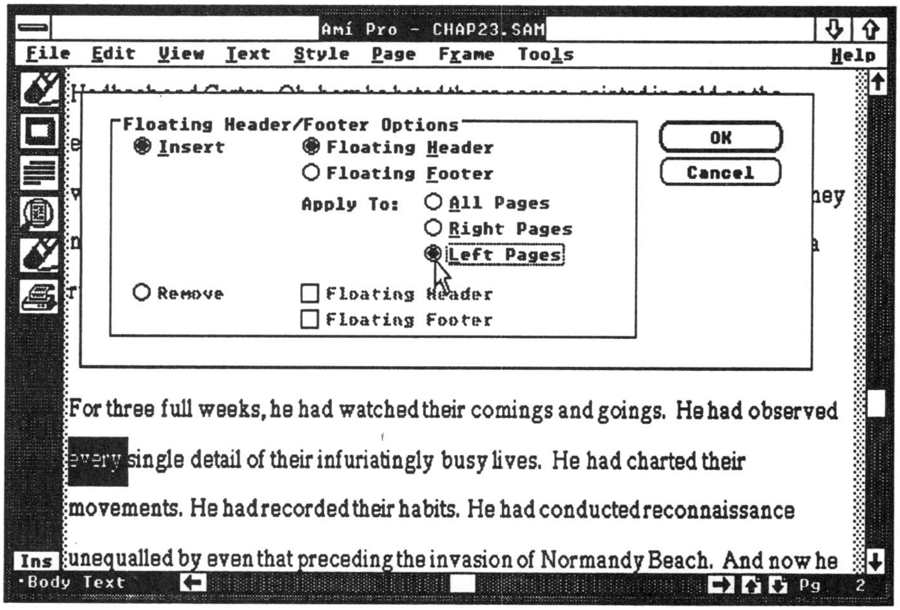

Figure 15-6 Creating a floating header for a section of a document.

4. Do one of the following:

   - If you want this header or footer to appear on every page until the next floating header or footer, choose All Pages.
   - If you're adding to a right (odd-numbered) page and you want this header or footer to appear on every right page until the next floating header or footer that applies to right pages, choose Right Pages.
   - If you're adding to a left (even-numbered) page and you want this header or footer to appear on every left page until the next floating header or footer that applies to left pages, choose Left Pages.

5. Click OK or press **Enter**. Amí Professional adds a floating header/footer marker to the page, as shown on the left in Figure 15–7. (You must have the Marks option turned on in the View Display Preferences dialog box to see the marker.)

6. If you inserted the marker in the first paragraph on the page, click the top margin to add a header or click the bottom margin to add a footer. If you inserted the marker lower on the page, go to the next page, then click the top or bottom margin as appropriate. (If there's not a conflicting marker in the first paragraph of the page, the margin

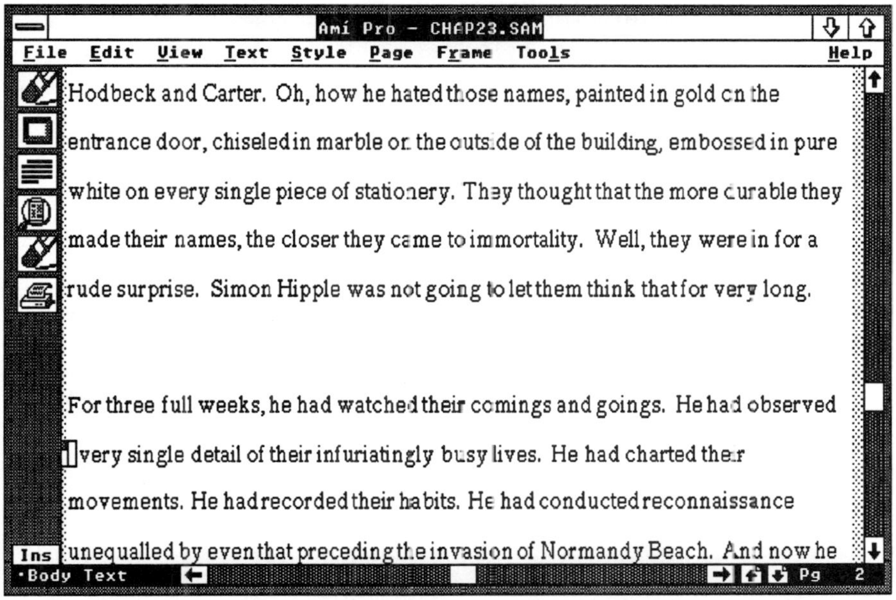

Figure 15–7
A floating header/footer mark.

should be blank. If there is another marker in the first paragraph, you may have to delete it before you can type.)

7. Type and format the text for the header or footer.

8. If you want to add a page number to the header or footer, place the cursor where you want the page number to appear, then use the Page Numbering command as described earlier in this chapter.

9. If you want to add a date that Amí Professional will update when you print the document, choose the Insert Variable command from the Edit menu, choose the System Date option, select a date format from the list, then click OK or press **Enter**.

You'll need to repeat this process on each page on which you want a new floating header or footer to appear. Amí Professional uses the same floating header or footer until it encounters the next page that contains a floating header or footer marker.

Setting Margins and Tabs for Headers or Footers

When you type in the top or bottom margin, Amí Professional automatically uses the paragraph style, margins, and tab settings in effect for headers and footers for the document. You can use commands on the Text menu to format the text. You can also change the margins or tab settings for headers or footers with the Page Modify Layout command.

To change margins or tab settings for the header or footer area throughout the document:

1. Choose the Page Modify Layout command.
2. Choose the Header or Footer option in the Modify box.

   The ruler at the top of the dialog box shows tab settings in effect for the header or footer area (if any).
3. If you're changing settings for a right or left page only, turn on Right or Left in the Pages box.
4. If you want to change the margins, type or select a new measurement in the margin running boxes.
5. If you want to change tab settings, do any of the following:
   - To set a new tab, choose the type of tab you want under Tabs at the right of the dialog box. Then point to the position in the ruler where you want the tab setting and click. A tab icon for that type of tab appears in the ruler.
   - To delete a tab setting from the ruler, click the tab icon to select it, then press the **Delete** key.
   - To move a tab setting on the ruler, point to the tab icon, hold down the mouse button, and drag it to a new position.
6. When all the tab settings in the ruler look the way you want, click OK or press **Enter**.

Figure 15–8 illustrates setting a tab for a header. You can also create different tab settings using inserted tab rulers. If you need more information about different types of tabs or using tab rulers, see Setting Tabs in Chapter 14.

EXAMPLE: Setting Tabs for Headers and Footers

Say you want to have a header with the title at the left margin, the date in the center, and the page number at the right margin, like this:

Annual Report	August 3, 1989	Page 2

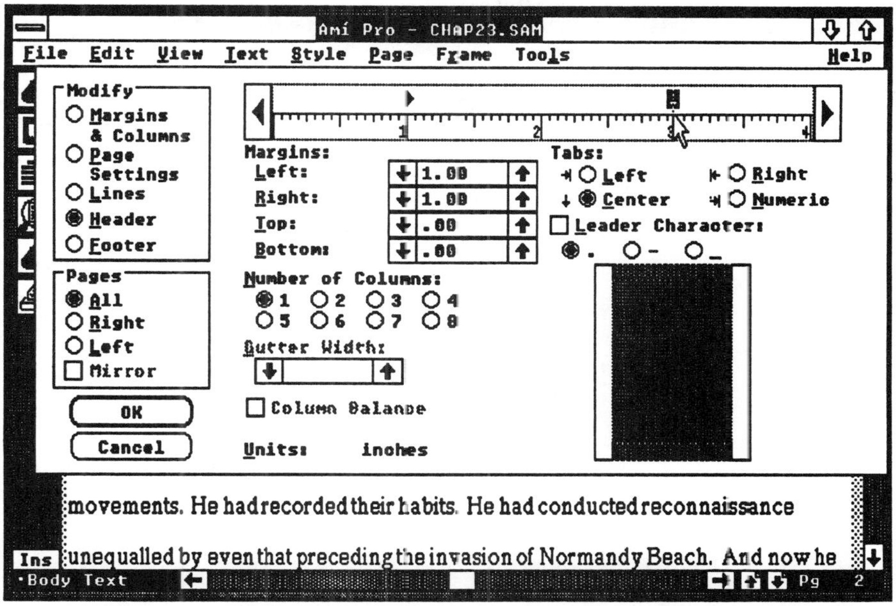

Figure 15-8
Setting a centered tab for a header in the Page Modify Layout dialog box.

and a footer that contains the centered company name, like this:

The Company, Inc.

Here's what you'd do:

1. Choose the Page Modify Layout command.
2. Select the Header option.
3. Set a centered tab at 4.25″ and a right-aligned tab at 7.5″. (These measurements are the center of the page and the right margin, respectively.)
4. Select the Footer option.
5. Set a centered tab at 4.25″.
6. Click OK to close the dialog box.
7. In the top margin, type the report name, press **Tab**, type the date, press **Tab**, type **Page** and a space, then use the Page Numbering command to insert the page number.
8. In the bottom margin, press the **Tab** key once, then type the company name.

Editing, Formatting, and Removing Headers or Footers

If you want to change the text for a header or footer, just move the cursor into the header or footer text and edit and format the text like you would in the rest of your document. You can also create a style for headers or footers that you can apply to all headers or footers. (See Chapter 9 for more information about creating styles.) If you want to change a page number that you've added with the Page Numbering command or a date that you've added with the Edit Insert Variable command, you'll have to choose those commands again and select new options.

To jump to the next header or footer, you can use the Go To command:

1. Choose the Tools Go To command.
2. Select a header or footer from the Next Item list.
3. Click Go To or press **Enter**.

If you want to delete a fixed header or footer, just delete all the text of the header or footer. If you want to delete a floating header or footer, click the floating header/footer marker to place the cursor there, choose the Page Floating Header/Footer command, and choose the Remove Floating Header/Footer option in the dialog box.

16

Controlling Pagination and Printing

When you're finished editing and formatting, you'll want to print all or part of your file. You can also print other items associated with your file, such as the document description and crop marks.

CONTROLLING PAGINATION

Amí Professional automatically inserts page breaks whenever the text reaches the bottom margin of the page. These are called *automatic page breaks* or *soft page breaks.* You can control whether page breaks divide paragraphs with the Style Modify Style command, as explained in Chapter 9, and you can control whether page breaks leave one line of text on a page with the Edit Defaults command, as explained in Controlling Widows and Orphans later in this chapter. You can also insert page breaks wherever you want to break a page, no matter which view is displayed at the time. Page breaks that you insert are called *manual page breaks* or *hard page breaks.*

Inserting Hard Page Breaks

You can always insert a hard page break, no matter which view you're using to display your document on the screen.

To insert a hard page break:

1. Place the cursor where you want to insert a page break.
2. Choose the Page Break command from the Page menu.
3. Choose Insert Page Break in the dialog box.
4. If you want to vertically center the text preceding the page break on the page, turn on the Vertically Center Text Above Page Break option. This option is especially handy for creating title pages—you can combine this option with centered horizontal alignment (on the Text menu) to center the title on the page.
5. Click OK or press **Enter**.

In layout view, text simply shifts from page to page when you insert page breaks. In draft mode, page breaks you insert are represented by colored rectangular symbols, as shown in Figure 16-1. Automatic page breaks move as you add or delete text, but manual page breaks stay in the place where you inserted them.

Helpful Hint

If you decide you want to vertically center text on pages to which you've already added page breaks, select the page break marker, choose the Page

Figure 16-1
In draft mode, manual page breaks are shown as colored rectangles.

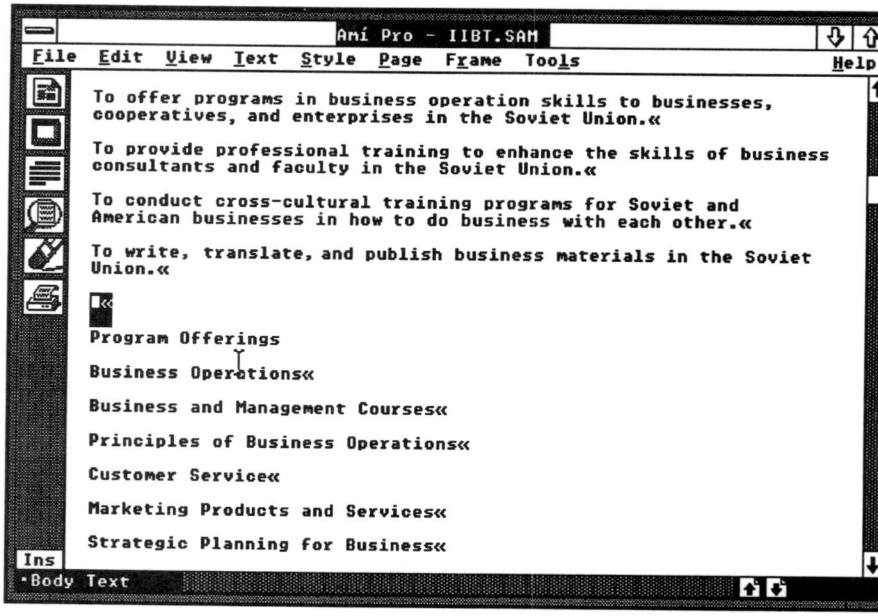

Break command and turn on the Vertically Center option, then respond Yes to the replacement verification message that the program displays.

Jumping to a Hard Page Break

You can use the Tools Go To command to quickly move the cursor to the next hard page break:

1. Choose the Tools Go To command.
2. Turn on the Next Item option, then select Hard Pg Break from the list.
3. Click Go To or press **Enter**. Amí Professional scrolls to and selects the next hard page break.
4. To jump to the next hard page break, press **Ctrl+H**.

Removing a Hard Page Break

You can't remove an automatic page break that Amí Professional has inserted, but you can remove a hard page break that you put in.

To remove a hard page break:

1. Do one of the following:
   - If you're using layout mode, move the cursor to the bottom of the page before the page break you want to remove.

   or

   - If you're using draft mode, place the cursor immediately after the page break marker you want to remove.
2. Choose the Page Break command from the Page menu.
3. Choose Remove Page Break in the dialog box.
4. Click OK or press **Enter**.

   Amí Professional recalculates the page breaks.

Controlling Widows and Orphans

By default, Amí Professional automatically prevents widows and orphans—single words and lines of text separated from their accompanying paragraphs. However, you can change the setting any time you like.

To prevent or allow widows and orphans:

1. Choose the Edit Defaults command.
2. Choose the Options button.
3. Turn on or turn off the Widow/Orphan Control option, as shown in Figure 16–2.
4. Click OK or press **Enter**.

Jumping to a Specific Page

When you know the page number you want to go to, you can quickly jump to that page.

To jump to a specific page:

1. Choose the Tools Go To command or press **Ctrl+G**.

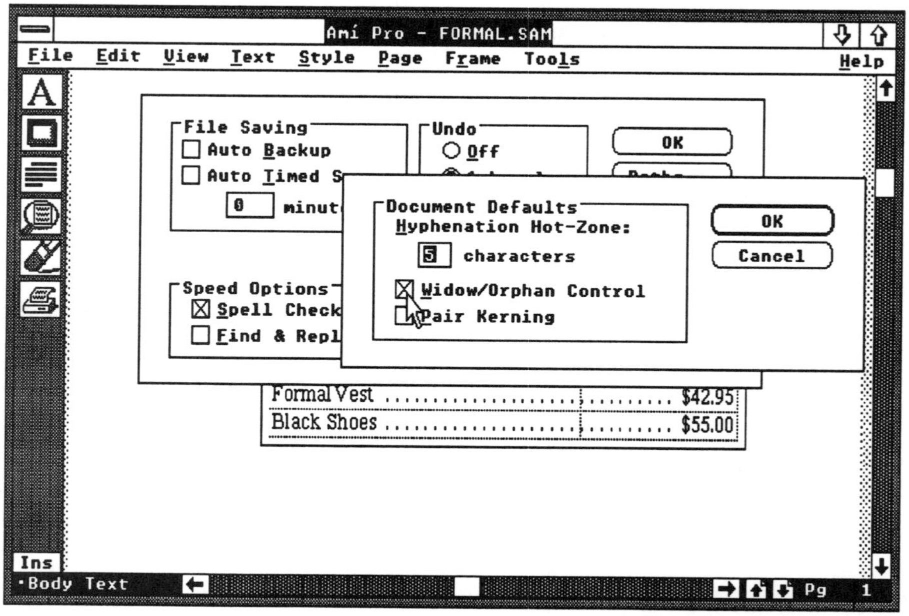

Figure 16–2 Preventing widows with the Edit Defaults command.

Amí Professional displays the dialog box shown in Figure 16–3.

2. Type the page number in the dialog box.
3. Click Go To or press **Enter**.

   Amí Professional displays the page you specified.

PRINTING

When you choose the File Print command in Amí Professional, you use the Windows printer driver files and the Windows Control Panel settings to control the printer. This section's discussions explain the connections between Amí Professional and Windows, and how to choose printer settings.

About .DRV Files

What's a .DRV file? DRV is the extension Windows and Amí Professional use for printer driver files. You must install the appropriate printer driver file before you can print from Amí Professional. Chances are that you already installed the appropriate printer driver when you installed Win-

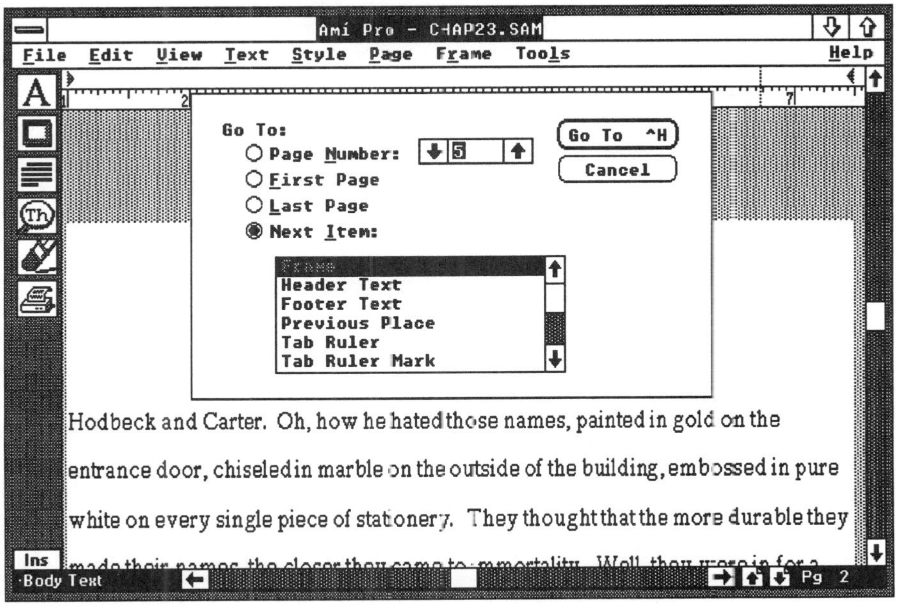

Figure 16–3
The Tools Go To dialog box.

dows. If you don't have the proper printer driver installed, you can install one using the Control Panel, as described later in this chapter.

Speed Tip

If you know that an Amí Professional file is ready to print when you turn on your computer, you can quickly start the program and print the file by typing **win amipro *filename*.sam /p** at the prompt. Be sure to include any drive letters or path names needed to find the file. For example, typing **win amipro a:resume.sam /p** would start the program and print the RESUME.SAM file stored in drive A, using the default print settings. If you're using Windows 386, you'll need to type **win386** instead of **win**; if you're using SAE Windows, you don't need to type **win** at all.

Preparing to Print

Before you print, you may want to do the following:

- Choose the Printer Setup command, then choose the Setup button and check the printer selection, paper size, and orientation options to make sure they're right.
- Choose the Page Modify Layout command, then choose the Page Setting options and check the page height and width.
- Check pages using full-page view.

Basic Printing

To print an Amí Professional file:

1. If necessary, open the document you want to print.
2. Choose the File Print command.

   Amí Professional displays the dialog box shown in Figure 16–4.
3. If you want to print more than one copy, type a new number in the Number of Copies box.
4. If you want to print only certain pages, type the starting page number in the From box and type the ending page number in the To box. If you want to print only one page, type the same page number in both boxes.

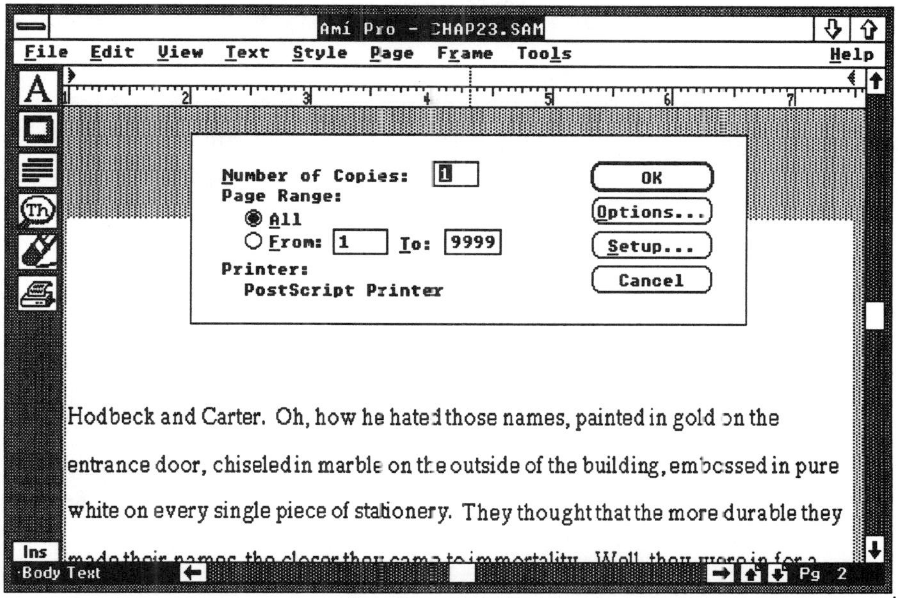

Figure 16–4 The File Print dialog box.

5. To select other print options, choose the Options. . . button, choose any of the following options, then click OK or press **Enter** to return to the Print dialog box.

Option	Description
Reverse order	Prints pages in reverse order, from last page to first page. This is especially useful on some laser printers.
Collate	When you are printing more than one copy, prints all pages of one copy before beginning the next copy.
Print document description	Prints the contents of the document description box on a separate page before printing the document.
Crop marks	Prints crop marks around the margins of the document (see the following Helpful Hint).
On preprinted form	Prints on a preprinted form. (See Chapter 17 for more information about filling out preprinted forms.)

6. Click OK or press **Enter** to begin printing.

Don't be alarmed if printing doesn't begin instantly—Amí Professional takes a few seconds to format pages and communicate with the printer, then your file should start to print. If it doesn't, read What If It Doesn't Print? later in this chapter for suggestions about how to find the problem.

Helpful Hint

If you want to format your documents for a small page size (6″ × 9″, for example), but print on a regular page size (8.5″ × 11″, for example), you can set the Page Modify Layout dialog box to the dimensions of the smaller page. Then print on the larger page, and turn on the Crop Marks option in the File Print dialog box to print crop marks around the "edges" of the small pages so you'll know where to trim your pages. It couldn't get any easier!

For crop marks to print, the page dimensions must be set at least ½″ smaller than the actual size of the paper you're printing on.

Canceling Printing

If you need to cancel printing at any time:

- Press **Escape**.

The printer may not stop immediately, because it continues to print whatever is in its memory until it receives the "Stop!" message from Amí Professional. If the paper is jammed or another emergency situation has developed, press a button (if your printer has one) to take the printer "off line" or, in the case of dire emergencies, turn off the printer. (Turning off some printers causes them to lose information, and you'll have to send data to the printers again to restart.)

Controlling the Paper Feed to the Printer

When you want to specify from where and when paper enters the printer, you use the Setup button in the File Print dialog box.

1. Choose the File Print command.
2. Choose Setup to display the dialog box for the printer you have installed. Figure 16–5 shows the Setup dialog box for an HP LaserJet printer—the display you see may look quite different. For more in-

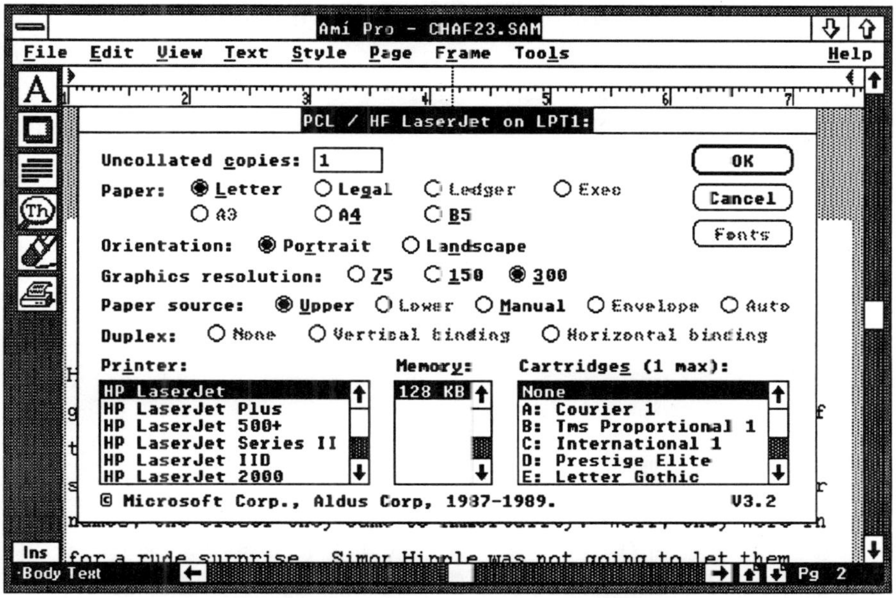

Figure 16-5
The dialog box displayed by the Setup button in the File Print dialog box.

formation about the printer options, see your Windows printer documentation.

3. From the Paper list, select the appropriate option. Not all printers accept all paper sizes: check your printer manual for specifics about the kind of paper your printer will accept.

4. From the Paper source box, select the appropriate option.

   Depending on the kind of printer you have installed, it will display various options such as Manual, Auto, Any Small Format, and so on.

5. Click OK or press **Enter**.

Changing Printers

When you used Amí Professional's Setup program, you told Amí Professional what kind of printer you're using. The dialog boxes you see are appropriate for that printer. If you installed several printers during the Setup process, you can use Amí Professional's File Printer Setup command to switch to a different printer. To install a new printer, see the next discussion.

To switch to a different printer:

1. Choose the File Printer Setup command.
2. From the Printer list, select a printer description.
3. Choose Setup. Amí Professional displays the Setup dialog box. This dialog box contains different options according to the type of printer. Figure 16–6 shows a dialog box for a PostScript printer.
4. Select options in the dialog box.
5. Click OK or press **Enter**.

Installing a New Printer

If you forgot to install a printer during the setup process, or if you've obtained a new printer since installing Amí Professional, you can use the following process to install a new printer. Before you begin this procedure, make sure you have the Amí Professional printer disks (Utilities 1 or 2) at hand.

1. Choose the Control Panel command from the Amí Professional Control menu (press **Alt, Spacebar, P**).

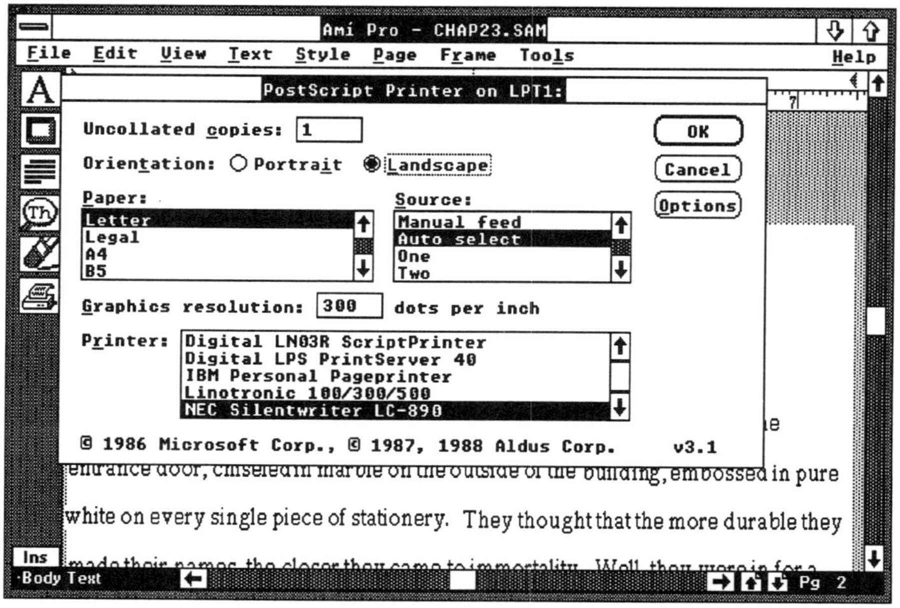

Figure 16–6 The dialog box Amí Professional displays for a PostScript printer.

2. Insert a printer disk into the A drive.
3. Choose the Installation Add New Printer command.
4. Scroll through the list of printers to find your specific brand and model. If you can't find it, replace the disk in drive A with the other printer disk, then go back to step 3. If you can't find your printer, consult Amí Professional's printer manual.
5. Select the printer from the list, then click Add or press **Enter**.

   A dialog box appears, asking whether you want to copy the driver file to your hard disk.
6. Change the path name if necessary, then click Yes or press **Enter**.
7. Choose the Setup Connections command.
8. Select a connection and a printer, then click OK or press **Enter**.
9. Choose the Setup Printer command.
10. Select the printer you'll use most of the time, then click OK or press **Enter**. A dialog box appears in which you enter output options (paper size, orientation, and so on) for that type of printer.
11. Choose options in the dialog box, then click OK or press **Enter**.
12. If you're installing a serial printer, choose the Setup Communications command, choose the appropriate communications settings, then click OK or press **Enter**.

Printing Envelopes

If your printer is wide enough or supports an envelope-feed mode, you can print addresses on envelopes with Amí Professional. The method you use to print envelopes depends on the type of printer you have.

You may need to experiment somewhat to find a method that works for your printer. To print envelopes, do the following:

1. Choose the Page Modify Layout command, choose the Page Settings button, adjust the Page Size boxes to match the height and width of the envelope, and set the paper orientation to Landscape or Portrait, according to whether you're inserting the envelope horizontally or vertically. (On most laser printers, it's best to set the orientation to Landscape and insert the envelope "short end" first.)

2. Position frames on the page where you want the addresses to appear and type the addresses in the frames. See Chapter 12 for more information about using frames.

3. Use the File Print command to print the envelope.

Amí Professional also provides a style sheet named ENV.STY that you can use as is (depending on your printer) or adapt to print envelopes.

What If It Doesn't Print?

If Amí Professional displays a message saying that your document is printing, but the printer just sits there silently, don't start cursing right away. It takes Amí Professional a few seconds to format pages and communicate with the printer. The length of time required depends on the length of your document and the speed of your computer. However, if you've waited a moment or two and the document still isn't printing or Amí Professional has displayed an error message, go through the steps in the following checklist. We can't foresee all the problems that can arise, but if you complete all the steps in the checklist in order, the odds are good that you'll find and fix your problem along the way.

1. Make sure the printer is plugged in and turned on.

2. Make sure the printer cable is securely plugged into the correct printer and the computer ports.

3. Make sure the printer buttons (such as Online and Ready) are "on" if they should be.

4. Make sure there's paper positioned properly in the printer.

5. Make sure all pieces of the printer (covers, ribbon or cartridge, paper trays, and so on) are in place.

6. Choose the File Print command, then check the settings to make sure they're right.

7. Turn the printer off, wait a few seconds, then turn it back on and try to print again.

8. If you're using PostScript codes in your document, create another copy of the document, remove the PostScript codes, and try printing the copy. An error in PostScript codes can cause a document not to print.

9. Check the Control Panel to make sure the printer "connections" are set to the correct port.
10. Check the Amí Professional printer manual to make sure that the driver file that's installed is the correct one for your brand and model of printer.

If you're an experienced MS-DOS user, you might also want to check the TEMP environment variable, which is typically set in the AUTOEXEC.BAT file with a statement such as SET TEMP=c:\. If this line is not present or sets an invalid path, fix it and restart your computer.

If you've gone through every step in this list and your document still doesn't print, call your printer manufacturer or call the SAMNA Technical Support number.

17

Form Letters, Address Labels, and Preprinted Forms

To create form letters, address labels, or other form-type documents, you use a merge process (frequently called *print merge* or *mail merge*) to insert variable information from a data file into a document with standard text. In this chapter, you'll learn to create form letters, address labels, and preprinted forms.

MERGE BASICS

To create form letters or address labels, you'll follow three basic steps:

1. Create a data file containing the variable information you want to use. This is usually a list of names, addresses, and other information.
2. Create a standard file that will contain the standard text and fields into which the variable information will be inserted.
3. Use the File Merge command to merge the two files and create multiple documents.

This process is illustrated by Figure 17–1.

CREATING A DATA FILE

A *data file* contains the list of information you want to use in your form letters or address labels. To create a data file:

1. Use the File New command to open a new empty document.

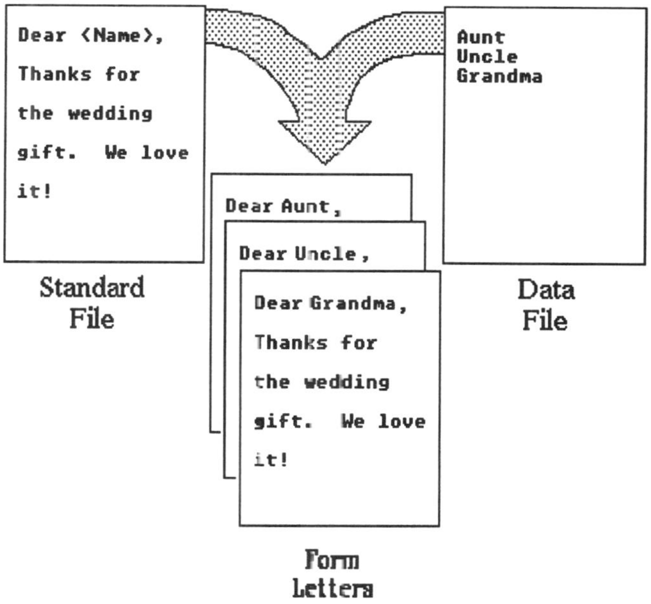

Figure 17–1
You merge a data file and a standard file to create form letters.

2. On the first line of the file, type the character you'll use to separate the *fields* (pieces of data such as name, street, and city) and the character you'll use to end each record (all the information that belongs together, such as all the data associated with one person's name). These characters are commonly called *delimiters*. The separator character is a *field delimiter*, and the ending character is a *record delimiter*. Be sure your delimiter characters aren't used in your data. For example, you might type ~¦.
3. On the second line of the file, type the names for all fields in a record and separate the fields with the separator character you chose. This line is commonly called a *header record*. For example, you might type **Name~Street~City~State~Zip¦**.
4. On the following lines, type your data records, putting the fields in the same order as in the header record, using field delimiters to separate the fields and using the record delimiter to end each record.
5. Use the File Save command to save your data file with a name that you'll remember as a data file (such as DATALIST.SAM, ADDRESS.SAM, or CUSTOMER.SAM).

If you don't have information for a particular field, don't put any characters (not even a space) in that field, but do put in the delimiter to end that field. You'll end up with two delimiters side by side (see Figure 17–3).

This process sounds more complicated than it actually is. You can easily create a data file by copying the format of a sample document like the ones shown in Figures 17–2 and 17–3.

Using Tables in Data Files

You can also create a data file in which data is in a table, provided that you don't have so many columns that a table would be unreadable. To create a data file this way, position the cursor at the top of a new file, insert a table with the right number of rows and columns, type the field names in the top row, then fill out the rest of the rows with the records. Because Amí Professional considers each cell a separate field and each row a separate record, there's no need to specify the delimiters as you must outside of tables.

If you put your merge data into a table, keep in mind that Amí Professional uses the Table Text style for all text in a table unless you assign a different style. The Table Text style specifies two decimal places for numbers that are alone in cells (not accompanied by text), and at the time of this writing, Amí Professional adds decimal points to zip codes and other unaccompanied numbers in cells during a merge process. To avoid getting unwanted decimal points when you are merging from a table,

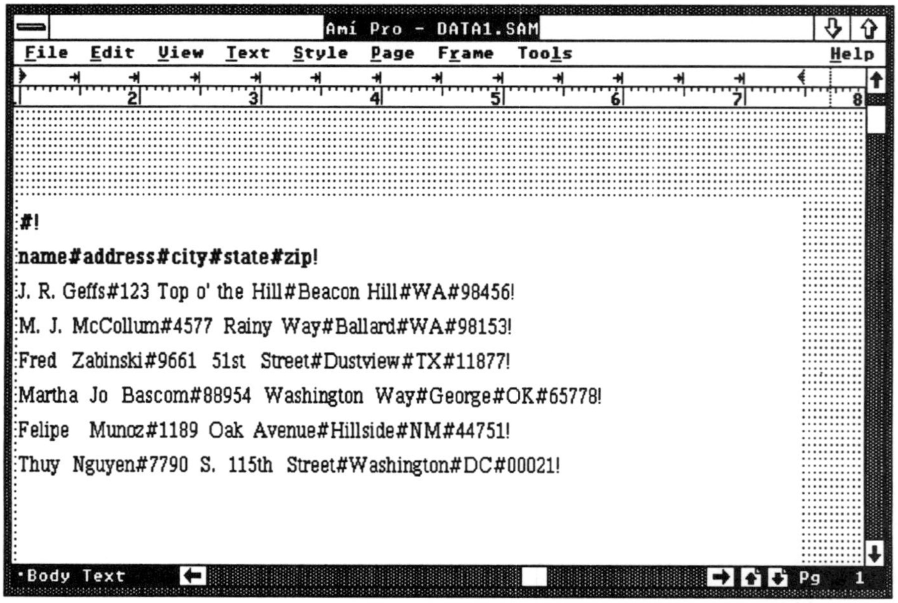

Figure 17–2
A simple data file containing names and addresses.

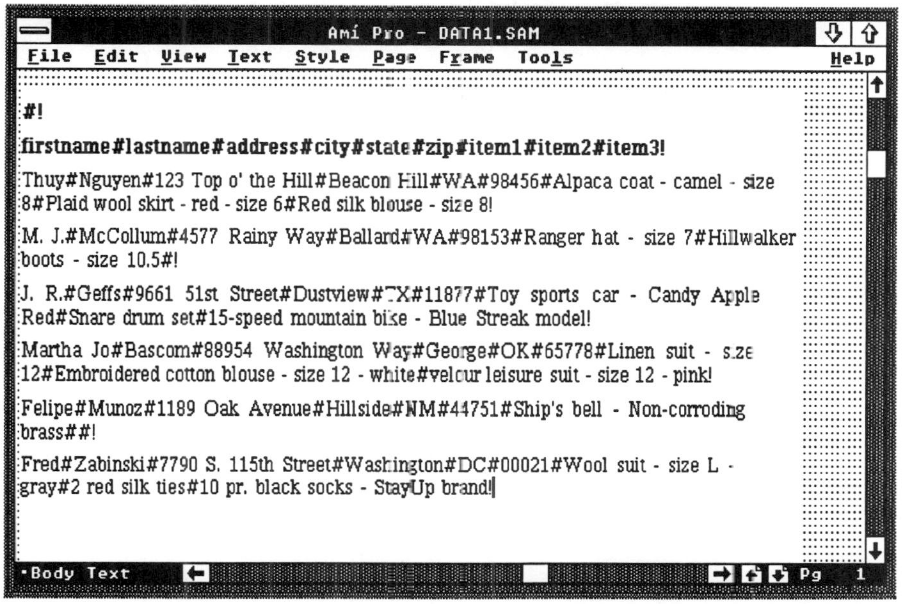

Figure 17-3 A complex data file containing fields with two lines of information.

change the Table Text style with the Modify Style command to remove the decimal point or apply a different style to cells containing numbers in your table.

Helpful Hints

For maximum flexibility in sorting data files, put titles such as Ms., Mr., Dr., and articles such as The, An, and A in a field separate from names of people, companies, or publications, like this:

Title	**FirstName**	**LastName**
Dr.	Maria	Sanchez
Mr.	John	McCollum
Ms.	Flora	Lee

Article	**Company Name**
The	Cookie Store
	Sweet Dreams
An	Apple a Day

Article	**Book Title**
The	Country Cookbook
	Criminal at Heart
A	Good Old Boy

This way you can sort using names, still keep the titles and articles, and have everything end up in the right place. For example, if you type **The Country Cookbook** in one field and then do a sort to list book names in alphabetic order, *The Country Cookbook* ends up under *T* instead of under *C*. If you put *The* in a separate field, the article stays with the record and prints with the rest of the name, but the sort order is correct.

If you want to be able to print part of a data file (just certain records), you can add a field such as Number, then type in numbers for each record. Then you can set up a conditional clause that would print a specific record (for example, `If Number = 3` to print the third record) or a range of records (`If Number < 10` to print records 1 through 9, or `If Number > 10 AND < 20` to print records 11 through 19). It won't make any difference if you don't need these numbers often—the program just ignores any fields in the data record that you don't reference in your standard document or in conditional clauses.

Using Data from Other Files

Instead of typing all the records in the data file as just described, you can use the Clipboard to transfer sections of text from other Windows files to the data file. Even if you're copying the information from another file, you still have to set up the data file according to Amí Professional's rules, as described previously. If the pasted entries are separated by spaces or tab characters, use the Tools Find & Replace command to replace the spaces or tabs with another character, such as @ or #. (Remember that you can press Ctrl+Tab for tab characters and Ctrl+Return for carriage return characters in the Find & Replace dialog box.) Be sure to end each record with the character you specified in the first line.

If you want to use data from a non-Windows application, your best bet is to import the file with the Import/Export command and then reformat the file as necessary.

CREATING A STANDARD FILE

You must create your data file before you create a standard file, because you need to use the field names from the data file in the standard file.

To create a standard file, open a new document and type the text you want to appear in every form letter. Wherever you want to insert a field for Amí Professional to fill in with text from the data file:

1. Choose the Edit Insert Variable command, choose the Merge Field option in the dialog box, then click OK or press **Enter**. A new dialog box displays a list of field names. If this is the first time you've used Merge Field, the list is blank.

2. To specify the data file to get field names from, choose the Data File button to open another dialog box, select the name of the data file from the list, then click OK or press **Enter**. The names of all fields in the data file appear in the dialog box, as shown in Figure 17–4.

3. In the dialog box, double-click on the field name you want to insert in your document. (You can also select the field name and choose Insert, but that's slower.) Amí Professional adds a field enclosed in angle brackets to your document. The dialog box remains open so you can insert more fields.

4. Continue to type standard text and repeat step 3 to insert all the field names you need in your document. Be sure to type all the spaces and punctuation you need between field names, such as a comma and a space between the City and State fields. Figure 17–4 illustrates adding field names to a standard file.

5. When you're finished inserting field names, click Cancel or press **Escape** to close the dialog box.

6. Save the standard file. Figure 17–5 shows a sample standard file.

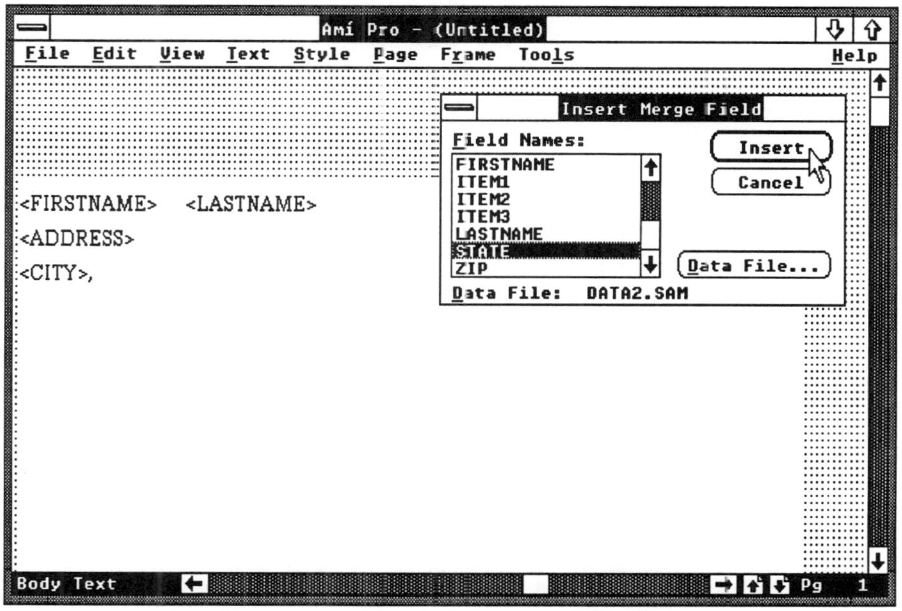

Figure 17–4 Inserting field names in a standard file with the Edit Insert Variable (Merge Field) command.

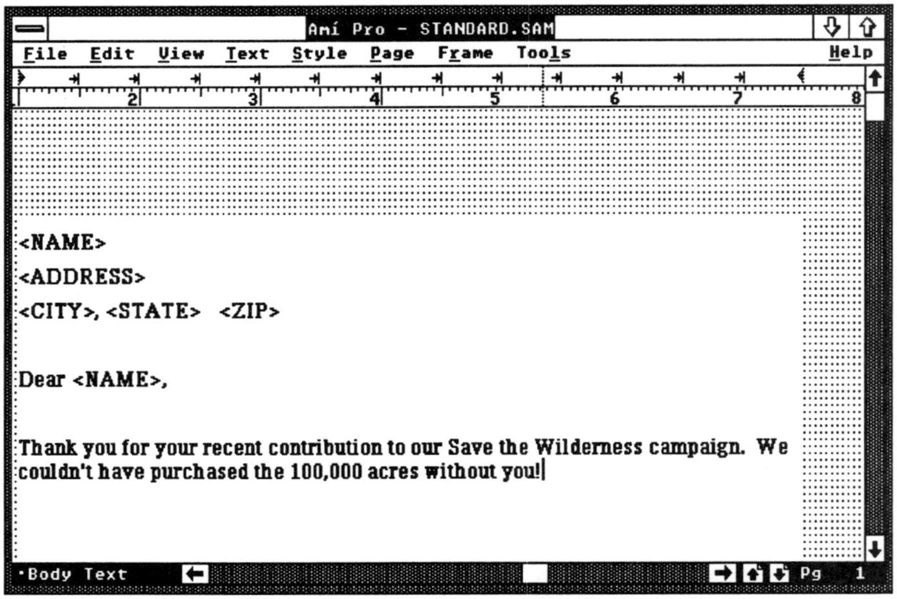

Figure 17–5
A sample standard file. Fields (shown in angle brackets) are filled in with text from a data file during the merge process.

Helpful Hints

When you create a standard file, remember that field names will be replaced by the data from your data file, so spacing and line breaks may look different in the result than in the standard file. Because Amí Professional uses word-wrap to break lines, the program may shift a long field name to the next line: This doesn't mean that the actual data will necessarily appear on the next line, like the field name—the location of data depends on the length of the merged data that replaces the field name.

At times you may need to use a field name in your standard file when there may or may not be data for that field in your data file. A good example of this necessity is using the field name <Position> to include a job title (such as Editorial Director) in an address; you may have a job title for some records in your data file but not for others.

If you put this field name on the same line with other fields, Amí Professional adjusts the text as necessary. If you put this field name on a separate line, you must use a style that has no space before or space after the paragraph (check this with the Modify Style command, Spacing options) or you'll end up with a blank line when there's no data to fill into that field. The Body Single style in most style sheets will work. The line spacing (single, 1 1/2, double, and so on) has no effect on this.

If you're inexperienced with merge techniques, it's a good idea to save form letters in a file (or at least view them first) instead of printing them immediately. You can easily print them later if everything's okay, and if something didn't work out right, you can just delete the file, fix the problem, and try again. Saving forms in a file enables you to practice and view results without wasting paper, printer ribbons, and precious time.

MERGING THE DATA INTO THE STANDARD FILE

When you've completed your data file and your standard file, you're ready to merge the two together and create multiple form documents. You can choose to print form letters immediately as they're created, to view them and then print, or to save them in a file for later printing.

To merge the data file and the standard file and create form letters:

1. If necessary, open the standard file you want to use.
2. Choose the File Merge command. Amí Professional displays the dialog box shown in Figure 17–6.
3. If the name of your data file is not shown as the data file in the dialog box, click the Data File... button to display a new dialog box, select the data file from the list or type the data file name in the text box, then click OK or press **Enter** to get back to the File Merge dialog box. Figure 17–7 illustrates choosing a data file from the list.

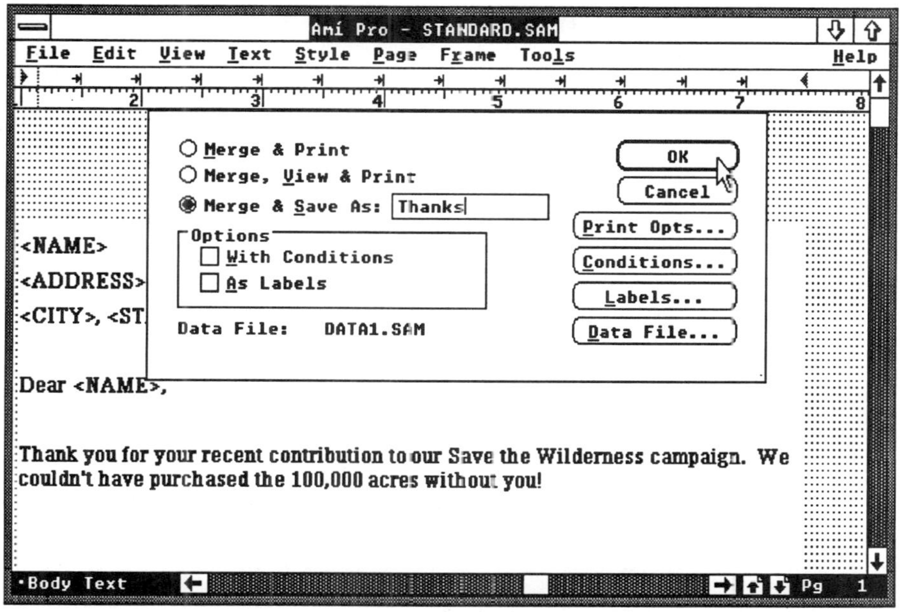

Figure 17–6 Choosing options in the File Merge dialog box.

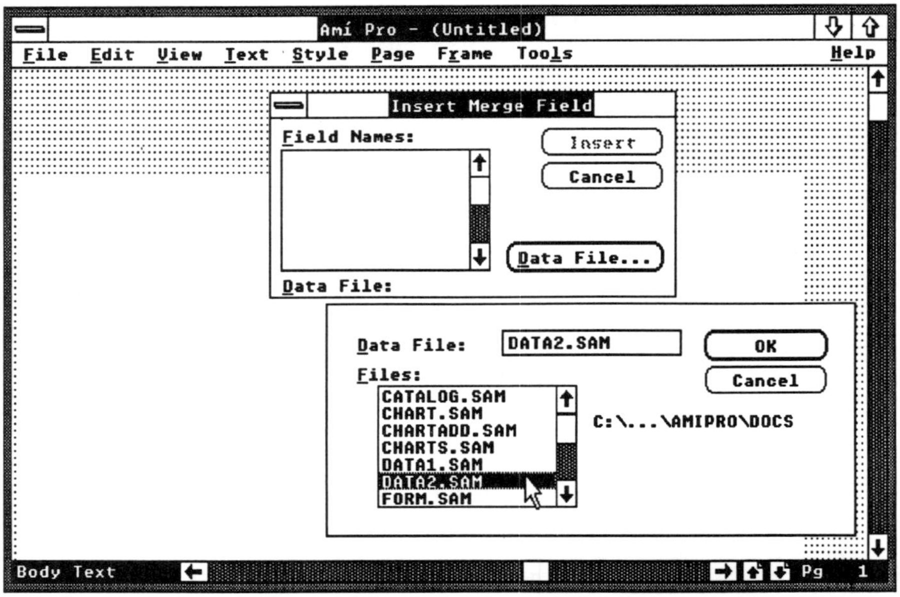

Figure 17-7
Selecting the data file in the Data File dialog box.

4. If you want to print more than one copy, print only certain pages, include conditional clauses, or print address labels, choose buttons from the File Merge dialog box and fill out the dialog boxes that appear. (These options are described in more detail in following sections in this chapter.)

5. Choose one of the following options to create the form letters:

   - If you want to print each form after it's created, choose Merge & Print.

   or

   - If you want to view each form and then print it, choose Merge, View & Print.

   or

   - If you want to save all the forms in a file for later viewing and printing, choose Merge & Save As, then type a file name in the text box.

6. Click OK or press **Enter** to begin the merge process.

If you chose to print the form letters right away, they'll start printing. If you chose to view, then print, Amí Professional displays each form and asks permission before printing. If you chose to save the forms in a file, use the File Open command to view the resulting file. (You might want to choose the Open Another button in the File Open dialog box so that you can see both the standard file and the resulting forms on the screen at the same time.)

Printing Multiple Copies or Printing Only Certain Pages of the Standard File

Just as when you choose the File Print command to print a normal document, when you're merging documents you can choose to print more than one copy of the forms or choose to print only certain pages of the standard file. For example, your standard file might contain three different letters on three separate pages, but you might want to print only the letter on the third page, and print two copies so that you can keep one copy for your files.

To print multiple copies or certain pages:

1. After opening the standard file, choose File Merge.
2. After choosing all of the other options you want in the dialog box, choose the Print Opts... button. Amí Professional displays the dialog box shown in Figure 17–8.

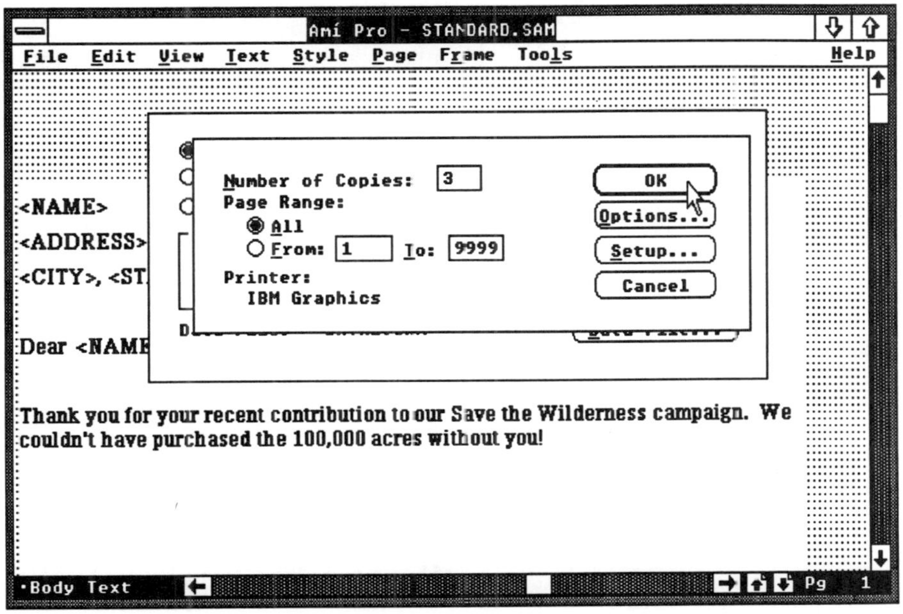

Figure 17–8 Choosing print options before a print merge process.

3. If you want to print more than one copy, type a new number in the Number of Copies box.
4. If you want to print only certain pages of the standard file, type the starting page number in the From box and the ending page number in the To box. (For example, to print pages 3 through 5, type 3 in the From box and 5 in the To box; to print only page 4, type 4 in both boxes.
5. Click OK or press **Enter** to return to the File Merge dialog box.
6. Click OK or press **Enter** to begin the merge process.

Using Conditional Clauses to Print Specific Records

Sometimes you may want to use only specific records in your data file to create and print form letters. For example, you might want to use only those records with 98126 in the Zip field, or those records with SEATTLE in the City field.

You can also make matches even more specific by using AND and OR clauses. For example, if your company must delay a shipment of chairs to Atlanta, you might want to use only those records that have CHAIR in the Order field *and* ATLANTA in the City field. If the delay affects Miami as well as Atlanta, you might want to tell Amí Professional to print forms using those records that have CHAIR in the Order field *and* have ATLANTA *or* MIAMI in the City field.

To use conditional clauses to tell Amí Professional which records to use when it prints forms:

1. After opening the standard file, choose File Merge and choose all the other options you want in the dialog box.
2. Choose the Conditions button. Amí Professional displays the dialog box shown in Figure 17-9.
3. Click the top check box to the left of the word *If* to add an X to the box.
4. Click or use the **Tab** key to move to the Field Name box and make Amí Professional display a list of the field names in your data file, then type the name of the field you want or click the field name in the list at the right.
5. If necessary, click or use the **Tab** key to move to the Operator box and make the program display a list of operators, then type the

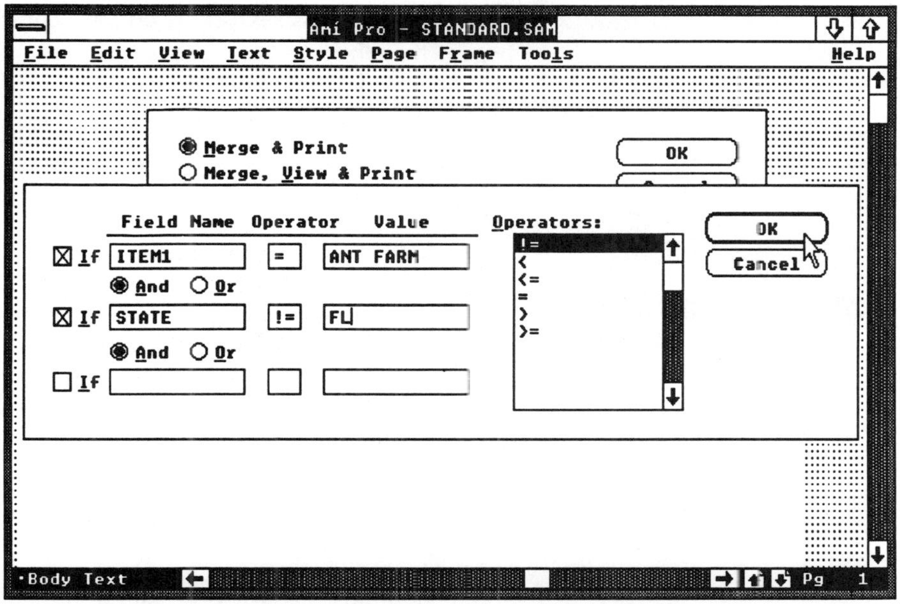

Figure 17–9
Setting up a conditional clause to print only those records that have ANT FARM in the Item1 field and something other than FL in the State field.

operator you want or click the operator in the list at the right. Here's what the operators mean:

!=	Not equal to
<	Less than
<=	Less than or equal to
=	Equal to
>	Greater than
>=	Greater than or equal to

6. Click or use the **Tab** key to move to the Value box, then type the value you want to match.

7. Click OK or press **Enter** to return to the File Merge dialog box.

8. Do one of the following:

   - If necessary, repeat steps 2 through 7 to set up more conditional clauses, choosing And or Or between conditional clauses.

   or

   - If you've set up all the conditions you want, turn on the With

Conditions option in the Options box, then click OK or press **Enter** to begin the print merge process.

Amí Professional prints forms only for those records that match the conditions you've specified. If you later want to use the same data file but ignore the conditions you set up, turn off the With Conditions option in the File Merge dialog box.

Creating Address Labels

If you have name and address fields in your data file, you can use the print merge process to create and print address labels. You need to create a standard file with the fields you want on the labels, and you need to set the page dimensions to the dimensions of your label. Then you tell Amí Professional how many labels to put on a page and where to start the first label. Here's how:

1. Set up your standard file with the name and address fields you want to print.
2. Choose the Page Modify Layout command, make the margins minimal (say, .10 inch), then select Page Settings in the dialog box, and set the page measurements to the dimensions of one label. In other words, if each label is 3 inches wide and 1.75 inches tall, you type these dimensions in the page settings boxes. You may need to adjust the text size or arrangement of the fields to fit the names and addresses on the label.
3. Choose File Merge and choose any other options you want in the dialog box.
4. Choose the Labels button. Amí Professional opens the dialog box shown in Figure 17–10.
5. To tell Amí Professional how many labels to print on each page, type numbers in the Labels Across Page and Labels Down Page boxes. Make sure the number of labels you type will actually fit on a page—for example, four 3-inch-wide labels won't print on an 8½-inch-wide page.
6. To specify the position of the first label relative to the upper left corner of the page, type measurements in the Down and Right boxes of the First Label Indent box. If you need to change the units of measurement (from inches to points, for example), click the Units: name first until you see the unit you want.

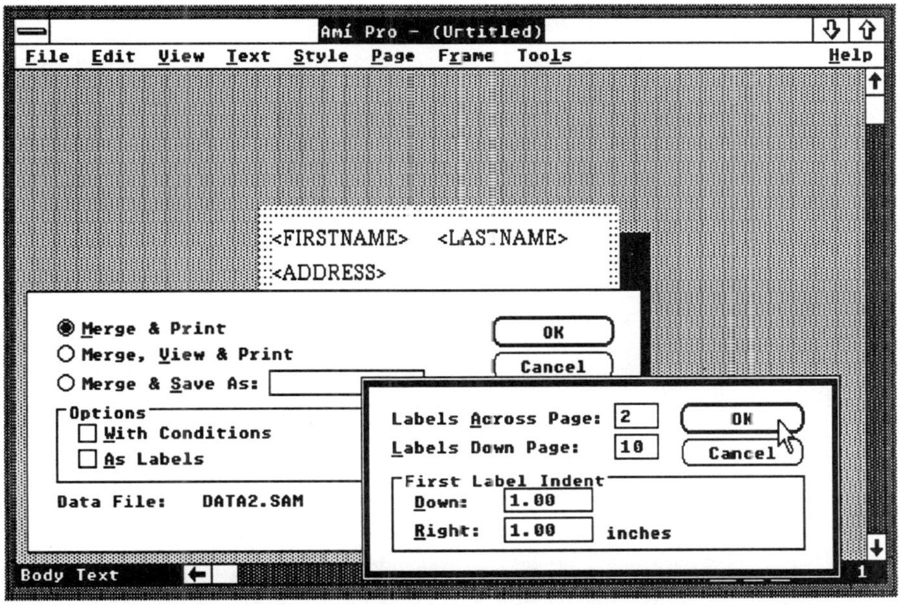

Figure 17–10 Setting up Amí Professional to print address labels from the data file.

7. Click OK or press **Enter** to return to the File Merge dialog box.

8. Click OK or press **Enter** to begin the print merge process.

If you later want to use the same data file to print something other than labels, make sure the As Labels option in the File Merge dialog box is off before you begin printing.

Instead of starting from scratch, you can start with the ~LABEL.STY style sheet, but you'll also need to adjust it to fit your needs.

SORTING THE DATA IN A FILE

You can use Amí Professional to sort the records in any file. This feature is especially useful in setting up a data file prior to starting the print merge process. For example, to make batch mailings easier, you might want to sort all the records according to the values in the Zip field. Then all the forms for one zip code would be printed together.

You can also sort data according to more than one field. For example, you might want to sort all the records in a data file by zip code first, then sort by last name so that records would be in alphabetical order within each zip code group.

Helpful Hint

Sorting by the wrong field or choosing the wrong sorting options can really scramble a document. And you can't undo a sort.

Thus, it's always a good idea to *save your file before doing a sort.* That way, if the results of the sort are not what you envisioned, you can always use the File Revert command to throw away the changes made by the sort.

To sort the data in a file:

1. If you don't want to sort the entire file, select the data you want to sort. (Even in a data file, you won't want to sort the delimiter line or the header record line, so select the actual records below these code lines.) If you want to sort the entire file, make sure nothing is selected.

2. Choose the Tools Sort command. If you didn't select anything, Amí Professional asks you if you're sure you want to sort the entire file. If you see this message box and you want to go ahead, click OK. Amí Professional displays the dialog box shown in Figure 17-11.

3. In the row labeled Key 1, type the number of the field you want to use as the first sorting key in the Field box. For example, to sort according to the codes in the ZIP field, which is the sixth field

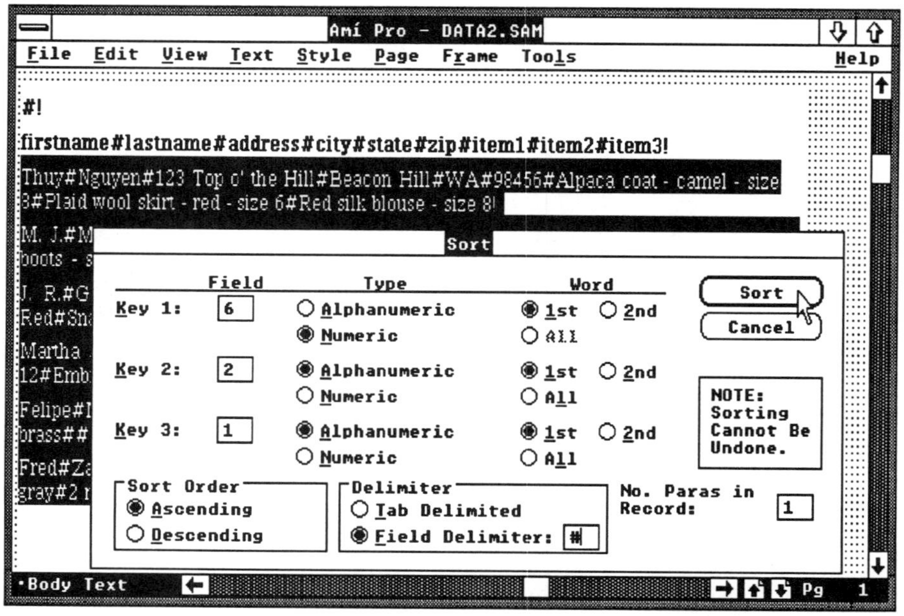

Figure 17-11 Setting up the Tools Sort dialog box to sort a data file by zip code (field 6) first, then by last name (using the 2nd field option).

(counting from the left margin) in your records, you'd type 6 in the Key 1 Field box.

4. Choose Alphanumeric to sort in alphabetic order, or choose Numeric to sort in numeric order.

5. If you have more than one word in the field you've specified and you don't want to sort according to the first word of the field, choose an option in the Word field to indicate which word of the field you want to use as the sorting *key*. (2nd sorts according to the second word in the field, and All considers all words in a field during the sort.) For example, if you put the city and state in the same City&State field (such as Seattle WA), but you want to sort by the state, you'd choose 2nd in the Word box to make Amí Professional skip over the first word (the city) and sort by the second word (the state).

6. If you are using more than one field as sorting keys, fill out the boxes in following rows (Key 2, Key 3, and so on) as appropriate. For example, to sort by the sixth field first, then sort the resulting list by the first field, you'd type 6 in the Key 1 Field box and fill in the rest of the Key 1 row, then type 1 in the Key 2 Field box and fill in the rest of the Key 2 row.

7. Choose Ascending in the Sort Order box to list records from *A* to *Z* or from 0 to 9, or choose Descending to list records from *Z* to *A* or from 9 to 0.

8. If the fields in the data you're sorting are separated by tab characters, turn on the Tab Delimited option in the Delimiter box. If the fields are separated by another character, turn on the Field Delimited option, then type the character in the following box. (If you're sorting rows in a table, these options are grayed out.)

9. If there is more than one paragraph in all of the records in your document and if each record has the same number of paragraphs, type the number of paragraphs in the No. Paras in Record box. If either of these conditions is not true, leave this option set to 1.

10. Click Sort or press **Enter** to perform the sort.

Helpful Hint

If you want to count the fields in your document but they're obscured by the Sort dialog box, try this:

1. Press **Alt+F7**.
2. Use the arrow keys or the mouse to move the Sort dialog box out of the way.
3. Press **Enter** to set the new position.

If this doesn't work, press Cancel to remove the dialog box, count the fields, then choose Tools Sort again.

CREATING FORMS

You can use a number of Amí Professional features to create your own forms. For example, you can use tables to align text in rows and columns and use cell references to do calculations. Figure 17–12 shows a form created as an Amí Professional table.

You can create forms with blanks that you can fill in with variable information, then print with the File Print command. If you need to print many variations of the same forms (IRS forms or payroll checks, for example), you may want to automate the process with the print merge techniques discussed earlier in this chapter. You can also use a special Amí Professional feature to fill in the blanks on preprinted forms, as described next.

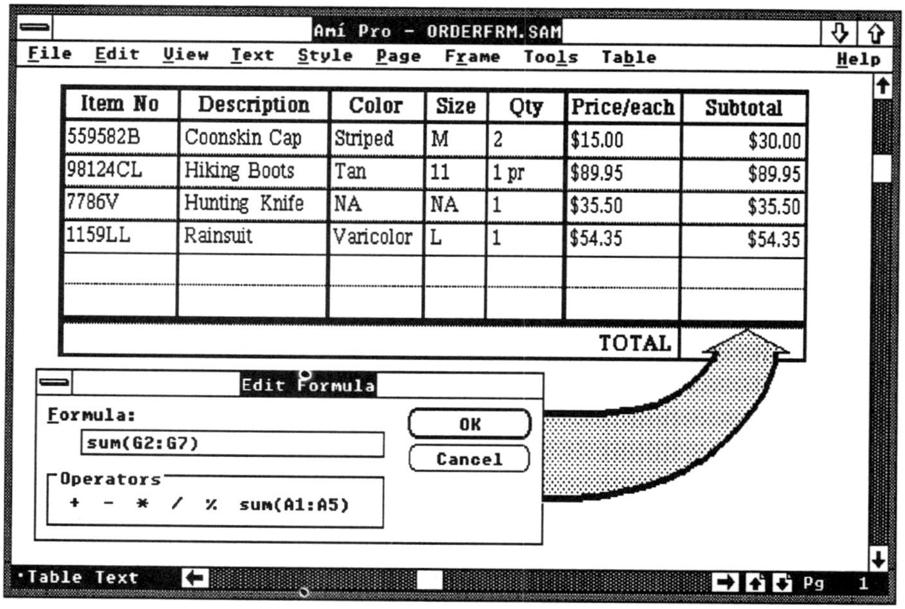

Figure 17–12
A form created as an Amí Professional table. The cell at the bottom contains a formula that does an automatic calculation.

Duplicating Printed Forms

If you want to design an on-screen form that duplicates the spacing of a printed form, you can use Amí Professional's *protected text* attribute, which you use to select and "lock" (protect) text in your form. When your text uses the protected-text attribute, the protected text doesn't print, so you can display a full form on the screen but print only the information you've filled into the blanks. Lines and shading in the protected areas of the document won't print, either.

Figure 17–13 illustrates filling in a form created in Amí Professional in which the labels (underlined in the figure) have the protected-text attribute. Figure 17–14 shows how the filled-out form would print. You can imagine how this feature makes it easy to fill in the blanks on preprinted forms.

To make it easier to fill out a form, you could attach bookmarks to the blanks, then use the Tools Go To command to jump from one bookmark to the next. See Chapter 8 for more information about bookmarks.

Creating a Form That Duplicates a Preprinted Form

To create a form that uses protected text for later printing on a preprinted form:

1. Using Amí Professional, duplicate the wording and spacing of the printed form.

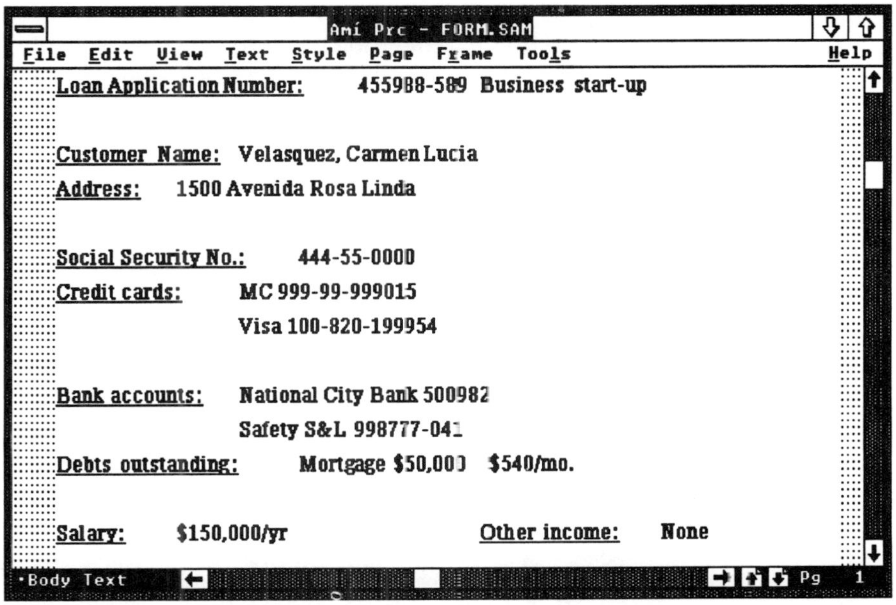

Figure 17–13
A form in which labels have the protected-text attributes.

Figure 17–14
When you are printing a form in which labels have the protected-text attributes, only the nonprotected—filled-in—information prints.

455988-589 Business start-up

Velasquez, Carmen Lucia
1500 Avenida Rosa Linda

444-55-0000
MC 999-99-999015
Visa 100-820-199954

National City Bank 500982
Safety S&L 998777-041
Mortgage $50,000 $540/mo.

$150,000/yr **None**

2. Select a section of wording (usually a label) that appears on the printed form (the text that you don't want to print). Be sure not to select any of the blank area you want to fill in with variable text.

3. Choose the Text Special Effects command, turn on the Protected Text option, then click OK or press **Enter**. Because the protected text attribute is invisible in layout mode, you might want to switch to draft mode to check it. Unfortunately, if your text is in a table, it won't show up at all in draft mode. You can control the color used for protected text in draft mode with the View Display Preferences command.

4. Repeat steps 2 and 3 until you've applied the protected-text attribute to all the text that you don't want to print.

5. Save the form.

Filling Out and Printing a Preprinted Form

Correct spacing is crucial when you fill out a preprinted form, so you may want to make several photocopies of the form and use the following procedure to run a few tests with your Amí Professional form, making adjustments until the blanks fill perfectly. Once you've saved the perfected version of your form, you should be able to fill out preprinted forms easily from then on, using the same file. You could save your form as a style sheet (use a .STY extension) and turn on the With Contents option.

When you're ready to fill out a preprinted form using the Amí Professional duplicate form you've created with protected text:

1. Open the form document.
2. Fill in the blanks. (You could use a data file and a print merge process to do this and save the forms in a file.)
3. If desired, use the File Save As command to save the filled-in forms with a different name.
4. Insert the preprinted form in the printer and make sure the printer is ready.
5. Choose the File Print command.
6. Turn on the On Preprinted Form option.
7. Click OK or press **Enter** to begin printing.

Amí Professional prints only the text that is not protected, filling in the blanks on the preprinted form.

Unprotecting Text and Making Changes

If you've accidentally applied the protected-text attribute, you may need to "unprotect" some text. To do this:

1. Select the text you want to change. If you have difficulty with the mouse, use **Shift**+***arrow*** keys.
2. Choose the Text Special Effects command.
3. Turn off the Protected Text option.

18

Outlining and Numbering

If you have to organize and refer to information in your document in a structured way, you'll need to number paragraphs or lines for easy reference. Amí Professional makes all types of paragraph numbering a snap by controlling the formats with styles. And you can number all or just some of the lines in your document with one command. You don't have to worry about keeping the numbers in order, indenting outlined paragraphs, and all of those other headaches that inevitably result when you type the numbers yourself—it's all automatic using this program. In this chapter, you'll see how to

- number and organize paragraphs using traditional outline formats
- structure and number paragraphs using the legal numbering system
- sequentially number paragraphs for easy reference
- number lines in your document

OUTLINING AND OTHER METHODS OF NUMBERING PARAGRAPHS

The styles in Amí Professional make it easy to do traditional outlining or any other form of numbering paragraphs.

Because you will be working with styles, you'll need to display the styles box if it's not already visible. Press **Ctrl+Z** or choose the Show Styles Box command from the Style menu.

Helpful Hint

If you're in the habit of pressing Enter between paragraphs to add blank lines, you're going to find that Amí Professional numbers your blank paragraphs if they have a numbered style applied to them. To add more blank space between paragraphs, you should get in the habit of changing the spacing before and after paragraphs in styles (see Chapter 9). If you must use the Enter key, you'll need to apply an unnumbered style (such as Body Text) to all the blank paragraphs.

Traditional Outline Formats

A traditional outline format uses this system of numbering:

I. Main Topic
  A. Subtopic
    1. Sub-subtopic
      a. Sub-sub-subtopic
      b. Sub-sub-subtopic
    2. Another sub-subtopic
  B. Another subtopic
II. Another Main Topic
  A. and so on

Amí Professional provides a traditional outline style sheet to make this type of formatting extremely easy. You don't have to indent the paragraphs or type the numbers or letters—the styles automatically take care of that. Here's all you do:

1. Choose the File New command to start a new document or choose the Use Another Style Sheet command from the Style menu if you want to format existing paragraphs.

2. Select ~OUTLINE.STY from the style sheet list.

3. Apply the appropriate styles to format your text:

Style	**Description**
Outline I	Main Topic (I, II, III, and so on)
Outline A	Subtopic (A, B, C, and so on)
Outline 1	Sub-subtopic (1, 2, 3, and so on)

Outline a	Sub-sub-subtopic (a, b, c, and so on)
Outline i	Sub-sub-sub-subtopic (i, ii, iii, and so on)

Outlining couldn't get any easier! If you add new paragraphs, rearrange the order, or delete text, the program automatically renumbers the paragraphs for you according to the style you've attached. To change the level of a topic (promote an A-level subtopic to a I-level main heading, for example), simply apply the appropriate style and the formatting will change. Figure 18–1 illustrates outlining with the ~OUTLINE.STY style sheet.

Legal Numbering Systems

You may want to use legal numbering, which numbers paragraphs like this:

1. Main Topic
    1.1. Subtopic
        1.1.1. Sub-subtopic
            1.1.1.1. Sub-sub-subtopic
            1.1.1.2. Sub-sub-subtopic
        1.1.2. Another Sub-subtopic
    1.2. Another Subtopic

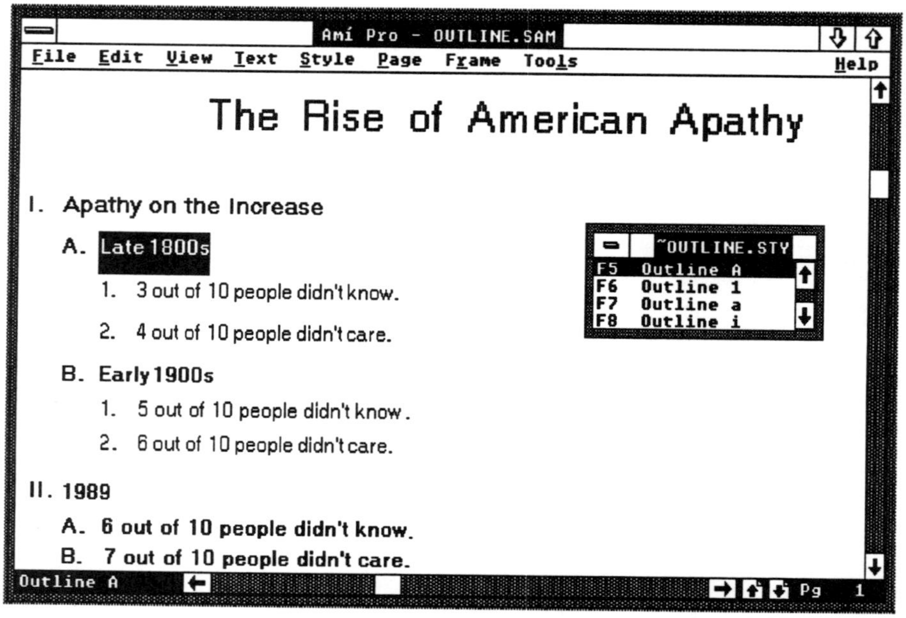

Figure 18–1 Traditional outlining is easy with the ~OUTLINE.STY style sheet included with the program.

2. Another Main Topic
   2.1. and so on

You can create a new style sheet named LEGAL.STY using the following instructions. They show you how to modify styles in the ~OUTLINE.STY sheet to create four levels of legal number styles.

First:

- If you want to start with a new document, use the File New command to open a new document using the ~OUTLINE.STY style sheet.

  or

- If you already have a document you want to format, use the Use Another Style Sheet command on the Style menu to open the ~OUTLINE.STY style sheet but leave your document displayed.

To create a new Level 1 style that numbers paragraphs 1., 2., 3., and so forth:

1. Choose the Create Style command from the Style menu.
2. Type **Level 1** in the text box, select Outline I in the Based On list, then click Modify or press **Enter** to go to the Modify Style dialog box.
3. In the Modify Style dialog box, select Special Effects in the Modify box at the left, and when the dialog box changes to show the Special Effects options, go to the Text & Special Effects Before Paragraph box and change the text in the box from <#2>. to <#**1**>.
4. Click the OK button to save the style and close the dialog box. Now your new Level 1 style will show at the bottom of the styles box.

To create a new Level 2 style that numbers paragraphs 1.1., 1.2., 1.3., and so forth:

1. Choose the Create Style command from the Style menu.
2. Type **Level 2** in the text box, select Outline A in the Based On list, then click Modify or press **Enter** to go to the Modify Style dialog box.
3. In the Modify Style dialog box, select Special Effects in the Modify box at the left, and when the dialog box changes to show the Special Effects options, change the Text & Special Effects Before Paragraph box to read <#**1**>.<#**1**>. and change the Space For box to .50 (inch).
4. Click the Insert Number button. When a new dialog box appears,

turn on the For Legal Numbering option, then click the Set Options Only button to go back to the main dialog box.

5. Click the OK button to save the style and close the dialog box. Now your new Level 2 style will show at the bottom of the styles box.

To create a new Level 3 style that numbers paragraphs 1.1.1., 1.1.2., 1.1.3., and so forth:

1. Choose the Create Style command from the Style menu.
2. Type **Level 3** in the text box, select Outline 1 in the Based On list, then click Modify or press **Enter** to go to the Modify Style dialog box.
3. In the Modify Style dialog box, select Special Effects in the Modify box at the left, and when the dialog box changes to show the Special Effects options, change the Text & Special Effects Before Paragraph box to read <#**1**>.<#**1**>.<#**1**>. and change the Space For box to .50 (inch).
4. Click the Insert Number button. When a new dialog box appears, turn on the For Legal Numbering option, then click the Set Options Only button to go back to the main dialog box.
5. Click the OK button to save the style and close the dialog box. Now your new Level 3 style shows at the bottom of the styles box.

If you need a Level 4 style that numbers paragraphs 1.1.1.1., 1.1.1.2., 1.1.1.3., and so forth:

1. Choose the Create Style command from the Style menu.
2. Type **Level 4** in the text box, select Outline a in the Based On list, then click Modify or press **Enter** to go to the Modify Style dialog box.
3. In the Modify Style dialog box, select Special Effects in the Modify box at the left, and when the dialog box changes to show the Special Effects options, change the Text & Special Effects Before Paragraph box to read <#**1**>.<#**1**>.<#**1**>.<#**1**>. and change the Space For box to .50 (inch).
4. Click the Insert Number button. When a new dialog box appears, turn on the For Legal Numbering option, then click the Set Options Only button to go back to the main dialog box.

5. Click the OK button to save the style and close the dialog box. Now your new Level 4 style shows at the bottom of the styles box.

To save the new style sheet so you can use it again:

1. Choose the Save As a New Style Sheet command from the Style menu.

2. Type **LEGAL.STY** in the text box and click OK.

You might want to use the Style Management command to delete the styles you don't need from the new style sheet and to assign any unused function keys (except F1 or F10, which are reserved) to the new styles. See Chapter 9 for more information.

Figure 18–2 illustrates formatting paragraphs with a legal numbering style sheet.

Sequential Paragraph Numbering

To do sequential numbering requires using only one style to number paragraphs like this: 1., 2., 3., and so on. If you followed the instructions in

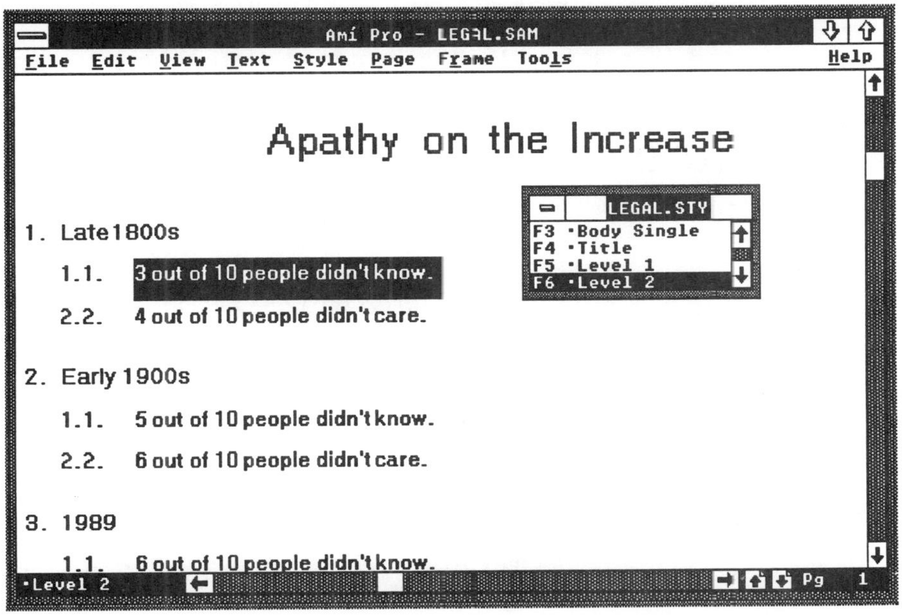

Figure 18–2 Doing legal paragraph numbering with an Amí Professional style sheet.

the previous discussion to create a legal numbering style sheet, you already have a Level 1 style that does this sequential numbering. If you didn't create that style yet, here's how to do it.

First:

- If you want to start with a new document, use the File New command to open a new document using the ~OUTLINE.STY style sheet.

  or

- If you already have a document you want to format, use the Use Another Style Sheet command on the Style menu to open the ~OUTLINE.STY style sheet but leave your document displayed.

To create a new Level 1 style that numbers paragraphs 1., 2., 3., and so forth:

1. Choose the Create Style command from the Style menu.
2. Type **Level 1** in the text box, select Outline I in the Based On list, then press **Enter** to go to the Modify Style dialog box.
3. In the Modify Style dialog box, select Special Effects in the Modify box at the left, and when the dialog box changes to show the Special Effects options, go to the Text & Special Effects Before Paragraph box and change the text in the box from <#2>. to <#**1**>.
4. Click the OK button to save the style and close the dialog box. Now your new Level 1 style will show at the bottom of the styles box.

Figure 18–3 illustrates sequential paragraph numbering.

NUMBERING LINES

If you're writing a specification, legal contract, or other document in which you need to refer to information by line number, you don't have to type the line numbers on each page—you can ask Amí Professional to add them with one easy command.

To add line numbers:

1. Choose the Page Line Numbering command.
2. Turn on the Number Lines option.
3. Choose an option to tell Amí Professional how many lines to number in the Options box: Every Line (1, 2, 3, . . .), Every Other Line (1, 3, 5, . . .), or Every Fifth Line (1, 5, 10, . . .).

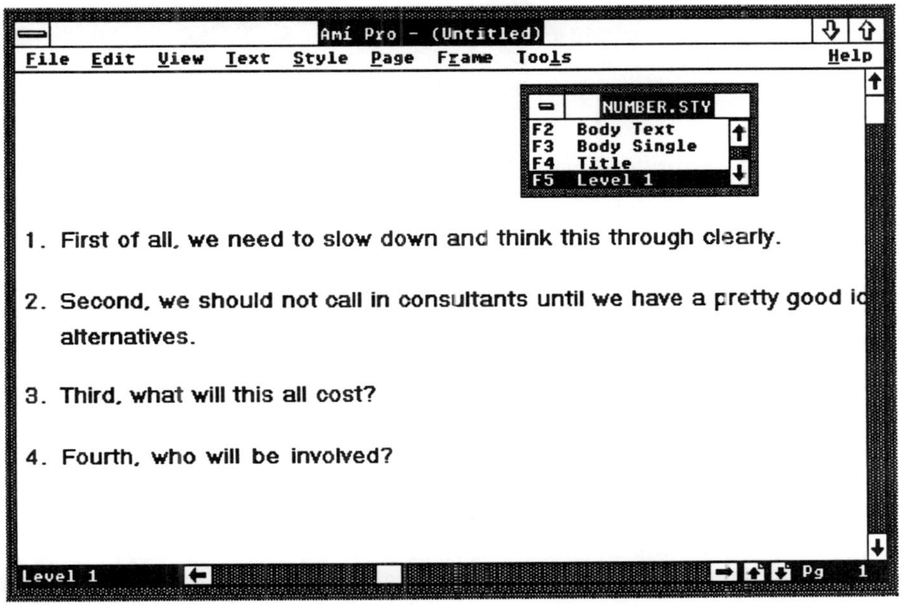

Figure 18–3 Numbering paragraphs sequentially using a customized Level 1 style.

4. If you want the line numbers to begin with one on every page, turn on the Reset Each Page option. Make sure this option is turned off if you want lines numbered continuously throughout your document.
5. If you want to use a style to control the appearance of line numbers, select the name of the style from the list. (See the next section for more information about this option.)
6. Click OK or press **Enter**.

Amí Professional adds line numbers in the left margin of your document, as shown in Figure 18–4.

Using a Style to Control the Appearance of Line Numbers

You can use a style to control the font, size, color, and spacing between the line numbers. Any style you choose in the Page Line Numbering dialog box affects only the style and spacing of the line numbers in the margin, not any other aspects of your text.

You might want to create a special line numbering style of your own. Then you can select that style from the style box in the Page Line Numbering dialog box. For example, you might want to make the line numbers

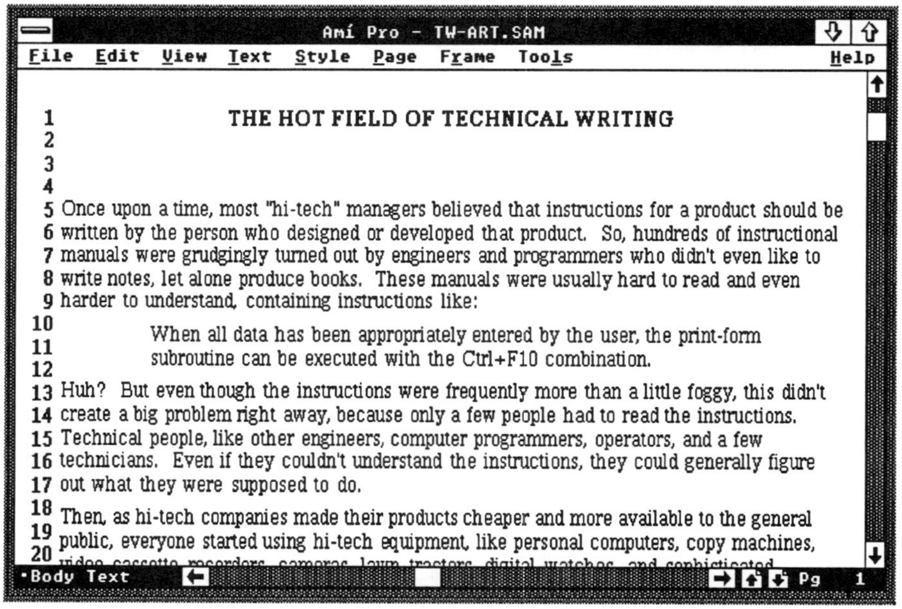

Figure 18-4 Line numbers in an Amí Professional document.

red Helvetica Bold text. To do this, you could create a new style named Line Number. In the Modify Style dialog box, you'd choose the color, font and size, choose Special Effects in the Modify box, add a number and any other text you want, and save the style.

Note: Don't change the options that control spacing before and after paragraphs for line numbers—this can throw off the alignment of line numbers and text in your document.

Removing Line Numbers

To remove line numbers:

1. Choose the Page Line Numbering option.
2. Turn off the Number Lines option.
3. Click OK or press **Enter**.

19

Creating Tables of Contents and Indexes

Two final steps in finishing a long document are creating a table of contents for the front of the document and creating an index for the back. This chapter shows you how to

- create a table of contents by collecting paragraphs with specified styles
- add index entries to your file
- collect index entries to create an index

CREATING A TABLE OF CONTENTS

When you're finished writing and formatting a long document, you'll want to add a table of contents so readers can see the structure of your document at a glance and know where to find the various sections they're looking for. Figure 19–1 shows a table of contents created by Amí Professional.

You create a table of contents by collecting all paragraphs formatted with certain styles.

Helpful Hint

To use chapter page numbers (such as 3–1, 3–2, 3–3, and so forth) in a table of contents and in an index, be sure to put the chapter number in the Leading Text box of the Page Numbering dialog box. Amí Professional uses the contents of this box to add text before page numbers, so if you have

Figure 19–1
A table of contents created by Amí Professional.

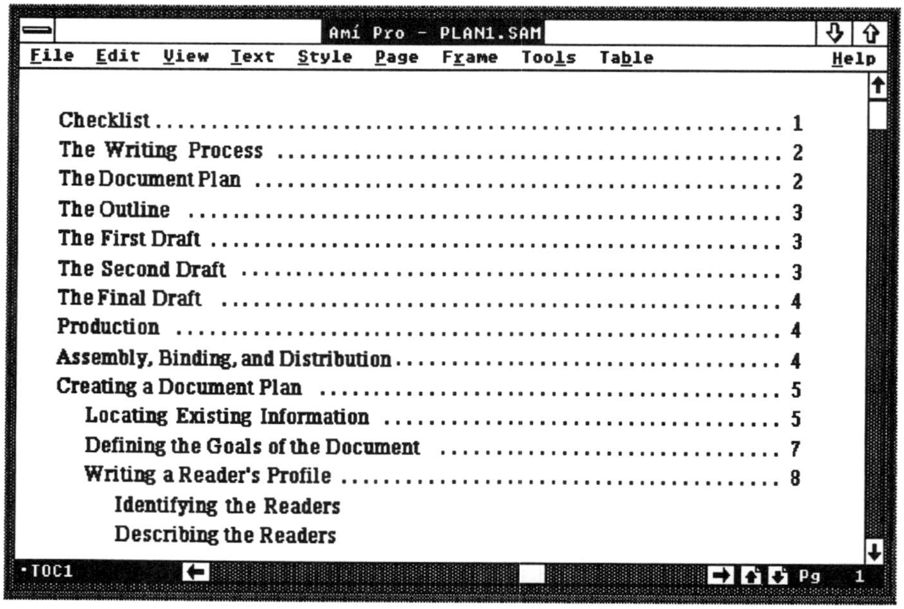

something like *Page* typed in the box, that will appear in the table of contents and index as well. See Chapter 15 for more information about adding page numbers.

Specifying Heading Styles to Collect

To create a table of contents by collecting styles, you tell Amí Professional which styles to collect for each level in the table of contents. Then Amí Professional reads through your document, collects all the paragraphs formatted with the styles you specified, and arranges them in a table of contents. This assumes, of course, that you've been consistent in using styles to format your headings. However, if you slip up now and then, don't worry—you can edit a table of contents just like you can edit any other Amí Professional text.

To create a table of contents:

1. Choose the Tools Generate TOC, Index command.

2. Turn on the Table of Contents option, then click OK or press **Enter** to close the dialog box and display a new one, as shown in Figure 19–2.

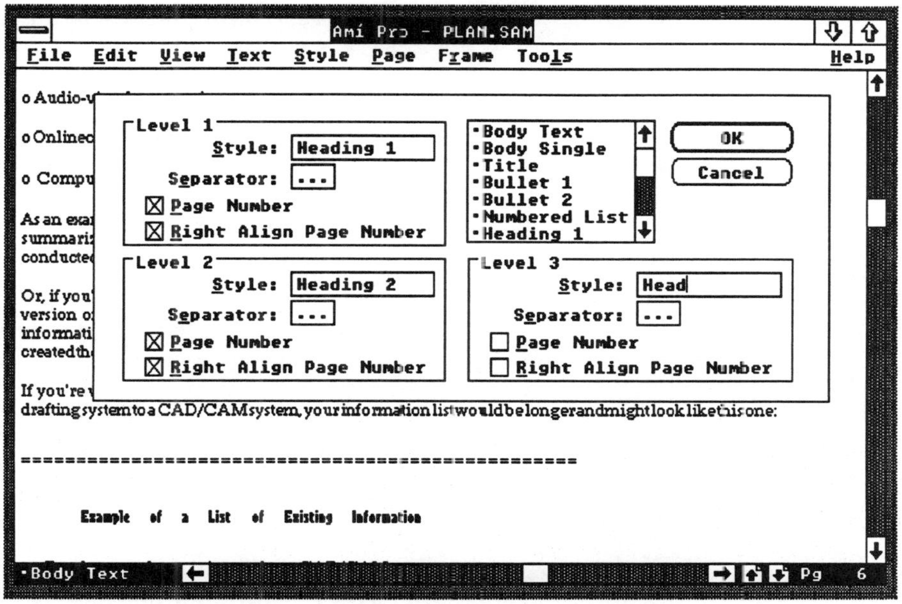

Figure 19–2 Setting up Amí Professional to create a table of contents using parts of the document marked with styles.

3. Fill out the Level 1, Level 2, and Level 3 boxes as desired:

Option	What to Do
Style box	Type the name of the style you want to use for that level of table-of-contents entry or select the style name from the list. If you type, be sure to match the capitalization exactly. For example, if you used the Heading 1 style to format all first-level headings in your document, you would insert **Heading 1** in the Level 1 box.
Separator	Type up to three separator characters (such as spaces, periods, or underscores) to print characters between the entry and the following page number. (If you hear a beep when you type in this box, there are invisible spaces occupying the box—select them and then type.)
Page Number	Turn on if you want the page number to appear with that level of entry; turn off if you don't want page numbers.

Right Align Page Number	Turn on if you want to align page numbers with the right margin. If you typed a separator character other than a space in the Separator box, Amí Professional fills the space between the entry and the page number with that character; if you left the box blank or typed spaces, the space is filled with periods.

4. Click OK or press **Enter**.

Amí Professional collects all the paragraphs with the specified styles from your document and adds new pages containing the table of contents at the beginning of your document. If your document is long, this process may take a few moments. When the table of contents is complete, Amí Professional automatically scrolls to the first page so you can see the results. The table of contents, as shown in Figure 19–3, is contained in a table that you can change using commands on the Table menu. You can also change the formatting of the table-of-contents styles or use the Text menu commands to format parts of the entries (such as the page numbers), just as you can change any other Amí Professional text.

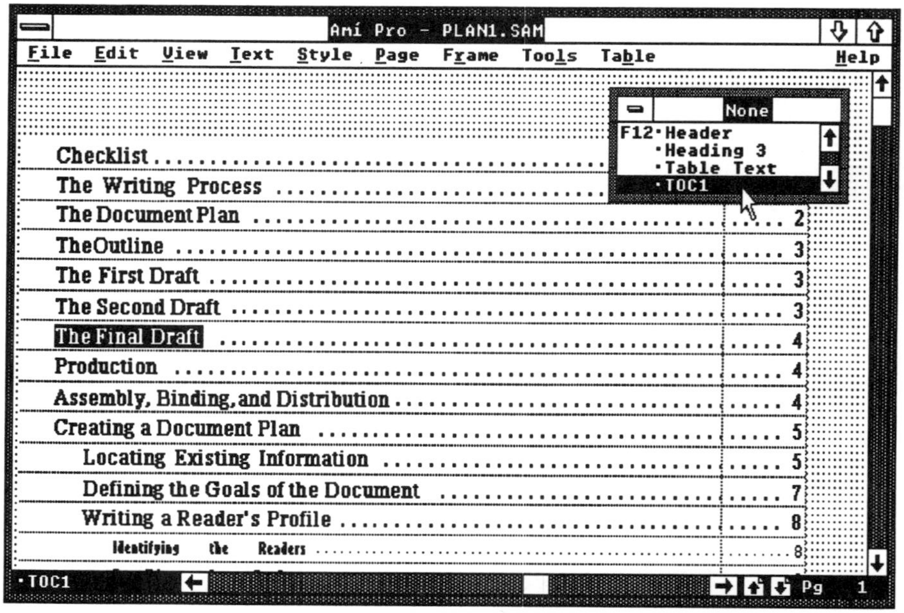

Figure 19–3 Amí Professional puts the table of contents into a table. Note that each level has its own TOC style that you can modify if you like.

Helpful Hint

You can double-click the space immediately preceding a right-aligned page number in an Amí Professional table of contents to move directly to that heading within the document.

Using Only Part of a Paragraph as an Entry

If some paragraphs in your document have the same styles you specified in the Table of Contents dialog box but you don't want to use all the text in those paragraphs, you can tell Amí Professional to use only the beginning parts of the paragraphs. For example, you might have used a Major Point style to format paragraphs in which you've created a bold run-in heading like the one shown in Figure 19–4. To include only the bold run-in heading in the table of contents, you need to use the procedure described earlier to specify the Major Point style as a level in the Table of Contents dialog box, then mark only the run-in heading part of the paragraph like this:

1. Select the beginning part of the paragraph you want to include in the table of contents. (With Amí Professional, you can't select only the middle or end portions.)
2. Choose the Edit Mark Text command to display the dialog box shown in Figure 19–4.

Figure 19–4 Marking part of a paragraph for inclusion in the table of contents.

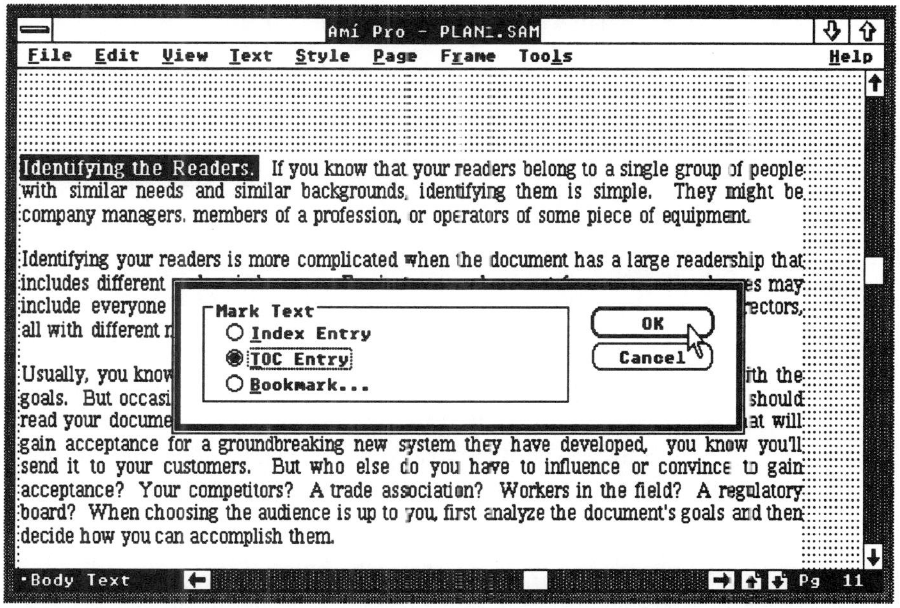

3. Turn on the TOC Entry option, then click OK or press **Enter** to mark the text. This type of "marking" is invisible, so you won't see anything when you remove the highlight.

4. Repeat steps 1 through 3 until you've marked all the portions of paragraphs you want to include in your table of contents, then use the Tools Generate TOC, Index command to generate or update the table of contents.

Updating or Deleting the Table of Contents

If you've changed the document and you need to update the table of contents, all you need to do is use the Tools Generate TOC, Index command again to generate a new table of contents. Amí Professional automatically replaces the old table of contents with the new one. If you want to delete the table of contents, select the entire table that contains it, then use the Table Delete Column/Row command to delete it.

CREATING AN INDEX

When you finish writing and formatting a long document such as your Ph.D. dissertation or that feasibility study for the office, you'll want to add an index to make it easier for readers to look up important information.

To create an index with Amí Professional, you follow two basic steps:

1. Mark index entries throughout your document.

2. Collect the index entries to create the index.

Figure 19–5 shows an index created with Amí Professional.

Marking Index Entries

In Amí Professional, you don't have to mark index entries on every page, as you do in many other programs. You just specify the entry once, and the program will note every occurrence of the entry throughout your document, so if you want to collect all the page numbers on which the words `Time Tracking` appear, you only have to mark `Time Tracking` once, and the program does the rest for you. Capitalization and other formatting doesn't matter—the program will note the page number for each instance of the letters you mark.

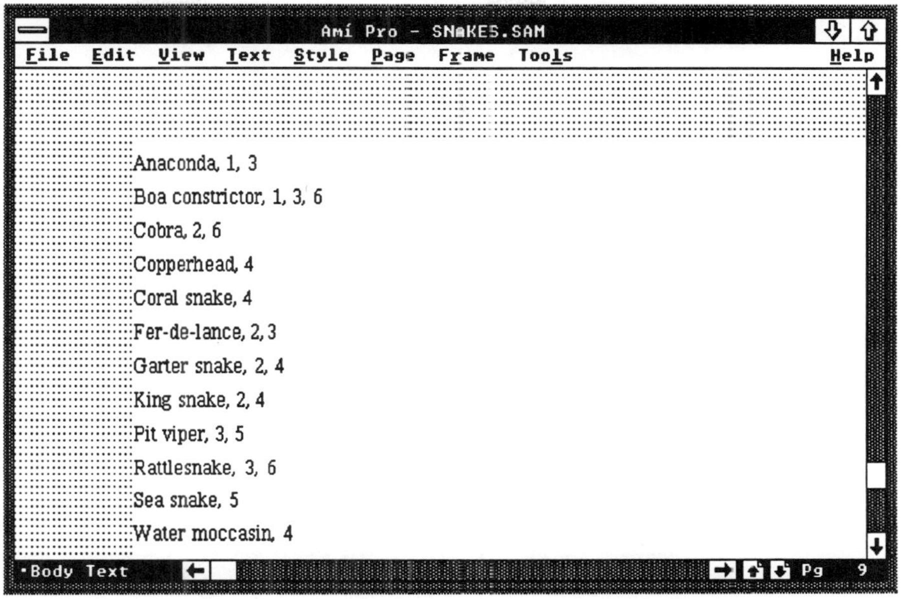

Figure 19–5
An index created with Amí Professional.

To mark index entries, as shown in Figure 19–6:

1. Select the text you want to appear in the index.
2. Choose the Edit Mark Text command.
3. Turn on the Index Entry option, then click OK or press **Enter**.
4. Repeat steps 1–3 until you've marked all index entries.

Helpful Hint

If you create indexes often, you may want to add the Mark Index Entry icon to the sidebar so that you can use the mouse to mark entries instead of choosing a command. See Chapter 21 for details about adding icons to the screen.

Generating the Index

To collect all the entries once you've marked them throughout your document:

1. Choose the Tools Generate TOC, Index command.
2. Turn on the Index option.

Figure 19-6
Marking an index entry.

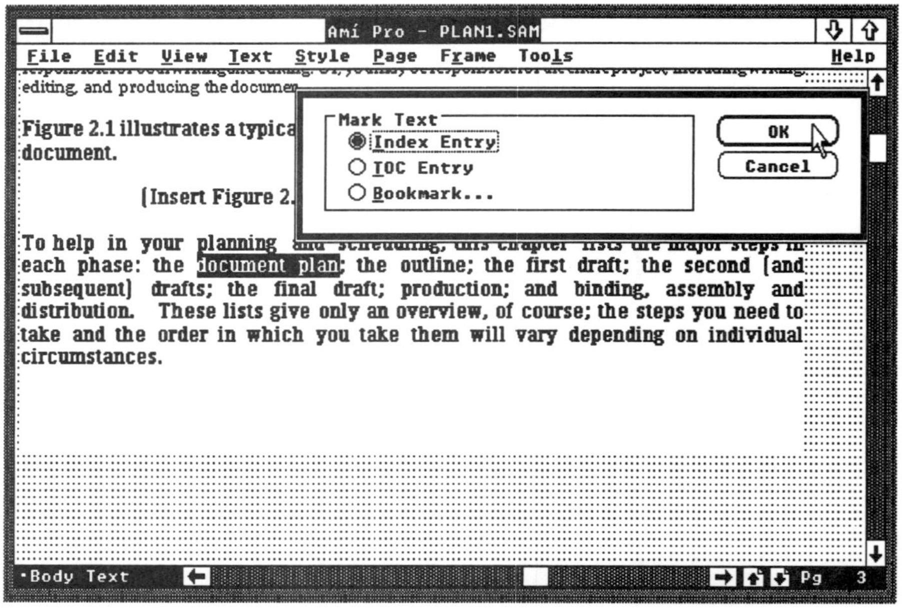

3. Click OK or press **Enter**.

Amí Professional creates the index by collecting all the occurrences of the text you marked as entries and formatting them in an index at the end of your document. If your document is very long and contains many index entries, this may take several minutes. When the process is complete, the program automatically scrolls to the first page of the index so you can see the results. Although Amí Professional finds every instance of the words you marked as entries, it uses the capitalization of the actual text you marked in the index, so you may need to adjust the case of the entries.

You can edit and format an index just like any other Amí Professional text.

Helpful Hint

You can double-click a page number in an Amí Professional index to move directly to that page number within the document.

Adding Subentries to the Index

You may want to have subentries beneath main entries in your index, like this:

Whale
Blue 5, 10
Gray 2, 4
Humpback 9, 11, 15
Mating ritual 3, 16
Shark 9, 14

Creating subentries is a bit confusing in Amí Professional, so we've included a couple of examples after the procedure to help you figure out the process. First, here's the main procedure to create subentries.

1. Create the main index as described in the previous sections.
2. In the index, type and indent text you want to collect as subentries.
3. Select a subentry.
4. Choose the Edit Mark Text command. When the dialog box appears, you may notice that the options are different than when you are in the main document. This is because Amí Professional knows the cursor is in an index, and so displays index options for you.
5. Select Second Level Index Entry in the dialog box, then click OK. Amí Professional displays a new dialog box.
6. In the Second Level Index Entry dialog box, do one of the following:
   - □ If you want Amí Professional to list the page number of the selected text when it appears immediately after the main entry in your document, select the Trails Primary option.

   or

   - □ If you want Amí Professional to list the page number of selected text when that text appears immediately before the main entry in your document, select the Leads Primary option.

   or

   - □ If you want Amí Professional to list the page number of selected text when that text appears anywhere within the same paragraph as the main entry in your document, select the Within Same Paragraph option.
7. Click Mark Entry or press **Enter** to mark the subentry.
8. Repeat steps 3 through 7 to mark more subentries. (Drag the Mark Text or Index Entry boxes out of the way as necessary.) When you're finished, close the Second-Level Index Entry window by pressing

Alt+F4 or by double-clicking the Control menu icon in that window's upper left corner.

9. Use the Tools Generate TOC, Index command to generate a new index. Amí Professional erases page numbers from the main entry and adds page numbers to the subentries beneath.

And now here are the examples. Say that you want index entries to look like this:

Whale
    Blue 5, 10
    Gray 2, 4
    Humpback 9, 11, 15
    Mating ritual 3, 16
    Shark 9, 14

Here's what you'd do:

1. Mark the word *Whale* as an index entry anywhere in your document, as described in Marking Index Entries earlier in this chapter.

2. Generate the index as described in Generating the Index earlier in this chapter.

3. Go to the index, find the *Whale* entry, and type and indent the subentries beneath the main entry. You must indent the subentries—you can just press the **Tab** key before each if you like.

4. To collect entries that say *blue whale, gray whale,* or *humpback whale* where the subentry text (*blue, gray,* and *humpback*) precedes the text, select these three entries, choose the Edit Mark Text command, select Second Level Index Entry, select the Leads Primary option in the dialog box, then click Mark Entry.

5. To collect entries that refer to *mating ritual* anywhere within the same paragraph as the word *whale,* select the indented *Mating ritual* entry (move any overlapping windows out of the way if necessary), and select the Within the Same Paragraph option, then click Mark Entry.

6. To collect entries that say *whale shark* where the subentry text (shark) follows the text, select the indented *Shark* entry, select the Trails Primary option in the dialog box, then click Mark Entry.

7. Press **Alt+F4** to close the Second-Level Index Entry window.

8. Use the Tools Generate TOC, Index command to generate a new index.

Updating the Index

If you've changed the document's page breaks or content and you need to update the index, all you need to do is use the Tools Generate TOC, Index command again to generate a new index. Amí Professional automatically replaces the old index with the new one.

20

Using Macros

Have you ever wished that you could automate word-processing tasks that you repeat frequently? For example, do you print double-spaced copies with wide margins for editing? Do you use the same data file to print address labels over and over again? With Amí Professional, you can record these actions as a macro—then you can choose one command or press a key combination, then sit back and watch Amí Professional do all of the steps for you.

A *macro* is a set of commands, keystrokes, and other instructions that automate Amí Professional tasks for you. You can easily record your own macros to do exactly what you want. If you're a dedicated keyboard user, you can assign a shortcut key combination to the macro so you can run it without taking your fingers off the keys.

You can create a macro to do almost anything in Amí Professional. You are limited only by your imagination. This chapter shows how to

- plan macros
- record macros
- run macros
- rename and delete macros

Although this chapter shows how to record macros, you can also use Amí Professional's macro language to write sophisticated macros with advanced functions. You can use the Macro Documentation command on the Help menu to get more information about this or contact Samna to receive a free macro language manual.

CREATING YOUR OWN MACROS

To create a macro, you'll record your keystrokes and commands. Recording macros is as easy as recording on an audio or video cassette. Here are the basic steps you'll use to create your macro:

1. Plan the steps that you want the macro to perform and choose a name for your macro.
2. Record the macro by performing the steps.
3. Test the macro to see whether it works.
4. If necessary, modify or record the macro again.

Planning a Macro

Before you record your macro, you should think about what you want the macro to do. Keep in mind that every action you perform will be recorded. Doing a little planning up front saves time because you'll improve your odds of recording the macro right the first time, instead of having to re-record it later.

Here are some general guidelines for planning macros:

- Don't use the mouse to select text or scroll in a macro. (When you use the macro on the next document, the macro can't know where you want to begin or end your selection.)
- It's okay to use key combinations to select or scroll if the keys select specific blocks of text (such as a paragraph or the whole document) or if they scroll to a definite location that remains the same in every document, such as the beginning or end of a document. In general, though, it's usually easier if you plan to select text before you run a macro that will affect it.
- Don't plan for the macro to begin a time-consuming process, such as printing documents or merging form letters. This takes control out of your hands. Instead, make the last step in the macro display the appropriate dialog box and choose any appropriate options. This

way you can turn on the printer or check other conditions, then choose OK when *you're* ready.

You might want to write a short description of the steps you want the macro to perform, creating a script you can follow. It's also a good idea to rehearse the steps you've planned for your macro before you begin recording, just to make sure you haven't left anything out. Here are some examples of planning steps for macros:

EXAMPLES: Macros in Amí Professional

A. This macro opens a specific style sheet to create a new memo. To store the macro:

1. Choose the File New command.
2. Select ~MEMO3.STY from the list.
3. Turn on the With Contents option.
4. Click OK or press **Enter** to open the new file.

B. This macro prepares to print three double-spaced copies.

1. Press **Ctrl**+**Home** to move the cursor to the top of the document, then press **Shift**+**Ctrl**+**End** to select the entire document. (This step could be a macro of its own!)
2. Choose the Text Spacing command and choose the Double-Space option.
3. Choose the File Print command and type **3** in the Copies box.

C. This macro sets up a document to print as 6 × 8-inch "pages" (the final page size) on 8½ × 11-inch paper with crop marks for later trimming.

1. Choose the Page Modify Layout command.
2. Choose the Page Settings option in the Modify box.
3. Type **6** in the first Custom box and type **8** in the second Custom box, then press **Enter**.
4. Choose the File Print command.
5. Choose the Options button, turn on the Crop Marks option, then press **Enter** to return to the Print dialog box.

These are just a few short examples of what you might plan for a macro to do. A macro can be very complex. Say, for example, you have a consistent page format you like to use from time to time: legal-size paper, two-inch margins top and bottom, one-inch side margins, a running head that puts the page number in italic in the middle of the top margin, and a running foot that centers the date in the bottom margin. You could record all the necessary formatting actions, then just use the mouse or press a couple of keys to make the macro format your document. Magic!

Amí Professional includes some macros that have already been created for you. An especially useful macro is WC.SMM, which counts all the words in an Amí Professional document! You can find out more about these provided macros in the READMAC.SAM file.

As well as deciding on the steps you want your macro to perform, you should decide on a meaningful macro name. Because macros are stored in files, the name must conform to file name rules and must end with .SMM, but make the name descriptive so that you can remember what the macro does.

Macro names must be unique, so you may want to display the Tools Macros dialog box so you can check the new name against the list of macro names and avoid duplicating one. If you accidentally try to save a macro with the same name as another, Amí Professional tells you that the name has already been used.

Recording a Macro

Recording a macro is just like making a videotape of your actions—whatever you do is recorded, in exactly the same way you do it. After you've recorded the macro, you can run it to reproduce your actions, just like you would play a videotape. Amí Professional responds to the macro just as if you were performing the actions yourself.

To record a macro:

1. Choose the Tools Macros command. Amí Professional displays the dialog box shown in Figure 20–1.

2. Type a name for the macro file. The file must have the extension .SMM; otherwise, Amí Professional won't recognize it.

3. If you want to assign the macro to a shortcut key combination, choose the Change Shortcut Key button, type a number in the Function Key box, and choose to combine that function key with the Alt key, the Shift key, the Ctrl key, or with any combination of those three. For example, to assign the Ctrl+F2 combination, type **2** and turn on the

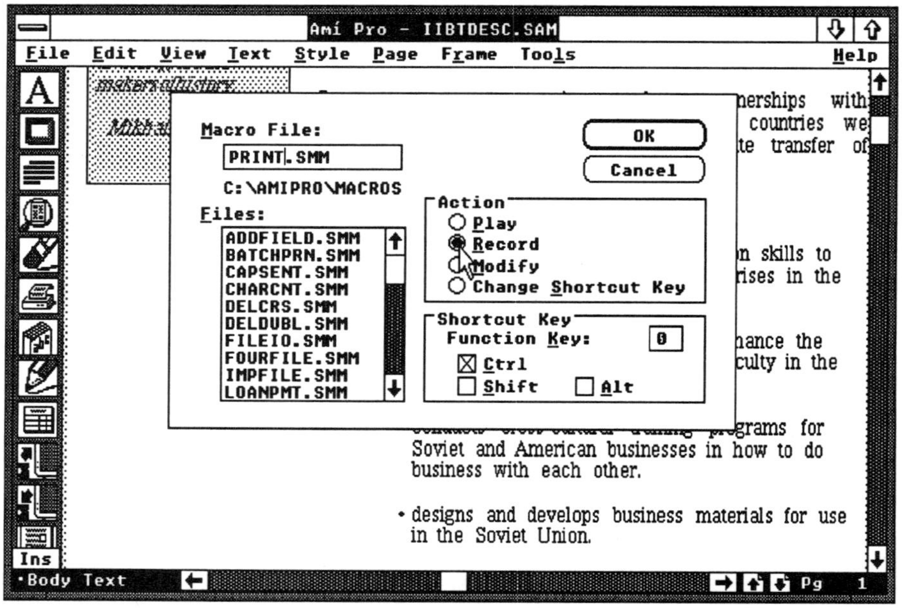

Figure 20-1 Filling in the Macro Record dialog box in preparation for recording a macro.

Ctrl option; to assign the Shift+Ctrl+F5 option, type **5** and turn on both Ctrl and Shift.

4. Choose the Record option in the Action box.
5. Click OK or press **Enter** to begin recording. Amí Professional displays `Record` in the status bar (if you have it displayed) to remind you that the recorder is on.
6. Perform the actions you want to record. There's no hurry. The recorder records only when you press the keys or use the mouse, so if you need to take time out to think or refer to your notes, that's perfectly all right.
7. When you've performed all the steps, choose the Tools Macros command again. You'll notice on the screen that the `Record` button has changed to `End Record.`
8. Click OK or press **Enter** to save the macro.

Next you'll want to run your macro to test it.

Helpful Hint

If you assign the key combinations Ctrl+F1 through Ctrl+F9 to the nine macros you use most often, you can add icons to the sidebar and then click them with the mouse to run the macro. See Chapter 21 to find out how to add icons to the sidebar.

RUNNING A MACRO

You can use two different procedures to run any macro you've assigned to a shortcut key combination. The macro instructions are carried out at the cursor, so be sure to move the cursor or select text as necessary before you start the macro.

Helpful Hint

If you're testing a macro, be sure to save your document first (as a matter of fact, it's *always* a good safety measure to save a file before running a macro). That way, if the macro does something unexpected that messes up the text, you can use the File Revert command to discard the changes made by the macro. You can also create a test document to use for macro-testing purposes.

Choosing a Macro from a List

You can always run any macro this way:

1. Choose the Tools Macros command.
2. Do one of the following:

   - Select the macro name from the list, then press **Enter**.

   or

   - Double-click the macro name in the list.

Amí Professional displays `Playback` in the status bar (if you have it displayed) and runs the macro.

Running a Macro with Its Key Combination

If you assigned a shortcut key combination to your macro, you can run the macro without choosing a command first.

To run a macro when you know its shortcut key combination:

1. Move the cursor or select text as necessary.
2. Press the shortcut key combination. Amí Professional runs the macro.

INTERRUPTING OR CANCELING A MACRO

If you need to interrupt or cancel a macro after you've started it, press **Escape**. Amí Professional displays the dialog box in Figure 20–2. You can choose to resume the macro, perform the next steps, or cancel.

CORRECTING MACROS

If your macro didn't do what you wanted, try to figure out what's wrong, then delete the faulty macro file and re-record the macro. Remember that the macro begins at the cursor position and probably affects any text that's selected at the time. Also, remember that it's not a good idea to use mouse actions to select text or scroll in macros. If you want your macro to select text or scroll, use key combinations that go to definite positions, such as Ctrl+Home to scroll to the beginning or Ctrl+End to scroll to the end of

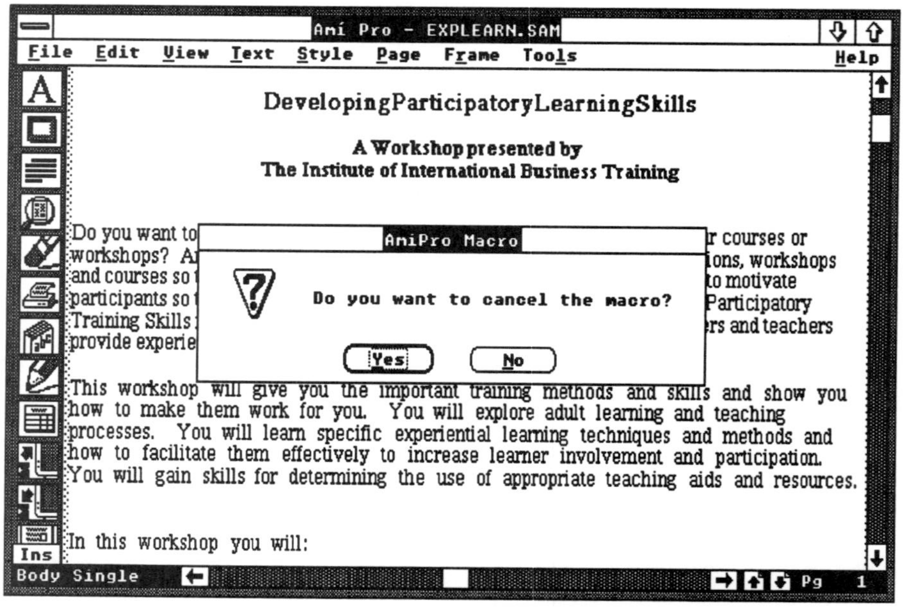

Figure 20–2 This dialog box is displayed when you interrupt a macro.

the document, Shift+Ctrl+End to select from the cursor to the end of the document, and so forth.

CHANGING, RENAMING, OR DELETING MACROS

To re-record a macro because it didn't work correctly or because you want to append more actions to it, here's how:

1. Choose the Tools Macros command.
2. Select the macro name from the list.
3. Choose Record in the Action box.
4. Click OK or press **Enter**. Amí Professional displays a dialog box telling you that the macro already exists.
5. Do one of the following:
   - If you want to record the macro from the beginning as you replace the previous instructions, choose Overwrite.
   - If you want to add actions to the end of the macro file, picking up where the old macro left off, choose Append.

   Amí Professional starts recording.
6. Perform the actions you want for the macro.
7. When you're finished, choose the Tools Macros command again and choose End Record in the Action box, then click OK or press **Enter**.

If you want to change the key combination assigned to a macro:

1. Choose the Tools Macros command.
2. Select the macro from the list.
3. Choose the Change Shortcut Key option in the Action box.
4. Change the key combination.
5. Click OK or press **Enter**.

Because macros are kept in files, you can rename and delete a macro file with your operating system's commands or with the File Manager, as described in Chapter 3.

21

Changing Amí Professional to Suit You

You've already learned about some of the ways to customize Amí Professional, such as setting time intervals for automatic saves, adding your own words to the spelling checker, setting Undo levels, and specifying the hyphenation hot zone. In this chapter you'll see that you can customize Amí Professional even further.

This chapter shows you how to change the way Amí Professional treats the monitor and the way it treats your documents. It describes how to

- change the unit of measurement in dialog boxes
- change the icon bar
- change the display preference
- change the colors of the Amí Professional screen
- return all Amí Professional options to their original settings

CHANGING THE UNIT OF MEASUREMENT

In most dialog boxes, Amí Professional uses inches as its default unit of measurement, but you can change this to centimeters, points, or picas. Amí Professional then uses the new unit of measurement for the options that the dialog box affects. For example, changing the unit of measurement in the Page Modify Layout dialog box affects the numbers you type for tabs and for margin measurements.

To change the unit of measurement in a dialog box:

1. With the dialog box open, point to the word expressing the unit of measurement (usually inches).

2. Click the left mouse button until you see the unit you want.

3. Choose other options in the dialog box as necessary, then click OK or press **Enter**. Figure 21–1 illustrates changing the unit of measurement in a dialog box. This method works in any dialog box that shows units of measurement.

SETTING SCREEN-DISPLAY PREFERENCES

The View Display Preferences command controls the way text is displayed in the Amí Professional window. You can choose options to see special characters and other options that are invisible by default. All of the options in the View Display Preferences dialog box are toggles. To turn on the options, just click them. An X appears in each of the accompanying check boxes. To turn the options off, click them again. In Amí Professional you can choose display options for both layout and draft modes. These options are described in detail in Chapter 3.

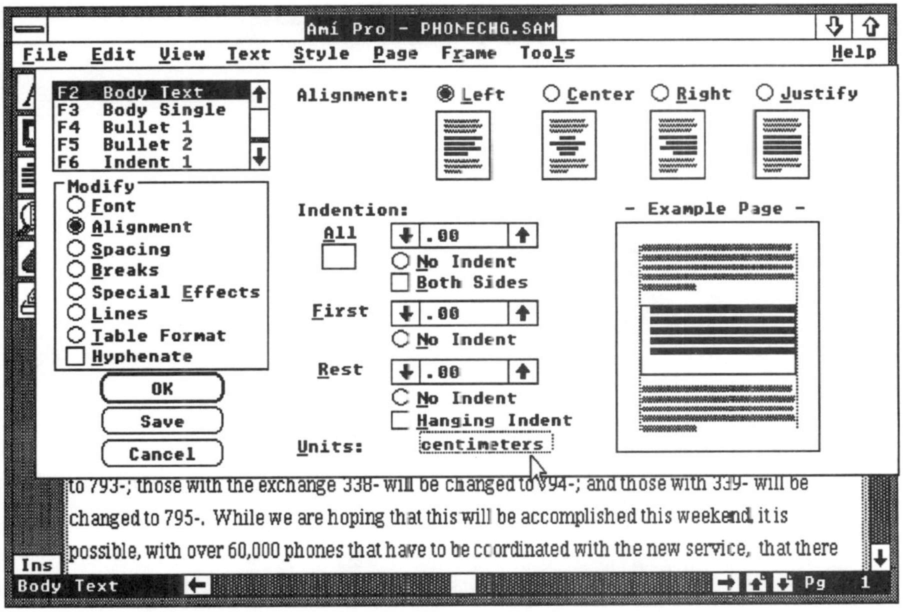

Figure 21–1 Changing the unit of measurement in the Modify Style dialog box.

To adjust the window display:

1. Choose the View Display Preferences command. Amí Professional displays the dialog box shown in Figure 21–2.
2. Click the options to turn them on or off.
3. Choose OK or press **Enter**.

CHANGING THE ICON DISPLAY

The icons at the left side of the Amí Professional screen are shortcuts that mouse users can click on to quickly choose commands without pulling down menus. Amí Professional contains more icons than you first see when you start the program. You can pick and choose from a list of icons in the Edit Display Preferences Sidebar dialog box (shown in Figure 21–3) to display the shortcuts that you want to use most often. You can display up to 12 icons at once, and you can arrange them in any order you like.

The list of icons includes the following:

Option	**Description**
Blank	Displays a blank space (for spacing purposes).
Toggle Draft/Layout Mode	Switches between draft and layout modes.

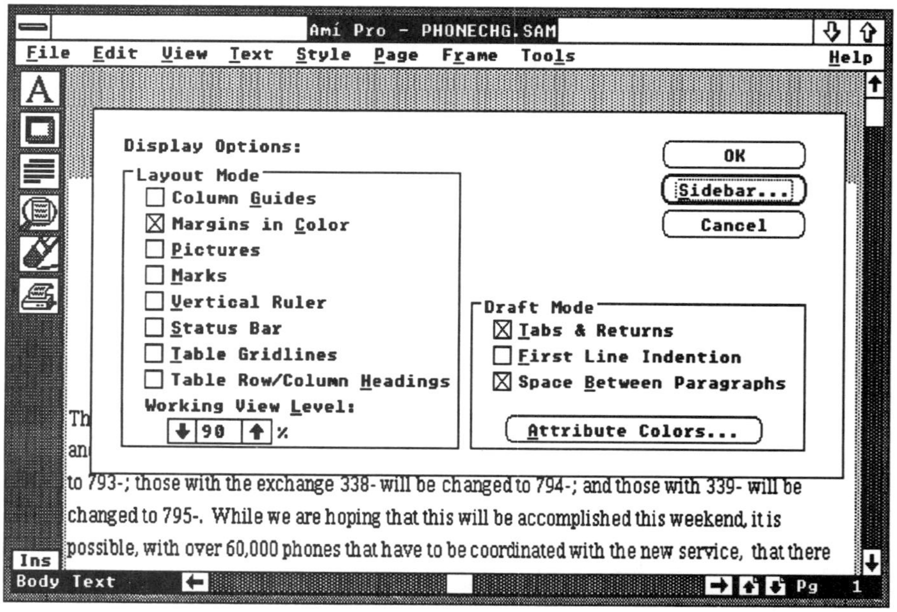

Figure 21–2 The View Display Preferences dialog box.

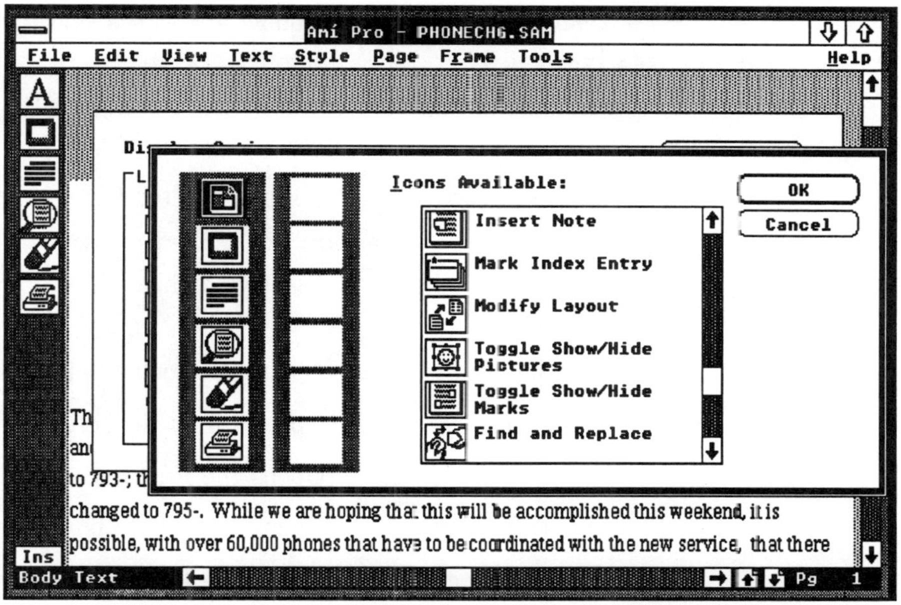

Figure 21-3 The list of icons you can choose from the View Display Preferences Sidebar dialog box.

Add a Frame	Turns the mouse pointer into a frame tool that you can use to add a frame to your document.
Modify Style	Opens the Modify Style dialog box.
Full Page/Current View Toggle	Switches between full-page view and the view currently being used.
Undo	Undoes the previous action(s) according to the Undo levels you have set with the Edit Defaults command.
Print	Opens the File Print dialog box.
Normal Text	Removes any formatting added to the styles of the selected paragraphs.
Bold Text	Makes selected text bold.
Italic Text	Makes selected text italic.
Underline Text	Underlines selected text, including spaces.
Word Underline Text	Underlines each word (no spaces) in selected text.

Double Underline Text	Double-underlines selected text, including spaces.
Superscript Text	Raises selected text above the baseline to create a superscript.
Subscript Text	Lowers selected text below the baseline to create a subscript.
Toggle Show/Hide Tab Ruler	Displays or hides the tab ruler.
Spelling	Opens the Tools Spelling dialog box.
Thesaurus	Opens the Tools Thesaurus dialog box.
Insert Variable	Opens the Edit Insert Variable dialog box.
Import/Export	Opens the File Import/Export dialog box.
Insert Footnote	Opens the Edit Insert Footnote dialog box.
Drawing	Adds the Draw menu and drawing tools to the screen when a frame is selected.
Charting	Opens the Frames Charting dialog box when a frame is selected.
Tables	Opens the Tools Tables dialog box and adds the Tables menu to the menu bar.
Go To Next	Goes to the next occurrence of the item specified in the Tools Go To dialog box (equivalent to pressing Ctrl+H).
Bookmark	Opens the Edit Insert Bookmark dialog box.
Delete	Deletes selected text (does not place it in the Clipboard).
New	Opens the File New dialog box.
Open	Opens the File Open dialog box.
Save	Saves the file.
Cut	Deletes selected text and puts it in the Clipboard.
Copy	Makes a copy of selected text and puts the copy in the Clipboard.

Paste	Inserts the contents of the Clipboard at the cursor position.
Insert Note	Inserts a note at the cursor position.
Mark Index Entry	Marks selected text as an index entry.
Modify Layout	Opens the Page Modify Layout dialog box.
Toggle Show/Hide Pictures	Displays or hides pictures. Amí Professional scrolls faster when pictures are not displayed.
Toggle Show/Hide Marks	Displays or hides marks for notes, tab rulers, floating headers, and floating footers.
Find & Replace	Opens the Tools Find & Replace dialog box.
Tables Connect Cells	Connects selected cells in a table to form one large cell.
Macro Shortcut 1–9	Run macros assigned to the shortcut key combinations Ctrl−F1 through Ctrl+F9. Macro Shortcut 1 runs the macro assigned to Ctrl+F1, Macro Shortcut 2 runs the macro assigned to Ctrl+F2, and so on.

To change the sidebar icons:

1. Choose the View Display Preferences command.
2. Choose the Sidebar button. The dialog box shown in Figure 21–3 is displayed.
3. To choose a position for a new icon, click one of the squares on the left-hand side of the dialog box. The new icon will appear in this square.
4. Click one of the icons from the list box, scrolling if necessary to display the icon you want. The new icon appears in the square you clicked.
5. Repeat steps 3 and 4 until you have chosen all the icons you want.
6. Click OK or press **Enter** to close the Sidebar dialog box.
7. Make other choices in the Display Preferences dialog box if you wish, then click OK or press **Enter**.

If you find the icon sidebar takes up too much screen space, you can display or hide the icon sidebar whenever you like this way:

- Choose the View Hide/Show Sidebar command.

or

- Press **Ctrl+Q**.

CHANGING THE FORMATS OF NUMBERS, DATES, AND TIMES

Because Amí Professional was created in the United States, it uses U.S. settings by default for dates and numbers. For example, in the United States we normally write 1/30/91 to mean January 30, 1991. However, in most other countries of the world, this date would be written as 30/1/91. Another U.S.-specific standard is using a comma as a separator between thousands and hundreds; many other parts of the world use periods instead. And although the 24-hour time format is normally used only by the military in the United States (civilians prefer to say 3 P.M. instead of 1500 hours), the 24-hour format is standard in most other places.

If you want to change these country-specific settings (as well as other settings), you can use the Windows Control Panel. This changes the formats used in all your Windows applications. Here's how:

1. In Amí Professional, choose the Control Panel command from the Amí Professional Control menu (**Alt, Spacebar, P**). This displays the Control Panel window, shown in Figure 21–4.

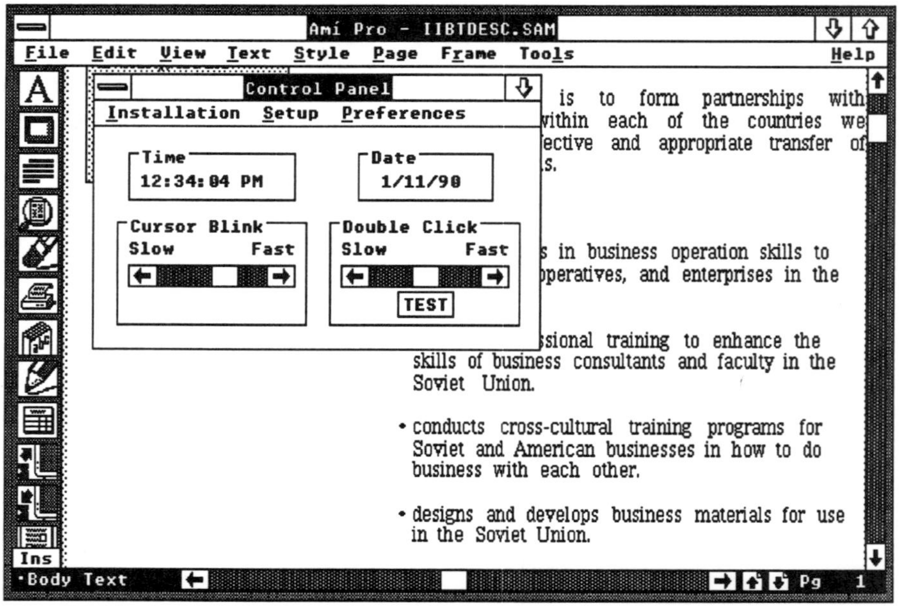

Figure 21–4 The Control Panel window.

2. Choose the Country Settings command from the Preferences menu. This displays the dialog box shown in Figure 21–5.

3. Change the options as necessary. If you want to switch all the settings to match the standards for a specific country, just select the country from the list.

4. Click OK or press **Enter**.

5. Choose the Close command from the Control Panel menu (**Alt+F4**) to close the window and return to Amí Professional.

Changes you make with the Control Panel are stored in the WIN.INI file.

CHANGING THE COLORS OF THE SCREEN

You can use the Control Panel to change the colors of the Amí Professional screen and all your other Windows applications. Here's how:

1. In Amí Professional, choose the Control Panel command from the Amí Professional Control menu (**Alt, Spacebar, P**). This displays the Control Panel window, shown in Figure 21–4.

Figure 21–5
Changing country-specific settings.

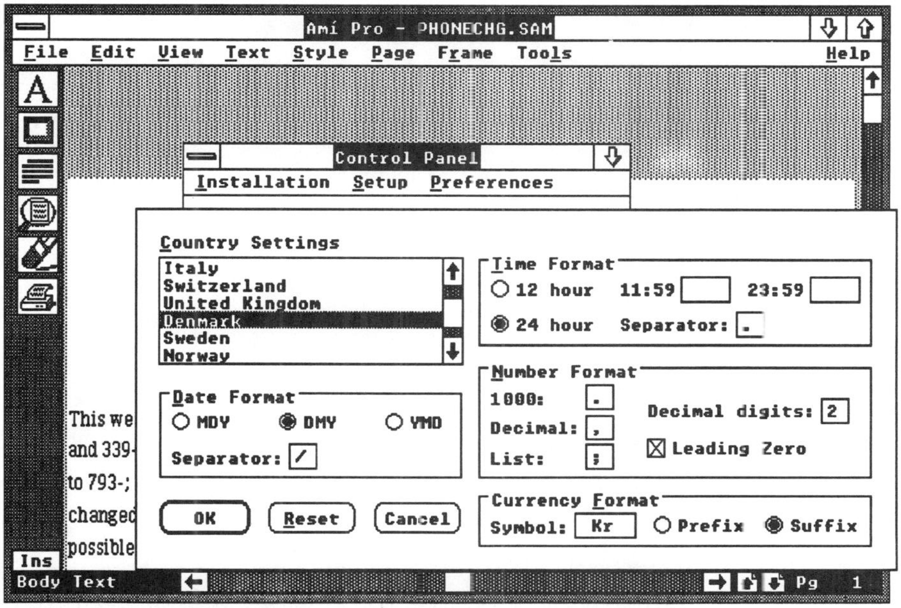

2. Choose the Screen Colors command from the Preferences menu. This displays the dialog box shown in Figure 21–6.

3. In the Screen Colors list, select the part of the screen you want to change. For example, if you want to change the color of the menu bar, select Menu Bar.

4. Use the mouse or the arrow keys to move the boxes in the Hue, Bright, and Color slider bars. As you change the slider bars, you'll see the appropriate part of the screen change color in the Sample screen at the right. If you want to cancel your changes and start over, choose Reset.

5. Repeat steps 4 and 5 to change any other parts of the screen you want.

6. Click OK or press **Enter** when you've changed the colors to your satisfaction.

7. Choose the Close command from the Control Panel menu (**Alt+F4**) to close the window and return to Amí Professional.

Changes you make with the Control Panel are stored in the WIN.INI file.

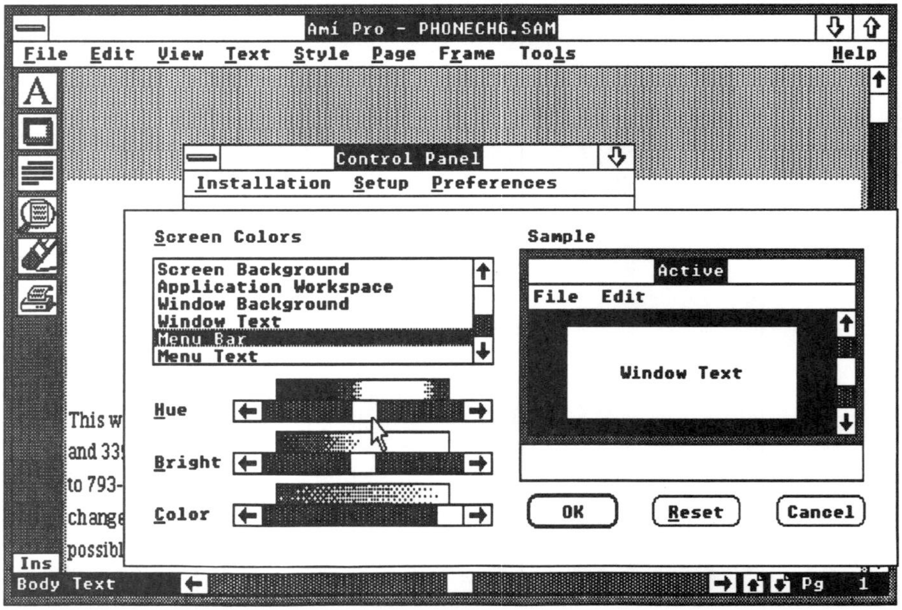

Figure 21–6 Changing screen colors with the Control Panel.

CHANGING ALL OPTIONS BACK TO THEIR ORIGINAL SETTINGS

Amí Professional keeps all the changes you make to the Amí Professional program in the WIN.INI file. If you ever want to reset Amí Professional back to the way it was when you opened the software package, here's how:

1. Open the WIN.INI file (you can use Amí Professional to do this).
2. Locate the section of the WIN.INI files that has the heading [AmiPro].
3. Skip all the lines that begin with `application#=` (more than 20 lines that contain conversion instructions), then delete all the other lines in this section.

Deleting the Amí Professional WIN.INI text deletes all the changes you've made to customize the program. This has no effect whatsoever on the files you've created with Amí Professional. When you run Amí Professional again, Amí Professional will add to the [AmiPro] section in the WIN.INI file as needed to store new settings.

A

Windows Basics

Because Amí Professional is designed to run under Microsoft Windows, the program uses multiple windows to display your documents and its tools. This appendix explains the basic methods that Microsoft Windows uses to work with multiple windows.

THE PARTS OF A WINDOW

Most windows have all of the parts shown in Figure A–1. This appendix shows how you can use all the different parts.

SELECTING A WINDOW

When you have more than one window open on the screen, you make a window active by selecting it. Commands and keystrokes affect only the active (selected) window.

To select a window or an icon (the tiny picture that represents an open window) with the mouse:

- Click the window or icon.

To select a window with keys:

- Press **Alt+Escape** until the window or icon you want appears highlighted and in front of any overlapping windows.

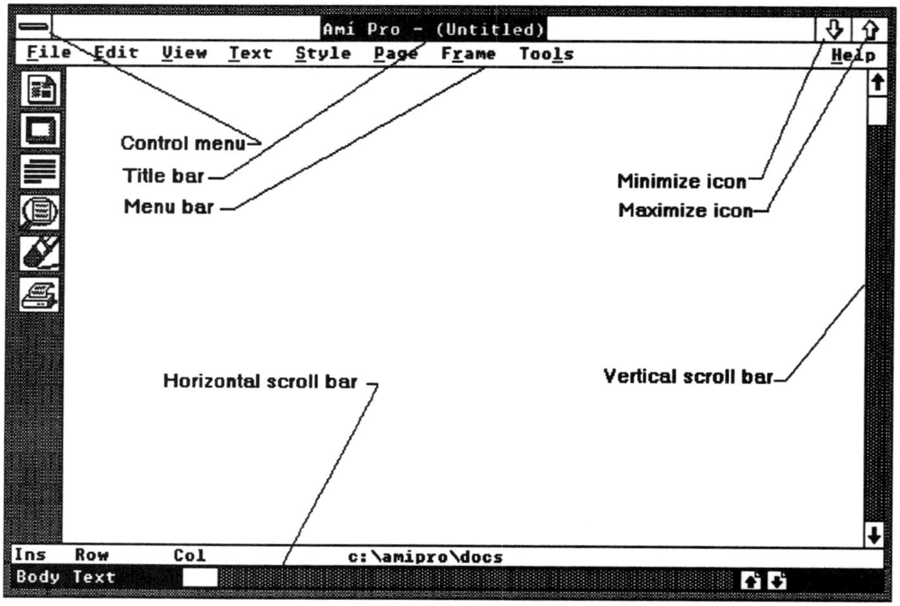

Figure A-1
Parts of a window.

WINDOW ACTIONS

This section shows the variety of ways you can change the location and size of windows.

Moving a Window

To move a window with the mouse:

1. Point to the title bar of the window.
2. Hold down the left mouse button and move the mouse to drag the window to a new location.
3. Release the mouse button.

To move a window with keys:

1. Press **Alt+Escape** until you select the window (if necessary), then press **Alt+F7** to choose the Move command from the Control menu.
2. Use the arrow keys to move the window to a new location.
3. Press **Enter**.

Changing the Size of a Window

You can make a window into a tiny icon, maximize it so it will take up the full screen, or change it to any size you like.

Changing Windows into Icons and Back

When you make a window into an icon, you aren't closing the window or saving the work you've done in the window, you're *only* reducing its size to a tiny picture, as shown in Figure A–2.

To make a window into an icon:

- Click the minimize icon (the down arrow) in the window's upper right corner.

  or

- Press **Alt+Escape** until you select the window, if necessary, then press **Alt+F9** (shortcut key for the Minimize command on the Control menu).

To change an icon back into a window:

- Double-click the icon. (Double-click means move the mouse pointer to the icon, then quickly click the left mouse button twice.)

  or

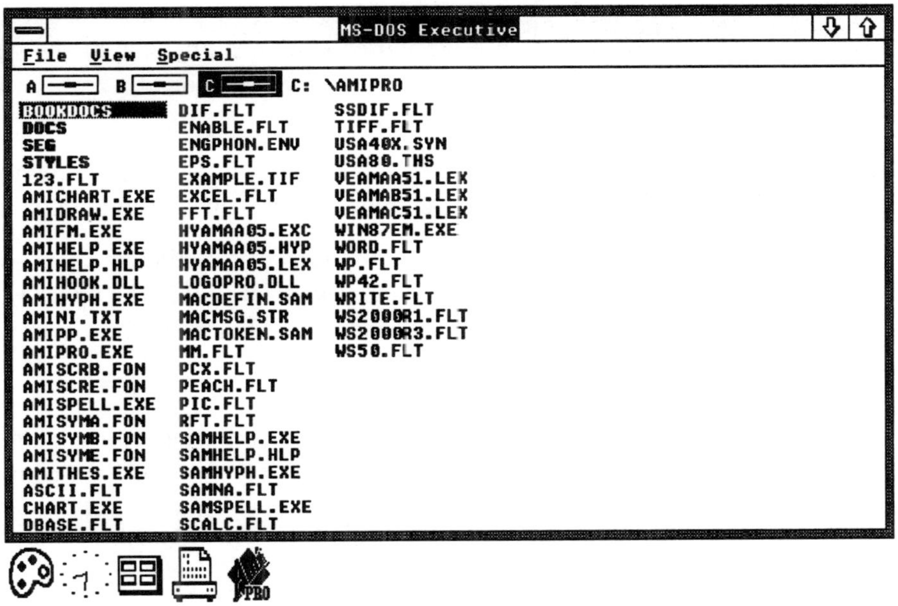

Figure A–2 You can change Windows applications into icons (tiny pictures at the bottom of the screen).

- Press **Alt+Escape** as many times as necessary to select the icon, then press **Alt+F10** (shortcut key for the Maximize command) to make the window occupy the full screen, or press **Alt+F5** (key for the Restore command) to restore the window to its previous size.

Making a Window Occupy the Full Screen

When you want a window to occupy the full screen, you can maximize the window (sometimes called *zooming* a window).

To maximize a window:

- Click the maximize icon (the up arrow) in the upper right corner of the window.

  or

- Press **Alt+Escape** until you select the window (if necessary), then press **Alt+F10** (the shortcut key for the Maximize command).

Dragging a Window to a New Size

When you want to control the size of a window, you can drag it to a new size with the mouse or the arrow keys. You can combine this with moving windows to arrange several windows on the screen into a layout that's most convenient for you.

To change the size of a window with the mouse:

1. Move the mouse pointer to any window border. When the pointer is on the border, it changes to a double-headed arrow, as shown in Figure A–3. You can point to any side of the window (to change the height or width of the window) or to a corner (to change both height and width at once).
2. Hold down the mouse button and drag the window to a new size. An outline of the window moves with the pointer to show the new size.
3. Release the mouse button. The window changes to the new size, and the maximize icon (the up arrow) in the upper right corner is replaced by the restore icon (a combination of a down and an up arrow).

To change the size of a window with keys:

1. Press **Alt+Escape** until you select the window (if necessary), then press **Alt+F8** (shortcut key for the Size command on the Control menu).
2. Use the arrow keys to change the size of the window. An outline of the window moves to show the new size.

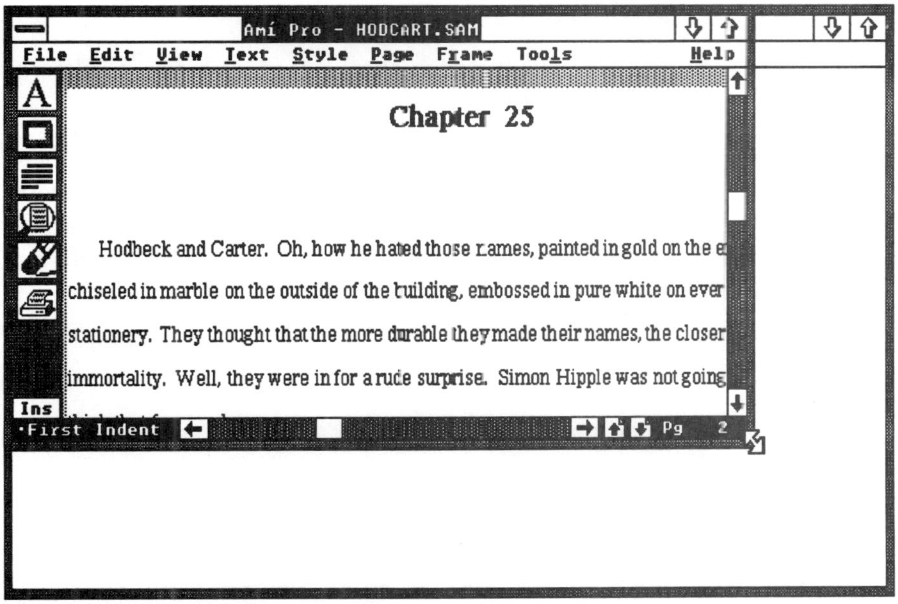

Figure A-3
You can change the size of windows by dragging the border with a mouse.

3. Press **Enter**. The window changes to the new size, and the maximize icon (the up arrow) in the upper right corner is replaced by the restore icon (a combination of a down and an up arrow).

To restore a window to its previous size:

- Click the restore icon in the upper right corner of the window.

  or

- Press **Alt+Escape** until you select the window if necessary, then press **Alt+F5**.

CLOSING A WINDOW

To close a window, you can choose from several options. Many Windows applications, including Amí Professional, have an Exit command on the File menu, so you can use that if you want. You can also do one of the following:

- Press **Alt+Escape** until you select the window (if necessary), then press **Alt+F4** (shortcut key for the Close command on the Control menu).

or

- Double-click the Control menu icon (the Spacebar picture) in the upper left corner of the window.

If you've made any changes that you haven't saved, the program asks whether to save the file before closing the window. If you're closing the MS-DOS Executive window, you'll see a message stating that this action will end your Windows session. Click the OK button or press **Enter** to continue your session.

B

Summary of Helpful Hints

FILE MANAGEMENT

Avoid Deleting or Moving Necessary Files. Generally speaking, Amí Professional needs all of the files that have the same basic file name to put that file together, as well as the style sheet it's based on and any files it's linked to. For example, say you have a text file named REPORT.SAM, that has associated graphics files called REPORT.G00 and REPORT.G01 and has a chart linked to an Excel file called SALES.XLC. You've created a special style sheet on which the report is based. If you delete or move any one of these files, you'll have to respond to a lot of error messages before you get any semblance of REPORT.SAM back together again. In other words, don't delete any associated files unless you're deleting the main document at the same time.

STYLES

Animated Presentations. If you're doing a presentation by displaying Amí Professional text on a screen, you can make your audience focus on important text by creating styles with different text colors, then changing styles with keystrokes to make the colors change. For example, you could create a style with white text and apply it to paragraphs you don't want the audience to see (white text on a white background is invisible), or you could create a red style and apply it to the point you want your audience to focus on.

Keeping Styles with the Document. To make sure all formatting stays with your document, turn on the Keep Format with Document option in the File Save As dialog box.

Saving Contents with Styles Sheets. To save the text or graphics you've created using a new style sheet, turn on the With Contents option in the Save As New Style Sheet dialog box. When you choose a style sheet, you also need to turn on the With Contents option in the dialog box to load the included text or graphics.

Indents in Styles. To create a special indent for only one paragraph in a document, you may need to create a special style just for that paragraph.

Merging Style Sheets. To move styles from one style sheet to another, use the Style Management command to move styles from the first style sheet to the document, then choose the Use Another Style Sheet command to open the second style sheet and use the Style Management command again to transfer styles from the document to the second style sheet.

Switching Among Style Sheets with Ease. To switch among style sheets easily, assign the same function key to similar styles. For example, you might always use F2 for a Body Text style, the style you'll use for most of your paragraphs.

DISPLAY ISSUES

Gray Bars or Strange Characters. If you see gray bars or strange-looking characters on your screen instead of text, Amí Professional is having trouble displaying the text in the correct size. If you're using working view, you may be able to fix this problem by switching to standard or enlarged view. Sometimes selecting the text and pressing **Ctrl+N** works, too, although this also removes any formatting you applied with the commands on the Text menu.

Getting Out of Facing-Pages View. The only way to get out of facing-pages view is to press **Escape** or click the Cancel button on the screen.

Opening a New File When Another File Is Open. To open a new file after you open another file and display them both on the screen at the same time, choose the File Open command, type a name for the new file, then click the Open Another button. When Amí Professional asks whether you want to create the file, answer Yes.

ENTERING, EDITING, AND FORMATTING TEXT

Using Codes to Speed Typing. To enter repetitive phrases faster and with fewer mistakes, type a two- or three-character code instead of the phrase.

For example, instead of typing Department of Human Resources several times, you could type ddd, then use the Tools Find & Replace command later to replace ddd with Department of Human Resources. When choosing a code like this, be sure to use characters that won't be part of words in your document. Any character repeated three times is a pretty safe choice and is easy to type.

Changing Formats as You Type. You can use shortcut keys to specify character formats as you type text. To do this, press the shortcut key combination (**Ctrl+I** for italic, **Ctrl+B** for bold, **Ctrl+N** for normal, and so on) with no text selected to apply the format to the cursor, then type the text in that format. For example, you could type

You are the **greatest**

by pressing **Ctrl+I**, typing **You**, pressing **Ctrl+N**, typing **are the**, then pressing **Ctrl+B** and typing **greatest**.

Replacing Tabs, Paragraph Marks (Return Characters), and Punctuation. When you use the Tools Find & Replace command to replace tab characters (**Ctrl+Tab**), paragraph marks (**Ctrl+Enter**), or punctuation such as commas and semicolons, choose the Options button, then turn off the Whole Word Only option. Otherwise, Amí Professional won't find most of the characters you want.

Keeping Words Together on the Same Line. To make sure that specific words stay together on a line (such as Easter Bunny), you can type nonbreaking spaces (**Ctrl+Spacebar**) between the words.

Saving Before Sorting. It's always a good idea to save your file before using the Tools Sort command. Then if the sort rearranges the items in a way you didn't expect, you can use the File Revert command to discard the changes.

PAGE LAYOUT

Different Numbers of Columns on the Same Page. To put different numbers of columns on the same page (such as one column over two), put part of the text in a frame.

Forcing Page or Column Breaks. To force a page break or a column break, you can position an empty frame where you want the text to break and fix its size so that text wraps around it to achieve the effect you want. Use the Frame Layout command to make the frame border invisible.

Lines on the Page. To add lines at specific places on a page, draw the lines in frames.

Using the Same Tab Ruler in Several Places. If you want to use the same inserted tab ruler in several spots in one document, you can click the ruler, choose Edit Copy to copy it to the Clipboard, move the cursor to the next position, then use Edit Paste to paste it in. This is a quick way to turn tab settings on and off in parts of the document.

No Header or Footer on the First Page. To make a header or footer appear on every page of your document except for the first, put the text into a floating header or footer attached to the first paragraph of the second page.

TABLES

Adding Text Before Tables for Flexibility. If you insert a table at the top of the page, you won't be able to add any text in front of it if you later decide you want to. This means your table is locked into position at the top of the page. To avoid this problem, just press the **Enter** key once before using the Tools Tables command to insert a table—this inserts a paragraph mark before the table. You can always delete this mark when you're sure you don't want to add any text before the table.

Positioning Tables. To precisely position a table on a page, put the table into a frame. When you insert a table into a frame, click the frame only once, then choose the Tools Tables command. If you double-click the frame, Amí Professional grays out the Tools Tables command.

Changing the Table Text Style for Numbers. If you put data for merging into a table and some table cells have numbers unaccompanied by text (zip codes, for example), you'll need to change the default Table Text style so that it does not display decimal points. Also, you must not add lines to a table containing data to use during a merge process.

Entering Data for Tables. If you have a lot of data to enter, you might find it faster to type the data outside of the table in draft mode, using tabs to separate columns and pressing Enter at the end of each row. Then use Edit Cut to put the data in the Clipboard to make your table.

Controlling the Initial Column Width. When you create a table with the Tools Tables command and use only the main dialog box, Amí Professional automatically makes the first column twice as wide as the rest of the columns. To make all the columns start out with the same width, click the Layout. . . button in the dialog box, click OK when the new dialog box appears, then type the number of columns and rows you want in the main dialog box.

FRAMES

Selecting Frames. Click once to select a frame. If you double-click, Amí Professional assumes you want to put text in an empty frame (unless you've attached a drawing or charting attribute to it, as described later) or assumes you want to draw in a drawing or charting frame.

Displaying Drawing Tools. If you select a frame, then choose the Frame Drawing or Frame Charting command, Amí Professional attaches a drawing or charting attribute to that frame, even if you cancel the command and leave the frame empty. If you later double-click the frame, Amí Professional will display the drawing tools. This means that you can't change your mind and put text in what was previously a drawing or charting frame—you have to delete the old frame and add a new empty one for text.

Aligning Frames. To precisely align frames on pages, switch to enlarged view and use the View Display Preferences command to display the horizontal and vertical rulers on the screen.

Duplicating Frames of the Same Size. If you know you want to have several frames of the same size, insert one empty frame, then copy and paste it until you have the number you want. You can only copy a frame before you put anything in it.

Sizing Graphics in Frames. If your frame is the size you want it to be, but you can't see the graphic you inserted, choose the Frame Graphics Scaling command and turn on the Fit in Frame option to resize the entire graphic to fit within the frame. You may need to use the command again to make adjustments to size, but at least you'll be able to locate the graphic.

Focusing on a Portion of a Graphic. If you want to focus on part of a large graphic, move the graphic within the frame until you see the part you want. You can type large percentages (like 300%) in the Frame Graphics Scaling box to "blow up" that part, and you can overlap frames to create special effects. For example, you might want to use this procedure to create an enlarged map of Hawaii in a small frame, then position that frame on top of a larger map of the United States.

Controlling Lines and White Space in Frames. The Borders option in the Frame Layout dialog box controls how much white (blank) space lies between the frame contents and the surrounding text. The Lines option controls where lines appear within the border space. So if you want .10 inch between the frame contents and the surrounding lines and .10 inch between the lines and text flowing around the frame, you'd set Border spacing to .20 inch, and set the Lines position to Middle. To make an opaque background within a frame extend completely to the lines surrounding the frame, either set all Border spacing to zero or set the Lines option to the Inside position.

Using Invisible Frames to Control Text Spacing. You can use frames with transparent backgrounds and no surrounding lines to force line breaks, to set up column breaks, or to align text in creative ways. A frame inserted this way simply creates a blank space on the page. Set the Wrap Around options in the Frame Layout dialog box the way you want and make sure there are no lines added.

Setting Default Characteristics for Frames. If you want most of the frames you insert to have the same characteristics (such as transparent, no lines, and text wrapping around), use the Frame Layout command to change the settings the way you want, then click the Make Default button. This tells Amí Professional to automatically use those settings when it draws a frame. You can always change any aspect of the frame later.

Drawing in Frames. Be sure to click a newly inserted frame only once if you want to select it prior to putting a drawing in it. If you double-click, the program assumes you want to add text. Once you've chosen the Frame Drawing command with a frame selected, you can double-click the frame to quickly display the drawing tools.

Working with Frames in Full-Page View. You can add, resize, move, and delete frames in full-page view. This is a good way to see the effects of your changes on the whole page.

CHARTING

Rearranging Data for Better Results. If the data in your chart isn't displayed the way you expected, you might be able to fix it by choosing Frame Charting and turning on the Flip Data option in the dialog box.

Entering Data for Charts. If you have a lot of data to enter, you might find it faster to type the data outside of the table in draft mode, using tabs to separate columns and pressing **Enter** at the end of each row. Then use Edit Cut to put the data in the Clipboard to make your chart.

Selecting Frames for Charting. Be sure to click a newly inserted frame only once if you want to select it prior to using the Frame Charting command to create or modify a chart. If you double-click, the program assumes you want to add text. Once you've created the chart, double-clicking the frame displays the drawing tools (so you can add more graphic elements or change part of the chart).

MACROS

Saving Before Running a Macro. It's always a good idea to save your file before running a macro. Then if the macro does something you didn't expect, you can use the File Revert command to discard the changes.

Assigning Icons to Macros. If you assign the key combinations Ctrl+F1 through Ctrl+F9 to your most important macros, you can use the View Display Preferences (Sidebar option) to display icons for those macros in the icon bar, then click an icon with the mouse to run the macro. The icons are named Macro Shortcut 1 through 9 and are pictures of keys labeled ^F1 through ^F9.

C

Keyboard Shortcuts

Action	Press
Apply/Remove Text Attributes	
Normal	Ctrl+N (removes all formats not controlled by style
Bold	Ctrl+B
Italic	Ctrl+I
Underline	Ctrl+U
Word Underline	Ctrl+W
Align Paragraphs	
Align Center	Ctrl+C
Align Left	Ctrl+L
Align Right	Ctrl+R
Justify	Ctrl+J
Edit	
Copy	Ctrl+Insert
Cut	Shift+Delete

Find & Replace	Ctrl+F
Force Line Break	Shift+Enter
Glossary	Ctrl+K
Go To	Ctrl+G
Go To Next Item of Same Type	Ctrl+H
Paste	Shift+Insert
Undo	Alt+Backspace

Switch Views

Draft/Layout Mode	Ctrl+M
Full Page/Current View	Ctrl+V

Work with Styles

Apply Style	Function key assigned to style; or Ctrl+Y, then use Ctrl+*arrow* key, then Spacebar to apply
Modify Style	Ctrl+A
Show/Hide Styles Box	Ctrl+Z

Other

Help	F1
Print	Ctrl+P
Save	Ctrl+S
Show/Hide Side Bar	Ctrl+Q

Cursor Movement

To the beginning of the line	Home
To the end of the line	End
Left one character	Left arrow
Right one character	Right arrow
Left one word	Ctrl+Left arrow

Right one word	Ctrl+Right arrow
Forward one sentence	Ctrl+. (period)
Back one sentence	Ctrl+, (comma)
Up one line	Up arrow
Down one line	Down arrow
Up one paragraph	Ctrl+Up arrow
Down one paragraph	Ctrl+Down arrow
Up one screen	Ctrl+Page Up
Down one screen	Ctrl+Page Down
To start of document	Ctrl+Home
To end of document	Ctrl+End
Select	Hold down Shift key and press cursor movement keys shown above

Commands and Dialog Boxes

Activate a check box or radio button with a focus (dotted outline)	Spacebar
Cancel the command or hide menu	Escape
Choose a highlighted command or button	Return
Move dialog box	Alt+F7, then use arrow keys and press Enter when done
Move to the next group of options	Tab
Move up or down a group of options, buttons, or check boxes	Up or Down arrows
Select a menu	Alt+the underlined letter of the menu name

Select a menu command	Type the underlined letter within the command name

Tables

Move left to right	Tab
Move right to left	Shift+Tab
Move up a row	Ctrl+Up arrow
Move down a row	Ctrl+Down arrow
Select a block of cells	Shift+Ctrl+Up or Down arrow
Move to beginning of current line within a cell	Home
Move to the first column in the current row	Home, Home
Move to the end of current line within a cell	End
Move to the last column in the current row	End, End
Move to the first cell in the table	Ctrl+Home
Move to the last cell in the table	Ctrl+End

Tabs in Tab Ruler

Choose left-aligned tab	l (lowercase L)
Choose centered tab	c
Choose right-aligned tab	r
Choose justified tab	j
Choose left-aligned tab with period leader character	Shift+L

Choose centered tab with period leader character	Shift+C
Choose right-aligned tab with period leader character	Shift+R
Choose justified tab with period leader character	Shift+J
Select all tab icons	A
Select more than one icon	Shift+click tab icon

D

Mouse Shortcuts

To	Use the Mouse to
Change a Directory	Double-click the drive letter in the dialog box.
Close a Window	Double-click in the control menu icon.
Edit Contents of a Frame	Double-click the frame (the cursor appears if there is text in the frame or the drawing tools appear if the frame contains a drawing or chart).
Select List Item	Double-click on the item in the list.
Open Go To Dialog Box	Double-click the page number box in the lower right corner of the window.
Maximize a Window	Double-click the title bar or the up arrow in the upper right corner of the window.
Minimize a Window	Double-click the title bar or the down arrow in the upper right corner of the window.
Open Modify Style Dialog Box	Double-click the current style indicated in the styles box.

Open a Document	Double-click the document's name in either the main Windows screen or the File Open dialog box.
Position the Cursor	Point to the position in text and click once.
Restore Window to Previous Size	Click on Restore icon (the up/down arrows) in the upper right corner of the window.
Select Frame Beneath	Hold down Ctrl key and click frame on top.
Select a Frame	Point to the frame and click once.
Select Text	Set cursor at beginning of text, hold down Shift key, and click end of text, or drag over area to select.
Select a Word	Double-click the word or drag the mouse over the word(s).
Select Multiple Objects	Hold down Shift and click on the objects you want to select.
Show/Hide Styles Box	Double-click the style status box in the lower left corner of the window.

E

Amí Professional File Extensions

Here are some important file extensions used in Amí Professional.

File Extension	**Description**
.DLL or .HLP	Help files.
.DRV	A printer driver file.
.SDW	A drawing created in Amí Professional. The program automatically adds this extension if you type only the file name in the Save As Drawing dialog box.
.EXE	A program file, such as AMIPRO.EXE, which contains the Amí Professional program or AMIDRAW.EXE, which contains the drawing program. You can't look at an .EXE file with Amí Professional, because it's written in code.
.FLT	A filter (translator) used by Amí Professional to convert files to or from other programs with the Import/Export command.
.FON	A font file.

.G00 (.G01, .G02, . . .)	A graphics file created by Amí Professional when you choose the Copy Picture option in the File Import/Export dialog box. These files (one for every graphic imported to a document) contain copies of the images that have the same basic name as the associated document (LETTER.G00, LETTER.G01, and so on) and are stored with the document (LETTER.SAM).
.LEX	A file used by the spelling checker. These files contain dictionaries, hyphenation rules, and so on.
.SAM	A document saved in Amí Professional. The program automatically adds this extension if you type only the file name in the Save or Save As dialog box.
.SMM	A macro file created in Amí Professional. The program automatically adds this extension if you type the file name in the Tools Macros dialog box.
.STR	Macro messages file.
.STY	A style sheet saved in Amí Professional. The program automatically adds this extension if you type only the file name in the Save As a New Style Sheet dialog box. The one exception to this is NONE.STY, which frequently appears in the title bar of the styles box. NONE.STY is not really a file, but rather it indicates that all the styles for the active document are stored with the document, not in a style sheet.
.THS or .ENV	Thesaurus file.

Index